THE
PSYCHOLOGY
—— OF ——
AWAKENING

ABOUT THE EDITORS

Gay Watson, Stephen Batchelor and Guy Claxton are all established authors whose books include: by Gay Watson *Resonance of Emptiness*; by Stephen Batchelor *Buddhism Without Belief*; *Jewel in the Lotus; Tibet: A Guide*; and by Guy Claxton *The Heart of Buddhism; Hare Brain, Tortoise Mind.*

THE
PSYCHOLOGY
—— OF ——
AWAKENING

Buddhism, Science, and our Day-to-Day Lives

edited by
Gay Watson, Stephen Batchelor, and Guy Claxton

SAMUEL WEISER, INC.

York Beach, Maine

This edition first published in 2000 by
Samuel Weiser, Inc.
P. O. Box 612
York Beach, ME 03910-0612
www.weiserbooks.com

Library of Congress Cataloging-in-Publication Data

The psychology of awakening : Buddhism, science, and our day-to-
day lives / edited by Gay Watson, Stephen Batchelor, Guy Claxton.
        p. cm.
    Includes bibliopraphical references.
    ISBN 1-57863-172-6 (pbk. : alk. paper)
    1. Buddhism--Psychology. 2. Enlightenment (Buddhism)--
Psychology. 3. Psychotherapy--Religious aspects--Buddhism.
I. Watson, Gay. II. Batchelor, Stephen. III. Claxton, Guy.
BQ4570.P76 P79 2000
294.3'375--dc21   99-059447

Printed in the United States of America
BJ

08 07 06 05 04 03 02 01 00
    9 8 7 6 5 4 3 2 1

Contents

Part III Buddhism and Psychotherapy

Part IV Practical Applications

Introduction

The psychology of awakening: to Western ears awakening, the goal of Buddhist practice, presents an unfamiliar concept. The idea of developing a psychology in order to cultivate ways to awaken is strange. What is awakening? What are we awakening from, what awakening to? One of the authors represented here suggests that the psychology of awakening is an oxymoron, that psychology and awakening do not and cannot belong together. Perhaps so, if one refers to psychology only in its narrowest sense, as it has been practised and taught throughout most of its short history, as a Western academic discipline sadly removed from subjective experience. Yet psychology, potentially and now more commonly, actually refers to the study of mind in its widest sense, the study of soul, cognition, emotion and consciousness. This study of mind as experienced from within has ever been the concern of Buddhism, a study which is inseparable from practice, a practice of cultivation in the service of awakening.

At this time, both practitioners of psychology and of the path of awakening realise that they have much to gain from each other. His Holiness the Dalai Lama has said: 'There are two general areas for which dialogue between Buddhism and psychology could be very valuable. One is the investigation of the nature of mind itself. The second is the investigation of the nature of mind specifically in relation to therapeutic purposes – how to bring people to better health.' How to live more peaceably, more wisely, more happily and with an open heart is a goal for all of us.

The long history of Buddhism's phenomenological exploration of experience points towards valid methods of exploring
subjectivity which may lead science away from one-sided objectivity and distance towards a science of embodiment and intersubjectivity, a path that contemporary cognitive science, as
Francisco Varela describes, is eager to understand. For spiritual
practitioners, Buddhism offers not only theory, a philosophy of
process much in tune with contemporary Western discourse, but,
most importantly, a way. This is a way of practice, a cultivation, a
path towards change and clear sight leading to happiness,
authenticity and connection. This Buddhist way is fast emerging
as a major influence on the development of Western culture. It is
the subject of Hollywood films; the Dalai Lama packs Madison
Square Gardens and the Royal Albert Hall. Athletes are advised
to meditate, business leaders to cultivate 'mindfulness' and
'intuition'. In a time of recession the retreat centre business is
booming. The Buddhist view of mind, how it works, how it errs
and how to put it right is being recognised as profound and
practical by scientists, therapists, aid workers, artists and
politicians.

Nor need the giving be only in one direction. Can Western
psychology's understanding of 'endarkenment' complement
Buddhism's quest for enlightenment? Can scientific studies of
consciousness and its relation to unconsciousness also help us to
live more happily, more wisely, and can they be used in the
service of spiritual progress? Maybe Western science may give to
Buddhism a clearer objective map of what is actually happening
on a neurological level while meditating. Most importantly the
West must bring its own strengths and skills to ancient Buddhist
wisdom if Buddhism is to flourish in the West. Just as it changed
its outer form and clothing in each culture to which it travelled –
Sri Lanka, Tibet, China and Japan – if it is to create a firm
foundation in the West, so Buddhism must find its Western dress.

Arising from the deliberations of two international conferences held at Dartington Hall in Devon, these essays come
from some of those who are most influential today in exploring
this dialogue between Buddhism and the West. They explore the
value of Buddhism's powerful vision of human nature and its
implications for personal and social life from many different
perspectives. They look backward to the history of the dialogue,
to successes and failures of understanding and interpretation,
they concern themselves with present dilemmas, and they look
forward to explore the way Buddhism and Western thought may

most fruitfully go forward to mutual understanding and benefit.

Part I is concerned with the more philosophical issues. Christopher Titmuss opens the debate with an examination of the concept of inquiry, which sums up the spirit of the collection as a whole. He emphasises the importance of genuine inquiry, the need to question and put aside all the views and identifications through which, consciously or unconsciously, we filter our experience. Such inquiry, he suggests, leads to an open mind and to liberation beyond the limitations of views and opinions. Geshe Thupten Jinpa, a scholar and long-time translator for the Dalai Lama, who, uniquely, holds doctoral degrees from both Tibetan and Western academic systems, follows with a consideration of the key philosophical presuppositions of the Buddhist psychology of awakening, of the conception of mind which emerges from them, and a comparison of this with Western theories. He suggests that while psychoanalysis aims at bringing about a coherent sense of self, Buddhist psychology aims to transcend the very concept of self. He reveals that Buddhism presents a concept of mind as process, one which is fundamentally positive and compassionate, and considers the implications of this for contemporary psychotherapy.

Stephen Batchelor presents an agnostic approach to Buddhism for the West, supporting Buddhism as a praxis rather than a religious institution. He proposes a way of life based on deep agnosticism, a passionate acceptance of unknowing in the face of the deepest questions of life and death, looking to Buddhism for a practice of existential confrontation rather than for a source of metaphors of consolation. Gay Watson considers the self that is to be awakened and liberated, finding that, although in theory Western views have come close to the no-self of Buddhism, in practice they have failed to consider the consequences of this knowledge in terms of emotion and possessiveness. Taking a similar theme, but attempting to show that psychotherapy may not be the discipline closest to Buddhism, Fred Pfeil compares Buddhist attitudes to self to those of postmodern theory. Most practically Helena Norberg-Hodge draws on her extended experience in Ladakh to show how Buddhist principles may influence and enhance our economic and ecological activities.

The second section of the book deals more specifically with the scientific perspective. Francisco Varela shows how leading edge conceptions of human beings in cognitive science are coming to resonate strongly with Buddhist views. Guy Claxton describes how Buddhism and psychology come together to account for everyday 'mystical experiences' and 'altered states of consciousness'. Susan Blackmore, explaining the striking parallels between Buddhism and Darwinism, amusingly invites us to awaken from the meme dream. Taking Richard Dawkin's concept of the meme, the unit of cultural transmission rather than natural selection, she considers the most persistent, and from the Buddhist point of view the most pernicious meme, that of the self. Finally in this section Terence Gaussen reviews research on infant development from neuroanatomy and physiology to emotion, cognition and social development, tracing factors seen to underlie the development of the individual self and consciousness. He links these new insights to the understanding of suffering, which religious practices seek to overcome.

Unsurprisingly, the greatest number of papers presented address issues of Dharma in action, arising from the interface of Buddhism and psychotherapy, whether in theory or in practice. Papers from both John Welwood and Mark Epstein show how profoundly Buddhist ideas and practices may influence the development of psychotherapy. John Welwood writes of psychological work in the service of spiritual development, arguing the often-ignored point that the paths and goals of Buddhism and psychotherapy while not incompatible are also not identical. He suggests that spiritual practitioners may often benefit from Western therapy, which should not be ignored as unnecessary or trifling within the spiritual path. He clearly addresses the areas of influence of both psychology and spiritual work and shows the ways they may work in harmony. Mark Epstein writes of openness and wholeness, encouraging us to go to pieces without falling apart. Leslie Todres uses vignettes from both psychotherapy and Zen to illustrate the maturation of liberating insight into tacit understanding, and the integration of both into everyday life. Maura Sills describes the practice of psychotherapy itself as a spiritual path, outlining the approach of core process psychotherapy. John Crook considers Zen teachings and practice in relation to a culture of dependency.

The final section is concerned with the applications of Buddhism in therapeutic practice and exemplifies the many different kinds of therapies with which Buddhism is now associated. Opening this section, David Brazier presents a clear exposition of different approaches and uses of Buddhism within psychotherapy. Jon Kabat-Zinn describes the development of his work of mindfulness-based stress reduction in medicine, health care institutions, school, prison and professional sports. James Low writes about structures of suffering from the perspectives of the Nyingma school of Tibetan Buddhism and Western cognitive-analytic therapy. Also from the point of view of Tibetan Buddhism, Tarab Tulku describes the use of lucid dreaming for therapeutic ends. Joy Manné tells of the use of breathing practices in the context of a psychotherapeutic case study. In more general terms Karen Kissel Wegela describes the inter-subjective way of working of contemplative psychotherapy as practised and taught at Naropa Institute. Lastly, Eric Hall explores the Four Noble Truths in the context of counselling and psychotherapy.

Since the writers represent many disciplines and styles, and the book is intended for the general reader, in the interests of simplicity and consistency, we have taken the decision to omit all diacritical marks.

Our thanks go to all the contributors for their work, and also to all those presenters and participants, who helped to make the conferences such significant events. We would like to thank the Dartington Hall Trust for providing such a beautiful venue for the conference, and the Dartington Hall Programme department under Helen Chaloner for their careful and considerate organisation. We very much hope that the work presented here will continue the multivoiced conversation between Buddhism and Western discourse, and further the development of a healthy and strong Buddhism both true to its origins and resonant with our time and culture.

Gay Watson
Stephen Batchelor
Guy Claxton

PART I

ASPECTS OF AWAKENING: BUDDHISM MEETS THE CONTEMPORARY MIND

Inquiry into Awakening

Christopher Titmuss

In recent years in Britain, the government has produced a number of charters for the public. One concerns health care and another concerns travel on the national railways. These charters provide the public with the opportunity to know the areas of responsibility of a particular utility or service. The consumer then has a right to take steps to address grievance and to have a clear understanding of the arrangement between the service and the consumer or patient. 2,500 years ago, the Buddha also provided a charter – a Charter of Inquiry. This charter provided thoughtful people with guidelines about what they needed to be aware of when exploring religious or spiritual values and beliefs. The Buddha provided a blueprint for the exploration and understanding of our relationship to our views.

In a celebrated talk of the Buddha to the Kalama people, the Buddha gave his Charter for Inquiry. The Kalama people had approached the Buddha and asked him, 'How do we know who is telling us the truth?' He replied: 'Do not accept anything because of

1. repeated oral transmission
2. lineage or tradition
3. it being widely stated
4. it being written in books such as scriptures
5. it being logical and reasonable

6. it inferring and drawing conclusions
7. it having been thought out
8. acceptance and conviction through thinking about a theory
9. the speaker appearing consistent
10. respect for the teacher

He then goes on to add that 'know what things would be censured by the wise and which, if pursued, would lead to harm and suffering.' The Buddha puts the emphasis on 'inquiry'. The word 'inquiry' means to 'investigate, to explore – with a view to resolution or realisation'.

When we look at this charter, we notice how easily we take up and cling to one or more of the ten points. Repeated oral transmission shows itself in secular and religious culture where the same message is passed on to us day in and day out through those who promote particular ends. How easily we identify with and subscribe to that transmission. Secular values indoctrinate us into believing that elevation of self and acquisition of wealth and luxury goods represents the mark of a successful life. We are even told that this is what it means to live in the 'real world'.

We may try to compensate for this extreme and narrow vision of life by identifying ourselves with a particular religion. We try to cover all eventualities through the maximisation of pleasure, and comfort for our sorrow and despair through a religious belief including some form of life after death.

We identify with particular views, conventional statements and agreements simply because countless others subscribe to it as well. Politicians, the corporate world, advertising, the media, hearsay and gossip influence our world view and standpoints. We agree with some, disagree with others and remain uncertain about others. Clinging to specific views generates an intolerance for the alternative outlook of others. Yet often we fail to ask ourselves how we have come by these views, or question the comfort we take from our beliefs, whether secular or religious.

We also invest books and scriptures with enormous authority. Scriptures claim to be the voice of God or the voice of Truth and therefore cannot be questioned. We identify with the views of science and its standpoints about what matters. We then neglect ethical considerations, grasping the constructive face of science whilst ignoring the destructive developments of scientific advancement. Certainly science has a legitimate view, but to claim or imply that science alone has access to true reality exposes an arrogance similar to any that religious authorities propound.

At times we draw conclusions based on inference and analysis and cut ourselves off from a non-conceptual awareness of the nature of things. We forget that for every theory and conviction that we uphold, there are others who will disagree with us, often profoundly.

Finally, the charisma, status, reputation and persuasive power of a speaker all influence us. A speaker may talk articulately and persuasively about an issue with apparent authority and understanding whilst the same issue may be unresolved in his or her life. Even though teachers of enlightenment may speak very well on the basis of their experience and understanding, it does not mean to say that they have insight and wisdom into every area of life. They may repeat some views wisely and skilfully but may need to observe noble silence in other areas. So unconditional respect may be unwise.

By not adopting any of the ten areas in the Charter for Inquiry, we safeguard ourselves from clinging and identifying with a particular standpoint, whether personal, philosophical, political, religious, social or scientific. It is in this light that we enter a spirit of inquiry while remaining vigilant with regard to what emerges out of it.

We need to understand that nothing whatsoever is worth clinging on to. Most religious teachings have strong elements of belief in them. One common feature uniting religions concerns certainty about what happens when we die. Religions in the Middle East state with conviction there is an afterlife in the form of going to heaven or hell according to our beliefs and behaviour. Or there is the widespread view in the Far East, subcontinent of India and other traditional teachings that we are reborn according to our karma, our deeds. On the other hand, the view of secular culture, under the influence of scientific materialism, states with equal certainty that there is only one existence. We are born once, we die once, with complete extinction at the end of life. Non-existence is one view. *When I am here death is not. When death is here I am not.* But is it necessary for us to carry any view whatsoever about the future – either extinction or continuity in one form or another? Continuity and extinction appear as extreme positions incompatible with the Buddha's teachings on the middle way. A mind preoccupied with the past and future invites extreme standpoints while the inquiry and meditation into the living present reveals the open door to enlightenment.

The Dharma, that is teachings concerned with liberation and enlightenment, encourages us to inquire deeply into the experience of living. It is necessary for us to explore what is, and our relationship to what is. The relationship to the here and now matters far more than taking up views about extinction or non-extinction when we die. Liberation means understanding the emptiness of the I, the ego, the substantial self – and thus resolving the issue of birth and death, past and future.

A young man came on a meditation retreat to Gaia House in South Devon. It was a period of transition in his life. He had the opportunity to go to university, find a job or travel, but most of all, he wanted to develop some deep experience and under-standing about who he was and what mattered. I asked him in an interview on the retreat what mattered. He said that he was concerned that his life would pass by and in ten or twenty years he might come to the conclusion that he was wasting his life. So I said to him that at the present moment the future mattered to him and the way that he would relate to the past. I then asked him if he felt that his life had been a waste of time so far.

He said 'No. So far, I have been doing what I wish to do.'

I asked him 'What do you want to do now?'

He said 'I want to live a conscious life.'

I said to him 'Conscious of what?'

He said, with a smile, 'Conscious of myself, conscious of my relationships with others, conscious of everything.'

I asked him if he was prepared to make sacrifices to live a clear and conscious life? He said that he was. This young man meditated on the here and now with a depth of dedication and commitment. I could see that he had a strong determination not to fall into habit patterns, fantasy, daydreams and speculation and to stay firmly grounded from moment to moment. Out of this discipline, the heart opens and consciousness awakens.

This young man is an example of the spirit of inquiry that is willing to question the demands and expectations of parents, educators and society upon him. That does not mean that we reject all values. Dharma teachings invite us to discover whether the pursuit of possessions, status and privilege can ever fully satisfy. That exploration will demand from us a great deal of awareness, an inquiry into our priorities, sacrifice and dedication. We will need to understand the nature of interconnectedness that reveals from moment to moment our relationship to the world.

It seems to me that if we take notice of the Buddha's Charter for Inquiry it will save us from getting stuck in a particular place. We can then keep our hearts and minds open. The natural outcome of such an inquiry is an authentic liberation free from self-deception. We neither cling to nor take pride in personal conditioning, social pressures and religious, political and social ideologies. Yet we have not withdrawn from the world, nor live in a detached cocoon. The Buddha's Charter of Inquiry undermines self-righteousness and selfishness. We see the tragic pain and conflict caused through our clinging to and identifying with particular standpoints.

One example of this occurs in the Middle East. Every year I have the privilege of going to Israel. I act as a facilitator with Israelis and Palestinians. There is a genuine spirit of inquiry and exploration taking place in these workshops. In order to inquire deeply, both Israelis and Palestinians have to be willing to make sacrifices. One of those sacrifices is learning to put aside the identification with being an Israeli or Palestinian. Both labels get highly emotionally charged due to a 3,000-year history of living together with conflict and uncertainty. In order to connect with each other, the labels *Palestinian* or *Israeli* must take second place to being a human being, to mutual understanding of suffering and its causes, and to coexistence.

If inquiry is to be a meaningful and profound experience, then it must be free from the propounding of views and opinions to impress others or ourselves. A deep interest in existence transforms our restrictions upon consciousness. If we inquire, we make a significant contribution to the resolution of suffering, finding of wisdom and generating compassion for others. Thus inquiry is not the pursuit of intellectual interests nor aimed to propound particular dogmas. In these teachings living in the real world means the recognition of suffering and working for its dissolution.

For more than twenty years I have been teaching Dharma retreats and insight meditation around the world. In regular afternoon sessions in the meditation hall, I facilitate an inquiry period. The principles of this are simple but effective:

1. Only one person can speak at a time.
2. She or he must speak from an area of direct concern to them or from their experience.
3. This may take the simple form of a question, an obvious form of inquiry. Or the person may have something he or she wishes to speak about.
4. I will then respond to that person. My response may take the form of asking that person questions or replying to their questions. A dialogue then gets underway.

5. My intention is to contribute to their insight and understanding.
6. It is important that we avoid abstractions or intellectual ideas.
7. When the inquiry is taking place I request everyone else to listen fully. That means both listening inwardly and outwardly. Inner listening is attending to the responses taking place in the inquiry. Is there empathy, interest or insight? Is there boredom, agitation or inner confusion?
8. The inquiry with the person may last for five minutes or half an hour. At any time either I, or the person who is speaking, can say thank you to bring the inquiry to a close.
9. When an inquiry with a person comes to its close, there is a period of silence. This period of silence lasts four or five minutes. This enables people to reflect on what was said, to digest, or to meditate on the here and now. It also generates a receptivity to the next person who wishes to speak.
10. After four or five minutes, I will invite another person to speak. Nobody is obliged to speak.

People are willing to speak about all manner of personal issues as well as explore their way of being in this world. I believe inquiry, with or without the aid of another, can dissolve immense problems and pressures, and make significant shifts of consciousness that are enlightening. Inquiry keeps our minds open, making a genuine and authentic difference to our life.

Profound insights can also emerge from reading, but all too often when we read, we only gain some intellectual satisfaction. Such understanding does not make for a real shift in our consciousness. In the East the traditional teachings required a genuine discipline and interest in what was read. It was not unusual for men and women of Dharma practice to have just a few verses from a book to read and reflect on.

There is a danger that the huge number of spiritual books available may inhibit inquiry rather than nourish it. If we are reading a book and a point in it genuinely touches us, we must feel the truth of it and see how it relates directly to our life. At that point we ought to be able to put the book down and just let the truth of that statement run deep into our being. It is this capacity to make the greatest journey in life from head to heart that matters so much. For that to take place, it requires from us a receptivity, a spaciousness and a willingness and ability to absorb. Meditation will heighten our receptivity. There are numerous questions of life that contribute to deep inquiry and the realisation of wisdom and enlightenment. For example:

What is love?
What is my relationship to impermanence?
Where is the clinging?
Is there any substance to the self?
What am I prepared to sacrifice to go deeply?
Am I in touch with my intentions?
What steps can I take to transform any greed, hate and fear within?
Do I want to realise a liberated and insightful life?
Am I willing to sustain inquiry and reflection until there is genuine enlightenment?

Dharma teachings are not a psychotherapy, philosophy or set of religious beliefs. They do not fall into those categories. It is a wonderful thing to explore and inquire into life. No stone is left unturned. When we discover the spirit and the skill in inquiry it means that we are willing to understand all the bitter-sweet experiences of life. It is all grist for the mill.

Genuine inquiry challenges us, makes us face up to ourselves and to see where we get stuck. We have the opportunity to go beyond absolutism, relativism, patterns of clinging and indecision. In liberation we know the limitations of views and opinions. The mind finds its rest in such a liberation.

May all beings live in peace
May all beings be free
May all beings be enlightened

The Foundations of a Buddhist Psychology of Awakening

Geshe Thupten Jinpa

I

At the heart of the Buddha's teaching is the message of liberation. This liberative transformation is characterised as *moksha* (freedom), *nirvana* (beyond sorrow) or, simply as *bodhi* (awakening or enlightenment). The Buddha's message of 'awakening' is often articulated in terms of a formula known as the Four Noble Truths. Briefly stated, the Four Truths are: (1) that there is suffering (2) that suffering comes from its origin (3) that there is a cessation of suffering and finally (4) that there is a path leading to such a cessation. According to Buddhism, the key to attaining this freedom is said to lie in gaining deep insight into what is perceived to be a fundamental truth of our existence. By this I am referring to the famous Buddhist doctrine of *anatman*, or 'no-self'. We can identify the key elements of the teaching on 'no-self' as follows:

a) the existence of self as an independent, eternal, and atemporal unifying principle is an illusion;

b) there is no need to posit an abiding principle like the *atman* (or soul) to explain the nature of our experience or the laws of causality;

c) the nature and existence of persons must be understood in terms of the five psycho-physical aggregates[1] which serve as the basis for our personal identity and existence;

d) that the grasping at such a notion of self lies at the root of our suffering and bondage, i.e. our unenlightened existence; and

e) the negation of this self constitutes the essence of the path to enlightenment.

This much seems to be common to most schools of Buddhism. As can be seen, Buddhism draws an interesting correlation between the self and *samsara* (or unenlightened existence) on the one hand, and 'no-self' and *nirvana* (freedom) on the other. The traditional Buddhist teachings on the twelve links of dependent origination is an elaborate illustration of this correlation. On this model, our existence is characterised by a perpetual cycle of confusion and dissatisfaction through interlocking chains of causes and conditions. At the root of all this is believed to lie an 'ignorance', a fundamental confusion pertaining to our own existence and the world. This, according to Buddhism, is the first link in the chain of twelve interlocking factors.

This 'ignorance', or *avidya* as it is called in the Buddhist parlance, is not a mere passive state of unknowing, nor is it a state of universal doubt along the lines of Cartesian universal scepticism. *Avidya* is directly related to one's own sense of self and identity. It is an attachment to a false notion of self, hence it is an active state of 'misknowing'. Unlike mere ignorance or unknowing it is in direct opposition to true knowledge. Tsongkhapa (1357-1419), the Tibetan Buddhist thinker and the founder of the Gelug school of Tibetan Buddhism, defines *avidya* as 'that which is the direct opposite of *vidya*, knowledge'. Like 'untruth' and 'unfriendliness' the negative particle *a* in *avidya* is a negation entailing a direct opposition to *vidya* (knowledge). It is thus a cognitive state, albeit an untrue one which can only be dispelled by generating the corresponding *vidya*. So, it can be said that this 'ignorance' is our deeply ingrained grasping mind that projects and apprehends intrinsic being or essence to our own selves and the various factors of existence.

With respect to understanding the function of *avidya* it is useful to recall a causal sequence which is encapsulated by Nagarjuna (second century CE), the founder of Madhyamaka (the Middle Way philosophy) school, in the following formula:

clinging to the factors of existence → grasping at the self;
grasping at the self → karmic action;
karmic action → birth-death cycle.[2]

The reversal of this causation, which is the process towards freedom, is beautifully captured in the following verses from *The Dhammapada*:

> I wandered through the rounds of countless rebirths,
> Seeking but not finding the builder of this house.
> Sorrowful indeed is birth again and again.
> Oh, housebuilder! You have now been seen.
> You shall build the house no longer.
> All your rafters of evils are broken,
> Your ridgepoles of ignorance are shattered.
> The fever of craving is past.
> My mind is joyful in the unconditioned freedom.[3]

What this causal process tells us is that a belief in the notion of self – i.e. an abiding, autonomous subject – gives rise to a clinging to an essence. This then leads to a pattern of existence where your whole *modus operandi* derives from a deep attachment to this inner core within you, which is your 'real self'. Every action is directed towards protecting and nurturing this precious core. Your interaction with others is judged in terms of whether it is beneficial or harmful towards this 'you'. Depending on how you judge the situation to be, you react either positively or negatively. This is of course accompanied by the occurrence of differing afflictive emotions within you motivating you to act in a particular way. Thus, a whole pattern of thought and action is set which becomes deeply habitual. This entire process need not necessarily be as conscious as the language of mental phenomena such as 'belief', 'judgement', 'clinging', etc., may suggest. In fact, much of this process should be understood as innate and functioning at what could be perhaps described as a precognitive level.

Tsongkhapa makes an important distinction between two types of *avidya*, which elucidates the nature of this so-called fundamental ignorance. One is the *avidya* that is acquired through thought processes such as rational thinking, and the other could be described as 'the natural, underlying tendencies inherent in all of us which instinctually seek grounding and solidity' for both the self and the world.[4] All the various metaphysical theories of self can be said to belong to the acquired category in that they are conscious, reactive attempts to certify and affirm our deeply ingrained notions of self and individuality. So, according to Buddhism, the task of the religious practitioner is to see through this deception and to reorient his or her personality so that there is no longer any felt need to seek an absolute ground. Therefore, it can be said that the acquired *avidya* is not the principal object of our critical analysis. The seeker's true opponent is himself or herself, albeit one's own sense of self that instinctually holds on to a notion of an abiding, individual core within oneself. This echoes the Buddha's dictum that you are your own worst enemy and also your own ultimate saviour.

Given that Buddhism defines its goal of 'awakening' in terms of an individual's journey from a state of fundamental confusion and suffering to that of 'knowledge' and freedom, much of the process involved in this transformation can be justifiably characterised as 'psychological'. It entails first and foremost a thorough understanding of one's own sense of self and its modes of operation. To a large extent, the process of discovering this can be said to be psychoanalytic in that its primary activity is to explore the psychodynamics of our mind. So the spirit of psychoanalysis does seem to be captured in the basic formula of the Four Noble Truths. First, the patient must be aware that he or she is ill. Secondly, he or she must identify what causes and sustains that illness; in other words, where the root of the illness lies. Only then can a cure be sought for the illness. This is how a process of healing begins.[5]

Having said this, I think it is vitally important not to succumb to the temptation of reducing Buddhism to a form of psycho-analysis or therapy. We should be aware of the fundamental differences between Buddhism and modern psychoanalytic disciplines, at least as they are popularly perceived today. To begin with, the goals of the two systems are different. Roughly speaking, psychoanalysis aims at bringing about a harmony between the various elements of individual's psyche so that a greater coherence can be achieved within the person's sense of self. In contrast, the aspiration in Buddhism is to transcend the bounds of the very concept of the self itself in that clinging to any sense of 'core' is seen as an obstruction. In contemporary language, we could say that what is being asked from us by the Buddhist doctrine of 'no-self' is not a mere change of an intellectual outlook, rather it is a radical transformation of our very being. Not only does this require a fundamental shift in our paradigm but also a radical reorientation of our frame of reference. One could say that, in a sense, Buddhism promises more than psychoanalysis. Furthermore, in Buddhism, there is an understanding that the existential insecurity at the heart of our being is so fundamental that it is beyond the content of any individual person's story. There is also no sense that the roots of many of our psychological ills can be traced to our childhood, although one could accept that certain aspects of them can be accentuated by unhealthy parenting. Therefore, Buddhist meditation tends to be less specific in its focus compared to psychoanalytic approaches. By specificity, I am referring to many of the contingent facts which make up our identity as an individual, such as gender, ethnicity, culture, language, and family environments. In addition, Buddhist meditation also demands the use of reason and philosophical reflections many of which are of a theoretical nature. This is, however, not to deny that there are significant parallels and overlaps between the concerns and approaches of Buddhism and that of modern psychoanalysis.

So, what *is* this freedom or awakening that Buddhism so consistently speaks of? In other words, how does Buddhism define its concept of awakening? The Buddhist *nirvana* is not just a psychological or epistemological state characterised by a temporary suspension of clinging to a self. More importantly, it is an ontological state, a mode of being where the person has effected a total transformation of his or her being. In such a person there is no longer any psychological and emotional need to grasp at any ground or solidity for security. Paradoxically, the realisation that there is no 'real' core to our being – that there is no essence – is said to liberate the mind! It is this essential *groundlessness* which becomes the source of security. As a Tibetan meditation text puts it: 'My mind, tired of the thoughts chasing after something, now rests at ease in the forest of the ineffable [truth].'[6]

Thus, we see that there is a direct connection between the search for freedom and the quest for the knowledge of the self (or its absence). In addition to the above, it is useful to take into account the mystical and aesthetical perspectives of the Vajrayana[7] Buddhism and its vision of enlightenment. According to this view, full enlightenment must encompass the perfection of not only all aspects of the human psyche but also the individual's 'physiology' as well. Principal amongst the elements transmuted is the sexual energy, which is seen as the key to spiritual freedom. *Nirvana* or 'awakening' here is defined in terms of perfection of the entire being. It is a state of non-duality in every sense of the word. The dichotomies that characterise our everyday existence in the *samsaric* world, such as 'subject and object', 'mind and matter', 'self and other', 'here and there', 'now and future', etc., – distinctions which are inescapable for our spatio-temporal existence – are believed to be totally transcended. In this view, not only must the tendency for grasping at one's own self and subjectivity be eliminated but more interestingly the Vajrayana teachings ask us to also transcend our very perception and identities of ordinary existence. If our deeply ingrained notions of self and individuality are at the root of our bondage, then surely these teachings are right in claiming that the habitual patterns which underlie our perception and the very understanding of the world become suspect as well. According to this view, it is believed that so long as we are imprisoned in our ordinary, 'normal' ways of perceiving the self and the world the tendency to cling at something secure and solid will always remain within us.

In summarising the Buddhist teachings on freedom, I have aimed to be as general as possible so that our understanding does not carry the prejudices which are too specific to an individual Buddhist school. Given that historically so many schools and traditions of Buddhism have evolved, the question could be raised about what makes a school of thought Buddhist. In other words, what binds all the various Buddhist denominations together as a family? Perhaps a useful way is to perceive that there is a certain 'orientation' of mind which is characteristic of most schools of Buddhism. Philosophically speaking, most Buddhist schools share a deep reluctance towards metaphysics. One could say that the Buddhists are minimalists with regard to metaphysical ideas. They postulate only the bare minimum. A form of an Asian Ockham's razor principle operates in Buddhist thinking. If Buddhists are to be philosophically labelled at all, their emphasis on validity of genuine experience means that we would have to call them 'empiricists'. In the ethical realm, they emphasise individual responsibility based on an understanding of the natural law of causality and also a deep appreciation of the interconnectedness of self and others. Soteriologically, the Buddhists' approach is to seek freedom through self-reliance. Salvation through a transcendent being external to personal existence has no real place in Buddhist religious praxis.

I shall now aim to identify and analyse what I see as key philosophical assumptions which underlie the Buddhist psychological theory of awakening. The aim of this enterprise is to bring into sharper focus the powerful metaphysical or religious ideas which appear to serve as the premises of the Buddhist teachings on awakening. This is crucial, for only by appreciating these underlying premises can we have a clearer understanding of what the Buddhist teachings on awakening entail.

II

As I see it, there are two fundamental premises to the Buddhist concept of awakening. First, there is the understanding that all defilements of our mind which the Buddhists call *klesha* or 'afflictions' are, in some profound sense, removable. These afflictions consist of a long list of emotions such as attachment, anger, and jealousy, and also what could be called cognitive events like false views, cynicism, and our deeply ingrained ego-consciousness. This is essentially a negative thesis in that its central claim has to do with what the essential nature of mind is not. Let us call this the *purifiability thesis*. There is, however, a positive thesis, which is our second premise. Buddhism appears to suggest that the potential for perfection exists naturally within the mind itself. Let us call this the *potentiality thesis*.

How does Buddhism argue for this purifiability thesis? It seems that there are two key arguments which together form the basis for this important Buddhist assumption. As can be inferred from the line of thinking so far, one line of important argument appears to be directed towards showing that the essential nature of mind is pure. In other words, Buddhism is asserting that the mind in its natural state is pure and unstained. The concept of the natural purity of consciousness is particularly developed as a systematic theory of mind in the Mahayana doctrine of Buddha-nature, the view that all sentient beings naturally possess the germinal seed for enlightenment. This purity should not be construed in any temporal terms; that is to say that there is no suggestion that in some remote past we were all pure and undefiled. The doctrine does not claim that our mind or consciousness has ever been free of the mental pollutants. It pertains more to a future possibility, a potential that is part of our mind's essential nature to be separable from these pollutants.

In one way or another, this notion of the essential purity of mind appears to be understood in terms of the fundamental nature of mind. We can see this particularly clearly if we perceive this thesis in the light of the Madhyamaka (Middle Way) theory of emptiness. According to this view, the mind in its natural mode of being is said to be essence-free, and devoid of any characteristics of 'thingness'. It is a mere absence, no-thing, open and fluid in its spontaneity. It is our deluded mind that projects on to it a form and the concept of 'thingness' thus obscuring the understanding of its genuine mode of being. Corollary to this is the argument that all defilements are rooted in a state of mind that is fundamentally confused. As shown before, Buddhism believes that at the root of all our afflictions is a fundamental ignorance, *avidya*, the Buddhist's own original sin. There is a sense that all our defilements are predicated upon this ignorance in that this confused state of being permeates the entire spectrum of our unenlightened existence. As the Madhyamika thinker Aryadeva says: 'As the bodily organ pervades our entire body so does ignorance reside in all.'[8] What is being claimed here is that all our afflictions such as attachment, hatred, jealousy, and so on arise from a deeply ingrained grasping to a sense of self that is held to be substantially 'real' and possesses intrinsic being.

How can we understand this claim? Analysis of our perception reveals that our normal, pre-philosophical world view appears to be close to that of what in contemporary Western philosophy is known as 'naive realism'. From this point of view, I am here and the world is there outside. 'I' as the subject is internal, private, and totally closed to others. Its reality cannot be questioned – it is 'here' within us, firmly established by our own experience, and provides the underlying unity to our diverse cognitive and physical experiences. In contrast, the world as object is external, quantifiable, and intersubjective. The gulf between these two is pre-given and nothing short of a miracle can bridge the abyss. It is the concept of an abiding self which serves as the core of our interpretation of the world around us and our relation to it. It is like a thread that weaves the myriad world of experience and helps enable us to make sense of the multiplicity. This mode of seeing the world is so pervasive that a serious observation of the nature of our experience in general will reveal that all coherent experiences are what one might call 'self-referential'.

Let us now examine the second premise, namely the potentiality thesis. According to this view, it is maintained that the potential for perfection lies naturally within the mind itself. Buddhism is saying that genuine 'awakening' comes from within. As the well-known Mahayana classic *Uttaratantra* (*The Sublime Continuum*) puts it: 'The qualities of the enlightened mind exist naturally within.'[9] We are also familiar with such typically Buddhist statements like 'no one "gives" awakening; nor does it come from outside', etc. I don't think that Buddhism is saying that we are all in actual fact fully awakened, only that we do not know it! Arguably, this is a Buddhist version of the doctrine of immanence. In order to appreciate this notion of immanence fully, it is crucial to have a basic understanding of the model of mind that emerges from Buddhist psychology. It is said that the essential nature of mind is 'luminous'. This is to say that the capacity to 'know' or to be aware is natural to the mind. The idea is that the mind in its natural state is a mere act of knowing; and it is our confusion which obstructs the full expression of this basic nature.

So, we can say that, in Buddhism, there is a clear sense that all sentient beings, though possessing equal potentials, are at different levels of cognitive capacity. This is dependent upon the level of the individual's mental development. The higher the level of mental discipline, the greater the development of the individual's power of discernment. For example, the Buddhist psychology and epistemology texts assert that an ordinary person's cognitive faculty is incapable of perceiving an event that lasts only a sixtieth of a snapping time.[10] His or her perception simply lacks the necessary power of attention that is able to arrest such a short instance. In contrast, the noble *aryas* (highly evolved beings) are said to be capable of arresting the moments even shorter than these instances. Certain Mahayana scriptures even speak of highly evolved Bodhisattvas who are able to 'stretch' an instance into an eon and contract an eon into an instance! Such are said to be the powers of discernment of a highly evolved mind.

Another way of seeing this theory of mind is to look at the Buddhist division of mental phenomena into primary mind and secondary mental factors. From its earliest history, Buddhist psychology has propounded a model of mind where qualities such as introspection (*samprajnaya*), mindfulness (*smrti*), understanding (*prajna*), concentration (*samadhi*) and so on are but different modalities of the mind. They are called *caitta* or 'mental factors' and are perceived to be natural aspects of our cognitive faculty. Those familiar with Buddhist psychology will be aware of the extensive discussion on the nature and function of these mental factors. Suffice here to state that it is these faculties which, in their perfection, become the qualities of the enlightened mind. There is also a sense that the fact that the quest for happiness appears to be innate to all suggests that ultimately there must be the possibility of its attainment.[11] So what we see here is a vision of a dual process: on the one hand the cleansing of the mind of its pollutants, while on the other, the qualities which enhance the capacities of the mind are developed. This dual process is exemplified in many of the Buddhist meditative practices aimed at overcoming afflictions of the mind.

So it could be said that according to Buddhism the mind cleanses itself of its own defilements. This 'cleansing' activity is not confined to what could be called the 'conscious', 'cognitive' level alone. There is a sense that through insight and prolonged reorientation even the latent tendencies which obstruct the expression of the mind's essential purity can be cleansed. In Buddhism, there is a complex understanding of the nature of afflictive emotions like anger. First and foremost, there is the conscious, reactive emotional experience itself. Then there is the underlying tendency towards anger which is natural to all of us. This could be called the anger in its subconscious form. Finally, there is the so-called seed of anger, which is the natural propensity to become angry to begin with. According to Buddhism, this propensity is created within our mind because of previous occurrences of anger. These three are intimately related to each other in that the first can be said to be a more obvious manifestation of the past two. In Tibetan, they are respectively known as 'manifest anger' (*khong tro ngon gyur*), 'subconscious anger' (*khong tro bag la nyal*), and finally, the 'seed of anger' (*khong throi sa bon*). Needless to say, the overcoming of the last two is considered to be more difficult than the first. In a Mahayana text the process of cleansing of these degrees of pollutants is likened to washing a cloth. The more one washes, the more likely one is able to get rid of even the slight traces of stains.[12]

We can now ask the question: 'What kind of a conception of mind emerges from the Buddhist psychology of awakening?' Perhaps it is useful here to look at some of the metaphors which are used in the Buddhist discourse on the nature of mind. Often, it is the metaphors that we live by which shed clearer light on the assumptions behind our basic concepts. A key metaphor in articulating the Buddhist concept of mind is the image of river or a stream. The use of this imagery is so embedded, especially in the Tibetan Buddhist conception of mind, that often the mind is referred to as simply 'the mind-stream' (*sem kyi gyu*). This notion of the continuity of consciousness has deep roots in the earliest writings of Buddhism. The Theravada classic *Visuddhimagga* compares consciousness to a 'flowing river'.[13] Vasubandhu (third century CE) invokes the concept to account for the phenomenon of memory.[14] Dharmakirti (seventh century CE) invokes it to reinforce the distinctness of identities of different persons in the light of his idealistic ontology.[15] Candrakirti (seventh century CE) invokes it to refute the intrinsic separateness of a mental event and its subsequent memory experience.[16] A corollary to this concept of continuum is the view that an individual's consciousness is unitary and indivisible. As a much quoted *sutra* states: 'The consciousness of sentient beings arise distinctly in single continuums.'[17] This is to say, that when a thought occurs, strictly speaking, only a single continuum of thought can occur at a given instance. This does not entail in any way the denial of the multiplicity of thoughts which quite naturally occur within us, an experience that is so characteristic of our everyday mental life. What it does imply is that all these thoughts are not discrete, unconnected, autonomous mental events; rather they are all various shades of the same spectrum of experience called consciousness.

Another image that often comes to mind when speaking of the mind in Buddhism is light. Just as light's primary feature is to illuminate, consciousness or mind is said to 'illuminate' its objects. There is a sense of natural clarity and reflexivity, without having to posit any notion of concreteness. In light, there is hardly any distinction between the act of illumination and that which illuminates. To some extent, we can say that the light is both the illuminator and the activity of illumination. The key idea here is the notion of activity. Similarly, in describing its content, the mind in its natural pure state is said to perceive only that which is ultimately true, which according to Buddhism is the absence of intrinsic being. So, it becomes clear that, in Buddhism, the mind or consciousness is not a static entity with characteristics of 'thingness'. All metaphors which convey a sense of spatial dimension are thus avoided in discourses pertaining to the mind.

It therefore emerges that the Buddhist conception of mind is best appreciated as a process rather than an entity. This calls into question many of the assumptions underlying spatial metaphors which appear to permeate the concepts of mind in many areas of contemporary Western thought. In some sense, one could argue that Buddhism questions any attempts to describe the nature of the mind in terms of the language of objects and things. This represents an important contrast from the way the mind is conceived in Western thought, at least in its classical forms. A second point of departure is the Buddhist notion of what I have called 'the singularity of continuum of consciousness'. This suggests that, in Buddhist psychology and philosophy of mind, various aspects of the psyche such as the cognitive aspects like thoughts, memory experiences, etc., and the affective aspects like emotion, including their underlying tendencies, are all perceived as belonging to one and the same continuum called consciousness. There is no concept of somewhat compartmentalised stark divisions as represented in the Freudian psychological model, at least in its popular form, of the ego and the unconscious. For, as we have seen, both the conscious levels of experience and its underlying tendencies which could be roughly characterised as subconscious are different degrees of mental activity within a single spectrum of experience. Even a brief glance at the etymology of the Buddhist terms reflect this way of thinking. To begin with, the Sanskrit word *citta* or the Tibetan equivalent *sem*, which is routinely translated as 'mind', has a broader connotation. It embraces both the cognitive and the affective aspects. In fact, there is a case to be made for suggesting that *citta* is translated as 'mind/heart'! Similarly, *mana* or *yid* (often translated as thought), and *vijnana* or *nam she* (which is translated as consciousness) have broader connotations than their English counterparts suggest. Because of this, Buddhist psychology tends not to speak in terms of the language of polarities, such as 'will versus passion', 'love versus hate', 'consciousness versus the unconscious', and so on.

III

The aim of this chapter has not been a comparative study of Buddhism and psychoanalysis. It has been to consider, as far as possible, the traditional Buddhist conception of 'awakening' and to explore its underlying philosophical assumptions. Admittedly, the summary of the philosophical arguments in the second part of the chapter reflects my own personal prejudice as someone who has been brought up in a tradition that adheres to the tenets of the Madhyamika school. One could say that the version I have argued for is one plausible way of understanding the premises of the Buddhist idea of awakening.

By way of conclusion, I will make a few brief observations. First, the concept of mind that emerges from Buddhist psychology and philosophy of mind suggests an understanding of our fundamental nature as being essentially positive and compassionate. This concept of human nature is, as we have seen, grounded within a rigorous philosophical framework. As the pervasive influence of popular assumptions about Darwinian evolutionary theory has shown, at the fundamental level, how we perceive ourselves has a powerful impact on how we relate to others and the world at large. So the ethical and social implications of embracing a more positive vision of human nature cannot be underestimated. Furthermore, Buddhism's claim as to the purifiability of mind can have significant implications for contemporary psychotherapy. Even in its weak form, the Buddhist understanding of the purifiablity thesis provides a theoretical framework within which many of the observable facts of psychotherapy can be better appreciated. With its explicit avowal of the essential groundlessness of our being, Buddhist theoretical models of the mind are better able to accommodate the existential discoveries of analysis and therapy. Furthermore, Buddhist psychology with its thorough-going analysis of the concept of self can help expand the horizons of contemporary psychoanalysis and its applications in therapy. For the Buddhists, the insights of psychoanalysis and therapy can help one appreciate the crucial importance of understanding the uniqueness of each individual's psyche in order to develop ways of countering the neuroses of his or her mind. After all, *who* or *what* we are cannot be disassociated from *where* we come from. This is an important lesson that the Buddhist meditation teachers must learn in particular, if their message is to have any significant effect on their students. Perhaps, most importantly for the Buddhist teachers and translators, psychoanalysis and psychotherapy may provide one of the most appropriate and effective languages to present the insights of Buddhism to a contemporary Western audience.

The Agnostic Buddhist

Stephen Batchelor

Something I've noticed recently is how I started out rebelling against Christianity (and the West in general) and found in Buddhism a vindication for my largely unconscious rebelliousness. But as we grow older, we begin to recover our past. I was not brought up a Christian. I grew up in an anti-Church environment, one which might loosely be termed humanistic. Now I find that I am returning to that culture in which I grew up. While I admire many of Christianity's ethical values, I have no natural sympathy with the Christian tradition. But I do find myself increasingly sympathetic to my own childhood experience as a humanist, a secularist, an agnostic.

The term 'agnostic' is perhaps the one with which I most closely identify. It was only coined in the late 1880s by the biologist Thomas Huxley. And it was coined as a joke. Huxley belonged to a small philosophical circle in London in which he increasingly felt out of place. While everybody else in the group could readily identify themselves as Christian or Rationalist or Schopenhauerian, or whatever, he felt perplexed that no such term seemed applicable to him. So he decided to call himself an 'agnostic' in order that he too could 'have a tail like all the other foxes'.

Huxley developed the idea. He saw agnosticism to be as demanding as any moral, philosophical, or religious creed. But he refused to see it as a creed in the traditional sense of the word;

he preferred to see it as a *method*. The method he had in mind is still broadly that which underpins scientific inquiry. It means, on the one hand, taking one's reason as far as it will go and, on the other, not accepting anything as true unless it is demonstrable. Here there are clear parallels with the Buddhist tradition. The Indo-Tibetan tradition lays a strong emphasis on rational inquiry. I spent many years as a young monk not puzzling on koans but studying formal logic and epistemology with Tibetan lamas. In any case, all traditions of Buddhism agree that one should not believe something simply for the sake of believing it, only if it can be realised in some practical way.

Huxley even described his view as 'the agnostic faith', thus giving it the kind of seriousness that one might otherwise expect only amongst religious people. And within fifteen years of Huxley coining the term, 'agnosticism' was already being linked with Buddhism. It was first applied by a man called Allan Bennett who became a *bhikkhu* in Burma in 1901 with the name Ananda Metteyya. Bennett was the first Englishman to be ordained as a Buddhist and the first European to articulate his understanding of the Dharma as a practising Buddhist rather than merely a scholar of Buddhism. In a magazine he issued in Rangoon in 1905, he spoke of Buddhism as 'exactly coincidental in its fundamental ideas with the modern agnostic philosophy of the West'.

At the beginning of the century, when Westerners were only just starting to embrace the teachings of the Buddha, why would this young English monk have regarded Buddhism as agnostic? I suspect that one of the key sources may have been this famous passage from the 'Cula Malunkya Sutta', the sixty-third discourse in the *Majjhima Nikaya* of the Pali canon. The Buddha says:

> Suppose Malunkyaputta, a man were wounded by an arrow thickly smeared with poison, and his friends and companions brought a surgeon to treat him. The man would say, 'I will not let the surgeon pull out the arrow until I know the name and clan of the man who wounded me; whether the bow that wounded me was a long bow or a cross bow; whether the arrow that wounded me was hoof-tipped or curved or barbed.' All this would still not be known to that man, and meanwhile he would die. So too, Malunkyaputta, if anyone should say, 'I will not lead the noble life under the Buddha until the Buddha declares to me whether the world is eternal or not eternal; finite or infinite; whether the soul is the same as or different from

the body; whether or not an awakened one continues or ceases to exist after death,' that would still remain undeclared by the Buddha, and meanwhile that person would die.

This passage shows quite clearly both the pragmatic nature of the Buddha's teaching, as well as its agnostic bent.

It is generally assumed that a religious person believes certain things about the nature of oneself and reality in general that are beyond the reach of reason and empirical verification. What happened before birth, what will happen after death, the nature of the soul and its relation to the body: these are first and foremost religious questions. And the Buddha was not interested in them. But if we look at Buddhism historically, we'll see that it has continuously tended to lose this agnostic dimension through becoming institutionalised as a religion, with all of the usual dogmatic belief systems that religions tend to have. So, ironically, if you were to go to many Asian countries today, you would find that the monks and priests who control the institutional bodies of Buddhism would have quite clear views on whether the world is eternal or not, what happens to the Buddha after death, the status of the mind in relation to the body, and so on.

In the West, this has led to Buddhism being automatically regarded as a religion. The very term 'Buddhism' is largely an invention of Western scholars. It suggests a creed to be lined up alongside other creeds. It's another set of beliefs about the nature of reality that we cannot know by other means than through faith. This assumption tends to distort or obscure the encounter of the Dharma with secular agnostic culture. Another problem is that today the very force of the term 'agnosticism' has been lost. If somebody says they're an agnostic, although they know it means that one claims not to know certain things, it usually goes hand in glove with an attitude that seems not to care about such things. 'I don't know what happens after death' becomes equivalent to: 'I don't care; I don't really want to know; I don't even want to think about it.' Modern agnosticism has lost the confidence that it seems to have had at the time of Huxley. Buddhism too has lost that critical edge that we find in the early Pali discourses, Madhyamaka philosophy and the Zen koans. Very often Buddhism as an institution has tended to lapse into religiosity.

I would suggest that an agnostic Buddhist would not regard the Dharma or the teachings of the Buddha as a source which would provide answers to questions of where we are going, where we are coming from, what is the nature of the universe, and so on. In this sense, an agnostic Buddhist would not be a believer with claims to revealed information about supernatural or paranormal phenomena and in this sense would not be religious. I've recently started saying to myself: 'I'm not a religious person', and I find it strangely liberating. You don't have to be a religious person in order to practise the Dharma.

An agnostic Buddhist would not look to the Dharma for metaphors of consolation. This is another great trait of religions: they provide consolation in the face of birth and death; they offer images of a better afterlife; they offer the kind of security that can be achieved through an act of faith. I'm not interested in that. The Buddha's teachings are confrontative; they're about truth-telling, not about painting some pretty picture of life elsewhere. They're saying: 'Look, existence is painful.' This is what is distinctive about the Buddhist attitude: it starts not from the promise of salvation, but from valuing that sense of existential anguish we tend to ignore, deny or avoid through distractions.

Buddhism is often misrepresented as something nihilistic or life-denying. This fails to recognise that the project of the Four Noble Truths is about resolving the dilemma of anguish, not about indulging human suffering. Again it's a praxis; it's something we can do. It starts with understanding the reality of anguish and uncertainty, and then applying a set of practices that work towards a resolution. But this kind of agnosticism is not based on disinterest; it's not saying, 'I just don't care about these great matters of birth and death.' It is a passionate recognition that *I do not know*. I really do not know where I came from; I do not know where I'm going. And that 'don't know' is a very different order of 'don't know' from that of a superficial agnosticism.

This process of stripping away consolatory illusions by holding true to this agnostic not-knowing, leads to what we might call 'deep agnosticism'. I like to think of Buddhism as the practice of deep agnosticism. This both leads away from the superficiality of contemporary Western agnosticism, and begins to tap a dimension that seems essential to the heart of Dharma practice. To illustrate this, here is the very first koan of the *Blue Cliff Record*:

Emperor Wu of Liang asked the great Master Bodhidharma, 'What is the highest meaning of the holy truths?' Bodhidharma said, 'Empty, without holiness.' The

Emperor said, 'Who is facing me?' Bodhidharma replied, 'I don't know.'

This kind of 'I don't know' deepens the notion of agnosticism. It gives agnosticism meditative depth. Such deep agnostic metaphors are likewise found in such terms as *wu hsin* (no-mind), and *wu nien* (no-thought), as well as in the more popular 'Don't Know Mind' of the Korean Zen master, Seung Sahn.

'I don't know' is likewise suggestive of no-self and emptiness. 'Emptiness' is a singularly unattractive term. But was it ever supposed to be attractive? Herbert Guenther once translated it as 'the open dimension of being', which sounds a lot more appealing. 'Transparency' is another term that likewise makes it sound more palatable. Yet we have to remember that even two thousand years ago Nagarjuna was having to defend himself against the nihilistic implications of emptiness. Chapter 24 of the *Mula Madhyamakakarika* opens with the objection: 'If everything's empty, nothing could happen.'

Emptiness, it is thought, is a terrible idea. It undermines all grounds for morality. It undermines everything the Buddha was speaking about. Clearly the word did not have a positive ring back then either. Might Nagarjuna have used it quite consciously as an unappealing term, which cuts through the whole fantasy of consolation that one might expect a religion to provide? Perhaps we need to recover this hard edge of emptiness, its unattractive aspect.

By inquiring honestly into his self-identity, Bodhidharma could find nothing he could ultimately grasp hold of and say: 'Yes, that's me. There it is. I've got it. I've defined it. I've realised it.' Instead, he discovers the ultimate unfindability of himself, and by implication the ultimate unfindability of everything and everyone else as well: 'I don't know.' This gives another clue to emptiness and 'no-mind'. It's not that there is literally no mind. If you try to understand the nature of anything in the deepest sense, you will not be able to arrive at any fixed view that defines it as this or that. The Dalai Lama uses a quaint expression in colloquial Tibetan: *dzugu dzug-sa mindoo*, which means literally: 'There is no finger-pointing-place.' Or as we would say: 'There's nothing you can put your finger on.' Again this doesn't imply that the thing in question does not exist at all. It simply exposes the fallacy of the deeply felt, almost instinctive assumption that our self, the mind or anything else must be secured in a permanent, metaphysical basis.

Yet the uniqueness of a person's mind or identity, the uniqueness of a flower that's growing in the garden outside, does not require any kind of felt-metaphysical basis peculiar to that person or thing. Emptiness indicates how everything that comes about does so through an unrepeatable matrix of contingencies, conditions, causes, as well as conceptual, linguistic and cultural frameworks. Everything arises from an complex combination of transient events that culminate, in this particular instance, in my saying these words to you.

Now, whether we follow the Indo-Tibetan analytical approach or the Zen approach of asking a koan like 'What is this?', such meditative inquiry leads to a mind that becomes more still and clear. But paradoxically this does not mean that things then become more clear-cut, that you reach some final understanding of who you are or of what makes the universe tick. As things become more vivid and clear, they also become more perplexing. A deep agnosticism would be one founded on this kind of unknowing: the acknowledgement that, in terms of what life *is*, I simply do not know. In such unknowing there is already a quality of questioning, of perplexity. And as the perplexity becomes stabilised through meditation, one comes to inhabit a world that is mysterious, in a sense magical, in the lived sense not reducible to things, ideas or concepts.

Emptiness is not where the practice ends. It's a halfway point. We discover in its open, ambiguous space the wellsprings of creativity and imagination. In Mahayana Buddhism the Buddha is not just someone who had a wonderful mystical experience, whose mind is freed, but also this being who spontaneously and compassionately manifests and is embodied in the world (*nirmanakaya*).

The Buddha's awakening is followed by this strange period where, according to tradition, he hesitates for about six weeks before being prompted, by a god in this case, to go out into the world and do something. This process is similar in many respects to the process of artistic creation. When faced with the task of articulating a deep intuitive vision in words, clay or paint, one might experience that same intense trepidation that one finds in meditation when the mind is very still but at the same time tremendously resistant about pursuing the inquiry any further. At this point the meditator usually lapses into fantasy, daydreams and drowsiness, which you may be familiar with. The writer might have an urgent compulsion to tidy up his desk. It's the same kind of evasion; the same kind of hesitation in the face of what is rather awesome.

We stand on the threshold of the imagination. We are

challenged to imagine something that has never quite been thought of in that way before. The Buddha's genius lies precisely in his imagination. When he experienced awakening, suddenly the Four Noble Truths did not appear – 1, 2, 3, 4 – in words of fire in the sky or anything like that. Rather, the awakening did not become real until he had to stammer it out to his five former companions in the deer-park in Sarnath. This model of awakening is that of a process, which is perhaps never completed. The process of articulating the Dharma goes on and on according to the needs of the different historical situations it encounters. We could read the whole history of Buddhism, from the moment of the Buddha's awakening until now, as a process of seeking to imagine a way to respond both wisely and compassionately to the situation at hand.

Historically, Buddhism has always had to find ways of responding effectively to the danger of becoming too acculturated, too absorbed into the assumptions of the host culture. Certainly such a danger exists here in the West: Buddhism might, for example, tend towards a kind of souped-up psychotherapy. But equally there's the danger of Buddhism holding on too fiercely to its Asian identity and remaining a marginal interest amongst a few eccentrics. Somehow we have to find a middle way between these two poles, and this is a challenge which is not going to be worked out by academics or Buddhist scholars; it's a challenge all are asked to meet in their own practice from day to day.

I, Mine and Views of the Self

Gay Watson

The idea of no-self is one of the most important teachings in Buddhism; it is also for Westerners one of the least understood and the most difficult to grasp. Yet even the most cursory survey of contemporary Western discourse reveals views of self coming from many directions, that, carefully considered, may not be so very different. They reveal a picture of selves which under examination lose their definition and singularity while retaining their power of action. So what is the self? And what is it not? What does Buddhism deny? What does the West assert? Are there any comparisons between the two which can usefully be made?

We should, perhaps, begin with terminology. Not only are we confronted with different conceptions of self, but also similar ideas expressed in different terms. One man's ego is another man's self.[1] The immediate response to the conception of self, I would suggest, is usually, or perhaps until very recently has been, that which philosopher Charles Taylor has called the 'punctual self', the point of self-awareness in abstraction, in isolation from its constitutive concerns. It is that self which John Locke described when he wrote: 'We must consider what Person stands for; which, I think, is a thinking intelligent Being, that has reason and reflection, and can consider it self as it self, the same thinking thing in different times and places.'[2] However, if we look more closely and follow recent studies we find, even in the

West, a sense of self that is not a thing but a construct, and one that appears to be considered as ever more widely distributed. One of the first to consider this was William James. In the early days of the century and of academic psychology, he suggested: 'In its widest possible sense, however, a man's Self is the sum total of all that he can call his.'[3]

Our view of the self will also affect our view of the world. Changes in contemporary views of the self not only move away from the punctual self to a more distributed one, but also display a shift away from the separation of epistemology from ontology, of how we know from what we know, so that the stance we take towards knowledge and reality becomes in time a feature of that very reality. Francisco Varela is amongst the foremost articulating this enactive view. In his own words together with those of his co-writers 'cognition is not the representation of a pregiven world by a pregiven mind but is rather the enactment of a world and a mind on the basis of a history of the variety of actions that a being in the world performs'.[4]

This could seem very far removed from the idea of self as an independent and isolated essence or thing. Is it so far from the Buddhist view of no-self? Thus, I would like to consider Buddhist views on the self, before returning to some contemporary ideas.

THE BUDDHIST VIEW OF THE SELF

The third of the three marks of existence relating to all Dharmas is *anatta* (Pali) or non-self, and the concept of selflessness is one of the distinguishing marks of Buddhism. Yet when we look at the life of the Buddha Sakyamuni we see a man who possessed personal continuity, identity and personality. What then is the self which is to be rejected, and what is it that Buddhism denies? The Tibetan dGe lugs pa tradition makes a distinction between the 'mere self', the transactional self which functions convention-ally in the world, and an absolute or essential self, a fictitious self, which is to be denied. As Buddhism presents it, the self we experience is comprised of five psychosomatic aggregates: material form or appearance (*rupa*), feelings (*vedana*), per-ceptions (*samjna*), determinations (*samskara*) and conscious-ness (*vijnana*). The self therefore arises from the interplay of these rather than existing as any permanent ontological entity. From the Buddhist point of view, due to basic ignorance of the interdependent nature of these aggregates and all phenomena, this process of selfing, this dynamic experience of everchanging process, is grasped at as an entity, as some kind of container of the ongoing experience, and identified with. In mindful awareness we can become aware of the arising and falling, coming and going of the discontinuous thoughts, perceptions, feelings and sensations which make up what we like to imagine as a single coherent and continuous self. Again this has been beautifully described by Varela, Thompson and Rosch:

> This arising and subsiding, emerging and decay, is just that emptiness of self in the aggregate of experience. In other words, the very fact that the aggregates are full of experience is the same as the fact that they are empty of self. If there were a solid, really existing self hidden in or behind the aggregates, its unchangeableness would prevent any experience from occurring; its static nature would make the constant arising and subsiding of experience come to a screeching halt.[5]

So in ordinary experience it is the identification and appropriation of these experiential processes by an allegedly solid sense of self that causes the suffering of *samsara*. Without them, one could perhaps, aspire to the purity of perception suggested in the Udana:

> In the seen there will just be the seen; in the heard, just the heard; in the reflected, just the reflected; in the cognized, just the cognized. This is how, Bahiya, you must train yourself. Now Bahiya, when in the seen there will be to you just the seen; . . . then, Bahiya, you will not identify with it. When you will not identify yourself with it, you will not locate yourself therein. When you do not locate yourself therein, it follows that you will have no 'here' or 'beyond' or 'midway-between' and this would be the end of suffering.[6]

Buddhist descriptions are descriptions of process, of how things are, rather than what they are. So how does the sense of self come about? In the twelvefold description of dependent origination (*pratityasamutpada*) relating to the development of suffering human life, the same factors or aggregates appear in a different order. From basic ignorance of the three marks of existence – impermanence, unsatisfactoriness and lack of essential self – arise the mental tendencies or determinations which we saw earlier as the fourth aggregate, *samskara*. These give rise to consciousness, which in turn gives rise to *nama/rupa*, another name for the five aggregates we have already discussed, since the last four are attributed to *nama*, which is often translated as mind, with *rupa* as body or form. A more helpful translation of the pair however as 'name' and 'physical form' sees them as the basis for a Buddhist theory of identity.[7] It is name as the entire conceptual identity of the individual, and physical form which individualise, identifying us to ourselves and to others, and creating the divisions between inner and outer identity. The concept of 'name' also introduces the function of language.

In another description the Buddha said that name was comprised of the five factors of intention (*cetana*), attention (*manasikara*), perception (*samjna*), stimulation or contact (*sparsa*) and feeling (*vedana*). These same five factors were given as the five constant factors of consciousness in the Theravada Abhidharma, and again in the Mahayana by Asanga. Thus they are the foundation for a working sense of self. The illusory self with its concomitant egoistic grasping is a superimposition, resulting primarily from ignorance of the three marks of existence, reinforced by the naming process of language. Ignorance of the three marks of existence conceives of this fluid transactional self as permanent, partless and autonomous. The process is described as working in three main ways, both instinctually and intellectually: craving occurring in the linguistic form 'This is mine', conceit manifesting in the linguistic form 'This I am', and false views manifesting in the linguistic form 'This is myself.'[8] Once one identifies with a permanent self-concept, the pride and craving adhering to this become the pivot from which an egocentric world arises.

The self then, which in Buddhism is to be negated, is an illusion; it is the imposition of a container self with attributes of independence and permanence upon the foundation of the conventional or transactional self of ever-changing mind states.

Central to this process of expansion and solidification is *prapanca*, often translated as conceptual proliferation. It is another difficult term to translate, and entire books have been devoted to the subject, such is its importance. The major locus for discussion of *prapanca* rests upon a passage describing another process, the development of visual awareness:

Dependent on the eye and forms, eye-consciousness arises.

> The meeting of the three is contact. With contact as con-
> dition there is feeling. What one feels, that one perceives.
> What one perceives, that one thinks about. What one
> thinks about, that one mentally proliferates. With what
> one has mentally proliferated as the source, perceptions
> and notions tinged by mental proliferation beset a man
> with respect to past, future and present forms cognizable
> through the eye.[9]

This description clearly shows how mental proliferation arises,
and how in turn, in circular fashion, it influences all subsequent
cognition.

Some commentators[10] point to the idea of separateness which
adheres to the term *prapanca*, implying, in fact, an erroneous
imposition of separateness upon things which are really dependently originated. The most important attribution of separate
independent existence is that to the self. The pivotal separation is
the statement 'I am' from which all further attributions of
separateness spring. As the Buddha taught in *Sutta Nipata*, 916:
'The wise man should put a stop to the thought "I am", which is
the root of all naming in terms of manifoldness.'

In Mahayana Yogacara philosophy Asanga unites discussion
of self, discursive reasoning (*vikalpa*) and consequent conceptual proliferation (*prapanca*).[11] Asanga describes how *samsara*
is founded upon three bases created by discursive reasoning.
These three bases are 1) things, 2) the self and 3) the obstruc-
tions: desire, hatred and delusion. Asanga states that these three
bases are closely interrelated: the view of self is only supported
when there is an object in contradistinction to which it is defined
in self/other dualism, and desire, hatred and delusion can only
arise in the presence of ideas of self and possession. The antidote
is to understand that discursive thought and the given thing
which becomes the support for such thought are mutually
dependent and without beginning. Through such close investigation one may learn the interdependence and thus, the ultimate
emptiness of both selves and given things, arising together
through discursive thought and conceptual proliferation.

Thus we see that for Buddhism it is not so much that there is
no self, as is often bluntly stated, but rather that the imposition of
a permanent, separate self on to the interaction of self processes
is an error. The experiencing of life from the perspective of
identification with this unchanging centre, this independent
separate identity, is the ignorant premise that underlies life in

samsara. If, as we are told in the Second Noble Truth, desire is the cause of continual suffering, it is fuelled by the erroneous perception which sees and separates one who desires, the object of desire, and desires themselves. When one no longer sees in this way and things are seen as they really are, such desires and the traces they leave on mental processes will cease since they are the result of thinking in terms of the separateness or selfhood of oneself and all phenomena. As one lets go of this grasping of separateness compassion will arise, a concern for that from which one is not separate. In the Mahayana specific attention is drawn to compassion as the necessary adjunct to the wisdom which sees the truth of emptiness and sees things and selves as dependently originated and devoid of separateness.

SOME WESTERN VIEWS ON THE DEVELOPMENT OF CONSCIOUSNESS

Turning to Western views on the development of consciousness and selfhood I have neither the time nor the specific knowledge to describe them with much detail, and others have done this much better than I can attempt. Both John Crook and Guy Claxton have written of the phylogenetic and individual development of a sense of self.[12] Both their descriptions distinguish between the development of a working sense of self or continuity and that of a self-concept which develops on top of this. Briefly, both in the development of the species and of the individual, bodily awareness comes first. This is followed by representation of one's own physical state; a move from self-monitoring to self-awareness, which leads to the imputation of a self within a system. Once this imputation is symbolised within language it is reinforced and reified by social structures and value systems of the cultural sphere. Self-image as process retaining a connectedness with the environment, gives way to a self-concept which becomes increasingly solid and autonomous.

Other models I could mention, such as those from Systems Theory, from psychologist Margaret Donaldson and from neuroscientist Gerald Edelman, also show this two-tier development from transactional self as process to a self-concept reinforced by language and culture. These descriptions draw a distinction between a transactional self and a self-concept which tends to become hypostatised; such a distinction between an ever-changing experiential response to the environment and the concept of a reified continuous self living in an objective world is not so far from the Buddhist perspective.

Turning to psychotherapy, we find many different models of self-development, which share the characteristic that they all see the self as a compound and a construct. Freudian models delineate conscious, preconscious and unconscious, ego, id and superego. Object Relations theory sees the development of self occurring through interaction with others. Perhaps one can say that different schools of psychotherapy – analytic, humanistic and transpersonal – see the image of the self as covering a wider area, intra, inter and transpersonal. Jack Engler who has written most perceptively about the often perceived difference between Buddhism and psychoanalysis in their approach to the self or ego, speaks of both as viewing self as a representation 'which is actually being constructed anew from moment to moment'.[13] From this perspective the task is to acquire a cohesive functioning sense of self and to acknowledge it as a construct, which to remain healthy needs to be reconstructed from moment to moment. Our suffering and psychological ill-health arise from identifying with a permanent self-concept, grasping it and seeing our life and world through the lens of this concept, refusing to move with change and impermanence. However, in actuality I believe that sometimes psychotherapies themselves often lose touch with acknowledging the self as a construct. Attempting to heal the defective self-image, or replace an inappropriate with a more appropriate one, they forget in the process that any self-concept, is just that, a concept, and that identification with that concept, however appropriate, will be ultimately unhealthy and unhelpful, in a changing world. Only Lacan consistently seems to see the image of the self as a whole as a *méconaissance*, as not only a construct, but in the way we relate to it, a false one.

Just as current scientific views of the development of the self appear to have taken us quite a way from any unitary, essential and 'punctual' view, in the worlds of theory and art too we follow the postmodern train of the vanishing subject. This may take many different forms, but in all cases a substantial representation of the self at the centre of its world is replaced with a more relational and distributed concept of subjectivity, and a more contingent one. As Charles Taylor has pointed out, citing Merleau Ponty, Michael Polanyi, Heidegger and the later Wittgenstein, much of the most insightful philosophy of the twentieth century has gone to refute the picture of the disengaged subject. The unified and separate subject in contemporary discourse is replaced by an impermanent, contingent and constructed subject, whose identity is constituted and changed continually in relationship. From selfhood, the emphasis has shifted to alterity, from unity and identity to difference. Again there is no time to delineate individual arguments, let me merely point to the deconstructions of Derrida, the importance of the other and relationship, albeit in different ways, in the work of Bakhtin and Levinas, to Heidegger's delineation of the immersion of beings in Being, and to Richard Rorty writing of the contingency of selfhood.

CONCLUSION

The views of self in contemporary Western discourse in philosophy and science do not seem inimical to that of Buddhism. If, according to the Buddhist view, the sense of self is upheld by craving, conceit and false views, perhaps Western approaches may be said to have come to terms intellectually with new views of self rather better than they have emotionally dealt with craving and conceit. Contemporary views of self are, as we have seen, most definitely no longer those of a single, unitary and permanent self, and everywhere we find a distinction between transactional self, and self-image or self-concept. Yet our conceit, of 'I', and our craving of 'mine' would not appear to have yet caught up with our intellectual knowledge. Does this matter? I believe that it does, on both the philosophical and personal levels. For if our changing views are not accompanied by attention to the emotional reinforcements of 'I' and 'mine', though views may have changed, our daily lives will not, and to the old suffering will be added new suffering of uncertainty and resistance to the new views. When the self is separated from the world and the other, so it appropriates and attempts to dominate both the world and other. Similar separations are mirrored even in the interior individual world, with the hegemony of head or intellect over body and feeling, until we are alienated not only from our environment externally, but also from our embodied existence and our own experience. We become afraid of living. Paradoxically, along with the weakening of the certainty of the world and of the punctual self, the West has seen both a rise in nihilistic thought and a reactionary emotional clinging to the concept of self.

Despite the increasing dispersal of self theoretically over a wide area, intrapersonal, interpersonal and even transpersonal, we also see an increased emphasis upon the self and on the actualisation of its potential. In practice the self as construct or even as process has itself been defensively reified and reconsolidated. The generation of humanistic psychology has been termed narcissistic in the most pejorative sense, the 'me' generation. Although the sense of self is no longer unitary, yet the operational view of it as an egocentric centre of operations has been strengthened: theoretical models of the widely distributed self seem to be accompanied by an ever stronger focus on the interiority and individuality of that self, as James Hillman has recently argued.[14]

Narcissism and egotism are a defence against inadequacy or loss. In Buddhist terms such a defence is unnecessary since the loss is illusory, a loss of something which never existed in the first place, for the self itself is not an existent reality but merely a mental construction which falsely experiences itself as separate and then feels its own perceived groundlessness as a lack. For Buddhism, an investigation of the mental constructions which give rise to this constructed sense of self, reveals its emptiness, loosening at one stroke both the conceptual proliferation which supports the sense of self, that self itself and the anxiety unconsciously defending its fragility. What is left is not nothing, but a greater non-egocentric grounding, as one writer, David Loy, beautifully describes:

> If each link of *pratitya-samutpada* is conditioned by all the others, then to become completely groundless is also to become completely grounded, not in some particular, but in the whole network of interdependent relations that constitute the world. The supreme irony of my struggle to ground myself is that it cannot succeed because I am already grounded *in the totality*.[15]

Buddhism has in its long history not only effected the intellectual deconstruction of substantial views of the world, self and their relationship but has also instituted methods of practice for vitiating the emotional attachment to such views. It engages with both the philosophical and psychological sense of lack and its concurrent desire, for the philosophical and the psychological are inextricably interwoven. Buddhism sees how belief in the self is upheld by the desire to be and to have a self, and how from the central pivot of identification with a self, the notion of mine and the entire egocentric world arises.

For the Western view the perceived loss of self may well lead either to nihilism or to a reactive narcissistic grasping of self.[16] For Buddhism the realisation that self and world are interdependent and ultimately empty allows one not merely to ride on the processive wave, but to be it. When the world is not viewed from an egocentric position, the self may be seen not as a solitary unit but as immanent and embedded within a larger network of one's relationship with the world, accordingly both self and even death take on a different aspect. For, as Gregory Bateson pointed out in a rare Western exposition of interdependence: 'the individual nexus of pathways which I call "me" is no longer so precious because that nexus is only part of a larger mind'.[17] The bridge between self and emptiness, which carries one over the abyss of nihilism, is interconnection and interdependence. Such an understanding in Buddhism is instantiated through the wisdom which understands dependent origination, non-self and emptiness, and through morality and meditation, which encourage disidentification with the ways of egocentricity, with the cries of 'I' and 'mine'.

This may lead to a middle way between subjectivity and objectivity, one that escapes the extremism of either side, a non-dual view which may evade the Western dilemma of embracing either an extreme objectivism or an equally extreme subjectivism.[18] The impoverishment of the egocentric view and an alternative to it, a description of both the self to be abandoned and the enlightened self, was most succinctly and beautifully expressed by the Japanese Buddhist Dogen in the thirteenth century:

> To practise and confirm all things by conveying one's self to them is illusion, for all things to advance forward and practise and confirm the self, is enlightenment . . . To learn the Buddha Way is to learn one's own self. To learn one's self is to forget one's self. To forget one's self is to be confirmed by all dharmas.[19]

Subjects Without Selves: Contemporary Theory Accounts for the 'I'

Fred Pfeil

Like many others of my class (middle), culture (American), and generation (baby-boom), I wasted a goodsized portion of my youth watching old movies, soap operas, and sitcoms on TV. And the trashy, 'small "m" mind' that resulted from the interplay of these causes, conditions and decidedly unskilful practices has consequently been unable to resist feeling a kinship between the tenor and timing of this essay, and that narrative convention which used to clock in quite reliably at the climax of the wedding scene, just after the vows and before the blessing, when the priest or preacher intones 'If there be anyone here who knows aught against the marriage of this woman to this man, let her or him speak now, or forever hold his peace . . .' and then, to the audience's groans or cheers, depending on whether the genre's comedy or melodrama, there arises from the back the single upstart cry.

The marriage much of what is now called 'Western Buddhism' gathers us to celebrate is of course some synthesis of one or more of the various traditions of Asian Buddhism that have made their way to the West with one or more seam or version of the Western psychotherapeutic view or construction of the self. And let me say at once, for whatever it's worth, that I myself am far from univocally opposed to any and all forms of such a union. Throughout Buddhism's long and wide career, wherever the Dharma has found a home, after all, it has perforce done so by tying its lot in with indigenous spiritual ideologies and blending its practices with those already on the ground, from those of the Vedic tradition itself in India in 500 BCE, to Bon in Tibet and Taoism in China centuries later. Given this history, then, and given the strength of the 'therapeutic ethos'[1] in our culture and time, it would seem both churlish and ignorant to insist this newest marriage be postponed or prohibited due to any fear that the purity of some transhistorically, transculturally 'true', 'authentic', or 'original' teaching will be despoiled or besmirched. Yet, as at any wedding that follows on the heels of such a brief and feverish courtship as this one between Eastern Buddhism and Western psychotherapy has been, and particularly when one of the happy couple has already enjoyed several previous foreign unions of this same kind, there ought at least to be a place – a distant table at the reception, anyhow, over the sourpuss corner – from which to mutter a little, under the dance music, about how it won't work. Or, worse, about how pathologically well it will.

But now I'm sure you'll agree it's time to drop this metaphor, and come more directly to my point. What is so dubious or disturbing about the general impulse within what we have come to call 'Western Buddhism' to perceive or construct an intimate relationship between psychotherapeutic practices and concerns and Buddhist ones? In this essay, I will first offer an answer to this question, then go on to advertise the virtues of another kind of indigenous thinking through the self available to us here in the West today, albeit one much less well known than those offered by the therapeutic paradigm. The answer I'll rehearse fairly summarily, mainly because I suspect in its most general form it will be at least familiar, if not congenial, to many readers of this volume; the advertisement, which I suspect may well be both less familiar and, to some degree, less agreeable, will require rather more elaboration on that account.

I am, indeed, encouraged to think my first point will raise no great hackles with you since I already half-articulated it a few sentences back, with those doughty words the 'ideological hegemony of the therapeutic ethos'. If, then or now, your culturally conditioned ears picked up the Marxist inflections of such phraseology, you've got the accent right – like His Holiness the Dalai Lama in this (and, alas, only this) respect, I too am prone to describe myself as 'half-Marxist, half-Buddhist'.[2] So I would like to think His Holiness would not be surprised to find the Left's historical and critical definition of that therapeutic ethos to be one which could just as readily have come from the perspective of a Buddhism which, like Marxism, is permanently sceptical of any fixed or naturalised view of the separate, individualised self. In the words of a contemporary left-feminist cultural critic, co-editor of the valuable anthology *Inventing the Psychological*:

> the mid- to late-twentieth century common languages of selfhood can be said to rest on a foundation of accepted 'truths' and practices that include the following: an arsenal of basic terms for the inner self and its dysfunctions . . .; a structure of the mind imagined in terms of rational 'conscious' processes and irrational 'unconscious' desire; a development through psychosocial stages; and a method of cure which depends on a patient's talks with a trained analyst, assumes the primary importance of a patient's family in the etiology of his or her symptoms, and presumes the possibility of a patient's self-improvement.[3]

The therapists among us will, no doubt, wish to quibble over some of the items on Nancy Schnog's list: isn't that 'structure of the mind' one we've long since declared woefully inadequate at best? Aren't we all hip nowadays to the limitations of the old so-called 'talking cure' and, conversely, to the importance, efficacy, perhaps even necessity of some non-verbal 'bodywork' instead? What remains, however, notwithstanding such side-quarrels, is nonetheless that 'common language of selfhood', that *common sense* of the self as being its own particular kind of thing: something that one *has*, has *individually*, and has *inside*: which individualised and inner type of thing, moreover, one can not only cure when ill or dysfunctional, but *improve* even when one is more or less functionally well.

Having arrived at this nest of assumptions at the base of the notion of the therapeutic self, I imagine my first point hardly needs stating. But I will state it anyhow just to make sure. The first reason I can see why Buddhists might want to resist, or at least sharply question, any easy or unproblematised commerce between psychotherapeutic and Dharmic perspectives and practices is that the former are built upon a set of foundational assumptions about the self towards which the latter must be incorrigibly sceptical at best. In a general sense the point is axiomatic, insofar as the teachings of the Dharma, and our own practice-centred experience, invite us to suspect the ultimate truth-value of any concept of self, however natural it might seem.

More specifically, though, I want to suggest that compared with, say, both premodern Western views and any number of non-Western views of the self, the *doxa* of the therapeutic self may be especially inimical to Dhammic teaching and practice, inasmuch as the therapeutic paradigm carries to a new extreme that dualistic opposition between inside and out, the inwardly vibrant individual, and the detached, unsympathetic, mechanically manipulable external world which has been intrinsic to Western bourgeois society since its first florescence in the seventeenth century. Here is how Robert Bellah and his associates, in their great work *Habits of the Heart: Individualism and Commitment in American Life*, describe the increasingly widespread attitude that the therapeutic paradigm helps foster within the high-intensity market setting of late capitalism:

> The therapeutic attitude . . . begins with the self, rather than with a set of external obligations. The individual must find and assert his or her true self because this self is the only source of genuine relationships to other people. External obligations, whether they come from religion, parents, or social conventions, can only interfere with the capacity for love and relatedness. Only by knowing and ultimately accepting one's self can one enter into valid relationships with other people.

> In its pure form, the therapeutic attitude denies all forms of obligation and commitment in relationships, replacing them only with the ideal of full, open, honest communication among self-actualized individuals.

> [T]he ideal therapeutic world is one in which impersonal bureaucratic rules guarantee free access to market choices and the opportunity for empathic communication in open and intense interpersonal relations. It is a world without politics and almost, it would seem, without community.[4]

Is this a world view any form of Buddhism worthy of the name can live with – that is, without itself becoming warped virtually beyond recognition by the ideological forcefield which has overcome and incorporated it, shrivelling our sense of such root concepts as the *skhandas* of the Pali Canon or mind/heart (*xin/hsin*) in Ch'an into just so many intrapsychic processes occurring solely within the individualised self? Likewise, is our sense of the community of the Sangha to be no more than that of just so many serialised groupings of individuals who, in Robert Putnam's unforgettable phrase, 'focus on themselves in the presence of others'? What can be the result of such reductions, distortions and dilutions but a Western Buddhism which, in effect, is just another 'lifestyle option' or 'enclave'?[5] And conversely, how would it be different if we were instead to understand the processes by which we are constituted in every moment as happening not only *within* but *outside* our conventionally separate selves, in a world which is not merely an external set of objects and processes, but rather, as Merleau-Ponty so beautifully put it, precisely what we *'live through'*?[6] How, likewise, would it be different if we who construe ourselves as Buddhists in the West were accordingly to understand our practice as the *collective* project of attempting to inherit, preserve, and creatively reconstruct what Batchelor calls a 'culture of awakening' in which 'Dharma practice' is understood to be performed primarily by communities, and to be less 'a private religious or psychotherapeutic process that offers solace in this [privatised, individual] life' than a 'cultural process of liberation that evolves over generations'?[7]

Just here, however, you will have noticed I am trembling on the brink of expressing the very kind of single-minded preference the highest forms of Buddhism and Marxism alike so sternly warn us against. So let me say again that we are not simply faced with a simple supermarket choice between two brands or flavours of Western Buddhism – one cheaper and more readily available, but chockful of additives and lots of refined sugar, the other the more organic high-priced spread. As the great Brazilian Marxist educator Paolo Freire put it, 'Only beings who can reflect on the fact that they are determined are capable of being free'.[8] Accordingly, if any communal vision of Western Buddhism as a long-term cultural project is to take root, more is needed than a demonisingly dualistic rejection of the regime of therapeutic individualism in the West. We also need some understanding of where this regime came from; what, within the long history of Western culture, are its 'long-wave' structural and 'short-wave' conjunctural causes and conditions; and of how and when its hegemony arose, why and for whom it first came, quite literally, to make widespread *common* sense. And likewise, we could also stand to know if there are anywhere on the cultural landscape some elements of a language of self-formation which could offer an alternative to the discourse of the therapeutic self: an alternative which ideally would, on the one hand, be more 'user-friendly' to the elusively unreified yet fundamental Buddhist concept of *anatman* and the sense it carries of any sense of self's inevitable suspension between the solidity of conventional truth and the emptiness of the ultimate.

And the good news is, on both these counts we are in luck. On the first, it suffices to point out that within the past fifteen years or so an extensive critical and historical literature has come into effect to provide us with a richly textured genealogical account of the causes and conditions subtending the construction of this goes-without-saying, psychological self – that is to say, of the multiple social, historical, and cultural sites of that construction here and there across the expanse of the ceaselessly modernising, rationalising, capitalist West. The range of this literature on the emergence and rise to hegemony of the therapeutic paradigm runs from the vast syntheses of Donald Lowe's *History of Bourgeois Perception*, Morris Berman's *The Reenchantment of the World*, or Charles Taylor's magisterial *Sources of the Self*, to the more finely grained local studies of Carl Schorske on the origin of the psyche in the political disappointments of Freud's Vienna, Ellen Herman's exemplary analysis of the promotion of psychological analyses of the social by a partnership of psychological professionals and the US Government throughout the 1940s, '50s, and '60s, and Joel Pfister's insightful look at the affinities and advantages of the therapeutic self as norm and ideal for an early twentieth-century professional-managerial class seeking cultural hegemony for itself.[9] To be sure, the 'causes and conditions' these cultural critics and historians explore are unlike those the Buddhism I have been taught typically invites us to look at; the former emphasising large-scale, structural determinations of culture and history, the latter the empty depths of one's immediate moment in time. But is this opposition itself not a false dichotomy constructed by our shared assumption of the unknowable, inviolable 'privacy' of our own 'individual', 'innermost' experience – an assumption which such scholarship helps us to see is itself historically produced? And conversely, is it not possible, at least at some moments within one's meditation practice, to know by taste and sense and feeling, not analytically but experientially, the culturally and historically specific contingency of each and all our senses of things, including and especially of those things we each and all call our separate selves?

In any case, though, what I want to focus on here is neither this first count nor this body of historical analyses, necessary and valuable as it may be, but on the extent to which we also have access to a relatively open-ended, unreified alternative to the therapeutic paradigm's account of the self. This contemporary way of thinking about self-formation owes much to Marxism – one of its foremost early practitioners, in fact, was the Marxist theorist Louis Althusser, particularly in his innovative expansions of the concept of 'ideology' – but just as much, if not more, to thinkers as diverse as Wittgenstein, Nietzsche and Foucault, and their disciples in fields as apparently far-flung as linguistic philosophy, gender studies, and political theory. Sometimes, its key terms and elements get lumped together with others like them under the umbrella name 'poststructuralism', or simply 'Theory' with a capital 'T'; other times, more egregiously and usually more pejoratively, they wind up being stuffed into the infinitely expandable maw of the 'postmodern'. Yet, despite what Wittgenstein would call its 'family resemblances' to the terms and emphases of other, similar methods and perspectives, there is enough that is both distinctive, and distinctively useful for us, about this one particular family of thought and discourse within these larger kinships that is worth trying to tug it loose from its neighbouring kin – especially if and insofar as some sort of dialogue or exchange between the terms and perspectives of Buddhism and this particular form of 'postmodern', 'poststructuralist' thought might help clear the ground on which a genuine Western Buddhist 'culture of awakening' might arise.

In a chapter this size – not to mention with a brain this small – I can hardly conduct a full survey of this perspective, much less render an adequate account of all the causes and conditions that have simultaneously made it possible within, and kept it largely confined to, the academies of the West. All I can offer instead are two gestures toward a sort of definition by evocation: the first an exploration of two of this new discourse's key terms, the second a description of some recent work of one particularly lively contemporary theorist whose questioning and thinking, I will seek to show, converges quite strikingly, even uncannily, with some of Buddhism's most central concerns.

The words I have in mind are 'subject' and 'discourse' – both terms whose newly mutated and expanded meanings have themselves provided the theme of many a recent article or book. Here, for example, from *The Subject of Semiotics*, is Kaja Silverman's capable summary of the inflections of the term 'subject', and of the kind of work within contemporary theory the term is now invoked to perform:

The term 'subject' designates a quite different semantic and ideological space from that indicated by the more familiar term 'individual'. The second of these terms dates from the Renaissance and . . . still bears the traces of the dominant philosophical systems of that time – systems which afforded to consciousness the very highest premium. The concept of subjectivity, as we shall see, marks a radical departure from this philosophical tradition by giving a more central place to the unconscious and to cultural overdetermination than it does to consciousness.

The term 'subject' . . . helps us to conceive of human reality as a construction, as the product of signifying activities which are both culturally specific and generally unconscious. [It] thus calls into question the notions both of the private, and of a self synonymous with consciousness. It suggests that even desire is culturally instigated, and hence collective; and it de-centers consciousness, relegating it . . . to a purely receptive capacity. Finally, by drawing attention to the divisions which separate one area of psychic activity from another, the term 'subject' challenges the value of stability attributed to the individual.[10]

At the risk of belabouring the obvious, let me point out a few of the most salient convergences between this use of 'subject' and traditional Buddhist ways of seeing through the self. There is, first of all, the same radical suspicion of that self's claims to sovereignty, fixity, and centredness, and of the identification of that self with what appears to and as consciousness. Secondly, and likewise, the term 'subject' carries the implication that far from our being individually distinct single agents, each replete with his/her own customised psychology, and autonomously empowered to take action for ourselves (e.g. to get our own personal needs met), our very sense of our being selves of this 'individualised' kind is a product or, better still, *effect* of 'signifying activities which are both culturally specific and generally unconscious'.

Further still, in the above phrase you will notice the germ of a radically revised notion of the so-called 'unconscious': not as the naturally occurring deep structure or innermost chamber of the self, as in the therapeutic model, but rather as the site of *culturally specific signifying activities* which serve as ground or pre-text for what then comes to be felt and known as 'conscious' life – the unconscious as a 'cultural unconsciousness', in the words of Michel Foucault.[11] This new non- or even anti-psychological conception of the unconscious is most commonly associated with the teachings of the French psychoanalyst and philosopher Jacques Lacan, and rightly enough; yet the full history of this contestatory notion runs back well before the moment of Lacan, to the neo-Marxist critique of Freudianism published in Moscow by a mysterious, brilliant student of Bakhtin's, V.N. Volosinov, in 1927. Like any number of contemporary disciples of Lacan, Foucault, or Deleuze and Guattari today, but seventy years before them, Volosinov criticised the psychological *doxa* of his own time for presenting 'humans in an inherently false, individualistic, asocial and ahistorical setting', and suggested that 'virtually the entire psychosexual apparatus of psychoanalysis could be replaced beneficially by a semiotics with a sociological interface'.[12]

We will soon return to draw out one more crucial, Buddhist-relevant implication of this new term 'subject', but first let us take 'a semiotics with a sociological interface' as our segue into our second term, 'discourse'. The term is a notoriously slippery, even treacherous one within poststructuralist theory; but in at least one of its meanings and applications, it seems to me potentially as serviceable to Western Buddhism as 'subject' could be. Least usefully, in the works of Derrida I know of, and certainly in most deconstructionist work that has followed in his wake, the term suggests a view of the primacy and generativity of language itself. But this use of 'discourse' in contemporary theory needs to be distinguished from a second, much more complex and helpful usage – one that views semiotics, the study of signs and signifying practices, within a terrain bounded by the 'sociological', that is, by the grounding, production, and reproduction of those signifying practices within the structures, practices, and power relations of the institutions through which we live our lives.

From Wittgenstein to Bakhtin and Volosinov, from Nietzsche to the Marxist Althusser and his post-Marxist student Foucault, the urge to expose and examine speech, text, and language in this sense, as practices grounded in the materiality of the social realities and institutions (from schools and mass media to economic structures and forms of governance) which they in turn (mis)construct in reified form as the timeless True and the obvious Real, runs a long seam through twentieth-century Western philosophy and social theory. These, I want to claim, are all thinkers who invite us to 'see through' the self non-dualistically, as a culturally specific, historically grounded construction which is nonetheless not illusory, insofar as, like the other ideologies to which it is linked, *any* sense of self is secreted by actual social institutions and has inescapably real effects both for those who embody it and – *a fortiori* – for those who do not. Indeed, it is precisely to step back from common sense without offering any 'better', more accurate or comprehensive alternative sense, that the word 'subject' is brought in by contemporary theorists to supplant such terms as 'person', 'individual', or 'self', each and all terms as familiar and 'obvious' as they are ideological – each and all, that is, key terms in a discursive regime that binds us, naturally, obviously, to a sense of ourselves as single, psychologically deep, individualised beings. For, especially when employed together with its companion term 'discourse' in the fully historical sense I have just described, the term 'subject' runs off the infinitely renewable energy source of a constitutive, contradictory pun: that between 'subject' as agent or actor – as, for example, the subject of a sentence, or the self-author of one's own 'subjectivity' – and 'subject' as that which has been coerced or persuaded to give up its will in obedience to a sovereign power – for example, as the subject of the King. To believe oneself to be an independently powered *subject* in the first sense, in other words, one must have always already, albeit unconsciously, consented to *subject* oneself to authority in the second; indeed, on this view, as Lacan's single most famous remark ('The unconscious is structured like a language') suggests, the 'unconscious' becomes less the secret theatre of our own individualities than the unstable site of our necessarily queasy yet necessary agreement to colour within some set or other of culturally pre-given lines, to play by some set or other of social rules so deeply embedded they quite literally go without saying, yet are constantly reinforced nonetheless.

Necessarily queasy yet necessary, as the great teachers of the Buddhist tradition also try to convey to us, with their talk of 'conventional' and 'ultimate', of 'mountains and rivers' ceasing to be then becoming again, of *'samsara'* as *'nirvana'*, and with their famous warning that those who take *sunyata* as foundation for a new, better common sense of self are an especially hopeless lot. And to this list of affinities between the language and lessons of left, or materialist, or perhaps I should say simply *social* post-structuralism and those of Buddhism let me add one final, still more striking likeness or quality: the studied refusal of both to rest in any assumed boundary line between the inner and outer, self and co-constitutive world. This homeless, ceaseless resistance to philosophical idealism and materialism alike is every bit as hard-wired into the social dialogics of Bakhtin, into the Foucauldian notion of discursive regimes of power and knowledge and the Althusserian depiction of the subject's ambivalent relationship to the institutionalised ideologies through which it comes to be, as it is insisted by Theravadan Buddhism's *skhandas'* ceaseless co-constitution of a 'seamless, dynamic process of experience, where not only the body/mind split but also the subject/object split is dissolved',[13] or the Ch'an Buddhist conception of *xin/hsin* as referring not only to both feeling-heart and thought-mind, but to both alike without as well as within the individual self.

I have been arguing, then, that there exists a striking overlap or convergence between certain currents within modern and contemporary Western critical theory and Buddhist perspectives; and that one particularly relevant and promising aspect of that convergence lies in the resistant scepticism urged by those perspectives and enacted by the theory towards the notion of the therapeutically accessible, psychological, inner self which is otherwise so dominant within Western culture today. And I offer this argument in the hope that some of you might be as interested as I am in offering at least some part of ourselves as the site of a conversation between Dharma and Theory, East and West which could be quite different from those presently underway between Western psychology and Eastern spirituality; for the likelihood is all too great that the ultimate purpose or effect of the latter will be the subordination of spirituality to psychology – or, more specifically still, the subjection of Buddhist perspectives and practices to today's foremost 'perfection project', the improvement or cure of the therapeutic self. I know, however, that in my eagerness to recommend this conversation, I have kept silent so far about some key differences of intention and emphasis which have certainly helped to prevent Buddhism and contemporary left-critical theory from getting to know one another before now; so, by way of, or more accurately, in lieu of, a conclusion, I want to describe one particular recent work by a contemporary poststructuralist theorist in which, for me at least, both the differences and the convergences show up with special vividness and force.

The work I have in mind is a little book called, ambitiously, *The Psychic Life of Power: Theories of Subjection*, by Judith Butler. Butler is, you might say, the very model of a contemporary left-feminist-poststructuralist Theorist with that capital 'T'. Her career began with *Gender Trouble*, a remorseless critique of any and all inclinations to regard gender definitions as naturally given; and her admirable antidisciplinarity is for our purposes sufficiently signalled by the restless sprawl of back-jacket shelving suggestions for this and subsequent works, from 'Philosophy/ Women's Studies' to 'Philosophy/Gender Studies/Politics', from 'Philosophy/Politics/Cultural Studies' to 'Critical Theory/ Philosophy'. More to the point, her entire mode of investigation is openly indebted to the philosophical and theoretical tradition running from Hegel, Marx and Nietzsche through Althusser, and Foucault which I have tried to evoke here. Given Butler's intellectual location, then, at the contemporary tip of this alternative Western tendency or trajectory, and, conversely, given what I take to be her near-perfect ignorance of Buddhist teaching and practice, I have found it all the more uncannily amazing to discover formulations, questions, and concerns like the following, all taken from the opening pages of *The Psychic Life of Power*, her most recent book:

> Bound to seek recognition of its own existence in categories, terms, and names that are not of its own making, the subject seeks the sign of its own existence outside itself, in a discourse that is at once dominant and indifferent.

> [P]ower that first appears as external, pressed upon the subject, pressing the subject into subordination, assumes a psychic form that constitutes the subject's self-identity.

> The form this power takes is relentlessly marked by a figure of turning, a turning back upon oneself or even a turning *on* oneself. This figure operates as part of the explanation of how a subject is produced, and so there is no subject, strictly speaking, who makes this turn. On the contrary, the turn appears to function as a tropological inauguration of the subject, a founding moment whose ontological status remains permanently uncertain. Such a notion, then, appears difficult, if not impossible, to incorporate into the account of subject formation. What or who is said to turn, and what is the object of such a turn?

> The temporal paradox of the subject is such that, of necessity, we must lose the perspective of a subject already formed in order to account for our own becoming. That 'becoming' is no simple or continuous affair, but an uneasy practice of repetition and its risks, compelled yet

incomplete, wavering on the horizon of social being.

What would it mean for the subject to desire something other than its continued 'social existence'? If such an existence cannot be undone without falling into some kind of death, can existence nevertheless be risked, death courted or pursued, in order to expose and open to transformation the hold of social power on the conditions of life's persistence?

[W]ithout a repetition that risks life – in its current organization – how might we begin to imagine the contingency of that organization, and performatively reconfigure the contours of the conditions of life?[14]

Very schematically, I will now point out what I perceive to be the convergences with and divergences from Buddhism in the above snippets; then very quickly tell you why I find the divergences as potentially generative for Western Buddhism as the overlaps. For starters, there are the terms themselves – 'subject', 'subjection', 'discourse' – so akin, as we have seen, to Buddhist terms and usage in their resistance to any view of self as given or world as 'thinged', yet so different from them in the implicitly political and/or social concern the Western terms reflect and encourage. Yet another set of likenesses is cued by the similarity between Butler's description of what she calls 'becoming', as 'an uneasy practice of repetition and its risks, compelled yet incomplete, wavering on the horizon of social being', and Buddhist descriptions gained in study and practice alike of what goes on when and as we 'self'. Or, more obviously still, by the extraordinarily close similarity between Butler's question, and the koans one is urged to practise with in Rinzai and Korean Zen.

Indeed, if there is a difference between Butler's 'What or who is said to turn, and what is the object of such a turn?' and Zen's 'What was your original face before you were born?', between her fastidiously verbose '[W]ithout a repetition that risks life – in its current organization – how might we begin to imagine the contingency of that organization, and performatively reconfigure the contours of the conditions of life?' and Master Kusan Sunim's brutally concise 'What is it?', that difference lies, I think, less in the words employed than in the intended site and function of their workings. All such questions, of course, whether uttered by Butler or offered by the Zen master, are articulated in full foreknowledge of their unanswerability; yet Butler's sound to me as though they are still aimed at keeping the analytical, conscious, reason-bearing intellect moving, if only through the act of scratching its sores, while the Zen master's questions are aimed to shut that mind down.

Admittedly, like its more purely deconstructionist near relatives, the 'social poststructuralism' whose outlines I have been very lightly tracing here carries with its studied scepticism towards any and all forms of common sense a tendency towards elitist obscurantism. Admittedly, its rigorous suspicion of any and all social relations, institutional structures, or forms of experience as virtually by definition only so many ruses and reflexes of Power, runs the risk of falling into an equally elitist nihilism. But both these risks and charges will be familiar to any student of Asian Buddhism as well – and not without cause, as any honest student of the historic debates between, say, the Svatantrika and Prasangika schools within Madhyamika will attest. For are these not the risks taken, the faults never wholly avoided, by any tendency or practice of mind, East or West, which, while setting itself against all forms of reification, nonetheless seeks to articulate itself in whatever newly coined or rearticulated language as it makes for itself?

So I continue to view the prospect of some further and more dialogic relationship between this seam within Western critical theory and Eastern Buddhism not as a 'bad marriage' set of irreconcilable oppositions, as I have suggested may be the case between Buddhist teachings on *anatman* and *sunyata* and the therapeutic paradigm's postulation of a distinctive 'core' self, but rather as an 'odd couple' match between two potentially mutually stimulating tendencies. At such an intersection, in the course of such a dialogue, as I somewhat rosily imagine it, the risk of privatised complacency and torpor implicit in any form of contemplative spiritual practice might be met by the call towards social engagement, and invigilated by the inspections of the disciplined intellect. Likewise, and conversely, both the restless hubris of intellect and the encouragement any kind of social or political engagement provides to bitterness and/or arrogance might be tempered and enriched by the patience, equanimity, and unknowing bred in the immediate meditative experience of 'beginner's mind'. In such a partnering, of course, there would probably be fewer people around to whoop it up at the wedding – but more chance for the relationship to last as a true partnership, that is, without one party merely becoming yet another accessorised servant to the other's monstrously swollen, narcissistic mate. Or, to drop these matchmaking metaphors altogether (and good riddance to them!), we might well have a better chance of becoming ourselves and bequeathing to those who follow us a sense of Sangha as a cultural community to be cultivated and tended for the sake of all beings, rather than as a place where, alone together, each in her/his own separateness, we learn and practise new techniques for getting what the culture tells us we personally need.

ACKNOWLEDGEMENT

Thanks to all my fellow 'second-class students' and other Dharma friends at Sharpham College for the help and inspiration they provided to the author throughout the year when the idea of this essay was hatched; and special thanks to Stephen and Martine Batchelor and to Gay Watson for their encouragement, friendship, and support.

Compassion in the Age of the Global Economy

Helena Norberg-Hodge

THE RISE OF MATERIALISM

There can be no compassion without wisdom. Indeed Buddhism teaches that wisdom and compassion are the two wings of the bird of enlightenment. By nurturing a compassionate heart which supports and is supported by an awareness that all 'things' are empty of inherent existence, we can transcend our narrow sense of self and experience ourselves not as limited static entities but as part of a web of relationships.

Few have combined compassion and wisdom with the brilliance of the great ninth-century Buddhist sage Shantideva, who taught that all the joy that exists in the world comes from wishing for the happiness of other sentient beings, and all misery from narrow egotism. To the extent that we care only for ourselves, he assured us, our lives will be filled with suffering. Could this, the heart of Buddhist teaching, ever be more relevant than it is today?

Like never before, the consumer culture that is spreading around the world promotes the notion of the 'rugged individual' disconnected from virtually all meaningful, let alone compassionate, contact with other people and the environment beyond. Advertising and media images tell us that we can gain our happiness through self-gratification and the quest for narrow, short-term needs: material success, personal security, success for our children. Commercial pressures are taking us ever further away from a sense of community and connection to nature, away from a sense of participating in the rituals and cycles of the social and natural world.

Erich Fromm once noted that the rise of modern consumerism is a relatively recent phenomenon. Previously, society had been characterised by values such as frugality and caring for others. Only with the rise of the mass-producing industrial economy – dependent on endlessly increasing production and consumption – did unrestrained materialism become acceptable.

The result has been a dramatic change: today, to 'go for it!' to 'shop till you drop!' – to spend, consume, enjoy – are deemed unqualified goods. At Christmas, it has even become part of the festive tradition for TV news reporters to give updates from the consumer 'front line', on how much Christmas shoppers are spending. The emphasis always, quite openly, is that high spending is good news: good news for consumers, for the economy, for business, for everyone.

If Buddhism is correct, then this modern love affair with alienated materialism should be leading us down a very dark path indeed towards very great suffering. Such, tragically, would appear to be the case.

As materialism becomes more and more entrenched in our society, so greed becomes a more powerful force in the world. The price of this consumerism is an ever more atomised and fragmented society centred around large-scale globalising economic and political systems.

INSTITUTIONALISED GREED IN THE GLOBAL ECONOMY

Today, fifty of the world's largest economies are corporate, not national, economies; almost all primary commodities, such as coffee and cotton, are controlled by six giant companies. The global economy they control is managed by giant transnational institutions such as the World Bank, the IMF and the World Trade Organisation. These organisations are unaccountable to any democratic constituency.

Quite reasonable ideas have contributed to the rise of this system: the notion that trade is in everybody's interest, for example, lies at the heart of the global economy. As a consequence, a broad spectrum of institutional pressures – from investments in infrastructure and research to regulations and direct subsidies – all promote trade for the sake of trade. As national governments have invested so much in trade, they have in fact supported the development of a transnational corporate system.

Today's global economy, then, is made up of giant transnational corporations (TNCs) which by their very nature have but to generate maximum profits in as short a time as possible. Because of pressure from investors and shareholders, these corporations are forced to subordinate other priorities. There is little room for social, ecological or spiritual values.

The logical end result of a globalised economy dominated by giant corporations is a world of homogenous consumption in which people everywhere eat the same TNC food, wear the same TNC clothes and live in the same houses built by the same TNCs. Today, cultures based on very different values that have existed for millennia are being amalgamated into a consumer monoculture. Even Buddhist societies that have sought to embody the notion that kindness and compassion should be at the heart of all human speech and actions are being undermined by the rampant materialism of the global economy. An unceasing tide of Western media, advertising and cinematic propaganda is descending on these ancient cultures.

Cleverly targeting the youngest members of society, these images promote the 'new', 'modern', 'cool' way of life.

The effect of the Western monoculture in the Third World (or the 'South') is to effectively 'gut' local cultures and to replace them with versions of happiness that serve commercial interests at the expense of social and ecological needs. The feelings of boredom and emptiness that are such trademark features of the malaise of Western society, are ultimately rooted in this emptiness-for-profit feature of business values: we are persuaded to value our expensive house, car, annual holiday, mini-disk system above all else, but are blind to the fact that we are free to enjoy them in a world in which we are isolated from all deeper values, all deeper connections with ourselves, with each other, with the community and natural world around us – our technology empowers us to be impotent. The irony is that we have perfect quality TV pictures, video images and music, but the culture producing them is often so anaemic and shallow, that much of what we watch and hear is not worth attending to.

The problem for many Third World peoples, of course, is that, although they have been sold the dream, that is often all they are sold. While the foundations of their world view and culture have been torn from them, in their place there is only the mirage of Western-style happiness. Many have left rural communities for an urban, consumer dream, only to find themselves isolated and alone in dilapidated shanty towns, lost between two cultures.

Modern symbols also contribute to an increase in aggression. Young boys see violence glamorised on the screen. From Western-style films, they easily get the impression that if they want to be modern, they should smoke one cigarette after another, get a fast car, and race through the countryside shooting people left and right! Over the course of twenty-three years, I have witnessed changes wrought by Western 'development' on the trans-Himalayan society of Ladakh, or 'Little Tibet'. I have seen a gentle culture change, a culture in which men, even young men, were happy to cuddle a baby or be loving and soft with their grandmothers. Now the macho image reigns supreme and Rambo would not be seen dead with a baby, or with his grandmother, in his arms.

Social changes of this kind are ultimately the product of changes in the economy. The global economy favours big business over small, and large global producers and retailers demand centralised, large-scale production; they also need concentrated centres of distribution. Because they have the monopoly on money and jobs, these large corporations are able to draw whole populations into urban centres. The result is that families and communities are torn apart as wage earners leave to make a living in the city. Local economies wither and dry, and people are forced off the land.

The global consumer culture is also contributing to a growing sense of personal insecurity. In virtually every culture before industrialisation, there was lots of dancing, singing, and theatre, with people of all ages joining in. I have witnessed groups sitting round the fire, where even toddlers would dance, with the help of older siblings or friends. Everyone knew how to sing, to act, to play music. Now that the radio has come to traditional communities, you do not need to sing your own songs or tell your own stories. You can sit and listen to the best singer, the best storyteller. But the result is that people become inhibited and self-conscious. You are no longer comparing yourself to neighbours and friends, who are real people – some better than you at singing, but perhaps less good at dancing – and you are never as good as the stars on the radio. Community ties are also broken when people sit passively listening to the very best rather than making music or dancing together.

As they lose the sense of security and identity that springs from deep, long-lasting connections to others, people living in remote village communities are starting to develop doubts about who they are. At the same time, tourism and the media are presenting a new image of who they should be. They are meant to lead an essentially Western lifestyle: eating dinner at a dining-table, driving a car, using a washing-machine. The images are telling them to be different, to be better than they are.

Paradoxically, then, modernisation – so often associated with the triumph of individualism – has produced a loss of individuality. As people become self-conscious and insecure, they feel pressured to conform, to live up to an idealised image. By contrast, in the traditional village, where everyone wore the same clothes and looked the same to the casual observer, there seemed to be more freedom to relax and be who you really were. As part of a close-knit community, people felt secure enough to be themselves.

When local economic and political ties are broken, the people around you become more and more anonymous. At the same time 'progress' speeds life up and mobility increases – making even familiar relationships more superficial and brief. In Ladakh and other parts of the Himalayas, I have seen previously strong, outgoing women replaced by a new generation – unsure of themselves and extremely concerned with their appearance. Traditionally, the way a woman looked was important, but her capabilities – including tolerance and social skills – were much more appreciated. Today, in many parts of the South, where, previously, there was not even a trace of anorexia or bulimia, women are becoming obsessed with their weight and appearance in exactly the same way that is so prevalent among Western women.

Despite their new macho image, men do not actually feel more powerful. They clearly suffer as a result of the breakdown of family and community ties. When they are young, their obsession with looking 'cool' prevents them from showing affection and emotion, while in later life as fathers, their work keeps them away from home and deprives them of contact with their children.

It is a feature of the global economy that a culture of scarcity replaces the abundance of natural resources and human kindness typical of traditional cultures: in their search for scarce jobs, scarce money, scarce love, people become far more insecure and far less willing to do favours for other people who become competitors rather than neighbours. As people struggle to survive, ethnic and religious differences begin to take on a political dimension, causing bitterness and enmity on a scale hitherto unknown.

This new rivalry is one of the most painful divisions that I have seen in Ladakh. Within a few years, growing competition generated by economic insecurity actually culminated in violence. Earlier there had been individual cases of friction, but the first time I noticed any signs of group tension was in 1986, only ten years after the process of economic development had begun. At that time, I heard Ladakhi friends starting to define people according to whether they were Muslim or Buddhist. And then, in the summer of 1989, fighting suddenly broke out between the two groups. There were major disturbances in Leh bazaar, four people were shot dead by police, and much of Ladakh was placed under curfew. This in a place where, previously, there had not been a fight in living memory. Indeed, when I had asked a friend how everyone managed to live so peacefully together, he hardly comprehended the question: 'What a funny question,' he said, 'We just live with each other, that's all.'

Westerners often assume that ethnic and religious strife is increasing because modern democracy liberates people, allowing old prejudices and hatreds to be expressed. If there was peace earlier, they assume it was only the result of oppression. But after more than twenty years of firsthand experience on the Indian subcontinent, I am convinced that economic 'development' not only exacerbates existing tensions but in many cases actually creates them. Development causes artificial scarcity, which inevitably leads to greater competition, and puts pressure on people to conform to a standard Western model that they simply cannot emulate.

To strive for such an ideal is to reject one's own culture and roots – in effect to deny one's own identity. The resulting alienation gives rise to resentment and anger, and lies behind much of the violence and fundamentalism in the world today.

THE RESPONSE OF ENGAGED BUDDHISTS

In the difficult situation globalisation is creating, Buddhism's philosophical foundation and emphasis on compassion put practitioners of these profound teachings in a unique position to lead the way out. Buddhism also provides the intellectual tools needed to oppose the spread of a global consumer economy. More importantly, it can also help to illuminate a compassionate path towards a localisation of the economy based on human-scale structures. For how can we make wise judgements if the scale of the economy is so great that we cannot perceive the impact of our actions? How can we act out of compassion when the scale is so large that the chains of cause and effect are hidden, leading us to unwittingly contribute to the suffering of other sentient beings?

The challenge for Western Buddhists is to apply the Buddhist principles taught many centuries ago – in an age of relatively localised social and economic interactions – to the complex and increasingly globalised world in which we now live. In order to do so it is vital that we avoid the mental traps of conceptual thought and abstraction. It is easy, for example, to confound the ideals of the 'global village' and the borderless world of free trade with the Buddhist principle of interdependence – the unity of all life, the inextricable web in which nothing can claim completely separate or static existence. Buzzwords like 'harmonisation', 'integration', 'union', etc., sound as though globalisation is leaving us more interdependent with one another and with the natural world. In fact, it is furthering our dependence on large-scale economic structures and technologies, and on a shrinking number of ever-larger corporate monopolies. It would be a tragic mistake, indeed, to confuse this process with the cosmic inter-dependence described by the Buddha.

The three poisons of greed, hatred and delusion are to some extent present in every human being, but cultural systems either encourage or discourage these traits. Professor Noam Chomsky of the Massachusetts Institute of Technology argues that the modern consumerist status quo requires a highly self-centred mindset:

> It is necessary to destroy hope, idealism, solidarity, and concern for the poor and oppressed, to replace these dangerous feelings by self-centred egoism, a pervasive cynicism that holds that all change is for the worse, so that one should simply accept the state capitalist order with its inherent inequities and oppression as the best that can be achieved.[1]

Today's global consumer culture nurtures the three poisons on both an individual and societal level. At the moment, $450 billion is spent annually on advertising worldwide, with the aim of convincing three-year-old children that they need things they never knew existed – like Coca-Cola and plastic Rambos with machine guns. Before the rise of consumerism, cultures existed in which this type of greed was virtually non-existent. Thus we cannot conclude that the acquisitiveness and materialism of people trapped in the global economic system are an inevitable product of human nature. Instead we need to recognise the extra difficulty of uncovering our Buddha natures in a global culture of consumerism and social atomisation.

Buddhism can help us in this difficult situation by encouraging us to be compassionate and non-violent with ourselves as well as others. Many of us avoid an honest examination of our lives for fear of exposing our contribution to global problems. However, once we realise that it is the complex global economy which is creating a disconnected society, psychological deprivation and environmental breakdown, Buddhism can help us to focus on the system and its structural violence, instead of condemning ourselves or other individuals within that system.

Buddhism, in its holistic approach, can help us to see how various symptoms are interrelated; how the crises facing us are systemic and rooted in economic imperatives. Understanding the myriad connections between the problems can prevent us from wasting our efforts on the symptoms of the crises, rather than focusing on their fundamental causes. Under the surface, even such seemingly unconnected problems as ethnic violence, pollution of the air and water, broken families, and cultural disintegration are closely interlinked.

Psychologically, such a shift in our perception of the nature of the problems is deeply empowering: being faced with a never-ending litany of seemingly unrelated problems can be overwhelming, but finding the points at which they converge can make our strategy to tackle them more focused and effective. It is then just a question of pulling the right threads to affect the entire fabric, rather than having to deal with each problem individually.

STEPPING BACK FROM THE LOCAL ECONOMY

At a structural level, the fundamental problem is scale. The ever-expanding scope and scale of the global economy obscures the consequences of our actions: in effect, our arms have been so lengthened that we no longer see what our hands are doing. Our situation thus exacerbates and furthers our ignorance, preventing us from acting out of compassion and wisdom.

Smaller-scale communities inevitably nurture more intimate relations between people, which in turn promote values and actions rooted in compassion and wisdom. In his book, *The Island of Bali*, Miguel Covarrubias described how small-scale village life led to a situation in which cooperation was the norm amongst the Balinese with neighbours assisting each other in every task they were unable to perform alone, helping each other willingly and as a matter of duty, expecting no reward. The result, Covarrubias writes, was a village system which operated as 'a closely unified organism in which the communal policy is harmony and cooperation – a system that works to everybody's advantage'.[2]

Similarly, when Columbus 'discovered' Hispaniola in 1492, he found the Taino Indians living there to be astonishingly kind and generous. Most villages were small, consisting of between ten and fifteen families. The system worked so well that Taino society appears to have been entirely without war and even without conflict (the leading Spanish chronicler of the time, Las Casas, reported that no Spaniard had ever seen two Tainos fighting). Indeed, most remarkable to the invading Spaniards was the extraordinary kindness and generosity of the Tainos. As Columbus wrote at the time:

> They became so much our friends that it was a marvel . . . They traded and gave everything they had, with good will . . . They love their neighbours as themselves, and they have the sweetest talk in the world, and are gentle and always laughing.[3]

Countless examples the world over testify to the fact that many smaller-scale traditional cultures naturally adopted a compassion ethic as the optimal base of social life. On the other hand, the greedy, selfish and violent aspects of human nature appear to be massively exaggerated in people living alienated lives in larger-scale societies where intimate contact with the people around them has been reduced to vestigial levels. My own experience of life in Ladakh as well as many other cultures suggests that when people live in smaller-scale social and economic units, their natural happiness, friendliness and capacity for kindness are enhanced to levels almost unimaginable to the average Western city-dweller. As amongst the Tainos, fighting in traditional Ladakhi society was virtually unknown, any disputes were almost always settled quickly and peaceably.

An important aspect of moving toward smaller-scale human institutions is reaffirming a sense of place. Each community is unique in its environment, its people, its culture. Human scale minimises the need for rigid legislation and allows for more flexible decision-making; it gives rise to action in harmony with the laws of nature, based on the needs of the particular context. When individuals are at the mercy of faraway, inflexible bureaucracies and fluctuating markets, they feel passive and disempowered; more decentralised structures provide individuals with the power to respond to each unique situation.

Since the global economy is fuelled by transnational institutions that can now overpower any single government, the policy changes most urgently needed are at the international level. In theory, what is required is quite simple: the governments that ratified 'free trade' treaties like the Uruguay Round of GATT need to sit down around the same table again. This time instead of operating in secret – with transnational corporations at their side – they should be made to represent the interests of the majority. This can only happen if there is far more awareness at the grassroots, awareness that leads to real pressure on policy-makers.

Pressuring for policy change can seem a daunting task. Many today have abandoned any hope of meaningful political change, thinking that we no longer have any leverage over our political leaders. But it is important to remember that in the long term, blind adherence to the outdated dogma of free trade benefits no one, not even the political leaders and corporate CEOs that are promoting it today. Among its other effects, globalisation is eroding the tax base and power of nation states – and that means the budgets and influence of elected officials. It is also threatening the job security of individuals, even at the highest levels of the corporate world.

It is heartening to bear in mind that even the tiniest change in policy towards curtailing the movement of capital and diversifying economic activity at the local and national level would reap enormous systemic rewards. The ability to shift profits, operating costs and investment capital between far-flung operations has played a key role in the growth of ever more powerful transnational corporations. Rules that limited the free flow of capital would therefore help to reduce the advantage that huge corporations have over smaller, more local enterprises, and would make corporations more accountable to the places where they operate.

LOCALISATION: TOWARDS A BUDDHIST ECONOMICS

Even now, without the help from government and industry that a new direction in policy would provide, people are starting to change the economy from the bottom up. This process of localisation has begun spontaneously, in countless communities all around the world. Because economic localisation means an adaptation to cultural and biological diversity, no single 'blueprint' would be appropriate everywhere. The range of possibilities for local grassroots efforts is therefore as diverse as the locales in which they take place.

In many towns, for example, community banks and loan funds have been set up, thereby increasing the capital available to local residents and businesses and allowing people to invest in their neighbours and their community, rather than in a faceless global economy.

In other communities, 'buy-local' campaigns are helping locally owned businesses survive even when pitted against heavily subsidised corporate competitors. These campaigns not only help to keep money from leaking out of the local economy, but also help educate people about the hidden costs – to their own jobs, to the community and the environment – in purchasing cheaper but distantly produced products.

In some communities, Local Exchange and Trading Systems (LETS) have been established as an organised, large-scale bartering system. Thus, even people with little or no 'real' money can participate in and benefit from the local economy. LETS systems have been particularly beneficial in areas with high unemployment. The city government of Birmingham, England – where unemployment hovers at twenty per cent – has been a co-sponsor of a highly successful LETS scheme. These initiatives have psychological benefits that are just as important as the economic benefits: a large number of people who were once merely 'unemployed' – and therefore 'useless' – are becoming valued for their skills and knowledge.

These and countless other initiatives around the world are a reflection of a growing awareness, a realisation that it is far more sensible to depend on our neighbours and the living world around us than to depend on a global economic system built of technology and corporate institutions. As Buddhists faced with this same reality, the compassionate choice is to become engaged. Buddhism provides us with both the imperative and the tools to challenge the economic structures that are creating and perpetuating suffering the world over. We cannot claim to be Buddhist and simultaneously support structures which are so clearly contrary to Buddha's teachings, antithetical to life itself.

The economic and structural changes needed of course require shifts at the personal level as well. In part, these involve rediscovering the deep psychological benefits – the joy – of being embedded in community. Another fundamental shift involves reintroducing a sense of connection with the place where we live. The globalisation of culture and information has led to a way of life in which the nearby is treated with contempt. We get news from China but not next door, and at the touch of a TV button we have access to all the wildlife of Africa. As a consequence, our immediate surroundings seem dull and uninteresting by comparison. A sense of place means helping ourselves and our children to see the living environment around us: reconnecting with the sources of our food – perhaps even growing some of our own – learning to recognise the cycles of the seasons, the characteristics of flora and fauna.

Most Westerners would agree that we have lost our sense of community. Our lives are fragmented, and in spite of the number of people with whom we come into contact in the course of a day, we are often left feeling sadly alone, not even knowing our neighbours.

Community could be rekindled through localisation. Excessive mobility erodes community, but as we put down roots and feel attachment to a place, our human relationships deepen, become more secure, and, as they continue over time, more reliable.

Many people believe that a cooperative community is an unrealistic ideal: 'In the real world, you have to take care of yourself. Nobody else is going to do it for you.' But my experience in the South has shown me the extent to which the techno-economic structures of our society get in the way of cooperation there. I have seen people who were once cooperative become greedy and competitive under the influence of industrialisation. The broader sense of self in traditional societies contrasts with the individualism of Western culture. In the West we pride ourselves on our individualism, but sometimes individualism is a euphemism for isolation. We tend to believe that a person should be completely self-sufficient, shouldn't need anybody else.

The closely knit relationships I've experienced in the South seem liberating rather than oppressive and I have been forced to reconsider the whole concept of freedom. This is not as surprising as it might appear. Psychological research is verifying the importance of intimate, reliable and lasting relations with others in creating a positive self-image. We are beginning to recognise how this, in turn, is the foundation for healthy development.

CONCLUSION – PERSONAL IS POLITICAL

We are living in a society in which the flames of individual human greed and ignorance have been institutionalised in the furnaces of the global market place. If we are to combat this systemic destructiveness, we need to appreciate that personal and political issues are inseparable. As Stephen Batchelor writes:

> The contemporary social engagement of Dharma practice is rooted in awareness of how self-centred confusion and craving can no longer be adequately understood only as psychological drives that manifest themselves in subjective states of anguish. We find these drives embodied in the very economic, military, and political structures that influence the lives of the majority of people on earth.[4]

Our individual greed and ignorance certainly support greedy and destructive forces within our economic and political systems. On the other hand, in a kind of vicious circle, these political and economic systems are also powerfully reinforcing these negative tendencies in the individual. We need to constantly remind ourselves of the goals and logic of a system that so powerfully and insidiously affects our behaviour.

The economic and political forces driving the modern economy are powerful indeed. Ultimately, however, their power depends on our lack of awareness of the system of which we are a part. Movements rooted in wisdom and compassion could turn the tide.

PART II

BODY, MIND AND SPIRIT: THE SCIENTIFIC PERSPECTIVE

Steps to a Science of Inter-being: Unfolding the Dharma Implicit in Modern Cognitive Science

Francisco J. Varela

A few months ago, a French publisher called me up and said he wanted to talk to me about a book. 'You know there are lots of people out there who wonder what it is that the brain and cognitive sciences do. Does it matter to anybody what's going on there? What's the point? Couldn't you write a book that people could read in the metro and then say, "Oh, now I see why it matters."' As the days went by, I began thinking 'Why not?' and 'How could I do that?' To my astonishment I found myself formulating some principles, that seen from the inside, looked awfully like Dharmic principles, and yet there was no 'Buddhism' in them at all. That really struck me. Having been involved for a long time with the interface between science and Buddhism, I figured maybe I've been missing the point. Maybe it's not about having an interface or an encounter, it's more about *rediscovering* some fundamental insights of Buddhism from *within*. Let the science itself speak out fully, and maybe it will find its expression. It's not going to be the 'same', it's going to be a 're-saying'.

So that's my exercise here. Cognitive science today, what is it to *you*? You being anyone except a brain scientist. I have structured this in four main key points. I will present them as slogans of ideas, or to be more precise, fundamental insights which rest upon about fifty years of good research, and which I take to be established results. After spending a long time in cognitive science laboratories you could say that I'm presenting take-home messages. These are not very personal interpretations, but an attempt to squeeze out the fundamental messages that can be seriously defended. There is no space for the detailed empirical and theoretical arguments here, but the point is that these are statements which are not arbitrary but *can* be supported by evidence from the long process of research. They are not just something off the top of my head or my own private opinions. I'm trying to take a reading and make it congruent with the underpinning of empirical results.

A last preliminary point: science moves very fast, so these key points were thus shaped ten years ago. Most of these things are not to be found in textbooks today.

1. THE KEY POINT OF EMBODIMENT

The first point is what I call the key point of *embodiment*. This is in contrast to the prevailing view that is grounded on the computer metaphor; seeing mind as the software, with brain and body as hardware. Here, by 'mind' I mean anything that has to do with mentality, with cognition and ultimately with experience. One of the major key realisations over the last few years in science has been to understand that you cannot have anything close to a mind or a mental capacity without it being completely embodied, enfolded with the world. It arises through an immediate coping, inextricably bound in a body that is active, moving, and coping with the world.

This might sound obvious but is not so within the world of research where other ideas have been predominant especially the computational idea I discussed above. It is necessary to break away from that dominance. There is a long list of arguments to say that the mind is not a program, a software, a rule-based manipulation of symbols. To summarise them in a nutshell, here comes my first slogan: *The mind is not in the head*. This idea arises as a consequence of the rediscovery of the importance of embodiment.

Now why is this? The logic here is very precise: once you understand that in order to have a mind you have to have an active handling and coping with the world, then you have an embedded and an active phenomenon and whatever you call an object, a thing in the world, chairs and tables, people and faces and so on, is entirely dependent on this constant sensory motor handling. You cannot just see the object as independently being 'out-there'. The object arises because of your activity, so, in fact, you and the object are co-emerging, co-arising.

Here is a quick example to show that this is not a purely metaphorical thing: some time ago Held and Hein carried out a beautiful classical experiment with two little kittens, which are blind at birth, in two baskets. The baskets were moved around for a little tour some hours each day and both the kittens were exposed to the same environment. One kitten was allowed to have its feet out of the basket and walk, the other one was kept tucked up inside the basket. Two months later, the two kittens were released. The one that had its feet free behaved like a normal cat. The other one did not recognise objects, it fell down the stairs and bumped into chairs. To all intents and purposes, it behaved as if it was blind, although its eyes were intact. The conclusion *not* to draw is that cats see with their feet! The conclusion to draw is that space arises out of movement. It is an absolutely dramatic statement that space, this thing in front that seems the most objective, the pillar of objectivity in physics, is totally inseparable from the fact that we have to sensory-motor handle it. The same kind of argument can be developed from a number of other examples that I cannot describe here. In my book *The Embodied Mind* there is a detailed description of how this can be applied to the perception and quality of colour, again an entirely *co-emergent property*.[1]

Let us now turn this slogan *'The mind is not in the head'* into a more structured logic: *Cognition is enactively embodied.* 'Enactive' is a label used here in its literal sense. Cognition is something that you bring forth by the act of handling, by the fact of doing it actively. It is the very foundational principle of what mind is all about. That entails, as I tried to show above, that it is a deep co-implication, a co-determination of what seems to be outside and what seems to be inside. In other words, the world out there and what I do to find myself in that world, cannot be separated. The process itself makes them completely interdependent, quite literally so, as seen with the example of the kittens.

There are two consequences to this enactive embodiment. If the mind is not in the head, where the hell is it? It's precisely the point here: it is in this non-place of the co-determination of inner and outer, so one cannot say that is outside or inside. The other consequence that follows, which is less commonly noted, is that the mind cannot be separated from the *entire* organism. We tend to think that the mind is in the brain, in the head, but the fact is that the environment also includes the rest of the organism; includes the fact that the brain is intimately connected to all of the muscle, the skeletal system, the guts, the immune system, the hormonal balances and so on. It makes the whole thing into an extremely tight unity. In other words, the organism as a meshwork of entirely co-determining elements makes it so that our minds are, literally, inseparable, not only from the external environment, but also from what Claude Bernard already called the *mileu intérieur*, the fact that we have not only a brain but an entire body.

If you are coming from that tradition of philosophy of mind which does think that mind is something that happens in the head, this comes as something of a surprise. For example, philosophers in the past have amused themselves by speaking about 'brains in a bath', a brain in a test tube with little wires coming out of it. It's funny, the Anglo-American philosophical community has spent hours at conferences discussing this kind of thing, but when we look at the state of research today, the whole argument seems bizarre because with a brain in a bath there cannot *be* such thing as mind. It would be completely incoherent neural activity, because it could not have the functionality of what it actually does, the constant coping with the body and with the environment which makes sense of it.

So, in brief, that is the first key point of embodiment, the co-determination of inner and outer. And we should not forget that this refers as much to the outside environment as it does to the body itself.

1

The Key Point of Embodiment

The mind is not in the head

Cognition is <u>enactively embodied</u>
co-determination of inner/outer

2. The Key Point of Emergence

The second slogan is: *The mind neither exists nor does it not exist.* I call this the key point of *emergence*. This is a tough one, because this notion of emergence is quite fundamental and usually misunderstood. I use the term 'emergence' in a more or less technical sense. The more one looks into the way the brain works, or I should say, the way the process of cognition works, the more it becomes clear that one is dealing with very individual components, neurons or groups of neurons or populations of neurons. It is the job of the neuroscientist to poke into these cells, and try to understand the details of their workings, the awesome richness of the brain and the extraordinary intricacy of millions and millions of intricate connections. These local elements in interaction can be referred to as the local rules; these *local* rules and local interactions turn out to be not like passing information in computers – beep beep from here to there, the sending of messages in a syntactic or programmatic manner. These interactions are in real time very fast, dynamic and simultaneous.

What one gets as a consequence is something I still find absolutely astounding, which is that from this local element comes the establishment of a *global* process, a global state or global level, which is neither independent of these local inter-actions nor reducible to them. This is the emergence out from the local rules to a global level that has a different ontological status, because it brings about the creation of an individual, or a cognitive unity. So when you see an animal moving around, or myself speaking to you, I behave as a coherent unity, not a mere juxtaposition of movement, voice, sight, and posture. I'm an integrated, more or less harmonic unity that I call 'myself' or 'my' mind, and you interact with me at that level: 'Hi, Francisco.' That interaction is happening at the level of individuality, which is the global, the emergent. Yet we know that the global is at the same time cause and consequence of the local actions that are going on in my body all the time.

Now, I don't have access to the firing rate of my neuron 223 in the visual cortex, because that would be like breaking the law that the global is of a different ontological kind than the local. This point of emergence, a general principle that has pervaded all of science and not only neuroscience during the last twenty years, reveals the fundamental importance of conceiving of a new mode or kind of existence, of the way to characterise what something is. It's a mode of existence of which you cannot say it doesn't exist. ('Francisco doesn't exist.') I count for something, you are reading what I am writing. At the same time, what is the nature of my existence? We do not assume that there is something substantial or a special quality that is sitting somewhere in this or that area of my brain that makes Francisco Francisco. In fact this cognitive self is entirely the result of its dynamical links that embrace very single local component, yet at the same time it is not identifiable to any interaction in particular. So it's like saying it is and it isn't there.

It's like when you say 'England'. In some sense England exists, it has commerce, it has peace treaties, and it does all kinds of things qua nation. At the same time, where is it? England is in the pattern of interactions of people living there, and those conversations and actions are what makes it into a unity. So it neither exists nor does it not exist, that is, it exists only as a pattern in flux. Clearly it has a *mode* of existence which is not of the kind that we have inherited from theology or physics, conceived as substantiality or a materiality, a quality which can be found or localised some way or another. Yet emergent entities are the basis of complex entities typical of the realms of life and mind, extremely effective as a mode of action and a mode of presence in the world.

So, cognition is not only enactively embodied but is *enactively emergent*, in that technical sense that I just tried to sketch. Some people might call that by various names: self-organisation, complexity, or non-linear dynamics. The core principle is the same: the passage from the local to the global. It's a co-determination of neural elements and a global cognitive subject. The global cognitive subject belongs to that emergent level and it has that mode of existence.

Now the principle of emergence is normally interpreted with a rather reductionist twist. What I mean is that many will accept that the self is an emergent property arising from a neural/bodily base. However the *reverse* statement is typically missed. This is important. If the neural components and circuits act as local agents that can emergently give rise to a self, then it follows that this global level, the self, has direct *efficacious actions* over the local components. It's a two-way street: the local components give rise to this emergent mind, but, vice versa, the emergent mind constrains, affects directly these local components.

So from this point of view, the puzzle of psychosomatic phenomena is a false problem. Why should we be surprised that a global state of a cognitive mood or an attitude or a state of mind could have a direct effect on very, very minute local principles? And if you think this is just wishful thinking, let me give you one example. We have been working with epileptic patients who have electrodes implanted in their brain for future surgery. Thus we have access to very detailed electrical signals of the brain of a waking human. This makes it possible to also analyse the moments that precede the crisis and in fact to predict its occurrence some minutes before.[2] This is of course a good example of local properties (the local currents) leading to a global state (the crisis) in a lawful manner. But we were also able to obtain evidence for the converse: if a patient engages in purposeful, cognitive activity (such as recognising a visual form) we could see changes in the epileptic dynamics. This means the effect of a global state has downward effects over local electrical activity in a very precise fashion[3]. So let's talk about mind-body integration. For some funny reason there is this Western tradition, this odd perception that you can have matter being the support of mind, but you cannot have mind directly affecting matter. Well, this is demonstrably wrong, and this again is what this notion of emergence allows us to see, if you understand it properly as a two-way street, not just a one-way street.

So, cognition is enactively emergent and is the co-determination of local elements and the global cognitive subject. There are two corollaries I would like to draw from this key point. First corollary, if you put together key point one and key point two, embodiment and emergence, the mind is fundamentally a matter of *imagination and fantasy*. In other words, it's the internal activity of these rich emergent properties, plus the fact that you have an ongoing coupling that forms the core of what the mind is. The mind is not about representing some kind of state of affairs. The mind is about constantly secreting this coherent reality that constitutes a world, the coherence of the organising through the local-global transitions. Stated in other words, perception is as imaginary, as imagination is perception-based. There are some beautiful experiments showing that you can give an (enactively embodied) organism anything at all as an excuse for sensory-motor interaction, and it will immediately constitute a world which is shaped, which is fully formed. It's an amazing conceptual shift from thinking that there are properties of the world that you need to apprehend in order to make a coherent picture of reality, to the notion that almost anything would supply an excuse to invent a reality. Our world is imagination and fantasy, and that's why it is a fundamentally important point for children to develop theirs.

The second corollary of this principle is that, since mind is based on local to global emergence, there is nothing in the mind that you can separate into discrete separate elements. In other words, phenomenologically our minds do not present a clear division of memory here, affect there, and vision over there. As a consequence, one of the most striking discoveries over the last few years is the understanding that affect or emotion is at the very foundation of what we do every day as coping with the world; that reason or reasoning is almost like the icing on the cake. Reason is what occurs at the very last stage of the moment-to-moment emergence of mind. Mind is fundamentally something that arises out of the affective tonality, which is embedded in the body. It takes about a fraction of a second for the whole thing to happen, over and over and over again. In the process of a momentary arising of a mental state, the early stages are rooted in the sensory motor surfaces near the spinal cord in the mid-brain, then they sweep upwards on to the so-called limbic system, into the so-called superior cortex, so this emotional tone changes transforming into categories and distinct elements and chains of reasoning, which are the classical unities description of mind. But reason and categories are literally the tips of the mountain which are sitting on affect, particularly affect and e-motion. In fact, e-motion is already intrinsically cognitive. Once you change your perspective and stop looking for reason as the most central principle of mind, then you can see the emergence of moment of mind as it happens. It starts out from this soup, the entire organism in situation, and then it gives rise to this surge, which gradually spreads out like peaks of mountains.

That's why experience in a phenomenological footnote is so hard to articulate, since a large chunk of its base is pre-reflective, affective, non-conceptual, pre-noetic. It's hard to put it into words, precisely because it precedes words. To say it precedes words does not mean it's beyond words. It's the opposite, it's because it's so grounded that it has not yet become the elements of reason that we tend to think are the highest expression of mind.

So, to summarise the two corollaries. First, I say: 'Life is like a dream'. Second, to cite Pascal: 'The heart has its reasons that reason does not understand'.

2

The Key Point of Emergence

The mind neither exists nor does it not exist

Cognition is <u>enactively emergent</u>
co-determination of neural elements
(local) and cognitive subject (global)

3. THE KEY POINT OF INTERSUBJECTIVITY

With our next key point we enter into a domain which is not well charted yet. The slogan is: *This mind is* that *mind*. It has been a constant in cognitive and brain science to simply assume as obvious that a mind belongs inside a brain, and hence that the other's mind is impenetrable and opaque. Any violation of this spatial separation is taken as invoking some kind of hocus-pocus psychic energy which is to be avoided. Well, very recent research in cognitive science is beginning to show quite clearly that individuality and intersubjectivity are not in opposition, but necessarily *complementary*. Again, it does not cease to amaze me how some philosophers of mind have spent litres of ink on debates about how to prove that you have a consciousness, and that we are not surrounded by zombies. Quite frankly I find this ludicrous. The issue is squarely upside down: the presence and reality of other is so intimately close that the pertinent question is how can we ever come to have the notion that we are that separate and distinct?

I have already said that modern research in cognitive science gives ample evidence to the effect that all cognitive phenomena are also emotional-affective. That is, it has very naturally ended up considering the very ground of the genesis of mind as an affective-empathic phenomenon. This is particularly clear in studies of both higher primates and young children.

Thus, in a recent survey Provinelli and Preuss conclude that the key result of many decades of research on higher primates is not the language/non-language controversy.[4] It is that higher primates excel at providing an interpretation of the *other's mind*. This represents a peculiar type of intelligence related to understanding mental states such as desires, intentions and beliefs from the other's bodily presence: face, posture and sound. Behavioural studies in children and chimpanzees reveal striking similarities in their developmental pathways in this regard, although it is likely that humans have developed further refinements. The pioneering work of D. Stern in his studies on babies noticed already that the boundaries of self and others are not delineated even in perceptual events, and that being a 'me' and constituting a 'you' are concomitant events.[5] The baby's amazing capacity for empathic response emerges a few hours after birth. A final example concerns what everybody knows, that kids need love and care when they are little. Recently, there was a beautiful study published on how love and care affects the structure of the local elements in those children.[6] Astonishingly, they were able to show that holding and loving care was a direct determinant not only at the level of brain properties (i.e. synaptic and neurotransmitter changes), but also at the level of genetic expression. In other words, these kids are modified in their very bodily constitution by actions at the emotional level between human beings. We could multiply the further examples dealing for instance with studies on early infancy and their absorbed concern with faces. Or the recent neurophysiology that links the perception of one's body image to that of the other's body as in a mirror. The basic point is always the same, namely that cognition is *generatively enactive*, that is a co-determination of Me-Other.

There is, of course, a direct link between affect and empathy that is worth exploring here a little more as a closing point. Affect is a pre-reflective dynamic in self-constitution of the self, a self-affection in a literal sense. Affect is primordial, in the sense that I am affected or moved before any 'I' that knows. As I write now, I have a dispositional attitude that engages me in an anticipation of writing and shaping my thought into sentences. As I write this word now, the disposition is coloured by a play of emotional charge revealing a moderate resentment for not finding the proper expression. But that emotional tone appears against a background of an exalted mood of a productive day devoted to finishing this text. More explicitly, I want to distinguish three scales for affect. The first scale is *emotions* proper: the awareness of a tonal shift that is constitutive to the living present. The second is *affect*, a dispositional trend proper to a longer time (hours or days), a coherent sequence of embodied actions. Finally there is *mood*, the scale of narrative description over a long duration (many days or weeks).

The primordial or pre-verbal quality of affect makes it inseparable from the presence of others, and this is where I enter into the last stretch of my argument here. In order to see why this is so, it is best to focus on the *bodily* correlates of affect, which appear not merely as external behaviours, but also as directly felt, as part of our *lived body*. This trait of our lived body plays a decisive role in the manner in which I apprehend the other, not as a thing but as another subjectivity similar to mine as alter ego. It is through his/her body that I am linked to the other, first as an organism similar to mine, but also perceived as an embodied presence, site and means of an experiential field. This double dimension of the body (organic/lived; *Körper/Leib*) is part and parcel of *empathy*, the royal means of access to social conscious life, beyond the simple interaction, as fundamental inter-subjectivity.[7]

3

The Key Point of Intersubjectivity

This mind is that mind

Cognition is generatively enactive
co-determination of Me-Other.

---

4. THE KEY POINT OF CIRCULATION

The next key point moves us straight into a sharper turn but a necessary one, since it is also motivated by the internal dynamics of research itself. The slogan: *Consciousness is a public affair.* The direct background for this key point is the recent boom in the study of human consciousness as a legitimate domain for science. But the term 'consciousness' is vague enough that we need some clarification to start with.

The main intuition that animates this key point is this: the depth inherent in direct, lived experience permeates the natural roots of mind. I would like to develop this intuition in two steps. First, the very thrust of a proper scientific analysis of mind (i.e. in the context of the cognitive sciences) leads to the need for a detailed examination of *experience* itself. Secondly, examined experience and scientific analysis can have an explicit, non-dual relationship, a *mutual determination*, a circulation that avoids the extremes of both neuro-reductionism and some ineffability of consciousness.

A common trait in many spiritual traditions is that human experience is not taken at face value, but *examined* in one way or another. In contrast, cognitive science has been almost entirely interested in cognitive faculties in ordinary, *un*examined life. But this is beginning to change rapidly, and is not surprising since cognitive science faces the unique challenge of containing our own conscious life within its field and scope, and, *a fortiori*, the very act of examining our individual life. I have given elsewhere the arguments for the importance of developing such an experiential neuroscience, or *neurophenomenology*.[8] At the very core of that research programme is the crucial issue that if we are to avoid simply reducing experience (examined and unexamined) to neural accounts, a proper *methodology* is required for its examination.[9] It is typically here that the interface with spiritual traditions naturally presents itself. Next to the issue of methodology, there is the complementary question concerning the *nature* of the relationship between such external, scientific accounts coming from cognitive science and the first person, that is, phenomenological accounts directly anchored in lived experience. How do these two domains of observation and descriptions *mutually constrain, co-determine* each other? It is only fair to say this direction of work discloses a number of deep, disturbing challenges, which is why this key point is far less consensual than the preceding ones.

Concerning methodology, whether it be phenomenological or based on a contemplative tradition a major challenge is to lay bare each one of these aspects of the way of access of phenomena in the first person, in flesh and bone to establish a phenomenological *pragmatics* beyond vague usage. The failure to make phenomenological reduction into a concrete method is, in my eyes, the most undeveloped theme of phenomenology, and the greatest strength of the Buddhist tradition. As a result, a substantial amount of phenomenological literature has strayed into textual analysis and repetition of descriptions from Husserl or others, without the disciplined engagement to re-do such descriptions afresh. Beyond phenomenology there are the much-criticised introspectionist schools in the early twentieth-century psychology, which are having a second day in court,[10] and the non-Western wisdom traditions which have patiently cultivated highly detailed know-how (i.e. Buddhism, Taoism, Gnosticism). This discussion opens the question to what extent there is a unity underlying the multiplicity of methodologies for the examination of experience. (In such traditions the method of exploring one's experience is the key to the path if spiritual transformation is to be possible at all.) The challenge that this multiplicity of sources represents is this: is there a homology between these methods? Is there such a thing as a basic structure shared by these various pragmatics of experiencing?

As presented, the pragmatics of exploring experience is a very specific gesture. Its unicity lies not only in what is done, but also in the inescapable ontological region *where* it happens: the *lived body* (*Leib*), as we have discussed before. In both ordinary and even more so in spiritual experiences, the feeling-tone of intimacy and directness is essential. Experience is Janus-faced. On the one hand it is a 'pure' domain, which may be (or not) described by the invariant categories, and proper to inter-subjective life world. However, it is also an event linked to the temporality of the world and more precisely to the world as it is manifest in the biological rhythms of *my* body.

In this sense the practices of this examining experience unfold, I submit, a *distinct region of ontological reciprocity*. This region can be characterised by the manner in which specific entities show up as within it (i.e. what is *given*), and by its distinct immanent constitution (i.e. what is given is given in a sphere which is *mine*). This specific region is inhabited or discloses entities and events inseparable from the presence of the lived body in all of its complexity. Needless to say, the direction of work just sketched cannot be carried on an abstract, general basis, but needs to be based on case studies, conducted step by step. As an example we may consider a study of the central question of the neurophenomenology of the experience of time, the ever-present embodied now,[11] or the origin of the image of self.[12]

So the study of consciousness in the sense examined here opens regional ontologies of material or ideal objects which are inter-penetrated, trans-parent both towards their material basis (they would remain otherwise unbridgeably detached) and to the experiential domain (they would remain otherwise as floating, disembodied idealities). Clearly, the reciprocity *Leib/Körper* is not available in all its enormous import as long as we remain in an attitude of unexamined experience, that is, within the natural attitude. Going beyond requires sustained cultivation of the reductive attitude to be fully applied.

A main lesson is that the enterprise of neurophenomenology has taken us into the thicket of philosophical and methodological renewal. If this direction of research is to provide an answer to the otherwise unbridgeable explanatory gap between the cognitive and the phenomenological mind, it cannot ignore the very constitutive basis for the mutual reciprocity that makes the mental and experiential, and the bodily and neural, hang together. It is thus evident that only from this renewed basis can a neurophenomenology be other than a repetition of the past, in the form of searches for correspondence across the 'mystery' line.

This mutual reciprocity without residue is the very nature of the region unique to the *Körperleib*. In this ontological region where reciprocity manifests in all its vividness, three main threads need to be woven together on an equal footing to provide a seamless braid of continuity between the material and the experiential, the natural and the transcendental.[13] In other words, we have identified three poles in the mutual circulation we have been examining:

1. The *formal* level, since describing mental contents partakes of a mode of ideality and hence is effectively on common ground.
2. The *natural* (neural, bodily) process considered at the right level, spanning across global emergence and local mechanisms, that assures a direct relevance both to the psychological content and to a detailed neuroscientific examination.
3. The *pragmatic* level of examination that opens up to the *Leib/Körper* transition since it, and it alone, can give us access to a non-dual position, that excludes neither experience nor body, and provides the relevant basis or data for 1 and 2.

These three poles do not simply stand in a static or structural relation. They stand in a *mutually generative* relation in the sense that each one requires the other to make any sense. None of them in isolation can suffice. This triple braid provides, I propose, the foundation for an important renewal in philosophy and science to move towards a non-dual thinking which is not declarative or predefined by decree, but found at our very doorstep.

4

The Key Point of Circulation

Consciousness is a public affair

Consciousness is <u>ontologically</u> complex
co-determination of first- and third-
person descriptions.

---

5. CONCLUSION

Let me draw my conclusions by referring to the notion of a psychology of awakening, which gives the title to this book. In some basic sense it is an oxymoron, something like 'military intelligence'. For if psychology qua cognitive science has come to mean anything in its long history it is an understanding of mind that requires an underlying notion of *ego*, a self, an individual mind. In its current incarnation as part of cognitive science this can also be expressed as the functioning of a *cognitive agent*, body-bound and brain-encased. In contrast, awakening, if anything, is the expression of the human capacity to cultivate the expression of that which is not self-centred and ego-based, and certainly not incarnating a cognitive process simpliciter. Specifically, I am using 'awakened' in the Dharmic sense of *boddhicitta*, awakened heart or compassionate emptiness, an eminently other-centred, *selfless agency*. As such, this contrast is unresolvable, not only an oxymoron but for long stretches of history simply a contradiction, or at the very least a tension: a tension that a few have tried to resolve by negotiating the passages between the level of individual cognitive agent to living in the midst of *inter-being*, to use the apt phrase introduced by Thich Nhat Hahn.

My purpose in this paper has been to consider the links between the neuropsychology of an individual ego and awakened mind within the modern context of *cognitive science*. In a nutshell, my argument has been that, even if the tensions cannot be worked out within modern cognitive science even when considering what goes for its most 'advanced' trends, one is seeing the seeds, soft and budding, of what might be a further stage, a future cognitive science where inter-being may be thematised without contradiction. This stage is the description of changes that emerge from within science itself as we have traced with our four key points, and not the announcement of a programme to be imposed from the exterior.

I am ready now to close by drawing together the conclusion concerning the possibility of a future cognitive science of inter-being, a further stage in a history of the development of the field since its inception in the 1960s. This is easily done by considering the historical waves of development within cognitive science:

- Stage 1 is expressed in the early *computationalist* cognitive science, which views the mind as an information-processing system, a set of discrete symbols handled by rules for action.
- Stage 2 is *connectionist* cognitive science, the replacement of the discrete symbol by a set of network states, incorporating a dynamical view.
- Stage 3, *embodied* or enactive cognitive science, summed up in the first two key points, takes this dynamical view one step further by suspending any notion of appropriate action as based on an adequate representation of a pre-given external world, and starts from situated sensori-motor actions, the source of meaning.
- Stage 4 is *generative* cognitive science, where the neuro-phenomenological perspective is extended to include as foundational its intersubjective, empathic-affective dimension. At this stage, cognitive science begins to touch on the

sphere of interbeing whose experience is the basis of awakened mind.

- Stage 5 is *neurophenomenology* – a further extension of the embodied-emergent perspective accompanied by an explicit demand to include phenomenological data, where consciousness figures as a central theme. At this point cognitive science enters into a new phase, which is just beginning to emerge today. All the rest is the future.

These successive stages in science can be seen to correspond to an evolution in the understanding of the other. For computationalism and connectionism the other's mind is mostly a problem, an open question that needs proof. The self is seen as an isolated agent who has no direct evidence that others are not mere zombies. For embodied cognitive science and a purely static neurophenomenology, the other appears as inter-action, a given fact but still to be generated as a separate entity, for which links must be built between two independent, constituted minds. In a generative view, the other and I are a common ground, a joint tissue which is tangibly present in empathy and affect, which offer a possible level of analysis if we avail ourselves of the means to do so.

The psychology of awakening then *can* be a real possibility; not merely an oxymoron, but an optimistic future-oriented science of mind. There is a long way to go before such a level of analysis can fully enter into science. For this to happen, we require at least two massive changes. First, breaking with the taboo of using phenomenal data as valid, and training in the competencies demanded by phenomenological analysis as well as those demanded by classical scientific research. Second, breaking with the taboo of intersubjectivity as a ground from which a variety of experiences issues forth. These are heavily inertial assumptions that will move as slowly as continents. The natural attitude of the scientist and the public today is to see the mind as a distinct, brain-encased self. Breaking that illusion from within science seems, today, not a complete impossibility – some cracks are opening for a science of interbeing.

You will have noticed that the four key points presented here all have in common an elegant *reciprocal causality*; a reciprocal co-determination is always at centre-stage, holding the hands of two extremes to join them in mutual determination. This reciprocity is so pervasive in this vision that it is the very ground on which we stand, that is, a ground of groundlessness. Thus

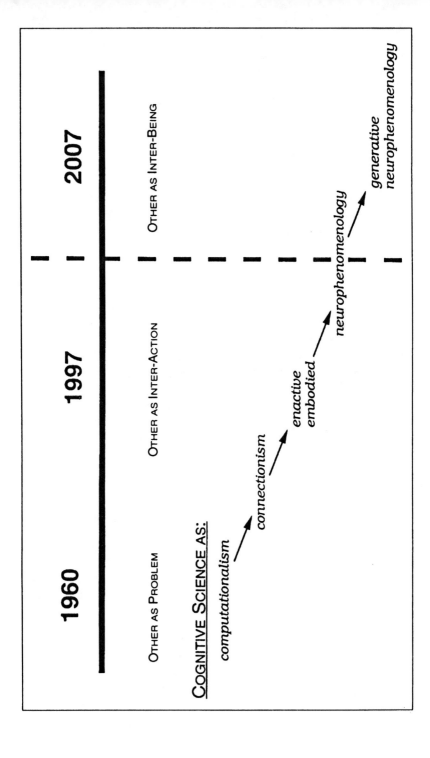

emptiness is rediscovered here as a force of scientific movement itself. Those familiar with Dharma may be tempted to continue the exercise of translating what we have said in this text into traditional Dharmic terms: the foundation of mindfulness, egolessness, interdependent origination, compassion, gross and subtle mind, and so on. It is a Dharma *implicit* in science that cries to be stated explicitly, to be restated yet again.

Neurotheology: Buddhism, Cognitive Science and Mystical Experience

Guy Claxton

'. . . But who are the grown-ups?'

'Don't ask me,' she answered, 'That's a question for a neurotheologian.'

'Meaning what?' he asked.

'Meaning precisely what it says. Someone who thinks about people in terms, simultaneously, of the Clear Light of the Void and the vegetative nervous system. The grown-ups are a mixture of Mind and physiology.'

Island, Aldous Huxley

The primordial ground of self-awareness is unceasing and unchanging.

The Dharmakaya's efflorescence of whatever arises is neither good nor bad.

Since awareness of Nowness is the real Buddha,

In openness and contentment we find the Lama in our heart.

When we realize that this unending Natural Mind *is* the very nature of the Lama,

There is no need for attached or grasping prayers or artificial complaints.

Simply by relaxing in uncontrived Awareness, the free and open natural state,

We obtain the blessing of aimless self-liberation of whatever arises.

Calling the Lama from Afar, H.H. Dudjom Rinpoche,
trs. Ven. Lama Sogyal Rinpoche

In his book *Clearing the Path* Nanavira Thera (1987) offers an analogy for the nature of mind based on the game of chess. In normal, or what Nanavira calls 'dispassionate', chess, a number of pieces move around on the familiar board of sixty-four squares according to fixed rules. But imagine a fiendish alternative, 'passionate chess', in which the moves that any piece makes depend upon the other pieces around it. The bishops, for example, being enamoured of the queen, are diverted from their usual diagonal path when passing close to her; while – perhaps out of fear of his jealousy – they take evasive action when in the vicinity of the king. The knights, being vain fellows, tend to be drawn into the company of any cluster of admiring pawns. The castles, owing to a mutual dislike, try to stay as far away from each other as possible. And so on. Although the normal rules continue to apply in general, 'passionate chess' is seriously complicated by the influence of each piece's likes and dislikes, attachments and aversions. Passionate chess is played by the normal mind, the mind of the *puthujjana*; while dispassionate chess reflects the *arahat's* mind, a mind freed of self-ish deformations. Buddhism is concerned with the transformation of the *puthujjana* into the *arahat*; that is to say, with liberating the mind from the intricate networks of fear and need brought into being by the illusion of 'self'.

Now consider the image used by British author and inventor of the concept of 'lateral thinking', Edward de Bono, in his psychology book *The Mechanism of Mind* (1969). Imagine the mind as a large sheet of some elastic material, rather like an enormous trampoline. The activity of the mind is represented by the way that steel ball-bearings, dropped on to the trampoline, roll along it. Experience wears the rubber thinner and it sags, so the balls tend to collect in the dips that represent the most familiar concepts. But suppose that someone is crawling about underneath this elasticated surface hooking weights to it at various points, so that, viewed from above, the surface becomes even more distorted. Now when the balls are dropped on to it, they will have no choice but to run along the valleys, and collect in the hollows that are created by these weights, as well as being channelled by the 'wear and tear' of experience. As a result of the added weights and biases, a mind-surface that has one intrinsic nature comes to behave as if it 'cared about' a very different set of priorities. The behaviour and the apparent significance of a ball dropped in exactly the same spot will vary, depending on the disposition of the invisible weights below. The more needs and threats one hooks underneath the trampoline, the more one's thoughts and perceptions will come to reflect these hopes and fears, and the less 'accurate' or 'objective' they will be.

A third analogy. Computerised banking systems have made possible a whole new kind of white-collar theft. A sub-program is installed in a bank's computer which tells the main program to skim off one penny from every transaction and deposit it into a specific account. As thousands of transactions are carried out every day, this swiftly mounts up. But such a fraudulent program, if unprotected, will be quickly discovered by the routine checking of the bank's own (honest) programmers. So the most sophisticated versions are designed to recognise when someone is checking (by the kinds of commands that are typed in, or the anti-virus sub-routines that are run), and when they do so they hide. They are capable of 'going to ground', of taking a vacation in a distant part of the computer network until the hunt is over, and then they creep back and resume their pilfering. Again, the behaviour of the system as a whole is perverted by influences that are themselves not directly observable.

Each of these analogies – the chess game, the trampoline, the computer virus – uses a modern artefact to dramatise the central psychological assertion of Buddhism: that there is a 'Natural Mind', a 'primordial ground of self-awareness', whose behaviour is distorted by misapprehensions about self in just the way (to use yet another image) that the picture on a TV screen can be distorted by the proximity of a powerful magnet. The activity of such a 'Self System' does not fundamentally damage the Natural Mind, any more than the magnet causes permanent damage to the television mechanism (or the weights to the elastic sheet), and when either magnet or self is 'switched off', the picture instantaneously regains its bright clear quality. When the passions of the chess-pieces are subdued, the game immediately reverts to its inherent form. If what we know about ourselves, when the Self System is 'on', is 'second nature' to us, what then is our *first* nature, Zen's 'original face'? And how is it to be recovered?

Posing the fundamental Buddhist questions in this way has the interesting consequence of providing a framework within which Buddhists and those who take a more scientific interest in the mind can converse. These analogies are by no means alien to those whose interest in the mind is more intellectual than soteriological: the collaborative teams of psychologists, neuro-scientists, philosophers and artificial intelligence modellers who work these days under the common banner of 'cognitive science'. In the last few years such teams have been mounting a new and vigorous assault on the fundamental, perennial questions of the human mind. How did it evolve? How does it work? How does it go wrong? What is its potential? And if the direct experiential insight of the Buddha, and the other mystics down the ages, is valid, should we not expect the painstaking rigor of empirical science to begin to point, in an objective way, to the same conclusions? It is the aim of this chapter to demonstrate one way in which this conversation can prove fruitful: precisely in showing how science can help us understand the nature and experience of the 'natural mind', the processes by which it becomes obscured or distorted, and how it may be released. Bracketing this detailed exposition, I shall have to make some more general remarks about the relationship between Buddhism – or, generically, 'spirituality' – and the scientific enterprise itself.

SCIENCE AND SPIRITUALITY: A CHECKERED HISTORY

The liaison between science and spirituality is a delicate and in some ways a dangerous one. Twenty years ago, with the publi-cation of Fritjof Capra's classic *The Tao of Physics*, there was a wave of enthusiasm for drawing strong parallels between physics and mysticism, based on the discovery of some striking simi-larities between the attempts of physicists such as Schrödinger and Heisenberg on the one hand, and the authors of *The Upanishads* and the *Tao Te Ching* on the other, to articulate their discoveries. Some commentators succumbed to the tempta-tion to conclude that the new theories of quantum physics and relativity had somehow proved, or at least added legitimacy to, the words of the mystics.

It soon transpired, though, that this use of science to lend credibility to spirituality was neither warranted nor wise. It was not warranted because, as Ken Wilber showed conclusively in his *Quantum Questions* (1984), the mystical writings of the great physicists arose not as inescapable corollaries of their theories, but from their appreciation of the *limits* of theory. Einstein and Planck were forced to embrace mysticism precisely at the point where their sophisticated physics could take them no further. And it was not wise because the discoveries of Buddha and Lao Tsu, if they *are* true, must be true regardless of intellectual fashion – and if there is one sure thing about science, it is that its theories are ephemeral. As particle physicist Jeremy Bernstein put it: 'If I were an Eastern mystic the last thing in the world I would want would be a reconciliation with modern science, [because] to hitch a religious philosophy to a contemporary science is a sure route to its obsolescence' (Wilber, 1982: 167).

The effort to 'explain' certain features and potentialities of human consciousness in terms of the apparent properties or behaviour of fundamental particles continues. Presently Danah Zohar (1990) is convinced that it is something called 'Bose-Einstein condensates' that need to be invoked. While Roger Penrose and Stuart Hameroff (Penrose, 1994) are arguing that consciousness arises as a result of quantum indeterminacies in arcane little filaments called microtubules that live inside neurons. But the effort is running out of plausibility, if not of steam. The superficial analogy between the indeterminacy of electrons and the elusive natures of self and consciousness is just that: a pun taken too seriously. The evidence for these, as opposed to dozens of other interesting speculations, is somewhere between extremely flimsy and non-existent. Yet such fancies have attracted much interest, perhaps, as Rick Grush and Patricia Churchland (1995) suggest, because the subjective and elusive mystery of mind seems to call for an equally slippery kind of explanation.

> Explanations of something as special as what makes me *me* should really involve, the feeling is, something more 'deep' and mysterious and 'other worldly' than mere neurons. Perhaps what is comforting about quantum physics is that it can be invoked to 'explain' a mysterious phenomenon without removing much of the mystery, quantum-physical explanations being highly mysterious themselves. (Grush and Churchland, 1995: 28)

Nanavira, as long ago as 1962, anticipated the current scepticism:

> The impossibility of making a definite assertion about an electron has nothing to do with the impossibility of making

a definite assertion about 'self'. The electron, in quantum theory, is defined in terms of *probabilities*, and a definite assertion about what is essentially indefinite cannot be made. But *atta* is not an *indefiniteness*; it is a *deception*, and a deception can be as definite as you please – the only thing is, that it is not what one takes it for. (Nanavira, 1987: 249)

The question is: should the failure of physics to live up to an unrealistic set of expectations cause us to retire, fingers burnt, from *any* attempt to bring science and Buddhism into conversation? I think not. The appropriate lesson to learn is not to give up, but to proceed with caution, and to choose one's science more carefully. As the most salient characteristics of humankind are that we are biological, social and psychological beings, it might, after all, be more profitable to look to the sciences that treat us as such, rather than as peculiar constellations of complicated mathematical equations and hypothetical particles.

If to do so we need to overcome a reflex aversion to the presupposition that quintessentially human properties, like hope and fear, self and consciousness, may reflect the intricate workings of the special kinds of meat of which we are composed, then so be it. Some people assume that to approach the 'higher', in human experience, in terms of the 'lower' is to attempt to degrade or belittle the former, and necessarily commits the error of ignoring its emergent or systemic properties. But reductionism seen as an *exploratory strategy* – investigating the extent to which concepts at one level of description can be used to generate interesting accounts of phenomena at the next level up – is quite different from reductionism as a belief system which insists that everything of interest about the 'whole' can be articulated in terms of properties of the 'parts'. The latter is a scientific or philosophical dogma; the former is the exploration of an open question.

This confusion about reductionism seems to have fuelled much of the fascination with the esoteric potential of quantum physics, many of whose enthusiasts seem to consider that an explanation of the human mind in terms of the brain is 'scary', 'degrading', or even 'inconceivable'. Why the collapse of a wave function is a less scary, reductionistic basis for explaining 'meness' than a filigree of neural fibres is a question usually left unaddressed.

BUDDHISM AND COGNITIVE SCIENCE: SOME PARALLELS

What, then, can we learn from cognitive science? As living organisms, we are fundamentally *embodied systems*. A body only exists and persists by virtue of its continual participation in a host of intricate dynamic interactions with the wider biological world. Systems theory tells us that a body is not so much a structure as a form of process; as Aldous Huxley said, a 'tune' rather than a 'pebble'. Internally, too, the body and all its constituents comprise a coherent, integrated system, a symphony of interpenetrating, self-maintaining processes in which the modulation of any one element affects the balance and the function of the whole. And this includes the brain and all the patterns that have been etched upon it by experience: all our knowledge and belief, all our foibles and fears. Neither brain nor mind ('mind' in the sense of all our conditionings) stands outside the system of which they are part, and to which they contribute – any more than the liver or the nose can claim a life apart from the world-body system of which they are aspects. Thus science tells us that the brain and its mind are essentially, ineradicably *ecological*. Whether we feel it or know it or not, it is a matter of scientific fact that we are 'children of the universe'. No matter how much we may long to belong, in truth we already do.

If the first Great Truth that science gives us is that we are ecological – approximate parts of an indissoluble whole – the second, which follows from it, is that we *care*. There is now good evidence to suppose that the human organism is designed to be considerate of the needs of its fellows and of its habitat. We have co-evolved both from, and as, ecosocial systems, so the body-brain-mind 'knows' that its well-being is intimately interlinked with the well-being of its human and natural surroundings. Our forebears' sense of identification – what it is 'my business' to promote and protect – would have extended outwards to embrace family, friends, other members of the species, and all living and non-living elements of the wider ecological system of which they were part. All other things being equal, it is in 'my' interest to look after my community and my environment, because, fundamentally, they are not really 'other'. Interestingly, it has been demonstrated that human babies, before they can have been influenced by conventional morality, show sympathetic distress to another distressed child. We are endowed, it appears, with *bodhisattva* genes as well as selfish ones (Dawkins, 1976).

The 'as well as' is important. We have evolved to care about both our own individual well-being, and about those around us. Often, these two priorities conflict, and then it is the brain's most crucial job to compute the best course of action. Sometimes it can find a way of being in which 'we' both win. Sometimes 'your' needs take precedence; sometimes mine. Is this feature of the Natural Mind at odds with the Buddhist ideals of selflessness and compassion? Apparently not, for we find in *The Dhammapada*:

> The welfare of oneself should not be neglected for the welfare of others, however great; recognising the welfare of oneself, one should be devoted to one's own welfare. (Nanavira, 1987: 210)

So sometimes the immediate commitment to personal survival must temporarily take precedence over concern for others. To what extent it does so will depend on how frequent and how severe these personal threats are. We might imagine that, for beings who live in a comfortable and abundant 'econiche', and who therefore experience genuine survival threats only rarely, compassion – concern to relieve the sufferings of others – would emerge as the predominant priority, not out of an overriding moral responsibility, but simply because, under these conditions, such generosity lacks competition from the other more individualistic motivations. Compassion is what social animals will manifest, naturally, when they are having it easy, while some of their fellows are not. *Enlightened* self-interest naturally embraces the welfare of others.

A third basic tenet of cognitive science is that there is no agent or homunculus outside the neuro-biological system, to kick-start it or help it out if it gets into trouble. The Canadian neuro-psychologist Donald Hebb, one of the pioneers of cognitive science, wrote in his 1949 book *The Organization of Behavior*:

> This discussion represents my attempt to be rid, once and for all, of the little man inside the skull who *approves* of some sensory events relayed to him by the nervous system, *disapproves* of others, and guides behaviour accordingly . . . By some such approach as the one suggested, it may become possible to understand the directedness and order in behaviour, and the variability of motivation, as produced by neural functioning alone. (Hebb, 1949: 234)

And this is echoed more recently by philosopher Patricia Churchland in her book *Neurophilosophy*:

> The cardinal background principle for the theorist is that there are no homunculi. There is no little person in the brain who 'sees' an inner television screen, 'hears' an inner voice, 'reads' the topographical maps, weighs reasons, decides actions, and so forth. There are just neurons and their connections. When a person sees it is because neurons, individually blind and individually stupid neurons, are collectively orchestrated in the appropriate manner. (Churchland, 1986: 12)

It appears, then, that cognitive science is implementing a programme of research that is strikingly Buddhist in philosophy and intent. Science (through experimentation and deduction) and Buddhism (through spiritual authority and direct experience) seem to agree that Who We Are is a selfless system which, perversely, 'thinks' it is/has a self. We, as conscious beings, very definitely *do* have a sense of ourselves – our 'selves' – as ghosts in the machine. Our everyday experience is precisely of ourselves as agents whose job it is to make high-level decisions: to choose, decide, reflect, initiate and plan. The central puzzle for both Buddhism and science is how can an eco-biological system which is essentially self-less – the Natural Mind – come to see itself as being chauffeured by some non-existent entity? And how does it continue to run when the chauffeur is shown to be a chimera?

The fourth and final feature of the mind, revealed by contemporary science, which I wish to mention here, is the priority of unconscious over conscious processes. In the everyday view of our culture, consciousness is where our sophisticated intelligence (and therefore our 'self') resides; and the unconscious is either a dumb menial, delegated only the most elementary (and alimentary) bodily tasks like circulating blood and digesting food, or it is Where the Wild Things Are. Recent research (reviewed in Claxton, 1997) shows that, contrary to popular belief, most of the interesting work of the human body-brain-mind goes on underground, in the dark, and consciousness tends to turn up late, puffing and panting, after the action has happened, trying to claim credit (or to shift the blame) for whatever transpired in its absence. In the clinical phenomenon of 'blindsight', for example, people 'see' without consciousness. In a series of experiments at the University of Tulsa people learnt unconsciously complex patterns of information that they could neither learn nor even detect when they were attending consciously. And perception in general has been shown to be not a direct registration of an external 'reality', but a more-or-less useful fabrication of the underground mind; a tapestry into which are woven dozens of unconscious assumptions and inferences. Consciousness receives a partial, and in many ways unreliable, print-out of what is going on down below.

Conscious mind has to be Don't Know Mind, because its contents are fed to it, moment by moment, from a deeper source – Natural Mind, Big Mind – to which it has no access. If Buddha Nature is essentially this bodily, ecological, compassionate, selfless, *and unconscious* source of deep intelligence, then it is inevitable that The World-Honoured One, and all the Buddhas and mystics down the ages, should either refuse to speculate about that to which they know they have no access, or should do so only indirectly, and with difficulty. D.T. Suzuki, in his book on Hui-Neng, *The Zen Doctrine of No Mind*, insists that Buddha nature:

> . . . is not to be conceived as something of substance. It is not the last residue left behind after all things relative and conditional have been extracted from the notion of an individual being. It is not the self, or the soul, or the spirit, as usually regarded. It is not something belonging to any categories of the understanding. It does not belong to this world of relativities. Nor is it the highest reality which is generally ascribed to God or to Atman or to Brahma. *It cannot be described or defined in any possible way*, but without it the world even as we see it and use it in our everyday life collapses. (Suzuki, 1969: 123)

One could go on elaborating the ways in which (what Harvard psychologist Howard Gardner calls) 'the mind's new science' is reasserting and rediscovering aspects of mind that have been lost from our 'common sense', or 'second nature', but which have always remained at the heart of Buddhist understanding, and indeed of all the great mystical traditions. Psychology is (re-)discovering how the Natural Mind can be intentional and purposeful, without at the same time falling into attachment, aversion and ignorance. New models of the brain are showing how the Natural Mind performs its vital task of integrating, adjudicating and prioritising human needs, without requiring any 'self'; indeed it does the job *better* – it produces clearer, faster, wiser cognition – when the Self System is 'taken out of the loop' (as George Bush used to say of those who were kept ignorant or impotent in the White House).

MYSTICAL EXPERIENCE

Before getting in to the neuroscience, though, it might be useful to recall in what ways experience changes when the Self System quietens down. What are the recurrent features of those passages of experience that people have referred to as 'mystical'? To articulate mystical experience is notoriously difficult. As Alan Watts (1961) wrote, it involves trying to speak the unspeakable, scrute the inscrutable and eff the ineffable. Yet the urge to try seems inexhaustible. We have a trail of mystical writings from the time of the Buddha and before, up to the present day. Each account is, of course, conditioned by the mystic's culture. If they are to communicate anything, they have to speak in terms of the language, the mythology and the life experience of their audiences. In particular their tales rely heavily on the use of metaphors – 'rebirth', 'the kingdom of heaven', 'the clear light of the void' – that are grounded in their own shared culture. Thus the poetry of Rumi, the parables of Christ, the Buddhist sutras and the spiritual guidance of *The Cloud of Unknowing* may seem, until they are unwrapped and reformulated in the language of our culture, to be speaking not just in different terms, but of different experiences.

Yet many scholars this century, from William James' *Varieties of Religious Experience* (1910, reprinted 1958) onward, have shown that it is possible to understand this diverse body of writing as pointing to experiences that share several core features. Below or beyond the contrasting 'exoteric' forms and rituals of the world's cultures and religions, there lies an 'esoteric' unity, a fluid quality of being which is tasted in mystical experience, but which has to be poured into the mould of one particular tradition, and thereby set and deformed, before it can be 'effed'. Wilber (1977), to name but one, makes the point by quoting from The First Epistle to the Corinthians (Chapter 12, 4-6): 'There are diversities of gifts, but the same Spirit. And there are differences of administrations, but the same Lord. And there are diversities of operations, but it is the same God which worketh in them all.'

My purpose here is not to argue further for this unity: the job is done. Rather I wish to review these common features, and to ask why it is that they go together. Let me illustrate some of these characteristics with this little gem of a poem by W.B. Yeats (1958).

> My fiftieth year had come and gone.
> I sat, a solitary man,
> In a crowded London shop,
> An open book and empty cup
> On the marble table top.
>
> While on the shop and street I gazed
> My body for a moment *blazed*,
> And twenty minutes, more or less,
> It seemed, so great my happiness,
> That I was blessed, and could bless.

What does this show us? First, mystical experiences often arise out of the blue, and in the most mundane settings. Although this 'altered state of consciousness' can be encouraged by the spiritual disciplines, and potentiated by exhaustion or privation, its appearance can neither be chosen, nor controlled, nor wilfully prolonged. Such experiences are often limited in time: from a minute or so up to an hour or two is common. Secondly, the mystic is 'blessed': there is joy, ecstasy, happiness, which suffuses whatever ordinary sights or activities happen to be occurring. Thirdly, there is equally the sense of being gifted with a form of kindly, even holy, wisdom. Not only was Yeats blessed; he 'could bless'. This upsurge of love and compassion is often described as being linked to a vivid appreciation of suffering; an appreciation which somehow is able to coexist with the sense of blessedness and bliss. And fourthly, there is a sense of unusual physical energy, and perceptual intensity, often captured, as here, by the metaphor of fire, or sometimes light.

While many of the non-Buddhist accounts draw on a 'transcendent' theological vocabulary, seeing the mystical experience as a direct encounter with a God who is 'other', the tendency this century has been to seek for an explanation of mysticism that takes a more immanent, psychological view. James himself, for example, notes that these experiences 'seemed to consist merely in the temporary obliteration of the conventionalities which usually surround and cover my life . . . What I felt on these occasions was a temporary loss of my own identity' (James, 1958). So the fifth characteristic of mystical experience, we might say, is a total or partial loss of the normal 'sense of self', one of the manifestations of which is a radically altered perception of *will*. One 'feels as if his own will is in abeyance, and indeed sometimes as if he were grasped and held by a superior power'. (James, 1958: 67) The sense of being a small, embattled and responsible self dissolves, and in its place comes the sixth feature: a recognition of what Brother David Steindl-Rast (Capra and Steindl-Rast, 1991) calls *belonging*. One is reconnected with one's ecological family; at home and 'at large' in one's natural communal living-room.

The last aspect of mystical experience I wish to draw attention to is perhaps the most ubiquitous: its mystery. There is a feeling of being in on a secret that is, paradoxically, not revealed, not made explicit. The mystical 'insight' is not the property of the verbal and conceptual levels of the brain-mind. The centre of gravity of the whole organism is shifted from the vaulting cupola of the intellect down towards the catacombs, the underground work-ings. William James talks of 'insight into depths of truth unplumbed by the discursive intellect'. (James, 1958: 68) Brother Henry in the Preface to *The American* refers, rather more elegantly, to the 'deep well of unconscious cerebration'. (James, 1990: ix) And Jung was emphatic about the relationship between mysticism and the unconscious, which he describes as 'simply the medium from which religious experience seems to flow. As to what the further cause of such experience may be, the answer to that lies beyond the range of human knowledge'. (Jung, 1958: 89)

Perhaps the richest source of writings that explicitly link religious experience to the unconscious and 'unknowing', richer even than Buddhism, is the apophatic tradition within Christian mysticism. The acknowledged 'father' of the apophatics was a sixth-century Syrian who, writing under the name of Dionysius the Areopagite, is reputed to have said: 'The most godly knowledge of God is that which is known by unknowing'. (quoted by Whyte, 1978: 80) The mystic is one who 'remains entirely in the impalpable and the invisible, belonging completely to him who is above all things, for he no longer belongs to anyone whether to himself or to another, but having renounced all knowledge, is united to the Unknowable in a better way, and knowing nothing, knows with a knowledge surpassing the intellect.' And God is 'the dazzling obscurity which outshines all brilliance with the intensity of its darkness'. (Ferguson, 1976:

116) One could quote from Meister Eckhart, Jacob Boehme, Teresa of Avila, and a dozen others, to show how ubiquitous are these close, safe encounters of an essentially mysterious kind.

The question I now want to address is: why do these particular attributes or qualities of experience seem to go together? Why is it that this encounter with mystery is reliably accompanied by a sun-burst of physical energy? Why is it that an incontrovertible sense of kinship with all creation should come hand in hand with a dramatic intensification of perception? Why is it that the 'right' course of action emerges so clearly, at exactly the same moment that one's sense of independent volition fades away? To see these qualities as 'gifts of God' fails to explain why God, in his/her/its wisdom, should choose so persistently just this particular portfolio of blessings to bestow. We can understand why the grace of a loving God should cause our own compassion to flower, and why our tight complexity should dissolve into a trusting sense of 'not my will but thine, O Lord'. But why should God make us *blaze* as well? Could it be that the answer to this question may be found in the very workings of the brain?

THE INTRINSIC MYSTERY OF THE BRAIN

Now we can return to the science. I do indeed propose that the peculiar conjunction of properties associated with mystical experience can be accounted for at the level of brain functioning, and particularly in terms of the way the human brain represents the 'self'. Recent work in cognitive science has constructed plausible models of the brain-mind which rely, not on the outmoded computer analogy, but on what is known, in neuroscientific terms, about the actual functioning of large systems of neurons (see Rumelhart, McClelland et al., 1986). Though the brain's interconnections are far too complex to describe at the level of individual neurons, it is possible to use the language of neuronal properties to describe higher levels of organisation, and to show how these general properties of cerebral functioning and architecture can give rise quite naturally to accounts of some widespread features of human behaviour and even experience.

The beauty of the human brain is that at birth it is unfinished, waiting for experience to tune it to the particular linguistic, cultural and social frequencies that it encounters. Events in the infant's world translate into activity in the nervous system which blazes trails through the dendritic jungle: in neural language, 'cells that 'glow' together, grow together'. Experience trains large, widely distributed, colonies of neurons to respond more or less as a unit, a 'concept'; and each concept is functionally hooked up to dozens of 'associates' of varying kinds and strengths. To become active, each concept requires concurrent inputs from a number of its 'upstream' associates, and when it, in its turn, is active, it sends stimulation to each of its 'downstream' associates.

One of the most important findings of neuroscience is that this stimulation is of two kinds. Most obviously, it can be *excitatory*. When a downstream associate receives a burst of excitatory energy from one of its upstream neighbours, that increases the likelihood that it will become active ('exceed its activation threshold') itself. But it will also be receiving *inhibitory* inputs from other upstream units, when they are active, and these tend to 'sedate' the downstream unit, making it harder for other, excitatory, inputs, to 'wake it up'. The more inhibition a unit is receiving, the greater the amount of excitation that will be required in order for it to become active. Thus the relative amounts of excitatory and inhibitory 'priming', distributed across a range of potential downstream units, will heavily influence which one of them will 'win the race' to become active, and will therefore serve to determine the direction that the flow of brain-energy will take.

Even within this simple sketch we can see that there are two very different ways in which the functioning of the brain-mind can be influenced by experience. The first modifies the *threshold* of each unit, so that it requires less (or more) net excitation to wake up. Each brain is born, we might suppose, with a framework of evolutionarily determined standard 'settings' to its thresholds, so-called 'default values' (Minsky, 1988), which can then be elaborated and modified by experience. But the effective sensitivity of each unit can also be modified in a second way: by the kind and amount of *priming* it is receiving from upstream – energy which is not sufficient to activate the unit by itself, but which affect the responsiveness of the unit to *other* inputs.

To illustrate: imagine that, downstream from unit A there are two other units B and C. The connection between A and B is basically stronger than that between A and C so that, all other things being equal, when A is active it will wake up B first, and the stream of energy (and sometimes of consciousness) will continue in a B-wards direction. But suppose now that, also upstream of B there is another unit S, which – all the time that it is active – sends a trickle-charge of inhibition downstream to B.

The effect of this is to tip the scales of relative excitability between B and C, so that now, when A is firing, it is C that reaches its own firing threshold first, and the flow of activation is thus diverted into a different path.

Now imagine a brain within which there is a unit (or constellation of units) S, of this kind, which is normally switched 'on', and which is upstream of a large, widely distributed set of units, some of which, as a result of S's influence, are rendered more sensitive than they would otherwise be (and therefore requiring less in the way of other excitatory inputs before they will wake up), and others are made less sensitive, and so more resistant to being woken up by their other inputs. The net effect of S's constant behind-the-scenes activity is to make a brain-mind with one set of basic – we might even say 'natural' – concerns or priorities behave as if it were a different brain-mind: one in which the priorities were of a different order. The underlying connections in the first brain would still be as they were; but while they continued to be overlaid with S's pattern of excitatory and inhibitory priming, they would not be visible.

Add another twist. Suppose that the total amount of 'energy' available within the brain-mind system is limited: not fixed, but subject at any one moment to a maximum which it cannot exceed (Kahneman, 1973). This limited pool of energy has to do two jobs: it has to be available to register new events, and to support the operations that are currently being performed; and it is also used to subserve all the patterns of priming that are currently 'setting' the system to select and notice some kinds of happenings, and to suppress others. These two uses, if either is extensive, may be in competition. The more energy that is tied up in priming, the less there will be left over to register (fully, subtly) whatever is going on. Thus if the S constellation, in order to imprint its pattern of preoccupations on the system-as-a-whole, has to syphon off a substantial proportion of the total energy, the amount of 'free energy' available for action, thought, perception and general alertness will be restricted. And the more active S is, the less free energy is left over to carry out both routine and non-routine processes.

THE SELF SYSTEM IN THE BRAIN

I suggest that the Self System – the nexus of conditioned needs, anxieties, and dispositions that make up who we think we are – is 'installed' in the brain in exactly the same way as the hypothetical

'S constellation' in the preceding discussion. The Self System (the SS) develops as a composite, mutually reinforcing set of tacit beliefs which filter and structure our interpretations of our own behaviour and experience; and of habits (of both action and perception) which are designed to serve up experience that appears to support those beliefs and interpretations. Many people have given detailed accounts of the structure of the self: see for example Wilber (1979), or, for a fuller exploration of my particular version, see Claxton (1994). But what I want to focus on here is not the 'anatta-my' of the SS (*anatta* being the Buddhist word for 'no-self'), but its functional status within the overall cognitive economy of the brain-mind.

When the SS is active – when it is 'switched on' – its effect is to overlay on the rest of the brain-mind network (or on selected portions of it) a pattern of both excitatory and inhibitory priming that fundamentally alters the functional characteristics of those areas. In particular the shifting balance of natural priorities, which it is the brain-mind's job to integrate, harmonise and 'adjudicate' between, becomes distorted and rigidified. 'Identification' may be defined as the state in which the preservation of the SS is interpreted as a basic survival need; and in which it, the SS, is therefore connected directly to the basic survival mechanisms. In this state preferences become necessities, disappointments are transmuted into disasters, and other people are seen primarily as resources (or threats).

Without the SS, it seems that the system-as-a-whole computes rapidly, and (for the most part) brilliantly, the best course of action, taking into account all the present priorities and predicted perturbations. The system functions in a way that is elastic and creative in incorporating and satisfying multiple concurrent needs and threats. But when the SS is active, the 'surface' of the brain-mind is 'tilted', in just the ways that the three analogies at the start of this chapter describe. Those needs/threats that are part of the SS pre-empt the integrative workings of the whole system. They are interpreted as being of overriding importance. They become members of the cognitive politburo, able to commandeer the resources of the body-brain-mind system for their own ends, however 'petty' those ends may seem to be. Only when the whims of the ruling elite of the SS have been satisfied do the other priorities of the State get a look in. (Anthony Greenwald (1980) has used a similar image in his paper 'The totalitarian ego'.) Thus the delicate, tacit negotiating ability of the brain-mind is blocked or perverted by the intransigent demands of the SS.

And worse, the portfolio of demands that the SS makes is itself likely to contain irreconcilable conflicts and inconsistencies. It may demand that I am both popular *and* honest, successful *and* relaxed, happy *and* sensitive. The size, complexity, longevity and incoherence of this portfolio of self-related priorities virtually guarantees that the typical state of the Western mind will be one of chronic low-grade alarm which continually threatens to, and periodically does, erupt into an emergency. When there is a constant queue of threats waiting to be taken care of, the SS is never going to be switched off (see Claxton, 1994).

Some emergencies can be effectively dealt with by a form of action – avoiding the sarcastic teacher, repairing the damaged reputation. Others, especially when the cause of the emergency is a prohibited state of the biopsychological organism itself – anger, fear, wild thoughts – can only be escaped via the defences of denial and self-deception (Goleman, 1985). Any aspect of one's own or another's distress, for example, which is experienced as discomfiting, will trigger such a self-protective response. These manoeuvres can be successfully accomplished only by the brain-mind dedicating yet more of its limited stock of energy to maintaining a constant 'force shield' of inhibition that prevents the flow of free energy from inadvertently straying into one of the danger zones. (Marcel Kinsbourne (1988) has recently argued that it is essential to the brain's working, for more general reasons, that it be able to throw up these inhibitory walls.)

Through such methods conscious awareness can be purged of threatening experience, but only at the dual cost of rendering consciousness itself incomplete and therefore unreliable, and of further depleting the free energy that is necessary for the brain-mind to perform its natural functions. When the SS becomes large enough to co-opt virtually the entire pool of energy, the brain-mind, starved of its vital resource, may collapse into depression or lethargy, step off the pavement into the path of an unnoticed truck, or dive unconsciously into the shallow end of the pool.

As well as raising preferences to the status of necessities, the SS can have the reverse effect. As I argued earlier, there is now good evolutionary and biological reason to suppose that the human organism is designed to be considerate of the needs of its con-specifics, and of its habitat. We have co-evolved both from, and as, ecosocial systems (see Lewontin, 1983). The body-brain-mind 'knows' that its well-being is intimately interlinked with the well-being of its human and natural surroundings; 'knows' in the sense that its design specification incorporates these as tried-and-tested working assumptions. The SS, however, is designed on the basis of different assumptions: that we are separate and, when push comes to shove, competitive. Thus the natural incorporation of *caring*, as a basic priority, into the brain-mind's computations, gets blocked when the SS is active, leaving compassion as a luxury.

TAKING THE SS OUT OF THE LOOP

What, then, would happen to a brain-mind in which a chronically active SS was all of a sudden switched off? Within an instant, the *modus operandi* of the brain would shift markedly. First, its intrinsic ability to harmonise and prioritise would be freed from the demands and vetoes of the SS, dissipating the sense of stuckness, and re-establishing a sense of *flow* – an experiential sense that mirrors the underlying change in the functioning of the brain-mind. Secondly, the sheer weight of needs, threats and preoccupations would drop dramatically, leaving a fresher, more peaceful quality to experience. In between periods of problem-solving or activity, there would now be interludes of genuine peace and relaxation, without the continual nagging sense of myriad things undone.

Thirdly, the disqualified senses of connectedness and belonging would be immediately rehabilitated, and the inhibited priorities of compassion and care would be released to take their place, not necessarily as overriding preoccupations, but as full participants in the tacit decision-making process. In fact we might imagine that, for beings who live in a comfortable and abundant econiche, and who therefore experience. genuine survival threats only rarely, a concern to relieve the sufferings of others would emerge as the predominant priority. Lucky beings, in other words, are genetically programmed to become *bodhisattvas* – provided the SS does not get in the way.

Fourthly, the sense of loss of self, of being taken over by a greater power or will, and of impenetrable (but trustworthy) mystery at the core of experience, arises as a result of the changed status of consciousness. One of the cornerstones of the SS is the identification of self with consciousness, thus concentrating attention in a conscious, rational pool of 'limelight', and ignoring the dark, mysterious ground from which experiences, decisions, intentions, feelings and thoughts arise. When the SS is taken out of the loop we are freed to acknowledge all that is going on at and beyond the horizon of awareness. The personal 'centre of gravity' falls below this horizon, and one naturally loses the anxious sense of conscious control, and inherits in its place faith and wonder. 'Not my (egotistical) will, but thine, O Ecosocial Organism' becomes the order of the day.

Fifthly, when the SS is switched off, all the energy which it had been using to keep the mindscape tilted is suddenly released. No longer tied up on sentry-duty, it is free to join the main stream of activity as it flows through the cerebral channels, and in doing so it is bound to increase both the brightness of experience and the subtlety and grace of movement. When the full energetic resources of the brain-mind are available to subserve action and perception, the accuracy and intensity of both must expand. No wonder the mystic imagines the body to be on fire, or the world to be full of bright marvellous light!

Sixthly, when the SS is disabled, so too are all its defensive inhibitions and evasions. Thus one sees oneself clearly and honestly, without distortion or prevarication; but because these characteristics are not referred to a central, identified-with self, they are no longer interpreted as shameful personal attributes, but as inherent parts of one's own dappled uniqueness. And freed of the sense of guilt, helplessness or anger which the SS manufactures in the presence of *others'* suffering, there is no need any more to pretend that things are not as they are. Both oneself and the world are experienced 'warts and all' – and, being at last in possession of 'the full facts', action is bound to be more skilful and appropriate.

It is beyond the scope of this paper to suggest how meditation and the other 'spiritual technologies' on the one hand, and psychotherapy and the other 'growth and healing technologies' on the other, influence the decathecting and/or deconstructing of the SS. But this is clearly a question of considerable practical importance. The nineteenth- and twentieth-century explosion of scientific technology (for good and ill) happened because of the development of a powerful system of ideas for explaining why natural phenomena behaved as they did. As yet there is no equivalent theoretical substructure (Buddhism notwithstanding) in the spiritual realm. If there were, and if new approaches, as yet undreamed of, were made available to us we would need to welcome them for our personal and social liberation, but, perhaps, with a cautious mixture of enthusiasm and trepidation.

There are many more intriguing aspects of the relationship between the brain-mind, as conceived of by cognitive science, and states of consciousness, both 'altered' and 'unaltered'. But this brief sketch may be sufficient to illustrate the value of the dialogue.

THE VALUE OF SCIENCE

Let me conclude by returning to the status of science in the context of spiritual inquiry. Though scientists are fallible, often insensible to their own mythology, prone to unwitting (and even occasionally quite deliberate) bias in their work, their enterprise is the honourable one of trying to observe the world in a way that is relatively (for that is all it can ever be) free of personal hopes and fears. In our everyday thinking, we rig the evidence, and deny that we have done so. If we are afraid that the world has an edge, we may *think* we are sailing in a straight line, while imperceptibly, unconsciously, steering in an arc. By navigating thus we are able to believe that we have put the world-edge theory to the test, while actually having preserved ourselves from the risk of falling off. Science, for all its tacking and jibing, may eventually live up to its promise of re-minding us of these ingrained forms of self-deception.

Thus the scientists are, along with the poets, the philosophers, the shamans and the mystics, part of a loose subversive alliance whose responsibility it is to keep society on its toes: to keep drawing to people's attention what it is that they have forgotten they believe; reminding them that their taken-for-granted views about what is sane, normal, obvious, natural, right and real are human constructions (to which there are therefore alternatives), not timeless and absolute truths. Sometimes, in a temporary fit of grandiosity (succumbing to one of the pervasive myths about science itself), scientists offer their theories as if they were 'reality'. They become mesmerised by the Holy Grail of Ultimate Truth, and Unified Theories of Everything, forgetting that the best they can do is offer a view that recaptures a part of the inscrutable whole that the previously dominant myth had excluded.

In the famous Zen Ox-Herding Pictures, the second picture shows the herdsman finding traces of the ox, and these traces are often understood as *intellectual* traces, accounts and descriptions of the ox, travel brochures for *nirvana*, which do not get one any nearer to realisation in themselves, but whose echoes of the Natural Mind overcome the scepticism of the conditioned, conscious mind, and allow it to entertain more seriously the possibility of liberation. For a culture brought up to treat scientific knowledge – falsely – as the highest form of knowledge, scientific theories and findings that seem to be fingers pointing to the same moon as the experiential truths of the Buddha may well serve to encourage people to give more respect to their own intimations of the Natural Mind, and thus to develop greater commitment to a path that will rapidly leave science itself far behind. For minds that are conditioned to need to *understand* before they will act – even in their own best interests – the power of science to persuade can be used in a good cause. This does not mean that Buddhism itself is given greater warrant by an alliance with science; only that certain kinds of mind will give it greater credence.

Waking from the Meme Dream

Susan Blackmore

Wake up! Wake up!
Errrr, ummmm, grrrrggr, Oh yes, I'm awake now. Wow, that was a weird dream. I really thought I had to escape from the slurb, and it mattered terribly to get to the cupboard in time. How silly! Of course, now I see it wasn't real at all.
Wake up! Wake up!
What do you mean, 'wake up', I'm already awake. This is *real*. This *does* matter. I can't wake up any more. Go away!
Wake up! Wake up!
But I don't understand – From what? And how?

These are the questions I want to tackle in this chapter. From what are we to awaken? And how? My answers will be 'From the meme dream' and 'By seeing that it is a meme dream'. But it may take me some time to explain!

There is a long history, in spiritual and religious traditions, of the idea that normal waking life is a dream or illusion. This makes no sense to someone who looks around and is convinced there is a real world out there and a self who perceives it. However, there are many clues that this ordinary view is false.

Some clues come from spontaneous mystical experiences in which people 'see the light!', realise that everything is one, and go 'beyond self' to see the world 'as it really is'. They feel certain that the new way of seeing is better and truer than the old (though of course they could be mistaken!).

Other clues come from spiritual practice. Probably the first thing that anybody discovers when they try to meditate, or be mindful, is that their mind is constantly full of thoughts. Typically these are not wise and wonderful thoughts, or even useful and productive thoughts, but just endless chatter. From the truly trivial to the emotionally entangling, they go on and on. And what's more they nearly all involve 'me'. It is a short step to wondering who this suffering self is, and why 'I' can't stop the thoughts.

Finally clues come from science. The most obvious (and scary) conclusion from modern neuroscience is that there is simply no one inside the brain. The more we learn about the way the brain functions the less it seems to need a central controller, a little person inside, a decider of decisions or an experiencer of experiences. These are just fictions – part of the story the brain tells itself about a self within (Churchland and Sejnowski, 1992; Dennett, 1991).

Some say there is no point in striving for an intellectual understanding of spiritual matters. I disagree. It is true that intellectual understanding is not the same as realisation, but this does not mean it is useless. In my own tradition of practice, Zen, there is much room for intellectual struggle; for example, in the cultivation of the 'Don't Know Mind', or in working with koans. You can bring a question to such a state of intellectual confusion that it can be held, poised, in all its complexity and simplicity. Like 'Who am I?', 'What is this?' or (one I have struggled with) 'What drives you?'

There is also a terrible danger in refusing to be intellectual about spiritual matters. That is, we may divorce our spiritual practice from the science on which our whole society depends. If this society is going to have any spiritual depths to it, they must fit happily with our growing understanding of the workings of the brain and the nature of mind. We cannot afford to have one world in which scientists understand the mind, and another in which special people become enlightened.

So I make no apologies for my approach. I am going to try to answer my questions using the best science I can find. We seem to live in a muddle that we think matters to a self that doesn't exist. I want to find out why.

DARWIN'S DANGEROUS IDEA

There is one scientific idea which, to my mind, excels all others. It is exquisitely simple and beautiful. It explains the origins of all life forms and all biological design. It does away with the need for God, for a designer, for a master plan or for a purpose in life. Only in the light of this idea does anything in biology make sense. It is, of course, Darwin's idea of evolution by natural selection.

The implications of natural selection are so profound that people have been awe-struck or maddened, fascinated or outraged, since it was first proposed in *The Origin of Species* in 1859. This is why Dennett (1995) calls it 'Darwin's Dangerous Idea'. Sadly, many people have misunderstood the idea and, even worse, have used it to defend indefensible political doctrines which have nothing to do with Darwinism. I therefore hope you will forgive me if I spend some time explaining it as clearly as I can.

All you need for natural selection to get started is a replicator in an appropriate environment. A replicator is something that copies itself, though not always perfectly. The environment must be one in which the replicator can create numerous copies of itself, not all of which can survive. That's it.

Can it really be that simple? Yes. All that happens is this – in any one copying generation, not all the copies are identical and some are better able to survive in that environment than others are. In consequence they make more copies of themselves and so that kind of copy becomes more numerous. Of course things then begin to get complicated. The rapidly expanding population of copies starts to change the environment and that changes the selective pressures. Local variations in the environment mean different kinds of copy will do well in different places and so more complexity arises. This way the process can produce all the kinds of organised complexity we see in the living world, yet all it needs is this one simple, elegant, beautiful, and obvious process – natural selection.

To make things more concrete let's imagine a primeval soup in which a simple chemical replicator has arisen. We'll call the replicators 'blobbies'. These blobbies, by virtue of their chemical constitution, just do make copies of themselves whenever they find the right chemicals. Now, put them in a rich chemical swamp and they start copying, though with occasional errors. A few million years go by and there are lots of kinds of blobbies.

The ones that need lots of *swampon* have used up all the supplies and are failing, so now the sort that can use *isoswampin* instead, are doing better. Soon there are several areas in which different chemicals predominate and different kinds of blobby appear. Competition for swamp chemicals gets fierce and most copies that are made die out. Only those that, by rare chance, turn out to have clever new properties, go on to copy themselves again.

Clever properties might include the ability to move around and *find* the *swampon*, to trap *isoswampin3-7* and hang on to it, or to build a membrane around themselves. Once blobbies with membranes appear, they will start winning out over free-floating ones and super-blobbies are made.

Another few million years go by and tricks are discovered like taking other blobbies inside the membrane, or joining several super-blobbies together. Super-dooper-blobbies appear, like multi-celled animals with power supplies and specialised parts for moving about and protecting themselves. However, these are only food to even bigger super-dooper-blobbies. It is only a matter of time before random variation and natural selection will create a vast living world. In the process billions and billions of unsuccessful blobbies have been created and died, but such a slow, blind process produces the goods. 'The goods' on our planet includes bacteria and plants, fish and frogs, duck-billed platypuses and us.

Design appears out of nothing. There is no need for a creator or a master plan, and no end point towards which creation is heading. Richard Dawkins (1996) calls it 'Climbing Mount Improbable'. It is just a simple but inexorable process by which unbelievably improbable things get created.

It is important to remember that evolution has no foresight and so doesn't necessarily produce the 'best' solution. Evolution can only go on from where it is now. That is why, among other things, we have such a daft design in our eyes, with all the neurons going out of the *front* of the retina and getting in the way of the light. Once evolution had started off on this kind of eye it was stuck with it. There was no creator around to say 'Hey, start again with that one, let's put the wires out the back'. Nor was there a creator around to say 'Hey, let's make it fun for the humans'. The genes simply do not care.

Understanding the fantastic process of natural selection we can see how our human bodies came to be the way they are. But what about our minds? Evolutionary psychology does not easily answer my questions.

For example, why do we think all the time? From a genetic point of view this seems extremely wasteful – and animals that waste energy don't survive. The brain uses about twenty per cent of the body's energy while weighing only two per cent. If we were thinking useful thoughts, or solving relevant problems there might be some point, but mostly we don't seem to be. So why can't we just sit down and not think?

Why do we believe in a self that does not exist? Someone may yet explain this in evolutionary terms, but at least superficially it appears pointless. Why construct a false idea of self, with all its mechanisms protecting self-esteem and its fear of failure and loss, when from the biological point of view it is the body that needs protecting. Note that if we thought of ourselves as the entire organism there would be no problem, but we don't; rather, we seem to believe in a separate self, something that is in charge of the body, something that has to be protected for its own sake. I bet if I asked you 'Which would you rather lose – your body or your mind?' you wouldn't spend long deciding.

Like many other scientists I would love to find a principle as simple, as beautiful and as elegant as natural selection that would explain the nature of the mind.

I think there is one. It is closely related to natural selection. Although it has been around for twenty years, it has not yet been put fully to use. It is the theory of memes.

A BRIEF HISTORY OF THE MEME

In 1976 Richard Dawkins wrote what is probably the most popular book ever on evolution – *The Selfish Gene*. The book gave a catchy name to the theory that evolution proceeds entirely for the sake of the selfish replicators. That is, evolution happens not for the good of the species, nor for the good of the group, nor even for the individual organism. It is all for the good of the genes. Genes that are successful spread and those that aren't don't. The rest is all a consequence of this fact.

Of course the main replicator he considered was the gene – a unit of information coded in the DNA and read out in protein synthesis. However, at the very end of the book he claimed that there is another replicator on this planet – the meme.

The meme is a unit of information (or instruction for behaviour) stored in a brain and passed on by imitation from one brain to another. Dawkins gave as examples – ideas, tunes, scientific theories, religious beliefs, clothes fashions, and skills, such as new ways of making pots or building arches.

The implications of this idea are staggering and Dawkins spelt some of them out. If memes are really replicators then they will, inevitably, behave selfishly. That is, ones that are good at spreading will spread and ones that are not will not. As a consequence the world of ideas – or memosphere – will not fill up with the best, truest, most hopeful or helpful ideas, but with the survivors. Memes are just survivors like genes.

In the process of surviving they will, just like genes, create mutually supportive meme groups. Remember the blobbies. In a few million years they began to get together into groups, because the ones in groups survived better than loners. The groups got bigger and better, and a complex ecosystem evolved. In the real world of biology, genes have grouped together to create enormous creatures that then mate and pass the groups on. In a similar way memes may group together in human brains and fill the world of ideas with their products.

If this view is correct, then the memes should be able to evolve quite independently of the genes (apart from needing a brain). There have been many attempts to study cultural evolution, but most of them implicitly treat ideas (or memes) as subservient to the genes (see Cavalli-Sforza and Feldman, 1981; Crook, 1995; Durham,1991; Lumsden and Wilson, 1981). The power of realising that memes are replicators is that they can be seen as working purely and simply in their own interest. Of course to some extent memes will be successful if they are useful to their hosts, but this is not the only way for a meme to survive – and we shall soon see some consequences of this.

Since he first suggested the idea of memes Dawkins has discussed the spread of such behaviours as wearing baseball caps back to front (my kids have recently turned theirs the right way round again!), the use of special clothing markers to identify gangs, and (most famously) the power of religions. Religions are, according to Dawkins (1993), huge co-adapted meme-complexes; that is groups of memes that hang around together for mutual support and thereby survive better than lone memes could do. Other meme-complexes include cults, political systems, alternative belief systems, and scientific theories and paradigms.

Religions are special because they use just about every meme-trick in the book (which is presumably why they last so long and infect so many brains). Think of it this way. The idea of hell is initially useful because the fear of hell reinforces socially desirable behaviour. Now add the idea that unbelievers go to hell, and the meme and any companions are well protected. The idea of God is a natural companion meme, assuaging fear and providing (spurious) comfort. The spread of the meme-complex is aided by exhortations to convert others and by tricks such as the celibate priesthood. Celibacy is a disaster for genes, but will help spread memes since a celibate priest has more time to spend promoting his faith.

Another trick is to value faith and suppress the doubt that leads every child to ask difficult questions like 'Where is hell?' and 'If God is so good why did those people get tortured?' Note that science (and some forms of Buddhism) do the opposite and encourage doubt.

Finally, once you've been infected with these meme-complexes they are hard to get rid of. If you try to throw them out, some even protect themselves with last-ditch threats of death, excommunication, or burning in hell-fire for eternity.

I shouldn't get carried away. The point I want to make is that these religious memes have not survived for centuries because they are true, because they are useful to the genes, or because they make us happy. In fact I think they are false and are responsible for the worst miseries in human history. No, they have survived because they are selfish memes and are good at surviving, they need no other reason.

Once you start to think this way a truly frightening prospect opens up. We have all become used to thinking of our bodies as biological organisms created by evolution. Yet we still like to think of our *selves* as something more. *We* are in charge of our bodies, we run the show, we decide which ideas to believe in and which to reject. But do we really? If you begin to think about selfish memes it becomes clear that our ideas are in our heads because they are successful memes. American philosopher Dan Dennett (1995) concludes that a 'person' is a particular sort of animal infested with memes. In other words you and I and all our friends are the products of two blind replicators, the genes and the memes.

I find these ideas absolutely stunning. Potentially we might be able to understand all of mental life in terms of the competition between memes, just as we can understand all biological life in terms of the competition between genes.

What I want to do now, finally, is apply the ideas of memetics to the questions I asked at the beginning. What are we waking up from and how do we do it?

Why is My Head So Full of Thoughts?

This question has a ridiculously easy answer once you start thinking in terms of memes. If a meme is going to survive it needs to be safely stored in a human brain and passed accurately on to more brains. A meme that buries itself deep in the memory and never shows itself again will simply fizzle out. A meme that gets terribly distorted in the memory or in transmission, will also fizzle out. One simple way of ensuring survival is for a meme to get itself repeatedly rehearsed inside your head.

Take two tunes. One of them is tricky to sing, and even harder to sing silently to yourself. The other is a catchy little number that you almost can't help humming to yourself. So you do. It goes round and round. Next time you feel like singing aloud this tune is more likely to be picked for the singing. And if anyone is listening they'll pick it up too. That's how it became successful, and that's why the world is so full of awful catchy tunes and advertising jingles.

But there is another consequence. Our brains get full up with them too. These successful memes hop from person to person, filling up their hosts' minds as they go. In this way all our minds get fuller and fuller.

We can apply the same logic to other kinds of meme. Ideas that go round and round in your head will be successful. Not only will they be well remembered, but when you are next talking to someone they will be the ideas 'on your mind' and so will get passed on. They may get to this position by being emotionally charged, exciting, easily memorable or relevant to your current concerns. It does not matter how they do it. The point is that memes that get themselves repeated will generally win out over ones that don't. The obvious consequence of this fact is that your head will soon fill up with ideas. Any attempt to clear the mind just creates spare processing capacity for other memes to grab.

This simple logic explains why it is so hard for us to sit down and 'not think'; why the battle to subdue 'our' thoughts is doomed. In a very real sense they are not 'our' thoughts at all. They are simply the memes that happen to be successfully exploiting our brain-ware at the moment.

This raises the tricky question of who is thinking or not thinking. Who is to do battle with the selfish memes? In other words, who am I?

WHO AM I?

I suppose you can tell by now what my answer to this one is going to be. We are just co-adapted meme-complexes. We, our precious, mythical 'selves', are just groups of selfish memes that have come together by and for themselves.

This is a truly startling idea and, in my experience, the better you understand it, the more fascinating and weird it becomes. It dismantles our ordinary way of thinking about ourselves and raises bizarre questions about the relationship of ourselves to our ideas. To understand it we need to think about how and why memes get together into groups at all.

Just as with blobbies or genes, memes in groups are safer than free-floating memes. An idea that is firmly embedded in a meme-complex is more likely to survive in the memosphere than is an isolated idea. This may be because ideas within meme-groups get passed on together (e.g. when someone is converted to a faith, theory or political creed), get mutual support (e.g. if you hate the free-market economy you are likely also to favour a generous welfare state), and they protect themselves from destruction. If they did not, they would not last and would not be around today. The meme-complexes we come across are all the successful ones!

Like religions, astrology is a successful meme-complex. The idea that Leos get on well with Aquarians is unlikely to survive on its own, but as part of astrology it is easy to remember and pass on. Astrology has obvious appeal that gets it into your brain in the first place; it provides a nice (though spurious) explanation for human differences and a comforting (though false) sense of predictability. It is easily expandable (you can go on adding new ideas for ever!) and is highly resistant to being overturned by evidence. In fact the results of hundreds of experiments show that the claims of astrology are false but this has apparently not reduced belief in astrology one bit (Dean, Mather and Kelly, 1996). Clearly, once you believe in astrology it is hard work to root out all the beliefs and find alternatives. It may not be worth the effort. Thus we all become unwitting hosts to an enormous baggage of useless and even harmful meme-complexes.

One of those is myself.

Why do I say that the self is a meme-complex? Because it works the same way as other meme-complexes. As with astrology, the idea of 'self' has a good reason for getting installed in the first place. Then once it is in place, memes inside the complex are mutually supportive, can go on being added to almost infinitely, and the whole complex is resistant to evidence that it is false.

First the idea of self has to get in there. Imagine a highly intelligent and social creature without language. She will need a sense of self to predict others' behaviour (Humphrey, 1986) and to deal with ownership, deception, friendships and alliances (Crook, 1980). With this straightforward sense of self she may know that her daughter is afraid of a high-ranking female and take steps to protect her, but she does not have the language with which to think 'I believe that my daughter is afraid . . . etc.' It is with language that the memes really get going and with language that 'I' appears. Lots of simple memes can then become united as 'my' beliefs, desires and opinions.

As an example, let's consider the idea of sex differences in ability. As an abstract idea (or isolated meme) this is unlikely to be a winner. But get it into the form 'I believe in the equality of the sexes' and it suddenly has the enormous weight of 'self' behind it. 'I' will fight for this idea as though I were being threatened. I might argue with friends, write opinion pieces, or go on marches. The meme is safe inside the haven of 'self' even in the face of evidence against it. 'My' ideas are protected.

Then they start proliferating. Ideas that can get inside a self – that is, be 'my' ideas, or 'my' opinions, are winners. So we all get lots of them. Before we know it, 'we' are a vast conglomerate of successful memes. Of course there is no 'I' who 'has' the opinions. That is obviously a nonsense when you think clearly about it. Yes, of course there is a body that says 'I believe in being nice to people' and a body that is (or is not) nice to people, but there is not *in addition* a self who 'has' the belief.

Now we have a radically new idea of who we are. We are just temporary conglomerations of ideas, moulded together for their own protection. The analogy with our bodies is close. Bodies are the creations of temporary gene-complexes: although each of us is unique, the genes themselves have all come from previous creatures and will, if we reproduce, go on into future creatures. Our minds are the creations of temporary meme-complexes: although each of us is unique, the memes themselves have come from previous creatures and will, if we speak and write and communicate, go on into future creatures. That's all.

The problem is that we don't see it this way. We believe there really is someone inside to do the believing, and really someone who needs to be protected. This is the illusion – this is the meme dream from which we can wake up.

DISMANTLING THE MEME DREAM

There are two systems I know of that are capable of dismantling meme-complexes (though I am sure there are others). Of course these systems are memes themselves but they are, if you like, meme-disinfectants, meme-eating memes, or 'meme-complex destroying meme-complexes'. These two are science and Zen.

Science works this way because of its ideals of truth and seeking evidence. It doesn't always live up to these ideals, but in principle it is capable of destroying any untruthful meme-complex by putting it to the test, by demanding evidence, or by devising an experiment.

Zen does this too, though the methods are completely different. In Zen training every concept is held up to scrutiny, nothing is left uninvestigated, even the self who is doing the investigation is to be held up to the light and questioned. 'Who are you?'

After about fifteen years of Zen practice, and when reading *The Three Pillars of Zen* by Philip Kapleau, I began working with the koan 'Who . . .?' The experience was most interesting and I can best liken it to watching a meme unzipping other memes. Every thought that came up in meditation was met with 'Who is thinking that?' or 'Who is seeing this?' or 'Who is feeling that?' or just 'Who . . .?' Seeing the false self as a vast meme-complex seemed to help – for it is much easier to let go of passing memes than of a real, solid and permanent self. It is much easier to let the meme-unzipper do its stuff if you know that all it's doing is unzipping memes.

Another koan of mine fell to the memes. Q: 'Who drives you?' A: 'The memes of course.' This isn't just an intellectual answer, but a way into seeing yourself as a temporary passing construction. The question dissolves when both self and driver are seen as memes.

I have had to take a long route to answer my questions but I hope you can now understand my answers. From what are we to awaken? From the meme dream of course. And how? By seeing that it is a meme dream.

And who lets the meme-unzipper go its way? Who wakes up when the meme-dream is all dismantled? Ah, there's a question.

The Development of Personhood and the Brain

Terence Gaussen

As a psychologist working with children who have developmental disabilities, and indeed as a person myself, I have become ever-increasingly aware of the biological basis of our existence – of the sheer fact that we are 'incarnate', we live in our flesh, we are in the meat of our substance, we 'awaken' within our bodies in our sense of being a person. I would like to look at this form of awakening through recent understanding of how human infants come to develop in relation to the caregiving environment, and the indications this gives about how our 'selves' come to exist in our bodies.

Two texts set this scene. The first is a fragment from Eliot's *Four Quartets*:

> The hint half guessed, the gift
> Half understood, is
> Incarnation.
> Here the impossible union
> Of spheres is actual,
> Here the past and future
> Are conquered and reconciled

How does the incarnation happen in the human infant – how do we develop our sense of self? How do we exist in this incarnate moment between past and future?

My second text is from good old Sigmund Freud. I am no Freudian, but he did after all give a very distinctive bias to Western understanding of the human psyche and its development. So I was delighted to read that Freud, who was originally a neurologist, wrote that: 'All our provisional ideas in psychology will presumably some day be based on organic substructure' (quoted in Schore, 1994: 21).

This recognition by Freud that his theories of psychological development (which have been so powerful, but now are recognised as being based on retrospective understanding from clinical populations) must at some time be tied in with the biological and neurological processes and systems is central to the point of this chapter. Understanding of the organic substrate and pathways of development can help us to understand – or at least construe more effectively – the development of a sense of self. I will therefore consider what modern biology and developmental psychology offer to our understanding of human development and then compare the 'resonances' between this modern Western scientific understanding, and the wisdom of the ancient traditions – whether Buddhist or Christian-mystic or others, particularly in relation to concepts of 'attachment'. As an aside I should also like to throw in the observation that the major world religions have had little or nothing to say about the development of individual humans from infancy. My reading of Buddhist psychology is that it relates to adults, not the development of children who come to make adults – I assume because 'childhood' was hardly recognised in former times.

Before embarking on a consideration of recent advances in developmental psychology, I would like to make a point about systemic models and reductionism. When I was younger I used to teach biology, and we used a textbook with the poetic title *From Molecules to Man*, which encapsulated the idea of the levels and systems by which one can understand animal and human processes – from the biochemical to the whole organism, and the social, taking in the time dimension too, whether of individual development or the whole vast process of evolution. Similarly as a developmental psychologist now I need to understand phenomena at all levels of the system. I see children with genetic disorders, with autism, with the whole range of physically based disorders, who need to be understood in terms of their biochemistry, brain function, emotion, cognition, social relationships, family, and environment.

The work I am reporting here is at a truly multi-systemic level, in which one needs to have knowledge of all levels and understanding of how the levels of function interrelate. However, this is not necessarily a reductionist view. As Damasio expresses it in his marvellous book, *Descartes' Error: Emotion, Reason and the Human Brain*:

> In attempting to shed light on the complex phenomena of the human mind, we run the risk of . . . explaining them away. But that will happen only if we confuse a phenomenon itself with the separate components and operations that can be found behind its appearance . . . To discover that a particular feeling depends on activity in a number of specific brain systems does not diminish the status of that feeling as a human phenomenon . . . Our sense of wonder should increase before the intricate mechanisms that make such *magic* possible (Damasio, 1994: xvii-xviii).

More simply put Steve Turner's poem sums it up:

> My wife, she said:
> 'All things considered, we're just machines.'
> So, I chained her to the kitchen wall
> For future use – . . .
> And she cried!

A range of areas of study, from neuroscience, via ethology and evolutionary psychology, to anthropology and social constructionism have contributed to the development of these new perspectives. But central for me, and most exciting, is the recent flood of research on the role of emotion in human functioning, especially when linked to brain function (Lewis and Haviland, 1993; Oatley and Jenkins, 1996). Previously 'emotion' has been seen as something rather irrational, and certainly not the possible subject of scientific study, psychology having been concerned with 'behaviour', cognition, learning and perception. However, research and thinking on the role of emotion as a vital part of human psychological functioning is now becoming central. As Sara Meadow (1993) puts it succinctly: 'most of the literature on cognitive development pays no attention whatever to emotion . . . and emotion is the cinderella of cognitive development.' She applauds the recent recognition of the role of emotion in cognition.

In developmental psychology there have also been exciting

paradigm shifts, stemming from the radical realisation that far from being a *tabula rasa* the human infant has amazing competencies at birth, as evidenced in the publication of Stone, Smith and Murphy's *The Competent Infant* (1974). This was followed by studies of infant-caregiver interactions which recognised that the competent infant influences the caregiver. The baby is an active participant in the interaction and the early infant-parent transactions form the central driving force of development. *The Effect of the Infant on the Caregiver* (Lewis and Rosenblum, 1974) was a milestone publication and was followed by the work of Trevarthen and the Newsons on intersubjectivity. Alongside this came John Bowlby's (1971) attachment theory, in which individual human psychological development is seen in its evolutionary, biological, ethological and interactionist context.

These strands have now come together to produce a further very significant paradigm shift, with the publication of Allan Schore's *Affect Regulation and the Origin of Self: A Neurobiology of Emotional Development* (1994), which adds the neurobiology, neuroanatomy and neurophysiology of human development to our existing knowledge. This is the main work which I will outline, but it should be thought of in the context of the extraordinarily exciting new insights from adult neurology and brain sciences (see for instance Damasio (1994)).

The fascination here for me is the new view of brain function in the development of the individual and the central place which emotion is coming to occupy. The derivation of the word 'emotion' is after all 'that which moves us'.

Let us start by looking at Allan Schore's book title again:

Affect Regulation and the Origin of the Self:
a Neurobiology of Emotional Development

It is a very explanatory title, because it incorporates exactly his thesis that the origins of self lie in the manner in which, in the early years, the infant learns to regulate emotion and that this is, in part, a neurobiological process, but one which operates in interaction with the caregiver environment. (It is also very different from Piaget's emphasis on development as an essentially cognitive process.) The book covers the fields of neurochemistry and neuroanatomy in minute detail, but it is perhaps highly significant that Schore himself is a psychotherapist who welds this detail into an overarching picture from the biochemical level to the human function. He combines developmental neuroscience with attachment theory, developmental psychopathology and psychotherapy.

But we will start with the brain. Explaining and illustrating the brain is never very easy – and I am not a neurologist – but my understanding is as follows.

Evolutionarily, the oldest part is the brainstem, which controls vital functions. Then comes the mid-brain, including the limbic system, which has always been seen as the seat of the emotions. The third part is the 'new' brain, the neocortex, which is especially expanded in man. Koestler (1967) and others have argued that, whereas one might have expected the limbic system to evolve further, keeping pace with the evolution of more advanced mammals, in fact this did not occur and the limbic system is found as a kind of common denominator in all mammals, in contrast with the varied and expanded forms of the neocortex. Evolution superimposed a new, superior structure on an old one and we still carry the effects of this in our apparent split between feeling and thinking, emotion and reason, 'animal passions' and higher thoughts. At least this was the view until recently.

Schore summarises a range of studies, which show the crucially important role of the 'cortico-limbic system' within the orbitofrontal cortex in establishing the balance and pattern between the individual's emotional and cognitive functioning. This new understanding is of a bridge between old and new brain function and, arising from this, the 'sense of self' is seen as stemming from affect and its regulation. Emotion and reason are not so separate. I suppose it is more: 'I feel therefore I am' or possibly 'I feel therefore I think', rather than the Cartesian 'I think therefore I am'; this is certainly what Damasio (1994) seems to be suggesting when he argues that it is the brain's intimate connection with the body which engenders the sense of self, not the power of thought alone. (It should be noted that in this sense 'feeling' is the perception of an emotion in cognition, whilst the emotion is the biological event itself.) He explains that:

> The apparatus of rationality, traditionally presumed to be *neo*cortical, does not seem to work well without that of biological regulation, traditionally assumed to be *sub*-cortical. Nature appears to have built the apparatus of rationality not just on top of the apparatus of biological regulation, but also *from* it and *with* it . . . the neocortex

becomes engaged *along with* the older brain core, and rationality results from their concerted activity. (1994: 128, his emphasis)

Allan Schore shows how this 'neurological bridge' between emotion and reason is built as the infant develops. He stresses the role of the attachment processes in the infant-caregiver interactions in determining the detail of its structure and future functioning (he takes a truly developmental view, arriving at a similar conclusion to that stemming from Damasio's studies of acquired disorders). Schore emphasises the need to understand development in terms of all the levels of the system (physiology to social), to understand the systems in terms of their regulative functions (as dynamic processes which influence each other as they develop) and to understand the effect of the caregiving environment on the development of the infant's brain. A brain, he says, can in fact only develop in the context of another brain (or brains) and if isolated would become very atypical.

This is a very central point regarding the development of self, since it combines developmental neurology with the effects of caregiver interactions and the social environment, to produce the balance of cognition and affect within the individual. That is to say: infant and caregiver interactions modulate infant affective responses, which then produce changes in the infant's brain systems which become self-regulatory in the future. Schore argues that this affective interchange therefore constitutes a mechanism by which the social environment influences the development of psychobiological systems involved in homeostatic regulation and that if the process goes well, the individual develops with balanced affect and basically a good sense of self. If the environment is misattuned, high levels of negative affect are generated, affect is poorly regulated and these characteristics are laid down in the 'wiring' of the orbitofrontal cortex which is a key part of the cortico-limbic system. What is this system?

The findings which Shore reports show how the orbitofrontal cortex has connections *down* to the areas of the limbic system which govern autonomic body functions and emotion and *up* into the rest of the neocortex. Schore states: 'Its distinctive anatomical locus and its dense reciprocal interconnections with distant sites in both the cortex and subcortex account for its involvement in a number of critical functions, including affect regulation' and adds that 'the orbitofrontal cortex occupies a unique position between the cortex and the subcortex . . . and plays an essential adaptive role in emotional and motivational processes' (1996: 35). He concludes that 'recent neuroscience research shows that in the cerebral cortex, the orbitofrontal region is uniquely involved in social and emotional behaviours, in the regulation of body and motivational states and in the adjustment of emotional responses'. These processes must be relatively important since the prefrontal cortex, as a whole, accounts for some thirty per cent of the total cortical mass of the human brain (although it is engaged in other processes as well).

The orbitofrontal cortex is thus a central associative area for the integration of sensory perception, ideation and visceral/emotional experiences. And the development of the pathways in the system is altered by the individual's experiences during the first two years of life. (See for example, Kraemer, 1992; Trevarthen and Aitken, 1994.) Schore's central thesis is that: 'the early social environment, mediated by the primary caregiver, directly influences the evolution of structures in the brain that are responsible for the future socioemotional development of the child'.

The processes involved in parent-child interactions are familiar to us all: they are those in which, in fine-grain detail, a child acts, a parent interprets and responds, so the child obtains feedback and reconstrues or learns – at the levels of language or cognition, and of emotion. It is clear from much research that emotion provides the setting conditions (positive affect engenders mutual intersubjectivity and learning) and it is unsurprising that the first characteristic of an infant is indeed emotion – it cries and smiles and shows how it feels as a necessary part of engendering caregiving. In addition, babies are superbly adapted at reading and responding to adult emotions. A crucial role for the caregiver is to act in such a way as to help the infant to adjust its emotional state (a simple example is that of holding a baby when it cries).

However, one of the insights that the work reported by Schore offers is that the physical and social context provided by the caregiver to the infant is far more than merely a supportive framework of the developing human brain: *it is an essential substratum of the assembling neurological system*. Brains develop in a brain-brain interaction!

In illustration of this Schore cites Trevarthen's (1993) work on infant proto-conversations which shows a traffic of visual and auditory signals between parent and baby. These induce instantly observable emotional effects, namely excitement and pleasure, which build within the dyad. It is known from a range of interactional studies that a baby is 'hard-wired' to respond in this way to a parent's facial features and voice; this is what an infant attends to preferentially.The basis for this neurologically is that the frontolimbic brain structure contains neurons that selectively respond to faces and to emotional expressions in faces; it is involved in directing attention and in the tracking of emotionally relevant objects in extrapersonal space. Close study of such interactive sequences show that the baby learns affect regulation and state regulation through these interactions. In parallel, neurological studies show that the quality and timing of this interactive experience influences the developing patterns of neuronal connectivity that underlie the behaviour. If it goes well and with positive affect, the neuronal pattern grows richer and more effective in modulating affect.

Schore demonstrates how the detail of this can be traced out in anatomical changes in neural pathways (which may become richer or more impoverished, or develop connections that are more or less beneficial in aiding affect regulation). In addition the infant-caregiver interaction is regulating the infant's production of neurohormones. These influence the activation of systems that programme the structural growth of brain regions essential to the future socioemotional development of the child. He concludes that: 'It is now well established both that the affective state underlies and motivates attachment behaviour and that the combination of joy and interest motivates attachment bond formation' and that 'high levels of positive affect are vitally important for the infant's continuing neurobiological development' (1966: 63). Emotions seem to be pretty important in this context, to say the least!

It is vital to note here that the orbital prefrontal areas are known to grow rapidly postnatally, indicating that they are at least susceptible to (but possibly 'designed for') response to environmental influence. Put simply by Schore: 'The caregiver regulates the neurochemistry and neuroanatomy of the infant's maturing brain and the neural substrate for infant emotion' (1966: 66).

So where does this leave us in relation to the developing personality and *sense of self*? The neurological pattern built up in the developing brain appears to lay down enduring affective representations of interactions, which can be referred to and accessed in the future. They form, so to speak, a set of 'emotional memories' – which influence the individual for a lifetime. In evolutionary terms, amongst the mammals, this is an essential process since the organism requires the capability to make relatively fluid switches of internal body states to meet changes in the external environment which are personally meaningful. This process had selective advantage. Animals with a good orbito-frontal system for quickly switching into new emotional states for response to the environment would be more likely to survive. We humans have retained the same system of quick access to important regulative states laid down in infancy but the trouble is that depending on the early experiences, the states may include 'painful' emotions which we switch on when stressed. Various authors refer to this as 'the emotional core', 'affective core' or 'childlike central core'. It can contain positive emotional patterns or negative, unpleasant ones, which are called on as part of the emotional response pattern of the individual. They may be very powerful, and seem to be potentially part of the experience of suffering (*dukkha*), particularly of the need for attachment (since they were generated in the attachment relationship with care-givers).

The orbitofrontolimbic region of the brain is the essential part of this emotional core and it comes to act in the capacity of an executive control function for the entire right cortex – the right cortex being essentially non-verbal and playing a part in many unconscious processes. Once laid down in the first two years of life, this non-verbal, prerational stream of emotion that originally functioned to bind the infant to its parent continues throughout life to be 'a primary medium of intuitively felt affective-communication between persons' (Schore, 1996: 73).

Schore, along with Sroufe (1989) suggests that the *core of the sense of self* lies in the patterns of affect regulation and that this regulatory capacity is responsible for the maintenance of the sense of continuity of the affect of the individual.

This brings us to the final part of the picture in which Schore describes the manner in which the sense of 'self' may be thought of as being 'dialogic': that is, as emerging from the infant's initial interactive regulative dialogue with the caregiver, which then becomes internalised as the self-regulatory capacities of the child (in the second year of life). The sense of 'self' established through this internal dialogue mediates incoming environment informa-tion, organises internal information from activated bodily zones, selects and initiates relevant emotional states and motivational processes, and actively directs appropriate modes of relationship with others.

Most of this process is known to occur in the inter-relationship of the orbitofrontal system with the rest of the brain, principally within the right hemisphere, where it is not available to conscious control. Moreover, the cortico-limbic system operates to select, and maintain continuity in, affect states. Thus the 'sense of self' emerges as the effect of this 'integrating system' comparing internal and external events and the 'feelings/emotions' which result from them and the changes/continuities in these affects. In short, patterns of affect regulation integrate a sense of self across (emotional) state transitions, thereby allowing for a continuity of inner experience.

As we have already noted, this neurobiological system (the cortico-limbic system) evolved for good biological reasons in order to regulate and direct mammalian emotional readiness to deal with environmental (and internal) events, in a rapid and flexible manner. This led to the cortico-limbic system acting as a 'comparator' of internal events (Schore's state transitions) and external events (sensory information from the environment), which inevitably resulted in the 'comparator' developing a sense of 'an observer watching the events'.

A similar position, derived from a different set of data, is reached by Damasio who states that 'thinking is indeed caused by the structures and operation of being' (1994: 248) and suggests that it is in the 'triangulation' (my word, not his) which an organism makes (in a specific set of interconnections in its brain) between the acts of perceiving and responding to an object. The 'third party self' requires a neural device which can monitor comparisons between different processes, forming a moment-by-moment, non-verbal narrative of what is happening in receptors or effectors. This can be entirely non-verbal in mammals, with humans having the advantage that verbal labelling can be derived from the primary non-verbal narratives. Damasio comments that: 'language may not be the source of the self, but it is certainly the source of the "I"' (1994: 243).

So though it may help to have the rational capacity to label and verbalise in language, both Schore and Damasio suggest that the 'self' may be thought of as emerging as part of a biological process which is essentially dialogic – first between the infant's brain and its caregiver's brain, then within the internal dialogue which the brain necessarily performs to monitor information from outside and inside, in order to select appropriate responses.

'Mind' is thus conceived as arising in the *activity involved in the neurological process of monitoring an intersection of sen-*

sory and somatic experiences. Damasio states quite categorically that: 'At each moment the state of self is reconstructed, from the ground up. It is an evanescent reference state, so continuously and consistently *re*constructed that the owner never knows that it is being *re*made unless something goes wrong with the remaking' (1994: 240). This seems hardly more than a hair's breadth away from the Buddhist teaching of *anatta*, in which all things are devoid of a truly separate self, and the sense of 'I', of self, only exists in dualism, (as in the derivation of Schore's dialogic self). The possible Buddhist quotations to express this are endless, but in this context I like:

> I think that I act; an 'I' acts me,
> But all the time I am being dreamed by what-I-am
> (Wei Wu Wei, 1966)

As Anagarika Govinda explains:

> It is the *relations* of material, temporal and spatial kinds
> . . . that form the constant element. In the same way, the constancy of relations in the ever renewing process becoming conscious (*being* conscious does not exist in reality, but is only a constant *becoming*-conscious), creates the illusion of an 'ego-entity' or an unchangeable personality (1961: 129).

Similarly I see parallels between modern developmental psychology and Buddhist teaching. Stated very baldly, one can see that the bio-psychological processes of infant 'attachment' to caregivers, in which a strong emotional core forms, lay down very powerful feelings of need and gratification, which can then become expressed in attachment to many other things in life – money, sex, power or what-have-you! This seems at least resonant with the Buddhist concept of 'attachment' as being made up of the needs, cravings and desires which cause us to experience *dukkha* – suffering and unsatisfactoriness. I am entertained by the idea that Bowlby's 'attachment processes' may refer to the same human processes of 'attachment' which the Buddha recognised so long ago. The Buddha, Christ and all the other great teachers had brains and bodies, organised just as ours are, and had to over-come, I assume, just the same difficulties which I have portrayed here of being 'in the flesh', in our meat, truly in-carnate in the very structure of our brains, in our emotion and thinking.

Two things finally – for those interested in therapy. I have communicated with Allan Schore and he reassures me that his next book is called *Affect Regulation and the Repair of Self!*

And because I am so impressed with the emotional organisation and Buddha nature of my dog Figaro – who daily provides me with reminders of what attachment means, and what it means to 'live in the moment' and be 'mindful', since that is all he *can* be – he is utterly incarnate, with body and mind as one – I will leave you with his picture and this 'homage' from *The Tenth Man* by Wei Wu Wei:

> He is a better dog than I am a man, and sometimes
> a better man also.
> I do not pat him, I bow to him.
> I called him my dog, now I wonder if I am not his man?

Now that says something about dualism and the interface of minds – it is easier to experience inter-being with a dog!

PART III

BUDDHISM AND PSYCHOTHERAPY

Realisation and Embodiment: Psychological Work in the Service of Spiritual Development

John Welwood

The technique of a world-changing yoga has to be as multiform, sinuous, patient, all-including as the world itself. If it does not deal with all the difficulties or possibilities and carefully deal with each necessary element, does it have any chance of success?

Sri Aurobindo

The impersonal is a truth, the personal too is a truth; they are the same truth seen from two sides of our psychological activity; neither by itself gives the total account of Reality, and yet by either we can approach it.

Sri Aurobindo

My purpose in this chapter is to raise some challenging questions about the integration between two sides of human nature – relative and absolute, psyche and spirit – in the service of bringing the teachings and practices of spiritual awakening more fully into everyday life. Although my argument bears mainly on spiritual realisation as it is described by the Eastern non-dual contemplative traditions, it should apply in many ways to Western mystical paths as well. Nothing in this paper should be construed as a criticism or attempt to diminish the teachings or practices of the Eastern traditions. I have only the greatest respect and gratitude for the teachings I have received and for the teachers who have so generously shared them with me. My focus here is not on these teachings per se, but on how many Western practitioners understand and apply them. The question of how to incorporate these teachings into life in the West, and the Western psyche, is a challenging one, which raises a host of new issues that the founders of these traditions never had to contemplate. I have reached no final or definitive conclusions regarding any of the questions I raise here, but rather present them in a spirit of inquiry.

When I first encountered Zen through the writings of D.T. Suzuki and Alan Watts in the 1960s, I found myself especially drawn to the mysterious satori – that moment of seeing into one's own nature, when all the old blinders were said to fall away, so that one became an entirely new person, never to be the same again. In Suzuki's words, 'The opening of satori is the remaking of life itself . . . a complete revolution . . . cataclysmic' in its consequences. A revelation that led to a whole new way of being – I have found this prospect compelling enough to spend much of my life since then pursuing it.

Many of us who have been involved in meditative practices during the past few decades have had a direct taste of this realisation, which has brought great joy and gratitude, along with new insight and clarity. Yet at the same time I have also developed a profound respect for how difficult it is to fully embody such realisations in everyday life – especially for modern Western people who live in the world, rather than in monastic settings. Monastic or retreat situations are designed to help people devote themselves one-pointedly to seeing through the veils of the conditioned mind and realising Being, spirit, naked awareness as their true, intrinsic nature. Yet the full embodiment of such realisations – through a wise and balanced way of engaging in livelihood, intimate relationships, and the complex challenges of modern society – presents another type of hurdle altogether. We who live as householders, husbands, wives, parents, or working people may also need other methods to help us integrate spiritual realisation into our busy, demanding lives.

REALISATION AND TRANSFORMATION

The hard truth is that spiritual realisation is relatively easy compared with the much greater difficulty of *actualising* it, integrating it fully into the fabric of one's embodiment and one's life. By *realisation* here I mean the direct recognition of one's ultimate nature beyond the conventional ego, while *actualisation* refers to how we live that realisation in all the situations of our life. When people undergo major shifts during periods of intensive spiritual retreat, they often think that everything has changed and they will never be the same again. And indeed spiritual work can open people up profoundly and help them live free of the compulsions of their conditioning for long stretches of time. But at some point after the retreat ends, when they encounter circumstances that trigger their emotional reactivity, their unresolved psychological issues, their habitual tensions and defences, or their subconscious identifications, they may find that their spiritual practice has barely penetrated their conditioned personality, which remains mostly intact, generating the same tendencies it always has.

For some people, spiritual practice can even reinforce a tendency toward coldness, disengagement, or interpersonal distance. Others who develop a high degree of spiritual insight, power, even brilliance, may still remain consistently blind to islands of darkness and self-deception in themselves. They may even unconsciously use their spiritual powers to reinforce old defences and manipulative ways of relating to others. How is it possible for spiritual realisation to remain compartmentalised like this, leaving whole areas of the psyche apparently untouched? Why is it so hard to bring the awareness developed in meditation into all the areas of one's life?

Some would say that these problems are signs of deficiency or incompleteness in one's spiritual practice or realisation, and this is undoubtedly true. Yet since they are almost universal, they also point to the general difficulty of integrating spiritual awakenings into the entire fabric of our human embodiment. It is said in Dzogchen Buddhism that only the rare highly endowed person attains full liberation upon realising the essential nature of mind. For the rest of us, liberation does not follow quickly from realisation. As the Indian sage Aurobindo put it: 'Realization by itself does not necessarily transform the being as a whole . . . One may have some light of realization at the spiritual summit of consciousness but the parts below remain what they were. I have seen any number of instances of that' (nd: 98). Because problems with integration are so widespread, we need to consider more fully the relationship between these two different movements in spiritual development: realisation and transformation, liberation and complete integration of that liberation in all the different dimensions of one's life.

Realisation is the movement from personality to being – leading toward liberation from the prison of the conditioned self. *Transformation* involves drawing on this realisation to penetrate the dense conditioned patterns of body and mind, so that the spiritual can be fully integrated into the personal and the inter-personal, so that the personal life can become a transparent vessel for ultimate truth or divine revelation.

In the traditional paths of Asia, it was a viable and acceptable option for a yogi to pursue liberation or spiritual development as an end in itself, to live purely as the impersonal universal, without having much of a personal life or transforming the structures of that life. These older cultures provided a religious context that honoured and supported spiritual retreat, and placed little or no emphasis on the development of the individual.[1] As a result, spiritual attainment could often remain divorced from worldly life and personal development. In Asia, yogis and sadhus could live an otherworldly life, have little personal contact with people, or engage in highly eccentric behaviour, and still be accepted, supported, and venerated by the community at large.

Many Westerners have tried to take up this model, pursuing impersonal realisation while neglecting their personal life, but have found in the end that this was like wearing a suit of clothes that didn't quite fit. Such attempts at premature transcendence – taking refuge in the impersonal absolute as a way to avoid dealing with one's personal psychology, one's personal issues, feelings, or calling – leads to inner denial. And this can create monstrous shadow elements that have devastating consequences, as we have seen in many American spiritual communities in recent years. For whatever reasons, for better or for worse, it has become problematic in our culture to pursue spiritual develop-ment that is not fully integrated into the fabric of one's personal experience and interpersonal relationships.

Here is where psychological work might serve as an ally to spiritual practice – by helping to bring awareness into all the hidden nooks and crannies of our conditioned personality, so that it becomes more porous, more permeable to the larger being that is its ground. Of course, what I am describing here is a special kind of psychological work, which requires a larger framework, understanding, and aim than conventional psycho-therapy. I am hesitant to call this psychotherapy at all, for the word *therapy* has connotations of pathology, diagnosis and cure that place it in a medical, rather than a transformative, context. Moreover, conventional therapy often involves only talk, failing to recognise the ways in which the body holds defensive patterns and also manifests the energies of awakening. Truly transformative psychological work must also help us unlock the body's contractions and gain access to its larger energies.

Of course, spiritual work has a much larger aim than psychological work: liberation from narrow identification with the self-structure altogether and awakening into the expansive reality of primordial being. And it does seem possible to glimpse, and perhaps even fully realise this kind of awakening, whether or not one is happy, healthy, psychologically integrated, individuated, or interpersonally sensitive and attuned. Yet after centuries of divorce between the spiritual and the worldly life, *the increasingly desperate situation of a planet that human beings are rapidly destroying cries out for a new kind of psychospiritual integration*, which has only rarely existed before. Namely, an integration between liberation – the capacity to step beyond the individual psyche into the larger, non-personal space of pure awareness – and personal transformation – the capacity to bring that larger awareness to bear on all one's conditioned psychological structures, so that they become fully metabolised, freeing the energy and intelligence frozen inside them, thereby fuelling the development of a fuller, richer human presence that could fulfil the still unrealised potential of life on this earth.

For most of my career I have explored what the Eastern contemplative traditions have to offer Western psychology – an inquiry that has been extremely fruitful. Yet in recent years I have become equally interested in a different set of questions: How might Western psychological understandings and methods serve a sacred purpose, by furthering our capacity to embody our larger awakenings in a more personally integrated way? Is our individuality a hindrance on the path of awakening, as some spiritual teachings would claim, or can true individuation (as opposed to compulsive individualism) serve as a bridge between the spiritual path and ordinary life?

THE CHALLENGE OF PSYCHOSPIRITUAL INTEGRATION

The question of how psychological work could serve spiritual development forces us to consider the complex issue of the relationship between the psychological and the spiritual altogether. Confusions about this are rampant. Conventional therapists often look askance at spiritual practice, just as many spiritual teachers often look askance at psychotherapy. At the extremes, each camp tends to see the other as an avoidance and denial of the *real* issues.

For the most part, psychological and spiritual work address different levels of human existence. Psychological work addresses relative truth, personal meaning – the human realm, which is characterised by interpersonal relations and the issues arising out of them. At its best, it also reveals and helps deconstruct the conditioned structures, forms, and identifications that our consciousness becomes trapped within. Spiritual practice, especially of the mystical bent, looks beyond our conditioned structures, identifications, and ordinary human concerns toward the trans-human – the direct realisation of the ultimate. It sees what is timeless, unconditioned, and absolutely true, beyond all form, revealing the vast open-endedness, or emptiness, at the root and core of human existence. Yet must these two approaches to human suffering work in different directions? Or could they be compatible, even powerful allies?

If the domain of psychological work is *form*, the domain of spiritual work is *emptiness* – that unspeakable reality which lies beyond all contingent forms. Yet just as form and emptiness cannot be truly separated, so these two types of inner work cannot be kept entirely separate, but have important areas of overlap: psychological work can lead to spiritual insight and depth, while spiritual work, in its movement towards embodiment, transformation, and service, calls on us to come to grips with the conditioned personality patterns that block integration.

The question of whether and how psychological work might further spiritual development calls for a new type of inquiry that leads back and forth across the boundary of absolute and relative truth, taking us beyond orthodoxy and tradition into uncharted territory. If, instead of leaping to facile or definitive conclusions, we start by honouring the question itself in a spirit of open inquiry, it takes us right to the heart of the issue of how spirituality in general, and Eastern transplants such as Western Buddhism, in particular, need to develop if they are truly to take hold in, and transform, the modern world.

As a psychotherapist and student of Buddhism, I have been forced to consider this question deeply. My initial interest in psychotherapy developed in the 1960s, at the same time as my interest in the Eastern spiritual traditions. I was inspired to become a psychotherapist largely because I imagined that psychotherapy could be our Western version of a path of liberation. But I quickly found Western psychology too narrow and limited in its view of human nature. And I wondered how I could help anybody else if I didn't know the way out of the maze of human suffering myself. Although I had one great teacher – Eugene Gendlin, a pioneer in existential therapy, who taught me much of what has proved useful to me as a therapist – I became quite disillusioned with Western psychology as a whole.

In looking for a way to work on myself and understand my life more fully, I became increasingly drawn toward Buddhism. After finding a genuine teacher and beginning to practise meditation, I went through a period of aversion to Western psychology and therapy. Now that I had found 'the way', I became arrogant toward other paths, as new converts often do. I was also wary of getting trapped in my own personal process, addicted to endlessly examining and processing feelings and emotional issues. In my new-found spiritual fervour, however, I was falling into the opposite trap – of refusing to face the personal 'stuff' at all. In truth, I was much more comfortable with the impersonal, timeless reality I discovered through Buddhism than I was with my own personal feelings or interpersonal relationships, both of which seemed messy and entangling, compared with the peace and clarity of meditative equipoise – sitting still, following the breath, letting go of thoughts, and resting in the open space of awareness.

Yet as I went further with Tantric Buddhism, with its emphasis on respecting relative truth, I began to appreciate many aspects of Western psychology more fully, perhaps for the first time. Once I accepted that psychology could not describe my ultimate nature, and I no longer required it to provide answers about the nature of human existence, I began to see that it had an important place in the scheme of things. Facing some extremely painful relationship struggles, I began to do my own intensive psychological work. Despite my clinical training, I was surprised at the power of psychological inquiry to help me uncover blindspots, address leftover issues from the past, move through old fears, and open up in a more grounded, personal way, both with myself and with others. This work also helped me approach spiritual practice in a clearer way, not so encumbered by unconscious psychological motivations and agendas.

Cultural Factors East and West

Learning to appreciate the respective value of psychological and spiritual work brought up another set of questions for me: Why was it so easy to see the value of psychotherapy for Western people, yet so hard to imagine traditional Asian people finding benefit in the services of a psychotherapist? What accounts for this disparity?[2] And why did most of the Eastern spiritual teachers I knew have so much difficulty understanding psychological work and its potential value for a spiritual practitioner?

In presenting my hypotheses about this, I do not wish to idealise the societies of ancient India or Tibet, which certainly had serious problems of their own.[3] Rather, my intention is to explore some (admittedly generalised) social-cultural differences that help us consider whether and how we in the West may have a different course of psychospiritual development to follow than people in the cultures where the great meditative traditions first arose.

Some would argue that psychotherapy is a sign of how spoiled or narcissistic Westerners are – that we can afford the luxury of delving into our psyches and fiddling with our personal problems while Rome burns all around. Yet though industrial society has alleviated many of the grosser forms of physical pain, it has also created difficult kinds of personal and social fragmentation that were unknown in premodern society – generating a new kind of psychological suffering that has led to the development of modern psychotherapy.

Traditional Asian culture did not engender the pronounced split between mind and body that we in the West know so well. In giving priority to the welfare of the collective, Asian societies also did not foster the division between self and other, individual and society, that is endemic to the Western mind. There was neither a generation gap nor the pervasive social alienation that has become a hallmark of modern life. In this sense, the villages and extended families of traditional India or Tibet actually seem to have built sturdier ego structures, not so debilitated by the inner divisions – between mind/body, individual/society, parent/child, and weak ego/harsh, punishing superego – characteristic of the modern self. The 'upper storeys' of spiritual development in Asian culture could be built on a more stable and cohesive 'ground floor' human foundation.

Early childrearing practices in many traditional Asian cultures also seem more wholesome than in the West, as mothers usually provide their children with strong, sustained early bonding. Young Indian and Tibetan children, for instance, are continually held, often sharing their parents' bed for their first two or three years. Describing Indian childrearing, one researcher notes:

> Intense, prolonged maternal involvement in the first four or five years with the young child, with adoration of the young child to the extent of treating him or her as godlike, develops a central core of heightened well-being in the child. Mothers, grandmothers, aunts, servants, older sisters and cousin-sisters are all involved in the pervasive mirroring that is incorporated into an inner core of extremely high feelings of esteem . . . Indian child rearing and the inner structuralization of heightened esteem are profoundly psychologically congruent with the basic Hindu concept that the individual soul is essentially the godhead (atman-brahman). A heightened sense of inner regard and the premise that a person can strive to become godlike are strongly connected . . . This is in contrast to the Western Christian premise of original sin . . . (Roland, 1988: 250)

Growing up in an extended family, Asian children are exposed to a wide variety of role models and sources of nurturance, even if the primary parents are not so available. Extended families also mitigate the parents' tendency to possess their children psychologically. Tibetan tribal villages usually regard the children as belonging to everyone, and everyone's responsibility. By contrast, parents in nuclear families often have more investment in 'This is *my* child; my child is an extension of me', which contributes to narcissistic injury and an intense reactivity to parents that affects many Westerners throughout their lives. According to Alan Roland, a psychoanalyst who spent many years studying cross-cultural differences in Asian and Western self-development, the closeness and intimacy of the Indian extended family create an ego structure whose boundaries are 'on the whole more flexible and permeable than in most Westerners', and 'less rigorously drawn' (1988: 226).[4]

Certain developmental psychologists have argued that the internalised traces of the parents are much more pronounced in children whose parents were not attuned to their needs. This would explain why the Tibetans I know do not seem to suffer from the heavy parental fixations that many Westerners have. Their self-other (object-relational) patterns would not be as thick, rigid, or impaired as for Westerners who lack good early bonding, and who spend their first eighteen years in an isolated nuclear family with one or two adults who themselves are alienated from both folk wisdom and spiritual understanding. Asian children would be less burdened by what the psychologist Guntrip considers the emotional plague of modern civilisation: ego-weakness, the lack of a grounded, confident sense of oneself and one's abilities.

In observing Tibetans, I am often struck by how centred they are in the lower half of the body and how powerfully they are connected to the ground beneath their feet. Tibetans naturally seem to possess a great deal of *hara* – grounded presence in the belly – which is no doubt a result of the factors mentioned above. Westerners, by contrast, are generally more centred in the upper half of their body, and weak in their connection to the lower half.

Hara, which Karlfried Graf Dürckheim (1977) calls the *vital centre* or *earth centre*, is connected with issues of confidence, power, will, groundedness, trust, support, and equanimity. The childrearing deficiencies, disconnection from the earth, and overemphasis on rational intellect in Western culture all contribute to loss of *hara*. To compensate for the lack of a sense of support and trust in the belly, Westerners often try to achieve security and control by going 'upstairs' – trying to control life with their mind. But underneath the ego's attempts to control reality with the mind lies a pervasive sense of fear, anxiety, and insecurity.

In addition to fostering strong mother-infant bonding, intact extended families, and a life attuned to the rhythms of the natural world, traditional Asian societies have maintained the sacred at the centre of social life. A culture that provides individuals with shared myths, meanings, religious values and rituals provides a source of support and guidance that helps people make sense of their lives. By contrast, children today who grow up in front of television sets that continually transmit images of a spiritually lost, fragmented, and narcissistic world, lack a meaningful cultural context in which to situate their own lives.

Another difference between East and West is that Asian cultures place greater value on being, while Western cultures put more emphasis on doing. The paediatrician and psychoanalyst D.W. Winnicott pointed out the importance of allowing a young child to remain in unstructured states of being:

The mother's nondemanding presence makes the experience

of formlessness and comfortable solitude possible, and this capacity becomes a central feature in the development of a stable and personal self . . . This makes it possible for the infant to experience . . . a state of 'going-on-being' out of which . . . spontaneous gestures emerge. (Greenberg and Mitchell, 1983: 193)

Winnicott used the term *impingement* to describe a parent's tendency to interrupt these formless moments, forcing children to separate abruptly from the continuity of their 'going-on-being'. The child is:

wrenched from his quiescent state and forced to respond . . . and to mold himself to what is provided for him. The major consequence of prolonged impingement is fragmentation of the infant's experience. Out of necessity he becomes prematurely and compulsively attuned to the claims of others . . . He loses touch with his own spontaneous needs and gestures . . . [and develops] a false self on a compliant basis. (Greenberg and Mitchell, 1983: 193)

It seems that traditional Asian families often give the young child more room and permission just to be, in an unstructured way, free from the pressures to respond and perform that Western parents often place on their children at an early age. Allowed to be in that way, these children would be more comfortable with emptiness, which we could define here as *unstructured being*. But in our culture, which emphasises doing, having, and achieving at the expense of simply being, emptiness can seem quite alien, threatening, and terrifying. In a family or society that does not recognise or value being, children are more likely to interpret their own unstructured being as some kind of deficiency, as a failure to measure up, as an inadequacy or lack. Thus the Western ego structure seems to form in a more rigid and defended way, in part to ward off a terrifying sense of deficiency born of an inability to relate to the open, unstructured core of one's very being.

In sum, the traditional Asian family seems to foster more of an inner core of well-being than the modern Western family does, by providing more of what Winnicott defined as the two essential elements of parenting in early childhood: sustained emotional bonding and allowing the child to be, to rest in unstructured being. I am speaking here of influences in the first few years of childhood, when the ego structure first starts to coalesce. In later childhood, many Asian families exert strong pressure on children to conform and to subordinate their individuality to collective rules and roles. Thus Roland notes that most neurotic conflicts among modern Asians are found in the area of family enmeshment and difficulties with self-differentiation. Indeed, while Eastern culture more generally values and understands being and emptiness, as well as interconnectedness, the West values and has a deeper understanding of individuation.

Cultivating one's own individual vision, qualities, and potentials is of much greater significance in the West than in traditional Asia, where spiritual development could more easily coexist alongside a low level of individuation. Here is where psychological work may serve another important function for Westerners, by helping them to individuate – to listen to and trust their own experience, and develop an authentic personal vision, sense of direction, and way of relating to life.[5]

Buddhist scholar Robert Thurman has argued that Buddhism is a path of individuation, and thus it is inaccurate to characterise the East as not valuing and promoting individual development. However, as Roland notes, individuation in Asian cultures has usually been limited to the arena of spiritual practice, rather than supported as a general norm. Certainly the Buddha gave birth to a new vision that encouraged individuals to pursue their own spiritual development, instead of depending on conventional religious rituals. In that broad sense, Buddhism can be regarded as a path of individuation. But this is a different model of individuation from the one that has developed in the West.

The Western understanding of individuation involves finding one's own unique contribution, vision, and path and embodying that in the way one lives. To *become oneself* in this sense often involves innovation, experimentation, and the questioning of received knowledge. As Buddhist scholar Anne Klein notes: 'Tibetans, like many Asians who have grown up outside Western influence, do not cultivate this sense of individuality' (1995: 26).

In traditional Asia, the teachings of liberation were geared toward people who were, if anything, *too* earthbound, too involved in family roles and social obligations. The highest, nondual teachings of Buddhism and Hinduism – which show that who *you* really are *is* absolute reality, beyond *you* – provided a way out of the social maze, helping people discover the transhuman absolute that lies beyond all worldly concerns and entanglements. Yet these teachings rest on and presume a rich underpinning of human community, religious customs, and moral values, like a mountain arising out of a network of foothills and valleys below. The soulful social and religious customs of traditional India and Tibet provided a firm human base out of which spiritual aspirations for a trans-human absolute, beyond human relationships and human society, could arise.

Because the traditional Asian's sense of self is embedded in a soulful culture rich in tradition, ritual, close-knit family and community life, people in these cultures do not lose themselves or become alienated from their own humanness in the way that Westerners do. And since soul – the deep, rich, colourful qualities of our humanness – has always permeated the whole culture, the need to develop an individuated soul never assumed the importance that it did in the West.

In the modern West, it is quite common to feel alienated from the larger social whole – whose public spaces and architecture, celebrations, institutions, family life, and even food, are lacking in nourishing soul-qualities that allow people to feel deeply connected to these aspects of life as well as to one another. The good news, however, is that the soullessness of our culture is forcing us to develop a new consciousness about finding or forging an individuated soul – a deep inner source of personal vision, meaning, and purpose. One important outgrowth of this is a refined and sophisticated capacity for nuanced *personal* awareness, *personal* sensitivity, and *personal* presence.

This is not something the Asian traditions can teach us much about. If the great gift of the East is its focus on *absolute true nature* – impersonal and shared by all alike – the great gift of the West is the impetus it provides to develop an *individuated expression of true nature* – which we could also call *soul* or *personal presence.*[6] Individuated true nature is the unique way that each of us can serve as a vehicle for embodying the supra-personal wisdom, compassion, and truth of absolute true nature. For traditional Asians, cultivating individuated soul qualities has never been such a concern, because soul is already so thoroughly woven into the warp and woof of their culture. Never having lost their soul, they have not had to develop any consciousness about how to find it – that is, how to individuate in a distinctly personal way.

We in the West obviously have much to learn from the Eastern non-dual teachings. But if we only try to adhere to the Eastern focus on the trans-human, or suprapersonal, while failing to develop a grounded, personal way of relating to life, we may have a hard time integrating our larger nature into the way we actually live.

SPIRITUAL BYPASSING

While many Eastern teachers are extremely warm, loving, and personal in their own way, they often do not have much to say about the specifically personal qualities of human existence.[7] Coming out of traditional Asian societies, they may have a hard time recognising or assessing the personal, developmental challenges facing their Western students. They often do not understand the pervasive self-hatred, shame, and guilt, as well as the alienation and lack of confidence in these students. Still less do they detect the tendency toward spiritual bypassing – a term I have coined to describe the tendency to use spiritual ideas and practices to sidestep personal, emotional 'unfinished business', to shore up a shaky sense of self, or to belittle basic needs, feelings, and developmental tasks in the name of enlightenment (Welwood, 1984). And so they often teach self-transcendence to students who first of all need to find some ground to stand on.[8]

Spiritual practice involves freeing consciousness from its entanglement in form, matter, emotions, personality, and social conditioning. In a society like ours, where the whole earthly foundation is weak to begin with, it is tempting to use spirituality as a way of trying to rise above this shaky ground. However, when people use spiritual practice to compensate for low self-esteem, social alienation, or emotional immaturity, they wind up with neither a healthy spirituality nor a healthy psychology. And their spiritual practice tends to remain in a separate compartment, unintegrated with the rest of their life.

For example, one woman I know went to India at age seventeen to get away from a wealthy family that had provided her with little love or understanding. She spent seven years studying and practising with Tibetan teachers in India and Nepal, did many retreats, and had many powerful realisations. She experienced states of bliss and inner freedom lasting for long periods of time. Upon returning to Europe, however, she could barely function in the modern world. Nothing made any sense to her, and she did not know what to do with herself. She became involved with a charismatic man, and wound up having two children by him before she knew what had happened to her. In looking back at that time she said:

This man was my shadow. He represented all the parts of myself I had run away from. I found him totally fascinating and became swept up in a course of events over which I had no control. Clearly, all my spiritual practice had not touched the rest of me – all the old fears, confusions, and unconscious patterns that hit me in the face when I returned to the West.

Spiritual bypassing is a strong temptation in times like ours when achieving what were once ordinary developmental landmarks – earning a livelihood through dignified, meaningful work, raising a family, sustaining a long-term intimate relationship, belonging to a larger social community – has become increasingly difficult and elusive. Using spirituality to make up for failures of individuation – psychologically separating from parents, developing self-respect, or trusting one's own intelligence as a source of guidance – leads to many of the so-called 'perils of the path': spiritual materialism, inflation, 'us vs. them' mentality, groupthink, blind faith in charismatic teachers, and loss of discrimination.

In this way, spiritual communities can become a kind of substitute family, where the teacher is regarded as the good parent, while the students are striving to be good boys or good girls, by toeing the party line, trying to please the teacher-as-parent, or driving themselves to climb the ladder of spiritual success. And spiritual practice becomes co-opted by unconscious identities and used to reinforce unconscious defences.

For example, people who hide behind a schizoid defence (resorting to isolation and withdrawal because the interpersonal realm feels threatening) often use teachings about detachment and renunciation to rationalise their aloofness, impersonality, and disengagement, when what they really need is to become more fully embodied, more engaged with themselves, with others, and with life. Unfortunately, the Asian emphasis on impersonal realisation makes it easy for alienated Western students to imagine that the personal is of little significance compared with the vastness of the great beyond. Such students are often attracted to teachings about selflessness and ultimate states, which seem to provide a rationale for not dealing with their own psychological wounding. In this way, they use Eastern teachings to cover up their incapacity in the personal and interpersonal realm.

People with a dependent personality structure, who try to please others in order to gain approval and security, often perform unstinting service for the teacher or community in order to feel worthwhile and needed. They confuse a co-dependent version of self-negation with true selflessness. And those who need to see themselves as special (the narcissistic defence) will often use the specialness of spiritual insight and practice, or their special relation to their teacher, to shore up a sense of self-importance. Spiritual involvement is particularly tricky for people who are narcissistically injured, because they are using spirituality to shore up a shaky sense of self, while supposedly working on liberation from self.

Spiritual bypassing often develops a rationale based on using absolute truth to deny or disparage relative truth. Absolute truth is what is eternally true, now and forever, beyond any particular viewpoint. When we tap into absolute truth, we can recognise the divine beauty or larger perfection operating in the whole of reality. From this larger perspective, the murders going on in Brooklyn at this moment, for instance, do not diminish this divine perfection, for the absolute encompasses the whole panorama of life and death, in which suns, galaxies, and planets are continually being born and dying. However, from a *relative* point of view – if you are the wife of the man murdered in Brooklyn tonight – you will probably not be moved by the truth of ultimate perfection. Instead you will be feeling human grief.

There are two ways of confusing absolute and relative truth. If you use the murder or your grief to deny or insult the higher law of the universe, you would be committing the relativist error. You would be trying to apply what is true on the horizontal plane of *becoming* to the vertical dimension of pure *being*. The spiritual bypasser makes the reverse category error, the absolutist error: he draws on absolute truth to disparage relative truth. His logic might lead to a conclusion like this: since everything is ultimately perfect in the larger cosmic play, grieving the loss of someone you love is the sign of spiritual weakness.

Psychological realities represent relative truth. They are relative to particular individuals in particular circumstances. Even though one may know that no individual death is ultimately important on the absolute, trans-human level, one may still feel profound grief and regret about a friend's death – on the relative, human level. Because we live on both these levels, the opposite of whatever we assert is also true in some ways. Jesus' advice, 'Love thine enemies' and 'Turn the other cheek', did not prevent him from expressing his anger toward the money changers in the temple or the hypocritical Pharisees. Thus our everyday experiences may often appear to be at odds with the highest truth. This creates uncertainty and ambiguity. For many people, the disparity between these two levels of truth is confusing or disturbing. They think reality has to be all one way or the other. In trying to make everything conform to a single order, they become new age Pollyannas or else bitter cynics.

Since we live on two levels as human beings, we can never reduce reality to a single dimension. We are not just this relative body/mind organism; we are also absolute being/awareness/ presence, which is much larger than our bodily form or personal history. But we are also not *just* this larger, formless absolute; we are also incarnate as this particular individual. If we identify totally with form – our body/mind/personality – our life will remain confined to known, familiar structures. But if we try to live only as pure emptiness, or absolute being, we may have a hard time fully engaging with our humanity. At the level of absolute truth, the personal self is not ultimately real; at the relative level, it must be respected. If we use the truth of no-self to avoid ever having to make personal statements such as, 'I want to know you better' to someone we love, this would be a perversion.

A client of mine who was desperate about her marriage had gone to a spiritual teacher for advice. He advised her not to be so angry with her husband, but to be a compassionate friend instead. This was certainly sound spiritual advice. Compassion is a higher truth than anger; when we rest in the absolute nature of mind – pure open awareness – we discover compassion as the very core of our nature. From that perspective, feeling angry about being hurt only separates us from our true nature.

Yet the teacher who gave this woman this advice did not consider her *relative* situation – that she was someone who had swallowed her anger all her life. Her father had been abusive and would slap her and send her to her room whenever she showed any anger about the way he treated her. So she learned to suppress her anger, and always tried to please others and 'be a good girl' instead.

When the teacher advised her to feel compassion rather than anger, she felt relieved because this fitted right in with her defences. Since anger was terrifying and threatening to her, she used the teaching on compassion for spiritual bypassing – for refusing to deal with her anger or the message it contained. Yet this only increased her sense of frustration and powerlessness in her marriage.

As her therapist, taking account of her relative psychology, my aim was to help her acknowledge her anger and relate to it more fully. As a spiritual practitioner, I was also mindful that anger is ultimately empty – a wave arising in the ocean of consciousness, without any solidity or inherent meaning. Yet while that understanding may be true in the absolute sense, and be valuable for helping dissolve attachment to anger, it was not useful for this woman at this time. Instead, she needed to learn to pay more attention to her anger in order to move beyond a habitual pattern of self-suppression, to discover her inner strength and power, and to relate to her husband in a more active, assertive way.

Given that compassion is a finer and nobler feeling than anger, how do we arrive at genuine compassion? Spiritual bypassing involves imposing on oneself higher truths that lie far beyond one's immediate existential condition. My client's attempts at compassion were not entirely genuine because they were based on rejecting her own anger. Spiritual teachers often exhort us to be loving and compassionate, or to give up selfishness and aggression, but how can we do this if our habitual tendencies arise out of a whole system of psychological dynamics that we have never clearly seen or faced, much less worked with? People often have to feel, acknowledge, and come to terms with their anger before they can arrive at genuine forgiveness or compassion. That is relative truth.

Psychological work starts there, with relative truth – with whatever we are experiencing right now. It involves opening ourselves up to that experience and exploring the meaning of that experience, letting it unfold, step by step, without judging it according to preconceived ideas. As a therapist, I find that allowing whatever arises to be there as it is and gently inquiring into it leads naturally in the direction of deeper truth. This is what I call psychological work in the service of spiritual development.

Many people who seek out my services have done spiritual practice for many years. They do not suffer from traditional clinical syndromes, but from some impasse in their lives that their spiritual practice has failed to penetrate: they cannot maintain a long-term relationship, feel real joy, work productively or creatively, treat themselves with compassion, or understand why they continue to indulge in certain destructive behaviours.

I have often been struck by the huge gap between the sophistication of their spiritual practice and the level of their personal development. Some of them have spent years doing what were once considered the most advanced, esoteric practices, reserved only for the select few in traditional Asia, without developing the most rudimentary forms of self-love or interpersonal sensitivity. One woman who had undergone the rigours of a Tibetan-style three-year retreat had little ability to love herself. The rigorous training she had been through only seemed to reinforce an inner discontent that drove her to pursue high spiritual ideals, without showing any kindness toward herself or her own limitations.

Another woman had let an older teacher in her Sangha cruelly manipulate her. She had a habitual tendency from child-hood to disregard her own needs and feelings, which, using 'Dharma logic', she lumped in the category of *samsaric* hindrances. In another Sangha the head teacher had to step down because he had begun to feel like a fraud. In our work together he came to see that all his spiritual ambitions were infested with narcissistic motivation. They had been a way of avoiding his psychological wounding and achieving a position where others would see him as special and important, rather than the helpless person he felt like on the inside.

SPIRITUAL SUPEREGO

In addition to spiritual bypassing, another major problem for Western seekers is their susceptibility to the 'spiritual superego', a harsh inner voice that acts as relentless critic and judge telling them that nothing they do is ever quite good enough: 'You should meditate more and practice harder. You're too self-centred. You don't have enough devotion.' This critical voice keeps track of every failure to practise or live up to the teachings, so that practice becomes more oriented toward propitiating this judgemental part of themselves than opening unconditionally to life. They may subtly regard the saints and enlightened ones as father figures who are keeping a watchful eye on all the ways they are failing to live up to their commitments. So they strive to be 'dharmically correct', attempting to be more detached, com-passionate, or devoted than they really are. In trying to live up to high spiritual ideals, they deny their real feelings, becoming cut off from their bodily vitality, the truth of their own experience, and their ability to find their own authentic direction.

Spiritual seekers who try to be more impartial, unemotional, unselfish, and compassionate than they really are often secretly hate themselves for the ways they fail to live up to their high ideals. This makes their spirituality cold and solemn. Their self-hatred has not been created by the spiritual teaching; it already existed. But by pursuing spirituality in a way that widens the gap between how they are and how they think they should be, they wind up turning exquisite spiritual teachings on compassion and awakening into further fuel for self-hatred and inner bondage.

This raises the question of how much we can benefit from a spiritual teaching as a set of ideals, no matter how noble those ideals are. Often the striving after a spiritual ideal only serves to reinforce the critical superego – that inner voice that tells us we are never good enough, never honest enough, never loving enough. In a culture permeated by guilt and ambition, where people are desperately trying to rise above their shaky earthly foundation, the spiritual superego exerts a pervasive unconscious influence that calls for special attention and work. This requires an understanding of psychological dynamics that traditional spiritual teachings and teachers often lack.

OVERCOMING PRAISE AND BLAME: A CASE STUDY

I would like to present a case study that illustrates both how spiritual teaching and practice can be used to reinforce psychological defences, and how psychological work can be a useful aid to embodying spirituality in a more integrated way.

Paul had been a dedicated Buddhist practitioner for more than two decades. He was a husband, father, and successful businessman who had recently been promoted to a position that involved public speaking. At first, he took this as an interesting challenge, but after a few experiences in front of large audiences, he started feeling overwhelmed by anxiety, worry, tension, sleeplessness, and other physical symptoms. At first, he tried to deal with his distress by meditating more. While these periods of practice would help him regain some equilibrium, the same symptoms would start to recur when he was about to face an audience again. After a few months of this, he gave me a call.

From the Buddhist teachings, Paul knew the importance of not being attached to praise and blame, two of the eight worldly concerns – along with loss and gain, pleasure and pain, success and failure – that keep us chained to the wheel of suffering. Yet it was not until his fear of public speaking brought up intense anxiety about praise and blame that he realised just how concerned he was about how people saw him. Recognising this was extremely upsetting for him.

At first Paul waxed nostalgic about his periods of retreat, when he felt detached from such concerns, and we discussed how living in the world often brings up unresolved psychological issues that spiritual practice is not designed to address. As our work progressed, he realised that he used detachment as a defence, to deny a deeper, underlying fear about how other people saw him.

He had developed this defence in childhood as a way to cope with not feeling seen by his parents. His mother had lived in a state of permanent tension and anxiety, and regarded him as her potential saviour, rather than as a separate being with his own feelings and life apart from her. To shield himself from her pain and intrusiveness, Paul had developed a defensive stance of not feeling his need for her, and by extension, for other people in his life.

Having tried all his life not to care about how people regarded him, he was particularly attracted to the Buddhist teachings of no-self when he first encountered them. After all, in the light of absolute truth there is nobody to be seen, nobody to be praised, nobody to be blamed. Yet on the relative level he still carried within himself a denied and frustrated need to be seen and loved. In squelching this need, Paul was practising defensiveness, not true detachment. And he was using spiritual teachings as a rationale for remaining stuck in an old defensive posture.

How could Paul be truly detached from praise and blame as long as he had a buried wish to be loved and appreciated, which he couldn't admit because it felt too threatening? Before he could truly overcome his anxieties about praise and blame, he would first have to acknowledge this wish – which was frightening and risky.

Along with his conflicted feelings about being seen, Paul also had a fair share of buried self-hatred. As his mother's appointed saviour, he had desperately wanted her to be happy, and felt guilty about failing to save her. In fact, he was stuck in many of the ways his mother was stuck. His guilt and self-blame about this made him hypersensitive to blame from others.

So Paul was doubly trapped. As long as he could not acknowledge the part of him that felt, 'Yes, I want to be seen and appreciated', his frustrated need for love kept him tied in knots, secretly on the lookout for others' praise and confirmation. And his inability to say, 'No, I don't exist for your benefit', kept him susceptible to potential blame whenever he failed to please others.

Yes and *no* are expressions of desire and aggression – two life energies that philosophers, saints, and psychologists, from Plato and Buddha to Freud, have considered particularly problematic. Unfortunately, many spiritual teachers simply criticise passion and aggression instead of teaching people to unlock the potential intelligence hidden within them.

The intelligent impulse contained in the 'yes' of desire is the longing to expand, to meet and connect more fully with life. The intelligence contained in 'no' is the capacity to discriminate, differentiate, and protect oneself and others from harmful forces. The energy of the *genuine, powerful no* can be a doorway to strength and power, allowing us to separate from aspects of our conditioning we need to outgrow. Our capacity to express the basic power of yes and no often becomes damaged in childhood. And this incapacity becomes installed in our psychological makeup as a tendency to oscillate between compliance and defiance, as Paul exemplified in his attitude toward others – secretly wanting to please them, yet secretly hating them for this at the same time.

As long as Paul failed to address his unconscious dynamic of compliance and defiance, his spiritual practice could not help him stabilise any true equanimity, free from anxiety about praise and blame. Although he could experience freedom from praise and blame during periods of solitary spiritual practice, these realisations remained compartmentalised, and failed to carry over into his everyday functioning.

I want to describe two defining moments in our work together, in which Paul connected with his genuine yes and no. These two moments are also of interest in highlighting the difference between psychological and spiritual work.

Before Paul could find and express his genuine yes – to himself, to others, to life – he had to say no to the internalised mother whose influence remained alive within him: 'No, I don't exist to make you happy, to be your saviour, to give your life meaning.' But it was not easy for him to acknowledge his anger and hatred toward his mother for the ways he had become an object of her own narcissistic needs. Quoting spiritual doctrine, Paul believed it was wrong to hate. Yet in never letting himself feel the hatred he carried unconsciously in his body, he wound up expressing it in covert, self-sabotaging ways. I did not try to push past his inner taboo against this feeling, but only invited him to acknowledge his hatred when it was apparent in his speech or demeanour. When Paul could finally let himself feel his hatred directly, instead of judging or denying it, he came alive in a whole new way. He sat up straight and broke into laughter, the laughter of an awakening vitality and power.

Articulating his genuine no, the no of protection – 'I won't let you take advantage of me' – also freed him to acknowledge his hidden desire, his dormant yes – 'Yes, I want to be seen for who I am, the being I am in my own right, apart from what I do for you.' The second defining moment happened as Paul acknowledged this need to be seen and loved for who he was – which triggered a surge of energy coursing through him, filling his whole body. Yet this was also scary for him, for it felt as though he were becoming inflated. And for Paul, with his refined Buddhist sensibilities, self-inflation was the greatest sin of all, a symptom of ego-bloatedness, the way of the narcissist who is full of himself.

Seeing his resistance, I encouraged him to explore, if only for a few moments, what it would be like to let himself become inflated, to feel full of himself, and to stay present with that experience. As he let himself fill up and inflate, he experienced himself as large, rich, and radiant. He felt like a sun-king, receiving energy from the gods above and below, radiating light in all directions. He realised that he had always wanted to feel this way, but had never allowed himself to expand like this before! Yet now he was letting himself be infused by the fullness that had been missing in his life – the fullness of his own being. To his surprise, he found it a tremendous relief and release to allow this expansion at last.

As Paul got over his surprise, he laughed and said: 'Who would have thought that letting myself become inflated could be so liberating?' Of course, he wasn't acting out a state of ego-inflation, but rather feeling what it was like to let the energy of desire, fullness, and spontaneous self-valuing flow through his body. In this moment, since he was according himself the recognition he had secretly sought from others, he did not care about how others saw him. Nor was there any desire to lord his new-found strength over anyone. He was enjoying the pure radiation of his inner richness and warmth – let others respond as they may.

Many spiritual seekers who suffer, like Paul, from a deflated sense of self interpret spiritual teachings about selflessness to mean that they should keep a lid on themselves and not let themselves shine. Yet instead of overzealously guarding against ego-inflation, Paul needed to let his genie out of the bottle before he could clearly distinguish between genuine expressions of being such as power, joy, or celebration, and ego-distortions such as grandiosity and conceit.

Since *need* had been such a dirty word in Paul's world view, he had sought to overcome it through spiritual practice. However, trying to leap directly from denial of his need for love to a state of needlessness was only spiritual bypassing – using spiritual teachings to support an unconscious defence. When he stopped fighting his need, he was able to connect with a deeper force within it – *a genuine, powerful yes to life and love* – which lessened his fixation on outer praise and blame. Paul discovered that this essential yes was quite different from attachment and clinging; it contained a *holy longing* to give birth to himself in a new way. Indeed, as Paul discovered his inner fire, value, and power through unlocking his genuine yes and no, he became less defensive, more open to others and to the flow of love.

DIFFERENTIATED AND UNDIFFERENTIATED BEING

In this case example, we can see how unconscious psychological issues distorted Paul's understanding of spiritual teachings and interfered with his capacity to fully embody them. His ambivalence, self-denial, and self-blame cut off his access to deeper capacities such as strength, confidence, trust, and the ability to connect with others in a genuinely open way. We could call these capacities *differentiated qualities* or *expressions of being*. If the absolute side of our nature – undifferentiated being – is like clear light, the relative side – or differentiated being – is like a rainbow spectrum of colours contained within that light. *While realising undifferentiated being is the path of liberation, embodying qualities of differentiated being is the path of individuation* in its deepest sense: the unfolding of inherent human capacities that exist as seed potentials within us, but which are often blocked by psychological conflicts.

While realisation can happen at any moment, it does not necessarily lead, as we have seen, to actualisation. Although I may have access to the transparency of pure being, I may still not have access to the human capacities that will enable me to *actualise that realisation* in the world. I may not be able to access my generosity, for instance, in situations that require it, if it is obstructed by unconscious beliefs that reinforce an identity of impoverishment and deficiency. If these unconscious beliefs are not brought to light and worked with, generosity is unlikely to manifest in a full and genuine way.

In the Buddhist tradition, differentiated being is often described in terms of 'the qualities of a buddha' – wisdom, great clarity, compassion, patience, strength, or generosity. Although some lineages do not emphasise these qualities, others, such as Tibetan Vajrayana, have developed a wide range of transformational practices designed to cultivate various aspects of them.

Since these deeper capacities are often blocked by unresolved psychological issues, working with these conflicts directly can provide another way, particularly suited to Westerners, to gain access to these differentiated qualities of being and integrate them into our character and functioning. After all, most problems in living are the result of losing access to these capacities – power, love, flexibility, confidence, or trust – which allow us to respond creatively to the challenging situations at hand. As we see and work through our psychological conflicts, these missing capacities often become unveiled.

Because Western seekers generally suffer from a painful split between being and functioning, they need careful, specific guidance in bridging the gap between the radical openness of pure being and being-in-the-world. Unfortunately, even in spiritual traditions that emphasise the importance of integrating realisation into daily life, special instructions about how to accomplish this integration are often not very fully elaborated. Or else it is not clear how the instructions, formulated for simpler times and a simpler world, apply to handling the complexities of our fast-paced world, navigating the perils of Western-style intimate relationships, or overcoming the apparent gap many people feel between realising impersonal being and embodying it in personal functioning. By helping people work through their specific emotional conflicts, which cut them off from their deeper capacities, psychological work can be of real, practical help in tapping their larger intelligence and bringing it more fully into their lives. This kind of work is like cultivating the soil on which the seeds of spiritual realisation can 'land' and take root.[9]

Cultivating the powerful resources latent in our absolute true nature allows us to develop a fuller, richer quality of human, *personal presence*; that is, an individuated way of embodying our true nature. This kind of individuation goes far beyond the secular, humanistic ideal of developing one's uniqueness, being a creative innovator, or living out one's dreams. Instead, it involves forging a vessel – our capacity for personal presence, nourished by its rootedness in a full spectrum of human qualities – through which we can bring absolute true nature into form – the 'form' of our person. By *person* I do not mean some fixed structure or entity, but the way in which true nature can manifest and express itself in a uniquely personal way, as the ineffable suchness or 'youness' of you. How fully this suchness manifests – in our face, our speech, our actions, our personal qualities – is partly grace, but also partly a result of our work on ourselves. Thus individuation, which involves clarifying the psychological dynamics that interfere with our capacity to be fully personally present, is not opposed to spiritual realisation. It is, instead, a way of becoming a more transparent vessel – *a person who can bring through what is beyond the person in a uniquely personal way.*

The secular humanistic perspective sees individual development as an end in itself. In the view I am proposing here, individuation is not an end, but a path or means that can help us *give birth to our true form*, by cleaning up the distortions of our old false self. As we learn to be true to our deepest individual imperatives, rather than enslaved to past conditioning, our character structure no longer poses such an obstacle to recognising absolute true nature or embodying it. Our individuated nature becomes a window opening on to all that is beyond and greater than us.

CONSCIOUS AND UNCONSCIOUS IDENTITY

Spiritual traditions generally explain the cause of suffering in global, *epistemological* terms – as the result of ignorance, misperception, or sin – or in *ontological* terms – as a disconnection from our essential being. Buddhism, for instance, traces suffering to the mind's tendency to grasp and fixate – on thoughts, self-images, feelings such as attachment and aversion, and external perceptions coloured by these thoughts, feelings, and self-images – while at the same time ignoring the source of this whole panorama of experience – the luminous, expansive, and creative power of awareness itself. Western psychology, by contrast, offers a more specific *developmental* understanding. It shows how our suffering results from childhood conditioning; in particular, from frozen, distorted images of self and other (object relations) that we carry with us from the past. Since it understands these distorting identities as relational – formed in and through our relationships with others – psychotherapy explores these self-other structures in a relational context – in the healing environment of the client-therapist relationship.

Since the spiritual traditions generally do not recognise the way in which the ego-identity forms out of interpersonal relationships, they are unable to address the interpersonal nature of these structures directly. Instead, they offer practices – prayer, meditation, mantra, service, devotion to God or guru – that shift the attention to the universal ground of being in which the individual psyche moves, like a wave on the ocean. Thus it becomes possible to enter luminous states of transpersonal awakening, beyond personal conflicts and limitations, without having to address or work through specific psychological issues and conflicts. Yet while this kind of realisation may provide direct access to greater wisdom and compassion, it often does not touch or alter impaired relational patterns which, because they pervade everyday functioning, interfere with the integration of this realisation into the fabric of daily life.

Spiritual practice can certainly have a powerful global effect on the psyche by undermining its central lynchpin, the identification with the narrow egoic self-concept – what I call the *conscious identity* (Welwood, 1996). The conscious identity is a self-image whose function is to allow us to imagine that we are solid and substantial. From a Buddhist or ontological perspective, this egoic identity functions as a defence against the threat of emptiness – the open dimension of being, with all its uncertainty, impermanence, and insubstantiality – which the ego interprets as a threat to its existence. From a psychological perspective, the conscious identity can be seen as a defence against an underlying sense of threat or lack, originally experienced in childhood in response to lack of love, connection, or acceptance. Even though our conscious efforts maybe geared toward overcoming this sense of deficiency, inadequacy, or unworthiness, we nonetheless tend to identify subconsciously with the sense of lack itself. I call this the *subconscious identity*.

Because subconscious identities are more hidden and threatening than conscious identities, they are also much harder to dislodge and transform. If the whole conscious-subconscious identity structure is to be transformed, it seems necessary to address the interpersonal dynamics that are part of its fabric. The relational context of psychotherapy can often provide a direct, focused, and precise method of working through the subconscious dynamics that keep this whole identity structure intact.

Paul, for example, had developed a conscious identity based on being in control of his life and 'not caring what people think'. This conscious control structure was a way of compensating for a deeper, underlying sense of deficiency that caused him to feel overwhelmed in interpersonal relations. His spiritual practice had partially undermined the conscious identity – his defensive control structure – by providing direct access to his larger being. But since he also used spiritual practice as a way to bypass, or not deal with, his subconscious identity – the underlying sense of deficiency – it could not free him from the grip of his whole identity structure.

Since Paul did not like to feel his deficient identity and the feelings of anxiety, frustration, and tension that accompanied it, he was happy to practise spiritual methods that helped him move beyond, and thus avoid, this aspect of his ego structure. Indeed, it was much easier for him to be present with the open, spacious dimension of being than with his anxiety and helplessness when they were triggered. Since his capacity for presence did not extend into the totality of his psyche, it was not of much use to him when he was up against his worst demons. Because he regularly bypassed the most painful aspects of his conditioned personality through spiritual practice, his ego remained largely intact.

Through the psychological work we did together, Paul was able to acknowledge his underlying sense of lack and open up to the feelings of vulnerability and helplessness associated with it. In this way, he began to dismantle his identity structure from within, instead of just trying to dissolve or move beyond it. In conjunction with his meditative practice, this kind of psychological work helped Paul learn to relax in situations that triggered his subconscious identity.

Of course, some might argue that Paul's problem was that he failed to truly understand or apply the spiritual practices and teachings he had received. That may well be. But I don't believe his spiritual practice was a failure. It served him well in many ways. It also brought him to the point where his most primitive, unresolved psychological issues were fully exposed and ready to be worked with. Yet he needed another set of tools to address these issues directly, to penetrate the unconscious roots of his tendency to distort and compartmentalise the spiritual teachings he had received, and to become a more integrated human being.

In the end, Paul felt that his psychological and spiritual work were both of great benefit, in complementary ways. The psychological work also had a clarifying effect on his spiritual practice, by helping him make an important distinction between absolute emptiness – the ultimate reality beyond self – and relative, psychological emptiness – his inner sense of lack and deficiency. Because he had previously conflated these two types of emptiness, his spiritual practice had often served to reinforce his subconscious sense of unworthiness.

TOWARD A FRESH DIALOGUE BETWEEN EAST AND WEST

The essential difference between Western and Eastern psychology is their differing emphasis on the personal and the impersonal. Unfortunately, contemporary translations of the Eastern spiritual teachings often make *personal* a synonym for *egoic*, with the result that the capacity for a richly developed personal presence becomes lost. Although personal presence may not be as vast and boundless as impersonal presence, it has a mystery and beauty all its own. Martin Buber saw this 'personal making-present (*personale vergegenwaertigung*)' as an integral part of what he considered the primary unit of human experience: the I-Thou relationship (in Schlipp and Friedman, 1967: 117). Indeed, to appreciate the power and meaning of personal presence, we only need to look into the face of someone we love. As the Irish priest John O'Donohue once remarked, 'In the human face infinity becomes personal.' While impersonal presence is the source of an *equal* concern and compassion for all beings – *agape*, in Western terms – personal presence is the source of *eros* – the intimate resonance between oneself, as this particular person, and another, whose *particular* qualities we respond to in a very particular way.

We in the West have been exposed to the profoundest non-dual teachings and practices of the East for only a few short decades. Now that we have begun to digest and assimilate them, it is time for a new level of dialogue between East and West, in order to develop greater understanding about the relationship between the impersonal absolute and the human, personal dimension. Expressing absolute true nature in a thoroughly personal, human form may be one of the most important evolutionary potentials of the cross-fertilisation of East and West, of contemplative and psychological understanding. The great potential in bringing these approaches together is to learn how to transform our personality – developing it into an instrument of higher purpose – thus redeeming the whole personal realm, instead of just seeking liberation from it.

Buddhism for one has always grown by absorbing understandings and methods indigenous to the cultures to which it spread. If psychotherapy is our modern way of dealing with the psyche and its demons, analogous to the early Tibetan shamanic practices that Vajrayana Buddhism integrated into its larger framework, then the meditative traditions may only find a firmer footing in our culture if they recognise and relate to Western psychology more fully. A more open and penetrating dialogue between practitioners of meditative and psychological disciplines could help the ancient spiritual traditions find new and more powerful ways of addressing the Western situation and thus have a greater impact on the direction our world is taking.

In sum, we need a new framework of understanding that can help us appreciate how psychological and spiritual work might be mutually supportive allies in the liberation and complete embodiment of the human spirit. We need to revise both spiritual and psychological work for our time, so that psychological work can function in the service of spiritual development, while spiritual work can also take account of psychological development. These two convergent streams would then recognise each other as two vitally important limbs of an evolving humanity that is still moving toward realising its potential as:

– the being that can open, and know itself as belonging to the universal mystery and presence that surrounds and inhabits all things, and

– the being that can embody that greater openness as human presence in the world, through its capacity to manifest all the deeper resources implicit in its nature, thus serving as a crucial link between heaven and earth.

Going to Pieces without Falling Apart: A Buddhist Perspective on Wholeness

Mark Epstein

There is a story from the Buddha's time about a householder named Nakulapita who went to the Buddha for advice on peace of mind. 'I am old and decrepit,' he told the Buddha. 'I am sick and constantly ailing. My body hurts all the time. What can I do to find happiness?'

The Buddha took Nakulapita's complaints seriously. 'Even so,' he said to him right away. (The Buddha often said, 'Even so.' Like a good psychotherapist, he tended to agree with his patient's self-assessments, even when they might wish them to be challenged.) 'It is true, Nakulapita. Your body is old and sick. With a body like yours, even a moment of good health would be a miracle. Therefore, you should train yourself like this, "Though I am ill in body my mind shall not be ill."' Nakulapita felt refreshed by this possibility. His body was going to pieces but he did not have to fall apart. He went to one of the Buddha's chief disciples, Sariputta, for further instruction.

Sariputta built upon the Buddha's lesson in his subsequent teachings. 'Do not look upon your body as your self,' he told Nakulapita. 'Do not think that the body is the self or that the self is the body or that the self is in the body or that the body is in the self. Do not look upon your feelings as your self, your thoughts as your self, even your consciousness as your self. Your body can change and become otherwise,' he told him, 'but grief, lamentation, pain, dejection, and despair do not have to arise.'[1]

Sariputta was teaching something very radical: that it was possible to let the mind float free of identifications with any aspect of the mind-body process. This is a point that the Tantric Buddhists of many centuries later have also made in their secret teachings about orgasm and death. In both processes, they teach, the self is swallowed up in the intensity of the experience. If we do not resist, we have the opportunity to glimpse this freely floating mind.

But the Buddhist sages have also discovered that we are all afraid of this loss of self and that we unconsciously pull back from a complete immersion in the mind that peeks through in such situations. Even in sex, they say, we resist completely losing ourselves, while in death we are notoriously fearful. But they also believe, as the Buddha and Sariputta did, that it is possible to train the mind to sustain its awareness so that the bliss that naturally dawns in orgasm and in death can shine through and permeate our regular lives. Thus, while teaching the emptiness of all things (no self in the body, no self in feelings or thoughts, no self in consciousness), Buddhists also teach a positive emptiness, a luminous knowing that is sometimes called the clear light nature of mind. This is the mind that the Buddha was pointing out to Nakulapita, the mind that holds the key to relief.

In approaching old age, illness and death we are all faced with the need for a mind that can withstand disintegration. Our usual strategies of managing threats to our self-sufficiency do not work very well in these situations. We are trained to keep ourselves together but we do not get much teaching in falling apart. Only very occasionally do we find an exceptional individual who is not terrified of floating free in the abyss.

There is an apocryphal tale of James Joyce asking Carl Jung what the difference was between his own mind and that of his schizophrenic daughter that illustrates this point.

'She falls,' Jung is said to have replied. 'You jump!'

I had a sense of this unexpectedly on one of my last meditation retreats. I was in Western Massachusetts in a very cold February, sitting silently over a ten-day period. Every day after lunch, instead of taking my customary nap, I decided to put on five layers of clothing and walk in the surrounding countryside for an hour. I tried to time my excursions to be back in time for the first afternoon meditation. The winter had been filled with snowstorms and the rural forests and farmlands surrounding the meditation centre had taken on the ghostly and sparkling look of Alaskan tundra.

Each day I would walk briskly and meditatively with my eyes down and my attention focused on my body's movements. There were empty roads and paths leading every which way so that after thirty minutes I would always be in a completely different place. At that point I would stop and look around with the full force of my concentrated awareness before turning around and heading back.

The first day I found myself in the middle of a frozen lake with a windstorm swirling the snow in circles about me. The second day I was halfway up a hill looking up at the sky at the instant that the first flakes of a new snowfall came fluttering down in slow motion on to my upturned face. The next day I was standing silently in the middle of a completely still forest when, with a sudden whoosh, an owl swooped low over my head with one huge dark wing extended.

I began to think there was something awesome about my timing. How was it that at the exact moment of my stopping such incredible things were happening? It took me longer than I am prepared to admit to realise that such things were *always* happening. It was only that I was finally paying attention.

These walks have become a huge teaching for me about the function of meditation. My practice was like the methodical thirty-minute walk. It could take me somewhere but I had to remember to look around once I got there. Those moments of silent awareness in the forest were precious because of how open and connected I felt. Rather than feeling one with the universe, I still felt my own presence, yet my experience of myself was altered. Like a child whose mind is free to roam because he is secure in his mother's presence, I completely let down my guard. Relaxing my mind into its deeper nature, I could reach beyond my personality into something more open.

I first tasted this possibility close to twenty-five years ago when I was beginning to explore Buddhist meditation. I remember becoming inescapably aware of how much tension I was carrying in my shoulders. I had not yet turned twenty-one and had gone to Boulder, Colorado for a kind of spiritual summer camp organised by a young Tibetan Buddhist lama, Chogyam Trungpa, Rinpoche. A graduate student friend of mine had told me about the summer programme and I was impressed with how many of my cultural heros were teaching there. John Cage, Gregory Bateson, Ram Dass and Allen Ginsberg were among the faculty, as were American Buddhist teachers Jack Kornfield, Joseph Goldstein and Sharon Salzberg.

While there were scores of eminent and accomplished teachers in Boulder that summer, many of whose offerings I eagerly sampled, my first real teachers were a pair of twins from Long Island who had been randomly assigned to be my roommates. Sons of Jewish immigrants who had set up a family fruit and vegetable business, these twins had become expert in such esoteric knowledge as herbal medicine, diet, naturopathy, massage and Chinese philosophy. Eschewing most of the formal courses at Naropa, with a not so carefully disguised disdain for the egos of most of the faculty, they contented themselves with regular early morning drives to Denver's wholesale fruit and vegetable market.

I was taking classes in Buddhist meditation, Chinese Tai Chi, sensory awareness, and contact improvisation dance while they were accumulating boxes of ripe figs, peaches, nectarines and cherries. They watched me with amusement as I took course after course fruitlessly struggling to release the shoulder tension that I could no longer ignore. Finally, one of the twins offered to teach me to juggle.

My breakthrough that summer came not during any formal meditation practice but from my experience of juggling. As I finally became able to keep three balls in the air, I noticed suddenly how quiet my mind had become. My everyday thoughts had vanished, and the tension in my shoulders was gone. I was momentarily undefended and curiously at peace. I wasn't trying to relax and I wasn't trying not to relax. Everything was floating. I was no longer centred in my thinking mind and had surrendered, momentarily, to something beyond what I knew.

A well-known poem by Wallace Stevens, 'Thirteen Ways of Looking at a Blackbird' gives a sense of what this juggling experience did for me. The poem contains the following verse:

> I do not know which to prefer,
> The beauty of inflections
> Or the beauty of innuendoes,
> The blackbird whistling
> Or just after.[2]

When we speak of the self from the perspective of Western psychology we are most often taken with the beauty of inflection, with the self's whistle as it appears. But when we look at the self from the perspective of the Buddhist psychologies, we emphasise the beauty of the self's innuendo, of the space around the self.

So perhaps my juggling breakthrough was the equivalent of hearing the blackbird's whistle 'just after'. I did not need to leave my ego behind, merely to see around its edges. My shoulder tension and my reliance on my thinking mind were symptoms of a defensive reliance on only one aspect of my nature: a holding on to the reactive self 'as it appears'. While juggling, as sometimes happens in meditation, my perspective had been broadened. I had permitted a loosening that was neither transcendent nor regressive but that had allowed me to see in three dimensions instead of in two. I had glimpsed my ego's inherent unreality, or rather, I had permitted myself to simply be, without worrying about keeping myself together.

Only in the musings of the British child analyst D.W. Winnicott have I found an approach to these kinds of experiences that dovetails with a Buddhist understanding. 'In thinking of the psychology of mysticism, it is usual to concentrate on the understanding of the mystic's withdrawal into a personal inner world . . .' wrote Winnicott. 'Perhaps not enough attention has been paid to the mystic's retreat to a position in which he can communicate secretly with subjective . . . phenomena, the loss of contact with the world of shared reality being counterbalanced by a gain in terms of feeling real.'[3]

When Winnicott wrote of the mystical experience he was alluding to a mode of being that he described over and over again in his work. Opposing such a state to one of either ego *integration* or *disintegration*, Winnicott wrote instead of the experiences of *unintegration* or letting go. By *unintegrated* Winnicott meant something like what I had stumbled upon in my juggling where the usual needs for control are suspended and where the self can unwind. He meant losing oneself without feeling lost, hearing the self's innuendo rather than just its inflection. 'The opposite of integration would seem to be disintegration,' commented Winnicott. 'That is only partly true. The opposite, initially, requires a word like unintegration. Relaxation for an infant means not feeling a need to integrate, the mother's ego-supportive function being taken for granted.'[4] His conclusion that these experiences are necessary for 'feeling real' is borne out by many of our own meditative experiences. It is most common, I think, for meditation to rather inexplicably promote this capacity, at the same time as it undercuts the reality of the self.

It is the mother's function, in Winnicott's view, to create an environment for her baby in which it is safe to be nobody, because it is only out of such a place that the infant can begin to find herself. 'It is not so much a question of giving the baby satisfaction,' he wrote, 'as of letting the baby find and come to terms with the object (breast, bottle, milk, etc.).'[5] As in the Wallace Stevens poem about the blackbird, the mother must do more than just satisfy the baby's basic needs, she must also create a space in which the infant can discover herself.

The mother is responsible for background as well as foreground, Winnicott implied. When this space is offered to a child, it develops into the capacity for unrestricted, unimpaired awareness that becomes the foundation for looking *in* to the self in later years. By accessing this ability we are able to *feel* our way into our selves just as the infant learns to explore her early environment.

A friend of mine made his own version of this discovery once when he spoke to me of his difficulties in relating to his ten-month-old daughter. He had trouble, he said, finding 'the right voice' to talk to her in. He could talk baby talk, read to her, play games, and give her direction, but he worried that he sounded fake, like his own mother, when he talked to her. I suggested that he try being silent with her, that he was worrying too much about *how* he talked to her. There was other communication besides the verbal, I reminded him.

When my friend experienced a sense of falseness with his daughter, he was aware of the artificial nature of his interaction. On some level, he knew that he was not giving her the chance to relax. She had to remain on guard, mobilise to respond to her father's anxiety. She could not float away into her own experience. My friend was setting up a situation in which his daughter would have to stay too attentive to him and too afraid of the depths of her own self.

The capacity to be alone is a paradox since it can only be developed with someone else in the room. Once developed, the child trusts that she will not be intruded upon and permits herself a secret communication with private and personal phenomena. The best adult model that Winnicott could find for this is what he called 'after intercourse', when each person is content to be alone but is not withdrawn. This is such an unusual state because of how little anxiety exists. There are no questions about the other person's availability but there is also no need for active contact.

This kind of aloneness, proposed Winnicott, is the foundation of all creativity since it is only in such a state that it is possible to explore one's internal world. The point is that it is not possible if one is *too* alone, or too intruded upon. It can only develop when the *holding* environment is safe and unobtrusive.

Meditation is a way of resurrecting this inner holding environment that allows me a taste of the mind that underlies our
conventional experience. But I have also found that psychotherapy can be a vehicle for this kind of discovery. It too can
seem like a long walk that suddenly opens up into an extraordinary vision of something that has always been available but
has gone unrecognised. Let me give you a couple of examples
from my experience.

When I first entered psychotherapy, some years into my
embrace of Buddhism, it was still with a sense of wanting to
break out of myself in some way. Guided to a Gestalt therapist
named Michael Vincent Miller, I remember being asked in my
first session what I wanted to get out of therapy. It was a simple
question, but it shook me up. I had just arrived, after all. Wasn't it
enough that I was there? Couldn't I just surrender and let
therapy do its thing? Wasn't he supposed to help me plumb the
depths of my unconscious to find out what I was truly after? I did
not really know what I wanted but I was being asked by this
somewhat mercurial man to take responsibility for wanting
something. Wasn't this awfully *personal*?

I was intrigued enough by my predicament not to flee pre-
cipitously. I must have known on some level that what I wanted
was to be able to say what I wanted. I fumbled around for a while
and said something about wishing that I could be more spontaneous, or more original, or more dynamic in my expression of
myself. Michael nodded sympathetically, at which I took offence.
He then asked me if I was aware that I was sitting on the edge of
my seat.

I was not aware of it. I was sitting the way I always sat when
talking with someone. 'What is wrong with the way I'm sitting?' I
wanted to ask. But I remained silent, feeling suddenly trapped
and at the same time noticing a flicker of glee deep inside me.
This man was going to help me: I could feel it.

Michael waited, as if to give me time to get over my sudden
self-consciousness and to actually notice how I was sitting. He
was right. I was perched like a bird on the edge of my chair. I was
very uncomfortable there. 'You give yourself no support,' he said
softly.

I spent the rest of the session feeling what it was like to sit
back in my chair, making use of my whole body as I spoke. It
required a good deal of effort to not just float back up into my
head but I could feel already that I was forging a connection with

the physical environment that I had been denying myself. My body *was* the unconscious that I was so interested in plumbing. For all of my meditation training, I still needed the help of a therapist to show me where I was holding back.

'Form is emptiness,' the Buddhists teach, but form is also form. I would never be able to approach the emptiness of form if I continued to deny myself the experience of it.

In my own way, I was dramatising a very familiar scenario. Distanced from my own body and lodged somewhere in my thinking mind, I was as estranged from my own creative abilities as I was removed from the support of my chair. There was a connection between inhabiting my body and opening up a creative mental space from which I could use words to articulate myself.

My therapist could just as easily have been a Zen master in the manner in which he related to me, only he was not. For me, his teaching did not in any way contradict what I had already put together for myself from my years of practising meditation: it merely drove home the lesson on another front, in a particularly vivid and helpful way. The lesson about being more in my body was not particularly new, but it was presented to me in a new way. We do not get lots of realisations in our lives as much as we get the same ones over and over.

There was something about this therapy that was very different from what I had expected and that has influenced me tremendously in my own work. Michael did not present himself as an authority figure who 'analysed' my psychic configurations. He did not interpret my Oedipal dilemma, at least not in so many words. He was not remote and silent. He was very available, quite humorous and playful, and he was always wondering where I was. He paid particular attention to what prevented me from being part of the relationship with him.

Intuitively, I recognised that his ongoing question, of where I was, was my own question as well. It had driven my interest in meditation and had propelled me into therapy. Through the power of therapy I started to see that I was most identified with who I was when I was anxious, yet I felt most myself when I could relate unselfconsciously. This presented me with a bit of a paradox. Throughout the course of this therapy I would always arrive at a rather intimidating conclusion. The only way to find out where I was was to get out of the way and let myself happen.

This makes the process sound too passive, however. Getting out of the way was essential. But letting myself happen was not quite the voyeuristic process that it sounds. My therapist was asking something of me that was more on the order of improvisation. He was asking for meditation *in action*, not for a mere witnessing of psychic debris.

When I first discovered Buddhism I found that it authenticated a feeling of emptiness that I had long harboured. I had never felt as real as I thought I was supposed to feel but with the wisdom of Buddhism behind me I stopped trying to feel more real than I did. My initial experiences in meditation taught me a receptive kind of surrender that gave me a sense of deepening, opening and acceptance. This gave me back a tremendous freedom – the freedom to just be how I was. My therapy worked in harmony with this discovery, but added something essential that I was still missing. As I began to improvise myself without so much self-consciousness, I came to see that this was an active aspect of surrender. Rather than simply opening receptively into the unknown, this was more of a letting go into spontaneity and self-expression.

The relief that I felt at being able to engage in this way was nearly identical to the relief that I have at other times felt in meditation when making contact with my 'big sky' mind. The two experiences have more than a superficial similarity. Both therapy and meditation, as disciplines, require the gentle coaxing and cajoling of the mind from a contracted state to a momentarily open and playful one.

As we work to bring the lessons of meditation and psychotherapy to life we see that this second, more active, aspect of surrender is as crucial as its receptive counterpart. Without the ability to meditate in action, it is all too easy to use the mental training of Buddhism or the self-knowledge of therapy to reinforce defences instead of cutting through them.

A number of years after ending my therapy with Michael, I began a course of therapy and supervision with a senior Gestalt therapist in New York City, a man named Isadore From. I was already a therapist by this time and Isadore was renowned as a teacher of therapists. He was a lovely man but exquisitely sensitive to any note of artifice. If I were to say to him, for instance, 'I *really* like her!' he would immediately ask me what I did *not* like about the person in question. My use of 'really' would strike him as an exaggeration that hid an ulterior meaning and he would usually be right. He was a difficult man to hide from. In one of my first meetings with him, after completing a particular exchange, I reflexively prolonged my gaze, attempting to preserve and extend the eye contact that we had established. This was a strategy that, in retrospect, I believe I had cultivated over the years of meditative training, meaning to convey a sense of openness and availability, spiced with a dash of meaningfulness, a kind of soul-ful gaze.

'Are you aware that you are staring at me?' Isadore asked after a moment. 'Blink!' he commanded.

Once again, my fragile relationship to the capacity for being was revealed. I had turned it into something that I *did*, instead of letting it be something that I was. Made anxious by the impending loss of connection, I was attempting to forestall the inevitable return to my own separateness by artificially prolonging my eye contact. It was like refusing to stop eating ice cream, not wanting to give up the taste, even though I was already full. As Isadore made me see, my anxiety about losing that state introduced an artificial note into something that in its very nature is natural, spontaneous and fleeting. Connection may be our natural state, as Buddhism teaches, but it is not static. Part of trusting in it is to let our experience of it come and go. While I had become much more comfortable with my own capacity for silent communication, I still did not really trust that the connection I so valued was infinite and renewable. While he would never define himself as 'spiritual' (having the same disdain for that word as he did for 'really'), Isadore taught me a very subtle, but essential, spiritual lesson. To experience true connection I had to be willing to come back into myself.

Meditation encourages a *trust* that is difficult to find elsewhere, a trust that if we surrender to the moment naturally that connection will be there, that an emotional experience, no matter now threatening, is bearable. Yet what Isadore was showing me in his simple command to blink was that I tended to get in the way of that trust by clinging to my new-found ability as if it would vanish without constant reinforcement. As Buddhism reminds us, and as Isadore made me see, we can cling to anything, even letting go.

How Does Liberating Self-Insight Become Tacit Understanding?

Leslie Todres

Overview

This chapter attempts to clarify the question of how liberating self-insight becomes tacit understanding. I hope to show how the terms used in this question are useful and that they are able to clarify experiences that are central to both psychotherapy and spiritual awakening. The approach taken can broadly be called phenomenological in that the seamless flow of everyday experiences is used to give substance to concepts such as liberating self-insight, tacit understanding and integration. Descriptions from two sources are used – from the reported lives of well-known Zen masters and from experiences of clients in psychotherapy. Regarding the former I draw heavily on the biographical accounts of Zen masters that are summarised in the book, *Crazy Clouds* by Perle Besserman and Manfred Steger (1991). The vignettes from psychotherapy are taken from my PhD thesis on self-insight in psychotherapy (Todres, 1990) and have been modified to exclude possible identifying details.

The broad question is concerned with how insights that occur in psychotherapy or spiritual awakening may become integrated into one's everyday life. The pursuit of this question is assisted by an enquiry into a number of related questions:

1. What is liberating self-insight?

2. Is there a difference between the kinds of liberating self-insights that occur in psychotherapy and those that occur in Zen enlightenment experiences?
3. What is tacit understanding?

The chapter concludes with some thoughts on how Jung's notion of the transcendent function is useful in furthering our understanding of the awakening of consciousness.

WHAT IS LIBERATING SELF-INSIGHT?

A number of philosophical traditions such as Buddhism, postmodern thought, eco-systemic theory, and existential phenomenology (see Wilber, 1995) have pointed out in different ways how the 'self' is different from a thing. In a previous paper (Todres, 1993) I reflected on how Martin Heidegger unfolded an ontological perspective in which the rhythm of human identity is not just defined interpersonally, but participates in a vanishing depth which is fundamentally open:

> In characterising human existence as the 'shepherd of Being' he [Heidegger] wishes to indicate that human identity is most essentially and radically defined by not being enclosed upon itself. It is thus most basically characterised by metaphors such as 'openness', 'lighting' and the 'there'. In this vision, human existence has its essence in its transcendence; it is being itself most when it is 'lost' from itself, 'there' for the beings and things that are. In its fundamental nature, human identity can thus never be finally objectified; it is essentially no-thing. (Todres, 1993: 257)

This kind of consideration sets the scene for defining liberating self-insight as a *direction* which frees self-understanding from the objectification of self and other. How deep can this go? Well, very deep, if we take the life and thoughts of the Buddha seriously. Deep enough to look at each other without conclusion, open to what is arising as if for the first time.

However, there appears to be a difference between experiences of such a direction that commonly occur in psychotherapy and those which occur in Zen enlightenment. In psychotherapy, a person may have an experience in which the way one has become defined becomes more flexible so that new possibilities of living and feeling can be accommodated. For example, in psychotherapy, Michael realised that he always responded to criticism as if he deserved a reprimand. He had not realised before how much he was living according to a definition of himself in which he was stuck in time, as if still responding to a critical mother. He became aware that he had developed a 'self' in which he attempted in many ways always to be beyond criticism. For example, he was often preoccupied with the length of his beard and the cut of his suit. This insight helped him realise that he need not live and act as if he was still standing there trying to be perfect. The direction of this self-insight was a shift in personal identity in which he became less objectified as the 'potentially reprimanded one'. So his identity became less fixed, and he embraced a greater ambiguity in situations where he began to learn a balance that was neither self-demeaning nor overly self-assertive.

However, although such an insight was made possible by his intrinsic no-thingness, it was not an insight about his no-thingness i.e. the structure of the depth of his identity as a whole. There is a profound difference between the kind of insight that allows us to grasp a more flexible self-as-object and the kind of insight that relieves the quest for self-definition *per se*. And here we turn to the Zen tradition.

After serious Zen study and practice, Layman Pang encountered Baso with the question:

'What kind of man is it that has no companion among the ten thousand things?'
Baso said, 'Swallow up all the water in the West river in one gulp and I'll tell you.'

Layman Pang experienced an opening of identity. Into what? Nothing in particular. Implicit here are some of the principles of the Buddhist tradition – interdependence, emptiness, no boundary. Yet even these words did not define him or his experience.

This kind of self-insight indicates a shift in personal identity not just to where a person is less defined than previously but to where self-definition is not possible, to where it does not exist. In this phase of experience the emptiness of self is emphasised.

In a period of great social inequality, Rinzai talked of the 'true man of no rank'. Likewise, after much searching and committed meditation, Bankei was suddenly struck with the insight that 'all things are resolved in the unborn'. These experiences indicate a vanishing depth of personal identity in which one finds oneself with the birds and the trees, and even then: what is this? No clinging to self high or low. We may thus be ready to define liberating self-insight as an understanding which allows personal identity to shift in a direction that is less restricted by one's previous enacted definitions. In the case of psychotherapy, this can lead to a more flexible self-concept: one more in accord with the limits and freedoms of human existence. In the case of spiritual practice, this can lead to a fundamental re-evaluation of personal identity as a whole, where the boundaries of the self are experienced as 'convenient fictions' and understood as empty of independent existence. Liberating self-insight in this view is thus a wonderful solution. But in our lives it is also a problem and it is to this problem that we reluctantly turn.

When Things are Either/Or: The Problem of Dissociativeness

This problem refers to how someone can have a self-insight which does not appear to make a difference to the way he or she subsequently feels or lives. The term, 'dissociation' is used here, not in the narrow psychiatric sense, but in the broader way in which Wilber (1995) used it, to indicate a failure to adequately integrate emergent differences.

In psychotherapy, Sharon was exhilarated to realise that she had been living as if her older sister were a parent and that this need not be so. Her personal identity had been bound up excessively with either trying to please her sister or rebelling against her. This insight liberated her to acknowledge strengths within herself which were independent of her sister's judgement. This more flexible identity functioned to allow her to live a more independent life. However, this emerging independent identity functioned best when she was not in her sister's company. When with her sister they would fall into old mutual roles where her sense of strength was obscured by a sense of helplessness and frustration. It took time for her to apply her more flexible sense of herself to a number of specific situations. Her insight, even though she lost the full impact of it, became rooted enough to serve as a reference point by which new skills could be learned in specific situations. So she had to learn the nuances of things like 'Where is my strength when my sister flatters me?' or 'When do I sometimes allow dependence on her?' The moral of the story?

Liberating self-insights can occur generally, but do not always function locally. Or as the Zen idiom says: 'Where is your Zen when you tie your shoelace?'

Ikkyu, a Zen master of the fifteenth century, was uncompromising in his demonstration of freedom, metaphorical homelessness, no place to stand. He vociferously rebelled against the Zen institutions of his day, calling his brethren 'phoney monks in cow skirts'. When Ikkyu's Zen teacher was asked who his successor would be, he referred to Ikkyu by saying, 'It will be the mad one.' It could be said that he did not fit in. There are numerous indications in his utterances and deeds that he represented the essential emptiness of self and world. However, it was only when he was seventy-seven and settled down with his blind lover who was in her late thirties, that there are indications that he significantly integrated his freedom with the specific complexities of leading an interpersonally confirmed life. Towards the end of his life, Ikkyu commissioned a portrait of himself which indicates something of this integration. He is painted in a grey, empty circle denoting the essential emptiness of things, while his lover, Lady Shin, is dressed in professional finery and playing her musical instrument. This vignette should not be taken to value either absolute or relative values over each other, but rather raises the possibility that experiences of emptiness of self can remain dissociated from the world of form and mutual definition.

After a deep enlightenment experience Hakuin attempted to have his experience confirmed by a well-known Zen master, Dokyo Etan. In answer to a well-known koan from Dokyo, Hakuin responded, 'In Joshu's *mu* there is no place to put hands or feet.' Fair enough – swallowed the river. Dokyo immediately grabbed Hakuin's nose, gave it a good twist, and laughed saying: 'I found some place to put hands and feet.' Dokyo then continued to give him a hard time to prod him out of his 'emptiness addiction'. The general point is that in human development and spiritual awakening, dissociation happens. It happens after achieving more flexible self-definitions in psychotherapy and it happens after experiences of no-self. So if such experiences are only part of the story of awakening what else do we need to consider?

What is Tacit Understanding?

The notion of 'tacit understanding' is explored in order to indicate a form of functioning by which an insight or learning has been integrated into a person's everyday thoughts, feelings and actions. Philosophers such as Michael Polanyi (1996) and Hubert Dreyfus (1972) have penetrated deeply into how we learn very specific things like riding a bicycle or playing chess. Although different terms are used such as tacit knowledge, intuition, and implicit understanding, such authors are concerned with the application or functioning of knowledge in our everyday lives. In this vision we are not disengaged cognitive beings who have learned the rules of operating and then apply this to concrete situations in a pre-given world. We are seldom that separate or knowing-in-advance. Also, the world is seldom something objectively there, independent of how we reveal it.

In this regard Merleau-Ponty (1962) has indicated how we belong to the things we learn and how knowing is only one productive phase in which we distance ourselves from something in order to find a new relationship to it. For example, in learning how to relate to an elephant, what is it enough to know? The most fundamental things are taken for granted – that we share space, move with gravity, and have outsides and insides. In a certain sense, we belong together. As we learn about elephants, we learn helpful details such as when they need to eat and sleep. We develop discrete bits of information about them. But ultimately no amount of learning these discrete bits of information is sufficient for learning how to relate to an elephant. This is because, as Merleau-Ponty noted, perception and understanding are not based on our capacity for picking up rules but rather, on ongoing participation in which constant living adjustments are made, often before they are understood. We learn as participants, and the known (as approximate style rather than definitive bits of information) is in constant dialogue with the surprise and unknowingness of perception and participation. So what are the implications of this for liberating self-insight? Just this: that an experience of liberating self-insight does not necessarily function in specific situations, and that although a liberating focus has occurred, it may not yet belong or be tacit to a person's complex functioning in everyday living.

In noting five stages of skill acquisition, Dreyfus and Dreyfus (1986) write about the level of expertise in which we are intimately familiar with a situation where the specifics of the situation is tacitly informed by a background context of understanding that operates spontaneously without us having to remember or be conscious of the principle on which it is based. As they so succinctly put it: 'We seldom "choose our words" or "place our feet" we simply talk and walk' (Dreyfus and Dreyfus 1986: 32).

In psychotherapy, Shirley experienced a number of self-insights in which she understood that a deep sense of mistrust of others had been necessary when she was growing up, but was not necessary in her present life. This was a relief for her, and her sense of personal identity was experienced in a more complex way than previously. This more complex personal identity allowed her to become much more inviting of interpersonal relationships. However, it took time for her new understanding to become tacit and to function in a more open way without effort and conscious choice. She knew that such tacit understanding had begun to occur when, for the first time, she allowed someone else to see the level of her distress by weeping. This had not occurred for many years and when it happened with her boyfriend, she later realised that her body was beginning to respond organically and naturally to situations of trust without requiring much conscious processing.

This level of tacit response reflects a level of understanding that Eugene Gendlin (1962) calls a 'felt sense'. He uses this term to indicate a preconceptual understanding of one's specific experience that functions intelligibly. Such tacit understanding is felt, is there as a whole, and provides an intelligible referent for thinking about, feeling about, and acting from.

When Zen masters demonstrate tacit understanding of no-self, it can look really crazy – since it happens spontaneously, preconceptually. In retrospect, however, one can reflectively lift out the nature of the insight that was demonstrated.

Fuke, a Zen fool who was a contemporary of Rinzai, used to:

roam the streets ringing a bell and crying out: 'When it comes in brightness, I hit the brightness. When it comes in darkness, I hit the darkness. When it comes from all directions, I hit like a whirlwind, and when it comes out of the blue, I flail it'.

Hearing this, Rinzai instructed one of his monks to grab Fuke and demand, 'If it does not come in any of these ways, what then?'

The monk did as he was bid. But Fuke only wriggled out of his grasp and said, 'Tomorrow there's a nice free lunch at the Monastery of Great Compassion.'

When the monk returned and told Rinzai what had happened, Rinzai said, 'I was always intrigued by that guy.'
(Besserman and Steger, 1991: 35)

In responding to the monk's challenge, Fuke does not hesitate by trying to formulate or remember the insight in general. Rather, out of tacit understanding an answer comes which is transparent to a number of the implications of no-self – such as present-centredness, flexibility, great creativity, and inclusive love. Fuke responds from his 'felt sense' of all of this without necessarily taking time to 'know it' in an explicit way. In Fuke's case, the liberating self-insight of no-self appears to have become tacit and is trusted as a source of action.

INTEGRATION: THE TRANSCENDENT FUNCTION

Let me return to the title of this paper: how does liberating self-insight become tacit understanding?

In liberating self-insight, the context for one's personal identity broadens, and in the case of Zen enlightenment experiences, no-self is hit. Such shifts in personal identity may be sudden and contain a new holistic reference point for living. However, working out the implications for living in specific situations is more gradual, and requires time and refinement.

The sudden and the gradual need to converse; a creative tension is set up in which the general nature of the new position meets the specific nature of complex situations. Carl Jung referred to this process as the workings of the transcendent function. Although this term has been shown to be problematic (Dehing, 1993), the phenomenon of which Jung was writing is instructive. In Jung's view, there is a creative tension that can occur between divided parts of our functioning, and there appears to be a pull towards harmonising or integrating these divisions. So in the process of psychotherapy, a person eventually finds a way to 'walk their talk'. When this has happened sufficiently and becomes tacit understanding, the 'walk needs little talk'.

To illustrate, John had a series of dreams in psychotherapy in which he saw himself in a divided way – as a 'good guy' that represented his public face and as a 'bad guy', of whom he was ashamed and who lurked in the shadows. The 'good guy' was only able to function at the cost of great self-vigilance and lack of spontaneity. The dream of his divided selves initiated a creative tension in which the divisions 'stuck in his throat', demanding some kind of reconciliation. He could no longer simply pursue one side of himself, even though it seemed socially safer to do so.

A resolution began to occur, first as a liberating self-insight and then, more gradually, as tacit understanding. The liberating self-insight occurred suddenly in a further dream in which he saw his 'bad' self as merely 'instinctual' rather than 'bad'. This helped him to separate the phenomenon from the judgement. Tacit understanding grew gradually, as he found ways to enact a more complex self-image that was both social and instinctual. In the beginning he noticed that he would err on one side or the other. But by bumping his insight against specific life situations in actual encounters, he became less and less preoccupied with the implications of his insight. His new identity was an 'and' rather than an 'either/or'.

In the case of spiritual awakening, the creative tension can initially be very strong – like a leaden ball which can be neither swallowed nor spat out. The tension is between the ahistorical and the historical, the personal and the impersonal, the absolute and relative, all time and just-this-moment. And can such integration ever be complete? In the Zen tradition, there are many stories which will illustrate the drama of comfortably harmonising emptiness with form. In this area, the term 'harmony' is better than 'integration' as one is not trying to achieve a simple synthesis but rather a plurality which is co-dependently supportive.

What does comfortably exchanging this moment with emptiness look like? Again, it can look pretty crazy:

> One day when Tanka came to visit Pang in his cave, the Layman (Pang) didn't get up from his seat. Tanka raised his fly whisk, symbol of the Zen master's authority. Pang raised his wooden hammer.
>
> 'Just this or is there something else?' Tanka asked.
>
> 'Seeing you this time is not the same as seeing you before,' said Pang.
>
> 'Go and belittle my reputation as you please,' said Tanka.
>
> 'A little while ago, you were bested by my daughter,' replied the Layman.
>
> 'If that's so, then you've shut me up,' Tanka said.
>
> 'You're dumb because of your intrinsic nature and now you inflict me with dumbness.'
>
> Tanka threw down his fly whisk and left.
>
> 'Master Tanka! Master Tanka!' Pang called after him.
>
> Tanka did not look back.

'Now he's come down not only with dumbness, but with deafness too!' said the Layman.

(Besserman and Steger, 1991: 19)

So how does liberating self-insight become tacit understanding? In the case of psychotherapeutic development, new, less fixed possibilities for self are seen and serve as a helpful reference. The reference may be held as a symbol, metaphor or self-image and is enacted in different complex situations. Over time it comes to function skilfully and naturally without much thought. In the case of spiritual awakening, no-self is experienced and also serves as a helpful reference. However, the reference can never be held absolutely and one learns in specific complex situations to sustain the implications of enacting the unity of emptiness and love – groundless context and this care-ful moment. This enactment never ends, and tacit understanding and liberating self-insight become an ongoing dance of closeness and distance.

14

Licking Honey From the Razor's Edge

Maura Sills

(Co-authored with Judy Lown for publication)

Psychotherapy is changing in the West. Just as there are many different kinds of Buddhism around, there is a variety of kinds of psychotherapy including several which are informed by Buddhist practice and principles. The particular flavour of Core Process training is very much founded on the transformative nature of awareness. The fundamental exploration that we have been undertaking at the Karuna Institute over many years grows from the question: 'Could we turn a one-person practice based on awareness into a two-person practice or group practice?' In other words, how can we express the fundamental practice of mindfulness within the therapeutic encounter? That has been both the challenge and the opportunity.

The phrase in the title, 'Licking Honey from the Razor's Edge' comes from a student who offered it as an example of what we are trying to do at the Karuna Institute. For me, it gave rise to an image of trying to get the honey without cutting my tongue. There is an edge, so, you cannot get the honey without cutting your tongue. It's bloody honey. The fruits of the practice, when working psychotherapeutically, involve opening to another's suffering and anguish. Licking honey from the razor's edge is a very appropriate description of what is called for from the Buddhist-oriented practitioner in Core Process psychotherapy. It calls for a very personal challenge of being affected, of being involved, of being engaged, of being available. In particular, the call is to be available in relationship. This approach to psychotherapy is centrally based on an experiential belief in relationship. If we don't believe in relationship this particular form of psychotherapy is not actually going to be possible.

This kind of contemporary contemplative approach is not based on the old traditions of psychotherapy in the West. It can be informed and enriched by an exchange with the different psychotherapy traditions but it is important to emphasise that what I am describing is not psychoanalysis. We respect the other traditions but Core Process work is based on a completely different set of premises. The practice may sometimes look exactly the same but what is actually happening inside the experience makes the therapy different. This is particularly so for the therapist.

One of the fundamental premises of Buddhist principles and practice is that we are not separate and discrete as human beings. At the physical level, of course, our bodies are separate and discrete from each other. But at subtle and complex spiritual levels we are neither discrete nor separate: we are interrelating and intercommunicating at many levels all the time. These communications and interconnections, together with the complexity of the dynamics that arise from one person's experiences or actions, influence the whole field in which that person exists. The field in psychotherapy can quite often just be seen as the one-to-one field of sitting in a room in a rather narcissistic manner working at the problems of the individual. From a Buddhist perspective, however, the field is much wider than that particular one-to-one field. Even in this setting, where there are just two individuals, the therapist will be intending to hold a larger experiential picture of what actually may be implicate. This means being open to what may just be emerging from being in that place, at that time, with that person, with yourself, with all of your histories coming into that moment. It includes all your relatives who are in the room and all of your ancestors who are knocking on the door. It means being open to a whole archetypal or collective level of experience and, beyond that, to the spiritual dimensions of wise mind that are also arising – in fact, co-arising – in the moment.

So, although the one-to-one psychotherapeutic relationship can look quite narrow, reductive, narcissistic and particular, whilst being all those things it is also more than all of those things. From an ethical point of view, a Buddhist-based psychotherapy needs to be open to the consequences of all of our actions. In the West, especially with our industrious and over-focused tendencies, we tend to think that ethics have to do with judgement. Ethics that are grounded in a Buddhist perspective are nothing to do with either judgement or interpretation. The intention is not to grasp what is going on, but to develop an openness to receiving the information that is arising with an acknowledgement of all of our limitations and all our reductions of capacity.

Contemplative psychotherapy, therefore, includes an experiential agreement that whilst working with the reductive aspects of psychotherapy these are being held within a larger truth where there is no separation or discreteness between us. There is a recognition that of course our psychohistories, our pasts, condition our experience. This conditioning creates strategies and patterns of behaviour. We also recognise, though, that there is a quality in human beings which is inherently awake. This is the core of our being which is not conditioned nor influenced by this driven quality of personality – of 'I', 'me' and 'mine'.

Buddhism teaches that there are three factors of existence, three things that tell us we are alive. One is unsatisfactoriness. Was breakfast satisfactory? It could have been better. It was perfect but I ate too much. Was my digestion satisfactory? Our lives are continuously marked by anguish and uncertainty and these are frequent themes in psychotherapy. Another factor is impermanence. This is pivotal in Buddhist psychotherapy as most people present themselves because they feel stuck in something they think will never stop, or in what they think is the problem or the issue. If we actually paid attention to, for example, unhappiness, we would find that the moments that someone is unhappy are probably fewer than the moments that they are not because it does not continue. It actually arises and passes. It comes and goes; just as these words will arise and pass away. Even those of us who are Buddhists find it very challenging to actually let go of the imagined continuity of self. This imagined continuity of self is driven by our need to propel ourselves into the next moment of existence. As therapists we need to bring skilful means to address this factor of impermanence – and the forces which pull us away from its recognition – within ourselves and within the therapy.

The third sign of existence is the absence of self. The absence of self creates particular difficulties for a Buddhist psychotherapist. The intention of Buddhist practice is to let go of self-view and self-construct. Self is seen as impermanent and illusory.

Psychotherapy is about the actualised self or, at least, the good-enough self. It is about reframing our self-constructs, not about the emptiness of the self. So in a Buddhist psychotherapy the middle ground is where the self is seen and experienced as a process, where these processes need to be attended to and where these may even be a resource within the larger context of the selfless. In essence, you must have a clear foundation and sense of self in order to explore its emptiness.

Other premises which are central to contemplative psycho-therapy come from the Four Noble Truths. Stephen Batchelor has described these as 'Ennobling Truths' in that they are things to be acted on, not to be understood.[1] One of the greatest difficulties in working with Westerners is that they believe that because they have a concept of something they know it. A con-cept is not the truth, it is not experience. A concept can be helpful. It can point us to some enquiry. If I have a concept of spaciousness that is very helpful because it is there in my psyche wandering around. But if I don't have an experience of spacious-ness, of openness, then it is not alive, it is not real. Concepts probably have to be challenged far more within the Western psyche than in the psyches of other cultures. This is because Westerners tend to believe that cognitive understanding and con-ceptual awareness constitute reality. They also hold very firmly to these traditions. So any psychotherapy that is about experience and about direct enquiry through awareness has got, not only to include and embrace, but move beyond concepts. So this particular form of psychotherapy is a challenge to become aware of the actual moment of experience, not just conceptually but experientially, at subtle and more complex levels.

What makes a Buddhist psychotherapy practitioner different from other practitioners is intentionality. When one is working through enquiry into the nature of how things are in the moment there has to be an intention to be aware. This means just allowing awareness – full stop. If it was easy for people to be aware, to experience witness-consciousness, we wouldn't have so many clients. It is not easy to allow awareness, to live without defend-ing ourselves from the possibilities of the impacts of experience. So the therapist has the larger intention of pure awareness, of direct experience, of direct perception. Of course, our capacity for awareness fluctuates. This personal capacity has its limits. So for the therapist the practice becomes, to some extent, an intention to be aware of the obscurations of awareness. For example, if I'm sitting in a conference with a lot of people and in a moment of quietness see if I can become aware of what it is that holds me separate and slightly away from the impact of the gathering, the first thing that might come to me is how over-whelming it would be if I was just to be aware in this very minute of everybody's experience. I don't think I could cope. The thera-pist's obligation is to work systematically at seeing what obscures pure perception in the moment. We discover that what obscures can be our own histories, those issues which get restimulated in therapy, our difficulty in receiving things, our likes and dislikes, what is good to hear, what isn't good to hear. Our agendas can distort what is going on. We can get attached to feeling good about ourselves; our ego as a psychotherapist, our role and our position can all have an impact.

We all have a fluctuating capacity for awareness. I can have reactions that limit my awareness; I can have responses to my experience of the impact of the other and the situation; I can also occasionally be resonant. The message is there. I might not have the words to go with the message. There are 'three r's' in therapy: reaction, response and resonance. Therapists are working diligently, even when they look quite passive, at what keeps them away from just being open to this moment, what keeps them away from just receiving you, just now. That is the work. We might think 'Is that all it is?', but we know from sitting in meditation practice how much attention and effort this takes. What keeps me away from full openness, from embracing the wholeness of this potential moment? This is also how it is for the therapist sitting with the client in therapy.

Intentionality, therefore, can give us some sort of awareness at that point in time of our capacity for inclusiveness. What are we cutting out? What are we not paying attention to? These might take the appearance of external things or could be things which we find it difficult to be with, to befriend, to be available for, in our own responses and inner reactions. This of course will limit the movement towards wholeness, and the primary purpose of psychotherapy is a movement toward wholeness. This could also be applied to a spiritual practice. If there is any agenda at all in Core Process work it concerns that growing edge of expansion. The therapist intends to accept more and more experience within the moment. Expanded awareness includes what comes from the past, what comes from the moment and what comes from a larger picture.

Although psychotherapy has mainly emerged in the West and carries with it certain limitations, it can also be a response to

Buddha Dharma. It can be a particular response to how to embody, how to work with Buddha Dharma in the West. The Western psyche has specific needs and this can be seen in terms of spiritual process. By this I mean a way of looking into the way things are with an open heart and an open mind. This requires being available to the impact of that, to be affected by that. The underlying premises of particular spiritual practice inform the intentionality of the Buddhist psychotherapist and it is this that makes the work different from some other forms of psychotherapy. This is not to say one is right and one is wrong, but it is important to see what distinguishes this form from others.

Two other factors which are extremely important in this work are the factors of energy and effort. These, of course, are central to awakening. Without energy the best intention in the world will not be fuelled. There are many different levels of energy from very subtle forms of energy through to the personal resources of the therapist and the client. The therapist needs to have the energy to give life to the intention to be fully present and open to the client's experience and to what arises in the therapeutic relationship. This takes resourcing physically, emotionally and spiritually. It requires therapists to know where they are resourced and in what way they are resourced. As a Buddhist psychotherapist a lot of the resources may indeed come from Buddha Dharma: from spiritual practice. I see meditation as absolutely essential for Buddhist psychotherapy practitioners. I could not practise as a Buddhist psychotherapist without a sitting practice. That is one of the resources. It is the ground for entering into places in relationship with clients that can be deeply challenging.

Effort is equally important. Right effort is not a formula. It is not a matter of wilfully or forcefully making right effort to get the energy together to have this good intention. It does not arise separately: it co-arises. It is the same quality of effort that one can bring compassionately to one's own practice when we are having difficulty in initiating this process. So, pivotal to Buddhist psychotherapy is making effort, finding the resources and holding the intention to meet the person and the experience as fully as possible with as much of yourself available as possible.

How we resource ourselves as therapists is our responsibility. It is my responsibility to resource myself. However, I believe that I cannot do that on my own because I am not discrete and separate. For help with resourcing myself I can come back to Buddha, Dharma and Sangha. I believe that we cannot do this work – or go through life's journey as spiritual enquirers –

without Sangha. Sangha is being with others, without assumptions about beliefs or positions, with an open mind and good heart to jointly enquire at a deep level. All of us have our own journeys, with their own challenges and efforts. It is this willingness to share our journeys that provides the resource of Sangha.

In their work with clients Buddhist psychotherapists are directly offering to co-journey with them through their psychological and developmental experience and through their spiritual experience, spiritual anguish, spiritual struggle. In order to do that, the therapist needs also to be open to the arising of compassion, which is, of course, one of the four Illimitables (Brahma Viharas). If we are open to how things are, compassion is a natural arising. We are just impelled. It just comes. We find that it is just there inside us, especially if we are open to another person's experience as if it were our own. It's very important to emphasise the need to know another's suffering, another's anguish, as if it were our own. If we can do this we are not one step removed. We are being fully available. We are being as close to that other's experience as possible. We do this through the whole field of relationship, based on a profound understanding of equality in terms of spiritual journey. The therapist is not the boss. There is a profound equality and integrity of relationship despite the apparent deficiency, need or disturbance of the client.

So, to be really open to equality in this meeting, the therapist is profoundly affected in how they hold the client's experience and in how they meet the person. There is no hiding behind the role as a psychotherapist. The therapist is not the expert, but only hoping that practice and preparation have prepared him to meet the client as authentically and with as much integrity as possible. The significance and the potential for healing, of knowing another's experience of suffering as if it were your own is that you are no longer separate from it. The experience is no longer 'over there'. It may actually be somewhere in the middle or it may actually be right here. Some of the things that we get to know might be right here, inside us. Some of them might be very familiar and some might be very challenging. For instance, we might find ourselves re-entering our own painful places, because the client's place is so close. How many of us would choose to go back into hell?

So it is a kind of affirmation that the very least you can do is to prevent the person from being alone in that place. You can perhaps be doing a lot more than that, but it is most important to allow self to be available to experience the other's suffering. It is also important, of course, to be available to experience the other person's joy and bliss. This is the hard edge. This is where the psychotherapist is really stretched. It is based on a belief that there is a part of us all – no matter how lost it gets, or how far away from it we move, or how obscured it is – that is already free and wholesome. This part of us is moving toward health. It is moving towards emptiness, and is not holding on to those notions of permanent self which believe that life can be fully happy, always happy and never stop being happy, and if we do something right and if we get something right we will *be* all right. This inclination towards emptiness, which arises naturally and leans towards health, is arising all the time. The difficulty, of course, is that because of our personalities and the driven quality we experience, we very seldom give ourselves the time and space to know it. But even within the most entangled and complex person's history and distress, health is continuing to try and express itself.

This way of working is based, then, on the transformative power of relationship. Obviously love is involved too. But there is a lot that practitioners need to be doing in the relationship. They need to be able to receive a lot and they have got to hold both that place of health and well-being – no matter how much it is just in potential – alongside all of the difficulty and the personal aspects of the person. So we are standing with one foot in each territory. They are not separate; it's just that we have separated these territories inside ourselves. We have split them off. So the psychotherapist has to hold the tension between being both absolutely open to receive and being with things on a personal level. As myself – Maura – can I allow myself, here and now, to be affected by the client and not just say 'that's a projection, that is not my stuff. I don't have to bother with that'. We don't have to take it all on as if it's all our fault and we're responsible, but once we have got it it's ours. To illustrate this, my husband, myself and my older daughter recently went out to China to adopt our new daughter and it felt like once we'd got her, she was ours. We are hers. You can try and get out of it in many ways but you can't. Once you have taken something in and on, it's yours.

So the transformative nature of the relationship is sometimes quite an imbalance because the therapist is doing most of the practice, but that will still have an effect on the situation. It will also have an effect on the therapist. So it's all practice. It's practice, practice, practice. Some people ask when I come out of the session, 'How was it?' Sometimes I say, 'It was easy practice, it was enjoyable practice' and sometimes I come out and say, 'It's hard practice, I don't know if I am up to this one. This is getting places in me that I am really struggling with.' It is practice in relationship.

The language of Buddhism helps us to understand about non-attachment. One of the questions that comes up most of all when I try to describe what is happening in a therapy session is to do with how attached or involved or affected the person is becoming. The first part of working with attachment is to feel it, to know it, to be with it, and to find a way of surviving it sometimes. The way to deal with attachment is not to stop loving anyone ever again. There is something about opening one's heart to the other in a way which does become affected, attached, involved, entangled, engaged. That is part of the territory. That is part of being a human being in relationship. If we were only to go the route of the solely personal, we would continue perhaps to be entangled and confused to the detriment of ourselves because we would not be holding the other within the larger picture. We would make something personal – we would tie it down through making it personal and holding on to it. So it is a case of being deeply affected and involved and even overwhelmed, overcome and incompetent. I've left sessions where I couldn't find a glimpse of my own good. At these times I might think that I would rather be doing something else. And sometimes it is amazing where your good gets re-established or contact with that which is healthy and whole gets re-established. For me, one of my greatest and dearest resources is my teenage daughter. I can come out of a workshop or a session on my knees and she will say, 'Oh, it's one of those again and now what you need me to say is that you are a good person. I love you. It will be all right in a few minutes. Sleep on it and in the morning it will be much better.' Reassurance comes from all sorts of sources.

Psychotherapy needs to be truthful. It needs to really take on the conditions of the world, the human psyche and consciousness. To do this, we need to reframe psychotherapy and we also have to reframe the notion of what and who a psychotherapist is. Issues of money and payment are part of this but we need to start by trying to reframe the notion of psychotherapist more openly as Dharma friend. A Dharma friend is usually seen as someone who helps us in our search for reality and truthfulness. A Dharma friend offers companionship on the path of awakening, of coming in to the moment. Dharma friendship gives more of a flavour to this movement of the changing nature of psychotherapy. We need to try and shift the notion of the psychotherapist as being psychological, clinical and objective. The work is to bring us back into human kindness and human awareness and bring us back just into the challenge of human relationship.

ACKNOWLEDGEMENT

I would like to thank all my students and clients who have been involved in this work. I hope that in writing about the subject I in no way do any disservice to the actual relationships I have had with them.

15

Zen: The Challenge to Dependency

John Crook

INTRODUCTION

The systems of meditative training in Buddhist texts are primarily intended for monastic practice by monks and nuns yet the great majority of Western practitioners are not home leavers and remain deeply embedded in family and work relationships. Not only are they untutored in the basic skills of monastic life but they are products of a very different system of personal expectations, family ethics and social relations from either the ancient or modern extended families of the Eastern worlds. The anxieties, forms of distress, alienation and extremes of low and high self-esteem which produce the individualistic Western personality are specific to a particular world culture. To seek enlightenment from so contrasting a base requires a prior assessment of the meaning of Buddhist practice within this culture. In my view many errors of judgement have been made both by Westerners and by Eastern teachers in this area.[1] A major question, which I approach in this text, hinges on the relationship between Buddhism and self-knowledge as experienced and expressed by Westerners themselves. How are these two systems of understanding to be brought together? A particular issue concerns the psychological stance of individuals raised under the influence of typical Western families.

SELF AS DEPENDENCY

In the early sermon of the Buddha on the Four Noble Truths he stated that the universal nature of human suffering was dependent upon an addictive grasping that is the result of not-seeing or ignorance (*avidya*). Most of the Buddhist literature discusses this addictive grasping in terms of the holding on to particular sensations, likes, preferences. Even so, in the Mahasathipatthana Sutta, the Buddha makes clear that the practice of mindfulness extends all the way up from such matters as breathing sensations to interactions with others, attitudes and feelings in a social world.

Today, few Buddhist practitioners in the West are monks and our prime psychological difficulties lie in the context of our personal relations with others of which those with the opposite gender are commonly the most painful. It is important therefore to see how the Buddha and later masters might have approached this issue. There are in fact important parallels between some contemporary psychotherapeutic perspectives and the ancient approaches: this is perhaps particularly apparent in Zen, which indeed proclaims itself to be in any case a matter of everyday life.

Dependency has become a key word in important areas of contemporary psychotherapy. It connotes a lack of personal freedom in relation to another, either living and present or a past figure in a person's life, whose influence remains paramount and often unconsciously affects current relations with others. Dependency implies addiction: there is a bond, or better a bind, here that cannot be laid aside and the influence of which penetrates deeply into personal feeling, attitudes and actions. Addiction takes the form of a continuous or repetitive grasping for a particular object or mind state: to abandon the object of addiction is for many almost unthinkable and any threat to the bond-bind resisted or suppressed.

A prime psychotherapeutic concern as become focused on difficulties experienced by carers of those suffering from chemical addiction, especially alcohol. Such persons, being addicted to certain patterns of behaviour perceived as caring, are known as 'co-dependents'. The addiction here is not to alcohol itself but to behaviours felt to be appropriate or necessary in dealing with the addicted relative. Essentially these patterns are coping skills developed in situations of often continuous low level stress. The phenomenon is now known to be widespread and not limited to caring situations specifically concerned with alcoholism but found in many situations where life in family or professional circumstances means exposure to oppressive interpersonal rules and the suppression of feelings which are not allowed either expression or discussion. The dependency on matching others' requirements for attention becomes socially tolerated, indeed socially infectious, and the negative results remain unnoticed so that the problem spreads within whatever institution it affects.

Emotional dependents become so focused on the activities of others, their health, their approval, their control or punishment, that they come to feel their own being to have little meaning. Any meaning attributed to themselves comes from outside and their relationships are such that their clinging cannot be freed from the clung to. Personal boundaries become so weak that psychological invasion becomes inevitable, the emotionally dependent quickly responding like appropriating mirrors to the responses of others. To sustain their dependencies they are forever trying to manage the impressions they make on others and become cleverly sensitive to others' moods and adapt to meet them. The low self-esteem and insecurity associated with these habits leads to depression and the consequent induction of further dependency on others who may again respond as carers rather than as curers.

Behaviour such as this may appear in a range of mild to severe forms. In particular the widespread distribution of the milder versions suggests that most carers, including professionals, may be suspected of being to a degree caught in the very process they attempt to cure in others. This often becomes very apparent in the therapy of caring personnel. Psychotherapists, psychiatrists, counsellors, pastors and nurses may often be affected unknowingly. Whitfield indeed argues that the 'untreated professional' virtually characterises the staff of caring institutions and may be sustaining the malfunction of those they treat.[2]

While social conditions may sometimes precipitate dependencies of this type, one can usually trace the origins in a given individual to emotional dependencies in the family of childhood. In fact we need to admit that to varying degrees all of us suffer from aspects of familial dependency and that our lives are largely shaped by this. For example, where a little girl responds to her father's hidden wish for a son by developing an addiction to intellectual brilliance, she emerges as an adult forever demonstrating her cleverness and suffers when she is unable to do this or fails to do so. A boy with an anxious mother may respond by attempting at every turn to reduce her anxieties, perhaps wrongly thinking she is primarily anxious about him. Such a lad emerges as an adult who in perpetually trying to reduce his anxiety about the worries of women friends can never actually present his own feelings to them. Repeated failures of this kind lead downwards into depression. There are literally hundreds of subtly varying scenarios resembling these themes in all of which we spend our time not being ourselves but attempting to fit in with another's predilections, whether that person be alive or long dead; the pattern is freshly represented in new relationships.

Perhaps we can understand the Buddha's own life in such a perspective. His father was desperately anxious that his son would become a great king so that the boy was subjected to an extremely narrow and restrictive education which also allowed him every sort of possible indulgence. The intelligent lad, however, began to wonder about the meaning of his curious life. Faced with discovering that which had been hidden from him, the facts of sickness, death and the possibility of salvation offered by the religious life, he abandoned his home doubtless to the great distress of all. Suffering from the guilt so entailed he put himself through every sort of extreme asceticism until, realising he was killing himself, he called a halt. His passionate need for a resolution of the guilt he experienced due to his desertion of his family may have driven his enquiry into what constrained the sense of freedom he intuitively knew must exist. In this quest he discovered a new method of meditation; rather than inducing trancelike *samadhi* he focused on the accurate observation of the actual state of mind he was enduring from moment to moment. It was doubtless this extremely precise self-observation that led to his breakthrough. The verse in which this is expressed in *The Dhammapada*[3] reveals a breaking out of a structure of thought and behaviour rather than some kind of ecstasy. His was an insight into how things were and the consequent joy in an essentially simple freedom.

> O housebuilder! You have now been seen.
> You shall build the house no longer.
> All your rafters have been broken,
> Your ridgepole shattered.
> My mind has attained unconditional freedom.
> Achieved is the end of craving.

The housebuilder is the self held together by the ridgepoles and rafters of dependency. In dropping addiction to these tendencies and concerns he 'saw the nature' of his being in the world and all that that was then to entail. But what was it that he so clearly saw?

Contemporary psychological understanding tells us that the patterns of behaviour that express individual 'character' emerge in the infant as a consequence of interactions between the carer, usually the parents, and the baby. Babies come into the world as extremely immature mammals, physically they are totally dependent on immediate and full-time care. Freud argued that the first experiences of total attention at the breast become the roots of a primary narcissism in which the infant feels itself to be the focus of all attention. As this gratifying state becomes challenged in interactions which necessarily require a give and take with the needs of the carer, the baby's disappointment, frustration and gradual need to become separate leads to patterned reactions that express specific responses to the patterns of behaviour of the mother. These patterns congeal progressively into a way of life designed to cope with the pressurising, often oppressive and occasionally abusive, needs of the carer; the free expression of a naturally supported self is twisted by the need to compromise personal growth to sustain inevitable dependency upon the ways of the carer. A 'false self' is thereby generated which continues its habitual reactivity in later situations of intimacy in later life. These are the basic roots of distress which, because we cannot see through them to their meaning and origin, endlessly iterate in the production of suffering – not only for the performer but also for those for whom he/she performs. Mark Epstein[4] argues that these patterns usually take one of two forms – exaggerating personal grandiosity or the denial of negative feeling.

In gaining a clear insight into his false self and its implications the Buddha became witness to the cognitive relativity of the 'ego' empty of any inherent existence. Subsequently, either he or a later practitioner also saw that all components of the self-process are likewise empty. It was not so much a discovery of something new, for emptiness does not exist in itself, but is rather the nature of any object to which the mind attaches. It is a recognition of the pre-existent groundlessness of being that underlies all the reactivity of becoming. Such realisation destroys the hold of the false self thereby allowing 'freedom' from previous constraint. It is important to know that Buddhist practice takes one nowhere except into this freedom.

Epstein points out that the meaning of the Buddha's enlighten-ment is often misperceived as the ego latches on to some theme or idea that enables its basic dependency to continue. He lists four such misapprehensions:

1. Selflessness is conceived as a sort of orgasmic potency, an unreflective spontaneity of the sort encouraged by primal scream therapy or Reichian ideas. While these therapies doubtless help many, their outcome is not to be confused with enlightenment.
2. Loss of self is seen as a merging with a void or some oceanic condition. Again such experiences are valued aspects of one-pointed concentration in meditation but they do not constitute enlightenment. At worst the practitioner becomes addicted to specific states which are sought again and again.
3. Some theoretical idea is idealised as an ultimate state and sought for intellectually as an ideal. Such a pursuit can of course never realise its objective.
4. An individual acting as a teacher is romantically seen as a representative of an ideal state. Uncritical devotion to such a guru allows so close an identification that the addict is literally invaded by the guru's mind and ceases to be independent. Such a situation can lead to all sorts of abuse and then resentment as the illusory adoration crashes. The same applies to addictions to particular institutions seen as presenting the ideal.

In all such examples the problem lies in substituting an imagined state of perfection for real mindful observation of how things actually are – concretely locking on to the Bodhi tree instead of seeing its basic emptiness and reflexivity with personal need.

ZEN PRACTICE AND THE NEEDS OF PRACTITIONERS

Work with Zen practitioners over twenty years has alerted me to the fact that participation in retreats and subsequent return to daily life tends to have a yo-yo-like momentum: exaltation with freedom followed by attrition and exhaustion. Although many individuals do show progressive alleviation of personal distress, the underlying cause of everyday exhaustion with consequent deadening of feeling and a sense of alienation is not easily uprooted. We need to realise that Zen is here a lay person's practice. Few practitioners are monks or undergo a monk's parallel training in a community. Unlike monks there is no underlying lifestyle which follows from a relinquishment of the householding life with family and business commitments. It follows that all the social conditions that support the false self are sustained beyond the walls of an occasional retreat. I am concerned therefore to introduce into Zen training practices that may aid in a more radical re-establishment of value in being. To this end the embedding of psychotherapeutic intervention within the context of retreat seems a possibly helpful option. This is however in no way an attempt to reduce Buddhism to psychotherapy but it is an acknowledgement of the ways in which the latter can help within the former.

There are already useful similarities between the treatment of hard-core emotional dependency and Zen practice. Co-dependents train within a twelve-step process derived from the work on chemical dependency. These steps involve a direct observation of one's actual condition and behaviour with an acknowledgement that life has become unmanageable: a fearless inventory of personal behaviour is constructed with acceptance of negativities and awareness of the addictive quality of one's behaviour. Direct attempts are made to make amends in life and the whole work is placed within the context of a belief in a higher power and its influence for good. Christians will favour God for this role but Buddhists have recourse to the Dharma, the Refuges and the Vows.

Similarly, Zen training involves parallel steps including a direct acknowledgement of how one is, however negative that may seem to be. One simply says 'yes' to the negativity and holds it in the frame of meditative awareness. The practitioner accepts his personal inadequacy and explores exactly how it is, allowing this to come into consciousness in bare attention. When the vision of oneself is perceived as a unified set of contrasting realities and accepted as such the point comes when, in a natural humility, the individual grasps the truth of 'false' existence and a curiously apophatic self-affirmation arises – not this, not that, just such as it is. Herein lies both acceptance and a new-found freedom. During retreat, individuals, with varying degrees of clarity, move towards this liberating insight. A powerful vehicle for this work is the Western Zen retreat in which I have combined the practice of meditative concentration in *zazen* with the communication exercise of Charles Berner.

THE WESTERN ZEN RETREAT

In Zen it is pointed out that attachment to quiet sitting, however, agreeable it may be, is a 'cave of demons', an addiction to tranquillity that must be broken up. The essential task of awareness is not trance or samadhic states but the perception of actuality directly. This means that in meditation one faces in various ways the actuality of existence. Contemplating the koans is one way of doing this.

The koans are paradoxical questions which cannot be answered but which can be resolved. The most basic are the Who questions. 'Who am I?' Of course, at one level one knows exactly who one is but, at another, one realises much is hidden from one. There are several contrasting ways of using koans but the modern method developed by Charles Berner and known as the 'communication exercise' is especially valuable for beginners and I use it as an introduction to Zen in Western Zen retreats at my centre in Wales.[5] It leads through a vigorous examination of personal illusions to an exhaustion of opinion and language in an immediate apprehension of 'just being'. Finding this essential base line of existence throws all other concerns into a realm of mere relativity and the grip they have on one's life relaxes. Recalibration of a practitioner's attitudes and action in life then becomes possible from a phenomenological base that lies outside opinion. Since it cannot come from another it is also a rediscovery of an essential self and the basis for renewed autonomy.

The communication exercise is done in groups that divide into couples (dyads) who sit together. Over a thirty- to forty-minute period a bell is rung every five minutes. In each five-minute period one of the partners asks the other his or her question which may be: 'Tell me who you are', 'Tell me what life is', 'Tell me what love is', 'Tell me what another is', 'Who is dragging this old corpse along?', 'What was your face like before your parents were born?' etc. Most beginners and many others use the Who am I? formulation. It is basic. The practitioner works with his or her question throughout the retreat unless a resolution appears. After each period the partners change over. The rules are that the one who is questioning never says anything other than the question, only asks it a few times and maintains an open, interested demeanour without expressions of encouragement or scepticism. The one who answers is encouraged to respond in whatever way most truly expresses his or her state of mind. This need not be by words alone. The answerer is however asked to sustain contact with the partner through frequent eye contact. The five-minute alternation imposes emotional discipline as each partner occupies in turn the complementary role to the other. The exercise is repeated over a period of at least three days which, in the case of the Western Zen retreat (five days) also includes exercise, meditative sitting (*zazen*), meals, walks and periods in which the group process is reviewed and personal interviews with the director take place.

Individuals usually spend many hours describing their various roles in life and their experiences in these roles. They then begin to express their feelings under a range of remembered conditions until some feeling is actually engendered in the present moment. To express that feeling, sadness, tears, joy, anguish, self-doubt directly is to give one's self unreservedly to the other in trust. This is especially difficult when feelings of guilt or shame are around and a practitioner may spend many hours fearfully and cunningly editing his responses to the question. Finally, unless the practitioner is severely blocked, he trusts enough to share. Such sharing rapidly becomes mutual and personal secrets of a lifetime's duration may be shared for the very first time with accompanying emotion.

It is a fact that the rehearsal of the past within the session does not have to be repeated once full expression has been given to it. It is as if the latent energy locked up in an issue has been released. The consequence is a sensation of increasing freedom and openness both of which probably relate to the rising levels of trust in the group. Often, however, the flow of expression finally dries up and there is a silence but no feeling of having resolved the question. This is called 'crossing the desert'. It requires sensitive reappraisal of all that has been said and maybe just silent musing and waiting. The role of the retreat director or 'master' is to interview practitioners and to interact with them in such a way as to facilitate their process. Naturally this requires considerable skill and imagination and the interviews often play a very important role in freeing individuals from stuck positions. The role cannot be undertaken by an untrained or an inappropriately trained person.

When the practitioner is fortunate, has managed to focus the question well and penetrated blockages, the result is a gradual or sudden awareness that he or she is everything that has been said and, since the negative energies associated with the themes of life have been ex-pressed, there is a glowing sense that what one is is indeed all right after all. There is a moment of relief and acceptance in which the question drops away. One 'knows' who one is in the same way that one 'knows' water only when one tastes it. Such a person may be very joyful and experience a number of states of consciousness that may be entirely new – a spacious clarity, bliss, love, emptiness; words which in truth have meaning only for those who have been to the same spaces.

Most of these experiences are moments of personal integration around a sense of total oneness with what one is. In Zen this is called the 'one man'.[6] Such work facilitates but cannot in itself produce the experience known as *satori* or *kensho* in which self-reference itself disappears so that, 'empty-headed', one simply regards the world as it is, unfiltered, all personal bias gone. Such an experience, usually felt to be of inestimable value, may be said to arise through 'grace' since any egoistic quest for it is inevitably bound to fail.

The experiencing of integration in these retreats has allowed many to return to their everyday life with a new-found inter-dependence rather than dependence on others. They become better able to hold their ground against the pressure of their own dependency habits. Not everything is achieved at once however: as in much work on the self it may be a slow, repetitive, grinding process. The fact that a very high percentage of people attending Western Zen retreats are from the helping professions under-scores the point that carers are themselves often dependents and that these professionals do little to help their members.

OPTIONS FOR PSYCHOTHERAPEUTIC INCLUSION WITHIN ZEN RETREATS

The Western Zen retreat illustrates the possibility of introducing procedures additional to *zazen* within a retreat with positive effects in freeing a participant from stuck positions arising from the 'false self'. I am about to begin experimenting with the intro-duction of other interventions which may also help participants in the same or similar ways. It is important to stress however that the return to *zazen* after each exercise remains a vital prerequisite for sustaining a Zen atmosphere of contemplative openness.

A number of possibilities are available. While psychothera-peutic interviews which take a long time are not appropriate in a group process, simple group exercises which can have consider-able power can be very useful. Among these, exercises in Gestalt work, fantasy, and sensitivity training seem good options and can be culled from sources in psychosynthesis and humanistic psychology generally. Gestalt exercises offer much and their use on retreat was tested out with Malcolm Parlett, a leading gestalt therapist, as co-leader this summer.

One approach that looks especially promising is the 'Order of Love', which British therapists have been learning about in the last few years. This group process has resemblances to psychodrama but its internal dynamics seem to draw on rather different resources in participants. The system is the invention of Bert Hellinger of Germany and has been presented several times recently in Britain by Hunter Beaumont and Judith Hemming. Apart from a translation of a Hellinger lecture in German[7] there is so far only a sketchy literature on this approach in English and no critical research nor a precise account of methods in practice. The writing suggests an intuitive visionary rather than an operator in conventional group psychology or counselling practice. Hellinger is adamant that he does not work from principles but from direct observation. He 'sees' what seems to enable love to flow and what prevents it. Although he says he is not interested in theory, the observer can see certain principles at work.

The 'Order of Love' refers to the re-ordering of affection, 'love', within the family scheme as held in the mind of a protagonist. The image is of a river of affection flowing through family members down through the generations the course of which has commonly become distorted in varying ways and with varying degrees of severity.

Individuals assemble in a group and, rather as in psychodrama, someone offers himself (to work) as a 'protagonist'. The group leader or director then asks a few questions about the family of which the protagonist is a member. The nature of the individual's concern and distress is revealed and he is then asked to choose individuals from the group, men representing men and women women, to take the position of family members: father, mother, sister, etc., on an arena. Family members are positioned by the protagonist in a way that represents their relationship – this uses two basic dimensions: distance between individuals and the direction in which they are faced. Once the family group is sculpted in these terms, the director asks the protagonist to sit and watch. The director then inquires from each of the statuesque figures how they are feeling.

Remarkably, the feelings of each individual commonly come very close to the feelings that the protagonist believes that family member to have. It seems as if positioning in this way after having heard the merest outline of the family dynamic is sufficient for participants in the 'constellation' to intuit a feeling in an often very heartfelt manner. Indeed this can be heavy stuff; an individual in a position may be close to tears or suffer pain or cramps within a few minutes of his or her placing.

The director now moves an individual nearer to or further from another and may invite that person to say a few words (as given by the director) to another. The result of the move is then tested and the feeling in the constellation assessed. Often quite a simple move causes a reshaping of feeling throughout the whole group. The creation of these moves requires a highly creative and intuitive grasp by the director of the processes involved and they are made according to the principles worked out by Hellinger from his own experiences in creating the process.

As the interactions continue the tensions in the constellation lessen and the contortions in the relations between the members are ironed out. When a flow of natural affection through the group is largely achieved the protagonist is asked to take his/her place once more within his own family. This is commonly a highly emotional moment or realisation for the protagonist. She now finds herself in a situation where love flows without distortion by jealousy, distrust, resentment or any other of the many means whereby it has been formerly blocked. The participant can thereby experience membership of a radically transformed family and feels herself supported by others and open to others in a way that may be radically new. Such an outcome is however not guaranteed. The pattern is remoulded as best as can be but situations that state an unworkable truth may have to be accepted and seen for what they are. Even so the working through is profoundly valuable and can lead on to further work in the same or other ways.

The principles observed in Hellinger's work imply that human families operate within an innate or archetypical structure through which the affection natural between generations flows: affection channelled in time through a system linking the generations. The core system is that of a husband and a wife where each respects the other as man and as woman and honours other influences, such as a previous marriage in the life of the partner, so that their mutual regard is free from distortion. Second relationships cannot replicate the first; they have their own characteristics which need acknowledgement. Similar core principles focusing on a free acknowledgement of basic emotion are suggested as determining the quality of parent-child relating and between other family members. Although Hellinger puts orthodox styles of relationship, marriage for example, in the forefront of this system, there seems to be no reason why other forms of partnering cannot be perceived in similar ways. The moves within the constellation and suggestions for words to be said are made by the director in accordance with these principles, which are of a basically simple nature affirming Hellinger's intuitions about how, where and when love can flow without impedance.

In my experience this is a powerful approach to unravelling knotted attitudes that are long-standing. One of its striking features is the way in which the presence of supporting figures, such as long-dead parents or grandparents, can radically transform the feeling of a key individual. The feeling of support coming down through time strengthens the identity and enables the expression of openness to another to arise. The locked-in self-referential feelings of resentment, jealousy, etc., are thereby opened up to a new experience of another.

Hellinger's emphasis on a flow of affection, distorted or not, through time is of great interest in a Buddhistic perspective for individuals are merely the commonly distorting vehicles for this flow. This is a way of expressing the effect of karmic influences determining the 'reincarnation' of emotion in succeeding generations. The re-ordering of love may make a profound difference to the outcome of contemplative practice on retreat.

What then is love? The Tibetans have two terms for what we call love and compassion. Love is 'the wish for others to be happy' and compassion 'the wish for others to be free from pain'.[8] It seems to me that both these terms imply empathy, on the one hand with those who are joyful and, on the other, with those who are sorrowful. Empathy necessarily underlies both 'wishes' and this is naturally the quality of a relationship between a man and a woman who are in open intimacy with one another. Similarly it qualifies the relation between parent and child. But empathy depends on the self being open whereas we have seen that the self as ego reacts defensively to all kinds of behaviour by others, beginning as we have seen in early infancy. Where defensive anger or distress is not relieved or resolved then secondary feelings such as resentment or jealousy can arise and become somatically embedded. These then are the distortions through which affection flows necessarily with difficulty and impediment.

There is much further work to be done before the implications of the Order of Love process can be fully understood. Participants commonly find the process mysterious but this is perhaps only because it works with deep unconscious motivations that operate with the emotions somatically as much as cognitively. To me it seems that even though untested, unresearched and by no means clearly understood, the process may offer much to psychotherapy not least as a component of work within Zen retreats.

CONCLUSION

I have been exploring ways by which Western self-knowledge as represented in social, psychological and psychotherapeutic theory may play a useful role in the Dharma project of the Buddha. In coming to the West, Buddhism has not yet fully taken on the quite profound differences between the monastic cultures of its origin and postmodern Western lay culture in its grand confusion. Since Western and Eastern cultures are now all in the same global melting pot it behoves both Western and Eastern Buddhists to seek a mutual understanding.

We began this chapter by showing that the Buddha's notion of the suffering self as addictively craving is mirrored in contemporary concern about addictive attachments to behaviour shown in dependencies on others. The pervasiveness of such attachments in contemporary society suggests that it is a root cause of much psychological suffering. Both the Buddha's view and contemporary social psychiatry are anchored in relatively simple models of mind that again reflect one another surprisingly well. The Buddha categorised mental functions perceived in self-reflective meditation as sensation, perception, cognition and a category called *sankhara*, karmic predispositions, that shape volition and determine action. They represent the acquired distortions or cognitive formations restricting openness that bedevil meditational practice as well as operating in everyday life. The implication is that through experiences of pain certain complexes arise which predetermine or underlie action, literarily a conditioning of past karma. The tendency to be dependent is, in this light, itself a consequence of some karmic predisposition allied to circumstances that trigger its appearance. Such a view resembles modern notions that childhood experiences set up emotionally toned habits of behaviour that lie as a bedrock of individual reactivity to circumstance. Both in Buddhism and in contemporary psychotherapy a prime intent is to recognise and transcend such behaviour rooted in embodied memories.

We have argued that in contemporary retreats for non-monastic practitioners a major barrier is the arising of conditioned stress brought into the retreat situation from everyday life. To ask such people to 'sit' without addressing these issues is in many cases counterproductive. In the Western Zen retreat the participant is enabled to contact others and to communicate feelings as they arise. I believe Charles Berner is right (see Note 5) to emphasise the importance of such communication as a means of freeing oneself from continual self-concern. In the Zen-Gestalt workshop, conducted jointly with Malcolm Parlett, we also found that a number of Gestalt exercises helped people free themselves thus enabling them to 'sit' with less difficulty and inner disturbance. We feel therefore that to enhance a retreat process by the addition of such contemporary 'preliminaries' is likely to prove generally beneficial.

Again, however, it is vital to make clear that no reduction of Zen to psychotherapy is intended here, nor do Zen retreats for experienced practitioners have to be constructed in this way. The exploration in Zen retreat characteristically goes beyond that of much psychotherapy. Far from simply readjusting ego-related behaviour to circumstances, Zen challenges the subject with the experiential non-existence of the self as an entity. To encounter the emptiness of selfhood in the mere flow[9] of being can be an alarming experience. Prior understanding of habitual responses and their progressive release clears the mind of self-concerning preoccupations thus enabling an entry, less shadowed by fear, into the more selfless realms of meditative practice. Such preliminaries help lay practitioners to travel more deeply in their quest that would otherwise be possible within the time limits of short retreats and, furthermore, have beneficial effects that carry over into everyday life and later retreats.

PART IV

PRACTICAL APPLICATIONS

Buddhist Psychotherapy or Buddhism as Psychotherapy?

David Brazier

THE THERAPY OF THE SPIRIT AND THE SPIRIT OF THERAPY

Psychotherapy has its roots in concern for the human spirit. There is a border region between therapy and spirituality.[1] It is in border regions of this kind that the most creative things generally happen. Many of the great innovators in the field of psychotherapy, like Freud, Jung, Rogers and Moreno,[2] were drawing on their knowledge of a Christian or Jewish spiritual tradition. New developments are less common in the heartland of a profession (whether this term is taken in its modern sense of salaried expertise or its older meaning of expressed faith). Interesting as the heartlands are to visit, I like to spend a good deal of time in the border regions, where the air is still fresh and bracing.

Historically, the creative borderland was in the region between psychotherapy and the Judaeo-Christian tradition. In some ways this was a legacy of the nineteenth-century struggle between science and religion. Psychotherapy grew out of an attempt to be scientific about the soul. Recently, however, a new border region has opened up with the arrival of a very different spiritual tradition in the West, a tradition with its roots in India and many of its branches and flowers in the extreme Orient. Buddhism offers a new contrast. For psychotherapy, the arrival of this new yet also ancient approach to the exploration of the spirit, is both a challenge and a stimulation.

Challenge can invigorate both parties. In this life nothing is achieved without some dukkha.[3] Some awkwardness is required. No grit, no pearl. There is much potential for both Buddhism and psychotherapy to gain in vitality through this encounter. The borderland can be an exciting place to work.

There are many different ways to profit from this opportunity. I will list some of the things that are currently going on in due course. Personally, it has always seemed important to me to ask questions about basic assumptions. Where there is a contrast between two different presentations of truth, then there may be a deeper unifying factor to be unearthed. The process of excavation, however, often unsettles the foundations of many more shallowly rooted dwellings and this can be unpopular. Thus the quest for truth can make one into a kind of heretic, an asker of awkward questions. It seems like a risk worth running. As I just said, no grit, no pearl.

Of course, the oyster makes the pearl in an effort to feel comfortable again. There is a constant dialectic going on between the attempt to get everything sorted out and smooth so that we feel comfortable and the effort to penetrate deeply into the meaning of discord. In the Zen tradition, there is a well-established idea that the truth should always disturb. There is a need both for those who act like grit and for those who try to turn the grit into nice smooth pearls. This is how a culture, whether Buddhist, scientific, humanist or whatever, is constructed. Many of the truly great beings, however, have not been seen as pearls until they were safely dead and buried.

Psychotherapy and Buddhism are two recent developments in Western culture. Psychotherapy is already becoming an established profession in Britain and in many Western countries. As it does so it establishes institutions which regulate practice and ensure that nobody does things that have not been approved by those who trained a long time ago. This acts as some brake on malpractice. It also makes the heartland of the profession a bit arid: a bit too smooth.

Similarly, Buddhism is becoming an established religion in Britain and in many Western countries. Already we see schools of this faith becoming established which are profoundly conservative in their way of operating. Too smooth. It would be a shame if Buddhism in the West became a stifling influence upon the creative human spirit.

In the border region between Buddhism and therapy, however, a great deal of very creative work is going on. I do not, in this paper, want to catalogue everything that is happening. There are plenty of other people willing to do that, I am sure. My primary interest is in asking questions about it. What is going on here?

SCOPE FOR INNOVATION: AN EXAMPLE

In his own day, the Buddha was a very innovative person. He created quite a stir. Young people left their families in droves to join his movement. Some people were very upset about it. Some were very inspired. Many changed their lives profoundly and began doing things they would never have dreamt of before. One thing we have to consider is whether what we need to do is to enshrine his innovations or to adopt his spirit of innovativeness.

Let us look for a moment at an example of twentieth-century innovation in the borders between psychotherapy and Buddhism. The example I have in mind is Morita therapy (Reynolds, 1976, 1984). This approach was developed in Japan in the early 1900s by Shoma Morita who was a Japanese psychiatrist. He brought together Buddhist philosophy and his personal clinical experience and a small dose of ideas from Western psychological medicine and put together a regimen which helped many of his patients to overcome their neurotic handicaps.

Morita therapy draws from the basic Buddhist analysis. The Buddha's concern was how to live with dukkha. We know the Buddha story. His mother died when he was born. He could never escape from this distressing knowledge however much he indulged his senses or mortified his body. We know how he was driven by his concern about dukkha. Like many of us, he found it terribly distressing that there is so much dukkha in the world – not just his own, but that of all beings. Yet he could not get away from it. He tried very hard. He went to the limits of self-indulgence, but that did not work. So he tried the opposite approach of mind over matter. If all suffering was experienced in the body, then perhaps getting mastery over the body would solve the problem. It did not. The Buddha finally faced facts. He declared that suffering is a part of life, a respectable reality – a 'Noble Truth'.

Of course, since then, many people have tried to tell us quite the opposite. We have learned that Buddhism eliminates dukkha:

that eliminating dukkha is what it is all about. I personally have not, however, met anybody who has eliminated dukkha and, I suggest, nor have you. The Buddha did not teach the elimination of dukkha. He taught the noble path of living constructively in a world in which dukkha is part and parcel of human existence. We may, if we wish, look for the elimination of dukkha in the life to come. For the purpose of living skilfully here and now, however, the task is to live constructively and compassionately in a world where dukkha is ever-present reality. By not closing our eyes to dukkha, we also avoid closing them to joy, bliss, love, compassion and all the positive experiences of beauty and truth.

This line of thinking is fundamental to Morita therapy. In Morita therapy there is no *direct* attempt to help the client to eliminate suffering or feel good. It is a principle of this approach that if the client thinks that suffering could be eliminated, this very thought will stand in his way. It will tempt him to think there is an easy way out.

What is done is to help the person to accept suffering and live constructively. Of course, when one does so, much suffering does evaporate of its own accord. If I stop doing self-destructive things, I do start to feel better on the whole. If I act in more constructive ways toward the people around me, some of this comes back to me and there is a fair chance that my life will become easier and more pleasant. There is, however, no one-on-one correspondence here, and if I only act constructively *in order to* feel better, I am likely to have many disappointments. The idea is to accept what one cannot change and do something about what one can change. In this regard, feelings are, in Morita therapy, classified as things one can do little about, whereas behaviour is something one can do a lot about.

Morita therapy, therefore, is, it seems to me, one application of basic Buddhist principles to the art of helping people and it leads to something which can be called a psychotherapy, but which is very different in many respects from the great majority of therapies practised in the West. Western therapies tend to give a pre-eminent position to the study of feelings. Is teaching the art of skilful living psychotherapy? This is an important question. Of course, the divide does not have to be unbridgeable. There are Western therapies which focus on behaviour rather than feelings and the Moritist analysis is not the only way of interpreting the Buddhist message. Morita has grown out of one aspect of Buddhist teaching. There are many other aspects which might be emphasised more by other practitioners. Nonetheless, Morita therapy is a therapy based on Buddhist principles and it is very different in many respects from the majority of Western approaches.

The practitioners of Morita therapy have gone to some lengths to distance what they are doing from its Buddhist roots. These are acknowledged, but as history rather than current affiliation. The development of Morita therapy could, therefore, be seen as a venture in taking a central part of Buddhist teaching and teaching it to people under the name of psychotherapy without much more than a passing reference to the fact that this is Buddhism. It could be seen as a kind of covert Buddhism. There are pros and cons to this covert approach. Many people are able to benefit in this way who might not be willing to approach a more overtly Buddhist setting. On the other hand, taking the teaching out of context may mean that the client/student can only proceed so far.

Then there is the question of culture. To what extent is it possible to extract (or alienate) Buddhist teaching from Buddhist culture? Buddhism is not simply a philosophy. It is a practice, or a collection of practices. Practice is always easier within a supportive culture. To some extent therapies like Morita have created their own culture with support groups and ongoing supervision of people who have accepted their approach. This is also true of other therapies. As Reynolds says, 'every psychotherapy offers a lifeway whether explicitly set out or not' (Reynolds, 1989: p.19).

WHAT IS GOING ON?

Morita therapy is just one example. A few years ago I wrote a paper called 'Is Buddhism a Therapy?' (Brazier, 1994) in which I argued that since Buddhism claims to cure or alleviate mental suffering, then it has to be considered to be a psychotherapy of some kind, whatever else it may also be. I also concluded, however, that if we allow that Buddhism is a psychotherapy, we also have to say that it is a very different one from those procedures which are generally called psychotherapies in the contemporary West.

For instance, well-being is not, from the Buddhist perspective, going to be achieved by strengthening the client's sense of entitlement, reinforcing their ego, encouraging them to express their anger more forcefully, nor giving transient feelings a privileged status in the person's decision-making process about life choices.

Nor is it going to be particularly served by researching their early life history, analysing their early relationships with parents, nor interpreting the transference of these patterns on to the therapist-client scenario. Again, from a Buddhist perspective well-being is likely to be enhanced by a variety of meditative practices, by deep moral reflection, by contrition for wrongs actually committed, by constructive gratuitous action, by simplifying one's lifestyle, by developing a sense of gratitude, by respect for parents and teachers and by keeping the higher purpose of life ever in mind. It is perfectly credible, of course, to say that these differences do not disqualify Buddhism from being a psychotherapy: they simply mean it is a different sort of therapy.

The preferred methods of Buddhist practice on the one hand and those of Western therapy on the other may not always be incompatible simply because they are different. Various permutations of eclectic integration are imaginable and some are being attempted. These developments are exciting and have much potential beyond what has so far been explored. They also challenge us to inquire into the underlying rationale to resolve what appear on the face of it to be differences of theory and principle. By doing so we move toward a principled integration rather than mere eclecticism. The idea that, whatever else it may be, Buddhism is also a psychotherapy, is, for instance, a central concept in the work of the Amida Trust (Brazier, 1995) where we are using the principles of Buddhist psychology as a basis for trying to achieve a principled integration of psychotherapeutic methods, drawing on both Eastern and Western sources.

Let us, therefore, briefly review what is actually going on. What is on the march in the borderland?

Well, first, there are the indigenously developed therapies in Buddhist countries, like the Morita and Naikan therapies in Japan, which rely upon Buddhist principles and methods. These, as already mentioned, tend to be quite strongly rooted in Buddhist principles yet to distance themselves from their roots in their public presentation in order to increase professional and public acceptance of their work and ideas.

Then, secondly, there is an increasing use of meditation, conscious breathing, mindfulness, movement, massage, and other 'techniques' of Buddhist origin by psychotherapists. This we may call 'technical eclecticism'. It is based on the idea that it is legitimate to use anything that works. Although much borrowing goes on all the time between different schools of psychology and spirituality, something essential does get changed in the transitional process. Meditation taught by a Zen master is not the same thing as meditation taught by an out-patient clinical psychologist. For a technique to make a genuine contribution to a therapeutic approach it has to be embedded in a value system which is consistent with the general tenor of that approach. When a technique is lifted out of one spiritual environment and employed in another, many changes of terminology and orientation are introduced so that the method in the new setting is substantially a new method. We can perhaps say, therefore, that the use of Buddhist methods in a non-Buddhist context is not Buddhism. On the other hand, there is no doubt that the dissemination of methods which are known to have a Buddhist pedigree into prestigious domains of our society such as medicine, does indirectly enhance the reputation of Buddhism and its acceptability to and standing with the public at large. This may contribute, in the longer run, to other people being able to benefit from a more undiluted exposure to Dharma.

Then, thirdly, there is the practice of psychotherapy by people who are practising Buddhists. This has often come about as a result of their search for a right livelihood. Initially, people may practise a completely Western style of psychotherapy as part of their search for a lifestyle compatible with Buddhist principles. In time, such people generally feel an imperative to make some effort to square their spiritual practice with their professional work and vice versa. They find that there are differences of underlying philosophy between their Buddhist faith and their psychological approach and this feels awkward. On the other hand, they have learned that a therapist does not try to impose their views upon the client. They therefore often experience some tension as they wonder how far they can legitimately go in introducing what they really believe into their practice with clients.

Then, fourthly, there is the creation of new psychotherapies in the West out of a cross-fertilisation of Buddhist and Western ideas. This is one possible response to the dilemma described in the last paragraph. Core Process psychotherapy would be a well-known example of what we are talking about here. Of course, there are many different ways of cross-fertilising Buddhism and Western psychology. There are numerous schools of psychology and numerous schools of Buddhism, so there are many permutations. More importantly, perhaps, such a process of creativity depends strongly upon the genius of the particular person who effects the innovation. There is a personal equation at work. All theory is, in some sense, autobiography.

Fifthly, there are now a number of experienced practitioners who have achieved a personal integration of Western skills within a framework of Buddhist principle. This is really the ultimate fruition of the process described in the paragraph before last. Such people tend simply to call themselves Buddhist psychotherapists, as though Buddhism were simply another school of psychotherapy.

Sixthly, there is the use and adaptation of therapeutic language, culture and form by Buddhist teachers as a medium by means of which to get their message across. Here we see Sogyal Rimpoche giving teachings which make a direct appeal to people engaged in bereavement counselling and hospice work (Sogyal, 1992). We see Akong Rimpoche (1987) rewriting tantric methods in language which is strongly influenced by Western humanistic psychological terminology. We see Thich Nhat Hanh integrating forms of group encounter into the life of his communities, talking about 'deep listening' and writing commentaries upon the basic Buddhist texts which present them as, in some degree, psychotherapeutic manuals.[4]

These are some of the things that are currently going on. All of them contribute in different ways to making aspects of Buddhist teaching accessible to groups of people – clients, students, professionals or the public at large – who might otherwise be difficult to reach. So is the development of Buddhist psychotherapy essentially an exercise in propagating Buddhism itself? Is this the real motive underlying the efforts of many people to bring therapy and Buddhism into closer association? We might also ask whether it is a successful strategy and whether it is likely to continue to be so. Is the liaison between Dharma and therapy to the advantage of both parties? Is this a marriage of principle or a marriage of convenience? Will it last?

Or, are these developments a way of watering down the Buddhist message and making it palatable to a public which is not impressed by some of the cultural baggage and even some of the doctrines of Buddhism seen as a fully fledged religion? Or again, is what is going on a kind of 'asset-stripping' in which psychotherapy is extracting the elements of Buddhism which seem practically useful and discarding what is left? Again, we may ask, is this process of cross-fertilisation benefiting psychotherapy as a whole or is it limited to the fringe populated by people who are actual Buddhist practitioners? How far does the dissemination of the Buddhist seed go? Who is seducing who?

Another related set of questions worth considering concerns

the question of advantage. Has the interaction between Buddhism and therapy been more to the advantage of one party or the other? Is there likely to be continuing advantage to both parties? Is this a phenomenon which will continue to flourish or is it nearing the end of its usefulness to one party or to the other? Can or should it be usefully sustained?

There is no doubt that for a psychotherapy training programme to be overtly Buddhist in its orientation is now a great deal more acceptable publicly and professionally than would have been the case even as little as ten years ago. In fact, the weight of relative prestige may actually be tipping in Buddhism's favour. Buddhism may have allied itself with psychotherapy in order to gain acceptability, but there are now signs that Buddhism may, in some quarters at least, be attracting a higher level of public goodwill than psychotherapy. The latter's reputation is by no means untarnished. Buddhism's public reputation, despite some palpable scandals, seems to have come through relatively unscathed.

There is also some evidence that approaches to Buddhism which adopt a 'therapeutic' style of presentation attract more interest. This is undoubtedly not the only 'growth strategy' available to Buddhist movements, but it is one approach which seems to yield results, if by 'results' we mean widespread public acceptance.

CONCLUSIONS

It is clear that the interaction between Buddhism and psychotherapy is currently prolific with creative developments. It is important that this fertility not be inhibited. At present the relationship between Buddhism and psychotherapy is, so far, to the enrichment of both. There are forces within both camps which could stifle this process. There are many people, however, who are inspired by it.

Along the way there are both practical and theoretical questions to face. At the practical level there are questions about:

1. The efficacy of techniques and whether 'outcome research' on, say, meditation, is a meaningful procedure.
2. The wisdom of combining methods of very different provenance: mindfulness training with systematic desensitisation, say, or *kum nye* practice with reflective listening, etc. There is

much eclectic experimenting going on.

3. The extent to which a technique depends for its effectiveness upon the cultural and/or faith context in which it is used.

4. The nature of the therapeutic alliance in Buddhism and therapy – a vast subject in its own right.

In the theoretical arena the questions are endless. Buddhism and therapy both debate the nature of dukkha, the nature of the self, the meaning of salvation/health, the purpose of life, the mechanisms of dependency, the manifestations of impermanence, the meaning of process, the role of ethical integrity, the function of introspection, the boundary between experiencer and phenomena, the nature of moral causation and a myriad related subjects. They have traditionally done so within different parameters provided by cultural precedent. Now this separation is breaking down. Hopefully this will be to the enrichment of both.

What will emerge at the end of this process is unpredictable. For some, Buddhist psychology provides a basis for a principled approach to psychotherapy integration. For some, psychotherapy provides an avenue for the development of a Western, practical, up to date, application and evolution of Dharma practice. Is therapy becoming Buddhism or is Buddhism becoming a therapy? Or is something completely new emerging for which we do not yet have a name? Where there are names there is deception – if I may slightly paraphrase the Diamond Sutra. It is probably important that we do not answer any of these questions too firmly. It is the very fluidity of the situation which ensures its continuing fertility.

Indra's Net at Work: The Mainstreaming of Dharma Practice in Society

Jon Kabat-Zinn

I

The image this chapter invokes is that of the great net of Indra, described in the *Avatamsaka Sutra*. It's an image of the interconnectedness of the universe. This net hangs over the palace of the Vedic god, Indra, atop Mt. Meru, the world axis in ancient Indian cosmology. At each vertex there is a multifaceted jewel. Each jewel is reflected in each facet of every other jewel in the net. As soon as you touch one part, you've in some way captured the whole.

I'd like to use this image of Indra's net not only in its classical guise as representative of the absolute interconnectedness of all of experience and reality in the universe, but also in the sense of its being a network that is currently expanding and doing a certain kind of work in society, that is, creating conducive conduits for the universal elements of Dharma to be felt in ways that are (as Dharma always is) profoundly healing and compassionate.

The way I propose to do this is to tell you something about my own life trajectory and work. I embarked on this trajectory and continue to pursue it simply as one individual who has been deeply touched by the Dharma in his own life and who was looking for a vehicle for a right livelihood. Of course, now I have the privilege and deep pleasure of sharing this work with a group of extraordinary colleagues and friends at our institute, the

Center for Mindfulness in Medicine, Health Care and Society, and with people around the world who have appeared, past and present, as nodes in Indra's mysterious net.

In the late 1970s I longed to find work that had value and meaning to me, having come out of a long trajectory of interest in and study of science in general and molecular biology in particular. My father was a highly accomplished and honoured molecular immunologist, what you might call a truly hard-core scientist, and my mother was and is an artist. I grew up in the 1950s, the era of C.P. Snow and 'the two cultures', and so, from early on for me, there was a germ of intuitive yearning, mainly below the level of consciousness, for the possibility of bringing the worlds of art and science together.

When I eventually came upon meditation, I never thought of it in terms of bringing art and science together, although now I see that it has served me in that particular way because of my own karma. Meditation just struck me as something that was missing from my own life, emphasising as it did the importance of wakefulness and self-acceptance, a sense of being okay the way I was without having to be judged by how I performed.

In school, at least in the United States at that time, you were constantly being evaluated and judged for how you performed, and hardly ever acknowledged as being a whole person. At gatherings of professionals and at parties, the common way for male intellectuals and academics to reach out in conversation was to say 'Where are you?' Translated, that meant 'What recognisable institution are you affiliated with?' That, instead of perhaps, 'How are you?' or 'Who are you?'

It was a kind of discourse, a way of relating, that I always had a great deal of trouble with. I often had the impulse, which I usually recognised as hostile and kept in check, to say 'Why, I'm standing in front of you! Where do you think I am?'

When I came across meditation and the consciousness disciplines, they meant an enormous amount to me, in part because they emphasised so much a clear seeing and acceptance of the present moment rather than being so caught up in one's head that one literally lived there full-time. I dropped into meditation (that's another story), and started practising as much as I could. It was love at first sight.

Much of the direction our work at the hospital has taken over the past seventeen years came to me in a flash, maybe lasting fifteen seconds, on a retreat in the spring of 1979 at the Insight Meditation Society in Barre, Massachusetts. The retreat was led by Christopher Titmuss and Christina Feldman, who are guiding teachers at Gaia House in Devon. The flash had to do with the question of how to take the heart of something as meaningful, as sacred if you will, as Buddha Dharma and bring it into the world in a way that doesn't dilute, profane or distort it, but at the same time is not locked into a culturally and tradition-bound framework that would make it absolutely impenetrable to the vast majority of people, who are nevertheless suffering and who might find it extraordinarily useful and liberative.

Parenthetically, I had the occasion in 1990 to spend some time with His Holiness the Dalai Lama in Dharamsala at one of the Mind/Life Conferences that on occasion arrange discussions between Western scientists and His Holiness. At one point in our discussions, the question was put to His Holiness about the danger of bringing the Dharma into the world in ways that might require giving up much of the traditional form and vocabulary, and whether that was possible without destroying the religion and the culture from which it springs and also without, in some way, profaning and betraying the moral and ethical foundations of Dharma practice.

I had more than a little interest in the Dalai Lama's answer, since I had been involved in just that kind of effort for eleven years at that point, although I hadn't yet given my formal presentation of our work to the group in Dharamsala. I found myself sitting there wondering how I would take it if the Dalai Lama's response were that it was an unwise, perhaps even a sacrilegious thing to do. What would I do? Would I repudiate our efforts of eleven years in the face of his authoritative disapproval? I thought to myself, if this practice means anything to me, then I have to really examine my own direct experience and if it measures up, to trust it, even if I'm living in total delusion. My strong impression, perhaps delusion, was an ongoing sense that our work was having a profound effect on people in the hospital, who were coming to our clinic, referred by their doctors by the hundreds each year. So the question hung there for me for what seemed an eternity while His Holiness listened to the translation into Tibetan. Then he said something I'll never forget: 'There are four billion people on the planet. One billion are Buddhists, but four billion are suffering.'

The implication was clear. It made no sense to withhold the Dharma, which we know to be fundamentally universal, so that its teachings are only accessible to Buddhists. The challenge is to make it accessible to all human beings, and to do it in ways that are authentic, true to the heart of the Dharma but at the same time not so locked in or wedded to tradition and vocabulary that prevent the practice from assuming new forms over the years, to grow and deepen (as it has always done) as it encounters new cultures.

My colleagues and I have recently formed an institute known as the Center for Mindfulness in Medicine, Health Care and Society at the University of Massachusetts Medical Center. Our 'organisational mandala' is meant to display the range of different but interpenetrating elements that comprise the Center and its work: patient care, education, research and outreach/networking. But the heart of everything that we do, as exemplified by mindfulness being placed at the centre of the circle, is grounded in stillness and in the practice of meditation itself.

You might note that the very words 'medicine' and 'meditation' sound as though they might be related, and they are. They both derive from the Latin *mederi* meaning 'to cure'. But the deep Indo-European root meaning of *mederi* is 'to measure', not in the usual Western scientific sense of holding an external standard up to things and measuring them, but more the Platonic notion that everything has its own right inward measure; therefore medicine in this context is the restoring of right, inward measure when it is perturbed, and meditation is the direct perceiving of right inward measure.

At the beginning, I asked myself, what would be a skilful way to approach the introduction of meditation into medicine and health care? It felt like the least skilful way would be to call it the Meditation Center. The First Noble Truth suggests that everybody relates to suffering because it is universal. Most people who come to hospitals do so because they are suffering in one way or another, or somebody else close to them is suffering. Hospitals are not a big draw when you are feeling well. You've got to be suffering a lot before you are willing to go to the hospital on your own. But hospitals do function as '*dukkha* magnets' in our society. So they are logical places in which to do Dharma work.

In 1983 *Time* magazine ran a cover which showed the head of a man in agony exploding out of a block of concrete, with the heading: 'Stress: Seeking Cures for Modern Anxieties'. This is symbolical of our age. I find it of value with certain professional audiences to emphasise the correspondence between our concept of stress and the Buddhist understanding of *dukkha*. Indeed, some translators actually use stress in English as a translation of *dukkha*. Stress is something that everybody intuitively understands in our society. So calling our programme 'stress reduction' might give us direct entry into the realm of working with *dukkha*. It had universal appeal.

We wanted to target a 'stress reduction' programme toward those people who were not satisfied with the health care system, were not being cured by the promise of medicine, were not receiving the kind of cure or caring that they sought in coming to the hospital. The challenge was to establish the clinic we had in mind to serve as a kind of safety net, one which was capable of catching people falling through the cracks of the health care system and challenging them in a meaningful way to see if there was not something that they could do for themselves as a complement to what medicine would be trying to do for them.

So we call our service 'The Stress Reduction Clinic' and everybody intuitively gets it. The universal response to seeing the signs up in the hospital, among patients, physicians, surgeons, hospital administrators, everybody, is that they invariably think or say 'Oh, I could use that.'

Of course, the Buddha noticed this a very long time ago: the universality of that sense of things being not quite right, that we all have running through us a river of anguish or grief or dissonance. In our society, the term 'stress' captures that. Yet 'stress' is not a good term from the scientific point of view because it is ambiguous in most contexts as to whether one is speaking of it as a response or a stimulus. It can mean many different things to different people, and has to be reduced to a precisely defined condition for scientific study. So from that point of view, the term has its drawbacks. But from the point of view of the inescapable anguish of the human condition, from the point of view of actually reaching out to people who are suffering, the term 'stress reduction' is something people are intuitively attracted to. And that can be exceedingly useful if your aim is to offer them a resource which includes asking them to do something for themselves which is arduous and challenging. There is a need to elevate motivation and aspiration, and if a particular term can help to accomplish that aim, it becomes a skilful way to embark on what is really a journey of a lifetime. Moreover, 'stress reduction' comes free of a lot of the baggage that accompanies psychiatric labels, which triggers for many people the implication that your problem is 'all in your mind', that 'there is something wrong with you'. In the US now, there is no onus to admitting that you are under a lot of stress. That you might be doing something about it conveys, if anything, a sense of intelligence and of agency, rather than being inadequate or abnormal.

Since 1979, we have seen over ten thousand medical patients who have completed the programme in the clinic. We have coined the term 'Mindfulness-Based Stress Reduction' (MBSR) to differentiate this Dharma approach from other programmes that carry the label 'stress reduction', many of which have nothing to do with the cultivation of wisdom, very little to do with compassion, and a lot to do with a fairly formulaic behaviour modification approach and philosophy, where transformation and healing are virtually excluded from the vocabulary and the underlying theory and thought processes. Whether we are conscious of it or not, our models of what human beings are and what they are capable of always dictate how we approach people and what we think might be possible for them.

Our view is that people are fundamentally miraculous beings, geniuses in fact, and also, in many fundamental ways, mysterious. We see everybody as having their own inner and outer expressions of genius, related in its universality to what some Buddhists call one's 'true self'. If we are able to appeal in some way to that genius within everyone, each person will recognise it instantly and that will form a good foundation for the actual work of meditation practice.

When we speak of meditation, I like to emphasise that what we are really talking about is a particular way of paying attention, one that gives rise to a moment-to-moment, non-judging awareness, which is how we define mindfulness. There is an *intention* involved in how we pay attention in meditation. If you have some experience with meditation, you will understand what I am talking about. But the systematic and intentional cultivation of present-moment, non-judgemental awareness is something I go into in great detail when I am giving talks to physicians, for instance, because it is new to them. When one speaks of meditation in this way, I find that professional audiences understand it intuitively, because everybody has had the experience of paying attention, or not being able to pay attention.

Apart from the word 'Dharma', I have not used any Buddhist terminology in talking about meditation in this presentation. And I should stress that I do not use the word 'Dharma' with our patients, or when I am talking to a group of mainstream professionals, although even that may change in the coming years as the world becomes more receptive and open to such concepts. But paying attention, and what it means to be truly human, and mindfulness, and states of mind such as wakefulness: people understand such concepts without any resistance, and without having to appeal to an ideological or cultural shift in perspective. Attention and wakefulness are key concepts in exploring meditation and the whole question of the 'psychology of awakening'.

A lot of the time you will notice, even if you have been meditating for some time, that there is a tendency to run around on automatic pilot, to be not quite here, with your children, at work, or wherever you are. We can operate in a kind of mechanical mode a good deal of the time, perhaps more than a little bit out of touch. There's a wonderful line in James Joyce's *Dubliners* that goes something like this: 'Mr Duffy lived a short distance from his body.' We may be capable of living a short distance from our bodies for decades at a time, all the while having all sorts of ideas in the mind about how our body is or should be or why it is inadequate or whatever it is, or too old or too young or too large or too small, or whatever. So our so-called everyday waking state can be a kind of dream. We are capable of living from day to day with an ongoing, persistent lack of awareness, a lack of consciousness. The implication is that you could go through life and never be where you actually are. You are always someplace else.

Now this is not just a Buddhist observation. Blaise Pascal, in his *Pensées*, said: 'All of man's difficulties are caused by his inability to sit quietly in a room by himself.' Henry David Thoreau, who lived in Concord, Massachusetts in the early part of the nineteenth century, said: 'I went to the woods because I wished to live deliberately, to confront only the essential facts of life and see if I could not learn what it had to teach and not, when I came to die, discover that I had not lived.'

Listening to the stories of hundreds of the people who have been referred to our clinic over the past eighteen years, and, of course, watching my own mind and my own leanings towards automaticity, it has become clear that many of us live caught up in this dream, in this fairly automatic and unconscious consensus trance that we think of as being awake. Yet, there are moments when we break through this dream state, often when we are ill, or dying, or when we receive a shock to the system, and we realise, 'My God, I got the rules of the game all wrong. I had no idea that I had a choice, that I didn't have to run over people or look cynically at people's motivations, or be preoccupied solely with my own pursuits, or withdraw into hurt, depression, isolation, and helplessness – that I have options, choices that can be exercised.'

Many of us may not come to such a 'rude' awakening until we have a heart attack, or are threatened with cancer, or are at death's door. Only then might we realise that we haven't really honoured our children or spouse, or that we didn't listen to our own heart. It might be a good idea, as Thoreau suggested, not to wait until you are about to die to realise that your life is yours. Perhaps it is not dying that we are afraid of in this life. Perhaps what we are really terrified of is living.

In 1939, Carl Jung wrote a foreword to D.T. Suzuki's *Introduction to Zen Buddhism*. Speaking of Zen meditation and practice, he said, 'As we know, this question of coming to wholeness has occupied the most adventurous minds of the East for more than two thousand years and in this respect methods and philosophical doctrines have been developed which simply put all Western attempts along these lines into the shade.' He knew something about it. But he also said that he did not think that it was possible for Westerners to really understand the heart of Zen and of Buddhist Dharma. That view is quite arguable now. Who could have predicted the incredible flowering of Buddhist practices and interest in Buddhism in the West that started in the 1960s or in the late 1950s with the Beatniks and with various meditation teachers coming to the West in large numbers for the first time? In 1996, it is not so inconceivable that Westerners might have an authentic meditation practice. And in an interesting cultural role reversal, on occasion we have Japanese, Chinese and Indian people coming to Westerners to learn something of the heart of their own traditions.

In America, meditation has even crept into the bubble gum comics: This is Bazooka Joe:

'What are you up to Mort?'
'Practicing meditation. It fills me with inner peace. After
    two minutes my mind is a complete blank.'
'Gee, and I thought he was born that way.'

Of course, this is a completely erroneous view of meditation – the idea, and it's very common, that meditation is a state change akin to simply flipping a light switch; switch into 'the meditative state' and your mind goes blank and stays that way. My point is simply that people who have no direct experience of meditation still have all kinds of ideas about it that they pick up from the culture at large.

Why have we chosen mindfulness to be the central focus of our work in the hospital with medical patients? I will answer that by first reviewing briefly the observation that in Pali, the classical language of Theravada Buddhism, the word most commonly used for 'meditation' is *bhavana*, which means 'development'. Meditation lies at the core of what is involved in the ongoing development of being human, or, if you will, the inquiry into what it means to be human and to have this apparatus – the body/mind – that has so much potential yet so much of the time we feel is weighing on us or falling apart or betraying us or getting us into trouble because we don't even know what is coming out of the mouth before it has come out, and even less what is going on in the mind. The 'apparatus' could, of course, work in our service, if only we paid attention to it and understood its potential for the ongoing development of awareness, of penetrative insight, of some degree of wisdom, and of compassion for others and for ourselves.

Even if you are thinking, 'I am a meditator, I know what I'm doing. I am cooking, or driving, or thinking . . .' there may still be a problem. The problem is not with the meditating, or the cooking. The problem is our relationship to the pronoun 'I' – as in 'I am a meditator'. In the practice of meditation we are dropping the notion of 'self' as we usually think about it. Mindfulness was taught by the Buddha in the *Mahasattipathana Sutta*, which speaks of the four foundations of mindfulness: the contemplation of the body, the contemplation of feelings (pleasant, unpleasant, and neutral sensations), the contemplation of mind states (including thoughts and emotions), and the contemplation of mind objects (suffering, impermanence, emptiness).

The text starts with the body, which is a really wonderful place to begin. If we are talking about interconnectedness and the true nature of the self, why not start the investigation close to home? If it is true that Mr Duffy lived a short distance from his body, maybe what would be required is to get back into the body. How do we cultivate mindfulness of the body?

We see meditation, yoga, Tai Chi, Qi Gong as what Roger Walsh, of the University of California at Irvine School of Medicine calls 'conscious disciplines'. These are methods for the systematic cultivation of our capacity to optimise functions that we hardly understand at all, including being in the body. Two major strands of practice are *samatha*, or *samadhi*, the strand of concentration (including calmness, stability of attention, one-pointedness), and *vipassana*, the strand of insight, mindfulness, awareness, discernment.

Our approach to practice aims to cultivate both strands

simultaneously. Yet we certainly don't use this vocabulary when we teach in the clinic. Practice taught in this way emphasises not trying to get anywhere but, for once in our lives, allowing ourselves to just be where we are, without any striving, without actually doing anything. Realising that in some way if you are already whole (the words 'health', 'healing', and 'holy' are all related to the word 'whole'), then there is no place to go, and nothing to do. In this sense, meditation is more a realising, a 'making real' what already is. That requires a certain kind of work, but we really don't have an appropriate verb for the process. 'Work' isn't quite right, and we can't really use the word 'doing' either.

We go by the term 'human beings' rather than 'human doings', but to watch us, one might wonder sometimes. Again, we are speaking of discernment, differentiated from judging. We are not talking about judging things, forming opinions then getting locked into one thing or another, but rather cultivating or developing our capacity for seeing more clearly, for letting go of opinions and accepting the actuality of what is unfolding, as best we can. This leads us to the cultivation and the spontaneous arising of compassion, including self-compassion, and of wisdom, which both have something to do with seeing the inter-connectedness of the world, the play if you will of Indra's Net, in virtually every aspect of life, every aspect of reality.

Now if we created a stress reduction programme based on such principles and practices, would anybody come? Would it become acceptable, in our case, to mainstream Americans and relevant to their concerns? Such an approach had, to our knowledge, never been tried before back in 1979. Could medical patients even be interested in such a thing? Would doctors refer people? Would hospital administrators do what was needed to support such a clinic? Would insurance cover it? And was what we had in mind truly universal? Could it be offered and seen as valuable by the people who are under the most stress in our society: the poor, recent immigrants, who do not even speak English, who face economic deprivation, bad living conditions, homelessness, joblessness, very often fragmented families? These are some of the questions we wished to explore in our research, and in our attempts to take a degree of responsibility for contributing to the emergent field of what has come to be called mind/body medicine.

The Stress Reduction Clinic or Stress Reduction and Relaxation Programme (SR&RP), as it was originally called, is a clinic in the form of a course. It is a course that is designed to teach people how to take better care of themselves and how to live more skilfully and more fully as a complement to whatever their medical treatments are, in other words how to move towards greater levels of health and well-being.

How do we know *how* individuals who come to the clinic with major medical problems and life stresses should move towards greater levels of health and well-being? The answer is, we don't. What we do is challenge each individual: 'If it makes sense to you, why don't you try engaging in what we offer, and see whether it would have any value? Together, we will try systematically to document your experience as we go along. The course is eight weeks long, and the commitment to take it requires that you would have to come to class once a week for two and a half hours.' There are about thirty to forty people in a class, all referred by physicians or, in perhaps ten per cent of cases, by other health care providers. They come with a vast range of different kinds of medical problems: heart disease, cancer, HIV, AIDS, chronic pain, irritable bowel syndrome, high blood pressure, skin problems, chronic anxiety, chronic panic disorder to name some of the major classes of diagnoses.

We challenge the people referred to the clinic to make a major commitment in taking this course. The commitment involves being willing to carve out at least forty-five minutes a day, six days a week, to practise the meditation and the yoga. To make matters worse, we tell people right up front, 'You don't have to like the meditation or the yoga, you just have to do it, and at the end of the eight weeks, you can tell us whether it was of any value or not. But in the middle, when the mind comes up with, ". . . this is so boring", or "this is not relaxing . . ." just keep up the practice, whether you like it or not. Because we can tell you right now, in advance, that you may find the meditation boring. You will no doubt also run into anxiety, ennui, irritability, in fact, you are going to run into every kind of human mental state that exists. Why? Because you are human, and mind moments, mental states keep coming up. It's got nothing to do with taking a stress reduction programme, although you can attribute it to the stress reduction programme if you want to. But, as we said, you don't have to like it, just suspend judgement as best you can and do it for the eight weeks, then we'll reassess.'

Participants also have to commit to doing awareness exercises in a workbook for about fifteen minutes a day, and attend an all-day silent retreat in the sixth week. In addition, they are required to attend individual interviews before and after taking the programme. I want to emphasise that the SR&RP is offered as a complement to medical treatment, not a substitute for it. We are not talking about an attitude of 'Oh, you have headaches. Why don't you meditate?' First it has to be established that the person doesn't have a brain tumour or something like that. So, all prospective participants are first worked up medically to the degree considered reasonable by their physician. Only then, when appropriate, are they referred to the stress reduction clinic. Of course, that is a lot of people because most people who have headaches don't have brain tumours. Brain tumours are relatively rare, but they do occur, so we want to be sure that people are getting appropriate medical treatment for their conditions at least concurrently as they launch into complementary, self-regulatory practices.

Meditation training is offered as a complement to traditional medical treatment, in part based on what we believe to be a core principle of the medicine of the future, namely, that twenty-first-century medicine will be fundamentally participatory. It will honour what I would call the sovereignty of the individual person, the patient as a whole human being. Many doctors have practised in this way throughout history. Now this principle is making its way into the training of all physicians from their first encounters with medical school. Ultimately, there is only one way to do it. You cannot honour who another person is without being present, and being present is not something that comes all that easily to most of us, especially if you are busy, stressed, and this person that you are seeing is one of twenty or thirty people that you have to see today, and each has a story that may be more painful and disturbing than the one before.

It is important to mention that, on the face of it, the MBSR approach takes the medical/psychiatric model – which rests on the development of specific treatments for specific problems – and appears to turn it on its head, in the sense that we are working with people with a wide range of different kinds of problems, yet we offer them all more or less the same inter-vention. The only way that that could possibly make any sense and be of any value is if we appeal to what is 'right' with them rather than focus on what is 'wrong' with them.

If you have thirty people in a room and they all have serious, sometimes horrible, problems of one kind or another: what do they have in common? Where could we possibly start to make a difference in their lives? Well, to begin with, you will have to get very basic. First grade is not good enough. You've got to drop down to kindergarten or day-care to really penetrate this koan. What do they have in common that is important, and a good foundation on which to build? For one, they all have bodies. Every single person has a body. Some may be partially or totally paralysed, some may not be able to walk, or see, or hear, but they all have a body. (Parenthetically, let's notice that it is a peculiar terminology to say that someone 'has' a body. Who is it that actually 'has' the body?) They are also all breathing. So that is where we start, with contemplation of the body. What's more, all the people in the room have minds too, in conventional parlance, and as we know, their minds are all waving to one degree or another and, to a large extent, they are unaware of it. It's absolutely news for most people that that's the case, that the mind is always waving. But ordinarily, without training in meditation, we don't think about it quite that way. And they are also all capable of paying attention to one degree or another.

Meditation, in the way we look at it, is a way of being. It's far more than a collection of techniques. Most clinically oriented people, if they think of meditation at all, think of it as just another relaxation technique. Nothing could be further from the truth. Meditation has little to do with relaxation. It has to do with being present and with seeing things as they are. What if you're tense in a particular moment? Is that bad, or is it just the way it is? If you are practising a relaxation exercise and you find you are tense at the end of it, then either you have failed, or the teacher has failed, or the exercise is no good, or the tape is no good; something is no good. But if you are practising meditation and your body feels as tense as can be, then you are just aware of the tension. That is just as good as if you were loose as a goose. So we sometimes tell people in the intake interview that we are going to teach them how to be so relaxed that it is okay to be tense. Then they have no place to go, nothing to attain. This is an effective attitude for furthering the inner work of attending to the present moment non-judgementally. Such a paradoxical tack can serve to help people to grow beyond the conventional mode of striving to get somewhere else to make progress. The Zen tradition mastered this approach a long time ago.

Imagine that you are guiding a meditation and you say: 'When you are ready, breathing in . . .' You haven't given anyone an imperative, an order. You've given them the freedom to breath in when they are ready. Sooner or later every person in the room is going to breathe in. So you have aligned yourself with something that is going to be part of everybody's immediate experience. '. . . and then watch the breath go out . . .' Sooner or later everyone is going to breathe out. All you are suggesting is that they be there for it. There is no coercion, no controlling them, no suggestion of what they 'should' experience. By the skilful use of language and pacing, you are actually empowering people, guiding them to become more awake to the present moment, to the body, to the mind, to the whole world. At some point, they may begin to see connections you have never mentioned; insights may begin to emerge that can be 're-incorporated' into their own body, in their own 'corpus'. So meditation practice goes far beyond a set of 'techniques'. It is a way of being, a way of relating to the entire field of awareness and experience.

We often use a variant of the Kalachakra mandala as a teaching device to talk about the extensive repercussions related to this work. At the centre of the mandala is a space we have labelled 'the room'. Once we get people into the room, we can do a certain type of work with them that can't be done unless they show up with certain expectations and motivation. In order to get people into the room, you need a staff of people to talk to the people you want to get into the room to help ignite and shape those expectations and motivations. This is depicted in the next level out, surrounding the space of the room. You also need skilled and caring meditation teachers who are going to do the work in the room with the people. That is the next level out from the centre.

Then you need a clinic to create a framework for what goes on in the room so you can call it stress reduction and people will come, and so you can bill their health insurance companies, and have a revenue stream to pay the teachers. Next level out: you need doctors and health care providers, nurses, psychologists, etc., who will refer the people to come to work in the room. In order to have the doctors, you need patients or people who come to the doctors, so that is the next level out. As we keep going out, we have levels such as the hospital, the medical centre, then medicine itself, and health care. Then, to pay for that, you have the health insurance level, then employers that contract with the insurance companies. Beyond that, there is the level of society as a whole, and beyond that, the politics of health care, and the economic life of the society. Beyond that is the world; beyond that, the universe. Moreover, the room is not just the physical space in which the classes are conducted. It represents the room one discovers in one's own heart as one practises mindfulness meditation.

This teaching mandala can readily remind us of the interconnectedness latent in 'doing' the work of *being*, right there in the room, with whoever shows up. The attitude that the instructor brings into the room, and whether he or she is aware of all these levels, ultimately influences absolutely everything in the world. Once you make the commitment, as Kabir put it, 'To stand firm in that which you are', to hold the central axis of your being human, the entire universe is different.

That is one of the repercussions of the physicist David Bohm's notion of the implicate order, the enfolded universe, of which Indra's net is such a powerful symbol. And seeing the world as fundamentally interconnected, one seamless whole, provides us with a very practical way to catalyse, both in individuals and in institutions and in the society as a whole, the emergence of unpredictable characteristics and events that reflect the underlying intrinsic wholeness of the world and are therefore both healing and transformative.

In 1979, the year that I set up the Stress Reduction Clinic, the Surgeon General of the United States issued a report called 'Healthy People'. It made the observation that half of the US mortality in 1976 was due to unhealthy behaviours or lifestyle, and twenty per cent to environment factors; in other words, things that people could do something about. The inner work we are speaking of here involves in some way taking charge of that which we can have some effect on. Rene Dubois, the great microbiologist/philosopher who worked at what was then the Rockefeller Institute, observed that 'human health transcends purely biological health because it depends primarily on those conscious and deliberate choices by which we select our mode of life and adapt creatively to its expression'. Adaptation is one of the key characteristics of being human, indeed, of all living systems.

When we begin to pay attention and cultivate awareness, our view of the world changes and we can begin to navigate in ways that are highly adaptive, highly supportive of healing, of health, and of a healthier way of being, not only in one's own body but in the world. We do that through the choices we make, through taking responsibility for ourselves to whatever degree is possible. Dr John Knowles, who was president of Massachusetts General Hospital, observed around the same time that: 'The next major advance in health of the American people will come from the assumption of individual responsibility'. That was in 1979, when the Stress Reduction Clinic first opened. In the autumn of 1996, there were over 120 MBSR programmes in the US and a few in other countries, including some in the UK, all based on the University of Massachusetts model we are speaking about. And that number is growing rapidly. The net is expanding. (As of June, 1997, there were over 240 centres worldwide offering MBSR.)

Taking a look at the fundamental training that goes on inside the room in the Stress Reduction Clinic's classes and at home, our patients cultivate mindfulness through both *formal* and *informal* meditation practices. Although it is crucial to keep in mind that meditation is a way of being and not a technique, we do make use of a number of formal meditation practices in MBSR, which involve a regular and, if possible, daily discipline. The big three are the body scan, sitting meditation, and mindful hatha yoga. These and other formal practices such as walking meditation are described in detail in *Full Catastrophe Living*, *Wherever You Go, There You Are*, and in my colleague, Saki Santorelli's book, *Heal Thy Self*. We ask the participants in the programme to make a strong commitment to practice at least 45 minutes per day, six days per week, using mindfulness meditation practice tapes that guide them in these various formal practices.

If people were to come in and observe what we are doing, from the outside it could well look like the Stress Reduction Clinic is the biggest joke in the world. Imagine: an observer would see people lying on the floor for long periods of time (practising the body scan), not talking, then they might spend more time sitting still (practising sitting meditation). What would not be intuitively obvious is that there is deep work going on here, and it is very hard to do. When physicians take the programme and gradually come to realise the enormity of what we are asking of the patients, their respect for their patients skyrockets, because they themselves may be having a terribly hard time just keeping their mind on the breath for even five minutes, or even five seconds! It become even more impressive to them that the dropout rates in this programme are extremely low. Our published studies show that the dropout rates average fifteen per cent.

The heart of the practice in MBSR lies in what we call informal mindfulness practice, i.e. mindfulness in everyday life. The true meditation practice is when life itself becomes the practice. We cultivate mindfulness systematically in daily life through paying attention to what we are doing, and bringing mindfulness of the breath into it is a very good way to develop this in whatever we find ourselves doing or experiencing: eating, standing, walking, routine activities like doing the dishes, taking out the garbage, cleaning the house, taking a shower, having words come out of your mouth. All these are occasions to which we can actually bring awareness, and notice how awareness itself actually changes how we relate to things.

I like to give people the following homework to drive the point of this practice home. The next time you are in the shower, check and see if you are in the shower. You can do the same checking in virtually every situation you find yourself in, driving a car, having a conversation, being with your children, even making love. It might be a rude awakening. Part of the curriculum of MBSR is to bring awareness to and examine with interest pleasant events, unpleasant events, neutral events, as they unfold in our lives.

II

I would like to switch gears at this point and discuss some of our research efforts in mind/body medicine and the outcome of MBSR training in medical patients over the past seventeen years. I'll begin by telling you very briefly about an experiment we did in the dermatology clinic with people with psoriasis. We asked ourselves the question: if people meditate, would it have a positive effect, not on just their stress levels or symptoms but on an actual disease process? Is there something that the mind does that is capable of actually healing the body or influencing healing in the body?

We decided to look at the skin disease psoriasis because it is known to be related to stress. We don't really understand the pathophysiology of psoriasis. It is known that stress is a part of it, but there are some very interesting things about the molecular biology of psoriasis that suggest that it would be a good model to study uncontrolled cell proliferation, which is closely related to cancer, and the genes known to be affected in psoriasis.

One standard treatment is phototherapy using ultraviolet light (UVB). The patient stands naked in a small, cylindrical light-booth and is bathed by ultraviolet light for short periods of time, no longer than fifteen minutes, often much less. The UV knocks out the rapidly growing epidermal cells, presumably by hitting the dividing DNA in the cell nucleus, and, over time, the skin clears. So we decided to teach standing meditation to people undergoing phototherapy. To maximise the connection between the meditation practice and the light treatment setting, and the patient's participation in his or her treatment process, we included instructions for visualising what the light is doing to help the skin clear.

We randomised people to two conditions: those who just received the light treatments, and those who got both the light and the meditation instructions, which were delivered through a guided meditation tape played from speakers on top of the booth while the person was standing in the lightbooth. The patients came for treatments three times a week, and we followed them and photographed their skin over time for up to about thirteen weeks. We looked not only at phototherapy as a treatment, but also photochemotherapy (PUVA) in which patients get ultra-violet light treatments plus a chemical called psoralen, which is thought to intercalate between base pairs in the DNA and creates covalent crosslinks between the strands when it is struck by the UV hitting the epidermis. The rapidly growing skin cells can no longer divide. Growth slows down, the scaly patches slough off and the skin clears.

In the first study that we did with a small number of people, we followed the meditators and the non-meditators. The survival curves were normalized to a hundred per cent for each patient. When a person came into the study, the degree of skin involvement at baseline for that patient was labelled a hundred per cent. Over time, it would go down. We defined five per cent or less of the initial skin involvement as clear. The five meditators, undergoing UVB in this case, cleared before the two people who were not meditating, and one non-meditator did not reach clearing at all. This pilot study had a very small number of subjects, twenty-three in all. We then produced a survival curve for the patients undergoing photochemotherapy. We found that only the meditators made it to clearing within forty treatment sessions.

We did this study back in the mid 1980s. It suggests that something that people are doing in the lightbooth is influencing the rate of skin clearing, having an effect on the healing process directly or indirectly. We didn't try to publish our findings at the time, except for a letter to the editor of the *Journal of the American Academy of Dermatology* in 1988 (Bernhard *et al*, 1988), because we felt it was potentially too important a result about which to make claims on the basis of one very small study, in which skin status was only assessed by the visual inspection and rating of nurses in the clinic who were not blinded to the patient's condition. We felt we should first try to replicate the

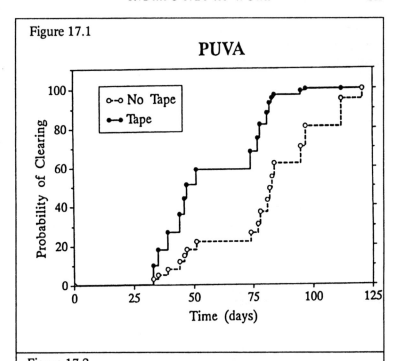

Figure 17.1

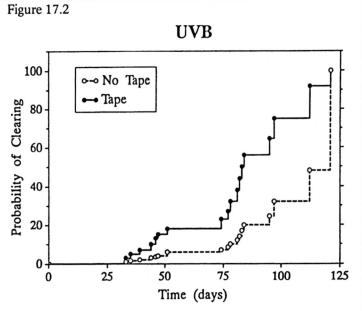

Figure 17.2

From Kabat-Zinn, Wheeler, Light *et al*, 1998. Reprinted with permission, *Psychosomatic Medicine*.

finding, with more people, and under more stringent experimental conditions, which would include blinded photographic verification of the nurses' ratings by the dermatologists. If we could see it twice, then perhaps we would be willing to believe it. It is good to be sceptical and cautious when making claims in this area.

So we designed a much more stringent study, although here too, the number of subjects, thirty-seven, was not as large as we would have liked. Nevertheless, the results are highly significant, both clinically and statistically, and show that the meditators cleared about four times as fast as the non-meditator controls (Kabat-Zinn, Wheeler, Light, et al, 1998). Figures 17.1 and 17.2 show you the Cox proportional hazard probability models of clearing as a function of time for both the meditation (tape) group and the regular treatment (light but no meditation) group. Notice that in the case of photochemotherapy (PUVA) (Figure 17.1), at a fifty per cent probability of clearing, there is about a thirty-day difference between the meditators and the non-meditators.

Figure 17.2 shows the results for phototherapy (UVB), the weaker treatment. Note that it takes longer for clearing to occur in general (because the treatment is weaker) but again you can see that here, too, there is about a thirty-day difference at the fifty per cent probability of clearing between meditators and non-meditators. When we plot it not as a function of time but as a function of total energy exposure of the skin, we see the same thing.

We interpret these findings as evidence that something that the meditators are doing is actually influencing cellular and molecular processes that are resulting in the clearing of the skin, in other words, in healing. There are enough suggestions about the molecular biology of psoriasis to actually begin looking at gene expression using this experimental system, so perhaps we can do science on the question of what the mind is doing all the way down to the cellular and even the gene expression level, in a way that might be able to tease out certain aspects of the underlying healing process in this case, and the mind's relationship to it. Moreover, this study suggests that the duration and cost of the light treatments might be substantially reduced if patients participated in the treatment by meditating. That would also reduce the risk of cancer associated with UV exposure.

In addition to studies such as this one that I have described, much of our research, especially in the early years, focused on clinical outcomes in the stress reduction programme itself, for medical patients with a range of different diagnoses. We have documented interesting, reproducible and long-lasting results in patients with a range of chronic pain conditions, with stress-related disorders and with people who, in addition to their medical conditions, suffer from anxiety and panic. Many of these findings are outlined in *Full Catastrophe Living* (Kabat-Zinn, 1996), and many have been published in the medical literature already (see references).

We also work in other venues. In 1992, the people in charge of the prison system in Massachusetts came to us, took the stress reduction programme themselves, and then proposed putting MBSR into the prisons for both inmates and correction staff. There is an enormous amount of suffering in and around prison. It is not just the inmates who are suffering, but also the people who are keeping them in prison. So to work in the prison system seemed like a very good opportunity to further the main-streaming of Dharma practice in society and perhaps contribute in a small way to the reduction of suffering and, ultimately, the reduction of recidivism, a huge problem in the criminal justice system in the US.

It takes an enormous degree of individual commitment and courage to walk into a prison, past three or four four-foot thick walls and barbed wire, to go through traps and random searches and everything else, and do this kind of work. Really, there is only one way you can do it and that is out of a love for the practice itself, and a deep respect for the human beings you encounter. The first rule in prison is that you never close your eyes in a group. Yet our instructors, many of whom were women, would often guide extended meditations for the inmates, every-one with their eyes closed! It is a very moving experience just to be in there on the floor with these folks, as they work on self-acceptance, letting go, being present, being non-judgemental, being non-reactive.

After four years and having had over 2,000 inmates and 200 staff go through the programme, our involvement with the prisons came to an end shortly after a big media uproar, with a front page editorial in the *Boston Herald*. Our work got caught up in a huge election year debate around 'coddling' prisoners as opposed to making them 'crush rocks', as our Governor put it (the very one whose appointed chairman of the Massachusetts Committee on Criminal Justice recruited us to do the work). Rehabilitation versus punishment was the issue. So the programme came to an end, which would have probably happened anyway because the funding was only there for that period of time. But the flap precluded any possibility of keeping it going, and made it very difficult for the wonderful instructors who were working in the prisons. At the time, we couldn't say much about scientifically validated outcomes because we hadn't completed the analysis of the data. But we had collected data on thousands of inmates and hundreds of staff and are currently in the process of analysing it. So, if the results are positive, as I imagine they will be from our personal experiences of working in the prisons, we will be able to make the case for the value of this approach in the criminal justice and corrections system.

MBSR is also making its way into the schools. One day, a fourth-grade teacher named Cherry Hamrick showed up at a talk I gave in Utah about our work in the hospital. She had gone through an MBSR programme at a hospital in Salt Lake City and said to me, 'I want to bring this into my classroom.' I said, 'Don't do it, the parents and the school system will misunderstand it and will eat you alive.' But like any good student, she did not listen to her teacher, she just went ahead and did it. Apparently she found a vocabulary and a way to do it such that, in this public elementary school in Utah, in a community which is ninety per cent Mormon, the children are practising a form of meditation that comes from the Buddhist tradition. Of course, they don't talk about it as Buddhist meditation, but they do know where it comes from. Not only that, the stress reduction was so popular with the students that it spread throughout the school.

I visited the class one time. The children and their parents came on a Saturday to meet me. One boy, who had ADHD (Attention Deficit Hyperactivity Disorder) and had been so problematic that he was described to me as having been the most hated kid in the school in earlier years, guided the sitting meditation for ten minutes. He did it very skilfully, and he didn't move a muscle. His mother sat right next to him. Later, when we had a chance to speak, she told me that her son is a different person now, and she and he attribute it to the meditation practice, which wasn't easy for him but which he pursued doggedly until he could be still for increasing periods of time and follow his breathing and watch his thoughts and impulses without reacting. This is just one personal story, but it suggests the potential value of a meditative approach within the classroom to enhance concentration, calmness, and engagement with the experience of learning when offered by a skilled and empathic and creative teacher.

(Another parenthetical observation: ADHD is running rampant through our society. I've seen studies that suggest that its incidence is quadrupling every four years, that perhaps ten per cent of children are on ritalin. One can't help wondering how much of this is for the sake of the children and how much for the sake of keeping order in the classroom rather than having a compelling educational environment that ignites a passion for learning and that excites the imagination.)

In this context, I think it is important to note that, from the meditative perspective, the entire society suffers from attention deficit disorder. Rather than medicating the whole society, which some doctors and the pharmaceutical industry are perfectly happy to contemplate, maybe what we really need to be doing is shifting one consonant in the word medication, to make it meditation. But not in some dime store, Mickey Mouse way, as just another behavioural modification technique to tune someone in and get them sort of straightened out so they will be more obedient and quiescent, but as a way of being, a way of inquiring into what it means to be human, a way of self-discovery.

Ms Hamrick once looked up what the Utah Board of Education said about the nature and practice of education in the state of Utah. It turns out that it is mandated to be directed to four different domains: the emotional, the intuitive, the somatic and the cognitive. The domain which dominates, of course, is overwhelmingly the cognitive. Often, sadly, even that domain is reduced to just bits of fragmented information thrown at the kids. They have to memorise the names of the states, the capitals of the states, the gross national product of the states. Ms Hamrick has taken the novel step of bringing mindfulness into every aspect of the curriculum, into Maths, English, Science and Social Studies. She works through poetry, through the body, through feelings, through experiments, to bring out the deeper meaning and interrelatedness and relevance of things in terms of body, feelings, intuition and thinking. It's virtually the four foundations of mindfulness and it's actually mandated by the state of Utah. This is her sixth year of offering the programme in her classroom (see Kabat-Zinn and Kabat-Zinn, 1997).

We also work with athletes. My colleague George Mumford has been working with the Chicago Bulls, world champions of basketball. For the past three years, George has been training them in mindfulness meditation and yoga. They do it because they believe that when they pay attention, they don't just get the basketball into the hoop more often, but they know more of what is going on the court, they know where each other is, they can feel it, they can sense it better in motion, and it gives them an edge over the competition, who may be playing in a less intentional and attuned state of awareness. The Bulls play with an awareness that is beyond what is usually thought of as possible, and they train to keep that a part of their game. It does not have to happen much more beyond the normal for it to be very effective. All you need is an edge of one or two per cent over the competition. We also trained the 1984 US Olympic Men's Rowing Team.

In closing, let me quote from Goethe: 'Whatever you can do, or dream you can, begin it. Boldness has genius, power and magic in it.' That has been a guiding principle in the work we have done, whether it has been with medical patients in the Stress Reduction Clinic, or with people in prison, with teachers and children, with athletes, judges or business leaders. It is very interesting to ask how it is that some of the world's best athletes and people who are awaiting heart transplants and liver transplants can find the very same practice of paying attention intentionally and non-judgementally to be of such value. It is extraordinary that they all report that mindfulness is in some way healing or transformative, worth the effort to cultivate it on an ongoing basis, and that it spills out into one's life, that it has more than one effect.

For, indeed, mindfulness has an enormous number of dimensions that can profoundly affect the lives of individuals and institutions. We have reached the point in the US where the hunger for inner peace, authentic experience and wisdom is huge. More and more people in our society are coming to meditation, and particularly to mindfulness meditation. Many are finding the practice within a wonderful constellation of meditative environments, such as the Insight Meditation Society and Spirit Rock in the US, and Gaia House in the UK. Others learn it through MBSR programmes in hospitals and in clinics. All of these environments, and many more, are simultaneously beginning to create an emergence of a new kind of possibility in the culture. It is filtering into virtually every aspect of society: politics, health care, education and parenting. For those of us who love the Dharma and deeply care about it, perhaps it is becoming more possible for us to ask ourselves how we might be more effective, more resonant nodes in Indra's net and perhaps take on a new level of work in and with the world. That work would be unique for each of us because of who each one of us is.

Maybe we can find new and imaginative ways to bring more of a universal Dharma element into our own lives in whatever we are already doing, and not be shy about bringing it more into the world for the sake of others as well as for ourselves.

If you are a physician, a psychotherapist, or work in the helping professions in other capacities, the opportunities are vast, and the possibility for creativity is also vast. The hunger is enormous. And let us note that there are huge potential pitfalls as well. They are usually one variant or another of the Buddha's big three: greed, hatred and ignorance. These are nothing new, of course, but they take on interesting new ramifications when working in the world with meditation because it is becoming so popular. But the challenge here, at the turn of not only the century but also of the millennium, is to see if it is not possible to shape ourselves in such a way that the net of Indra resonates as it has always resonated but with more and more people being drawn to the practice and to insight, wisdom and compassion. I think we have the potential to participate in and to help catalyse a flowering, not only of ourselves as individuals but of the society as a seamless whole. I like to think that we have the potential here and in all other places where such sparks exist, for a new renaissance, one of wholeness, birthed through the ceaseless mystery and beauty of the awakened mind and the awakened heart.

The Structures of Suffering: Tibetan Buddhist and Cognitive-Analytic Approaches

James Low

Suffering is something that concerns us all. We are marked by our own past sufferings, and the bruises we carry around in our hearts often keep us wary of what the world might bring. We are also marked by the sufferings of others and may rate our own and others' value as human beings in terms of our sensibility to, and efforts to alleviate, the sufferings of others.

On a more problematic level, psychotherapy has helped to highlight how much we wish to suffer, how deep our self-hatred can be and how committed we often are, both consciously and unconsciously, to maintaining the patterns of belief, cognition, affect and activity which bring us grief.

There are many similarities between Buddhist and psycho-therapeutic descriptions of the processes which lead to suffering. The main differences seem to be around the identification of initiatory causes. I am going to set out the basic structures of suffering according to two particular versions of Buddhism and psychotherapy: those of the Khordong lineage of the Nyingma[1] school of Tibetan Buddhism and the Cognitive-Analytic (CAT)[2] model of psychotherapy. These structures, though of precise provenance, do, I feel, have general relevance for the ongoing discussion of what Buddhism and psychotherapy might contribute to, and learn from, each other.

In both Buddhism and psychotherapy great emphasis is put on the process of the individual, the dynamic unfolding of experience – and clearly this is important. However an overview of the structures, particularly those which indicate cause and effect relations, whether linear and definitive, or contextually supportive (as in dependent co-origination), is also very important. When clarity about structure is established it provides a self-supervision support in the midst of process, a space for reflection, a means of reorientation, and particularly in the Buddhist context, an encouragement to enter fully into the disorientation from *samsara* that leads to awakening.

Although people come to psychotherapy for all sorts of reasons and with many different kinds of stories, problems and concerns, two basic blockages often seem to operate (Figure 18.1).

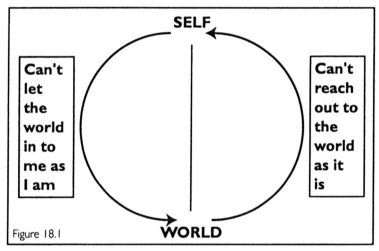

Figure 18.1

The individual, being absorbed in their own view of themselves, finds no gap in the world to enter, no way of speaking and connecting. And the world, other people, seem to present nothing but demands, criticism, shaming perceptions and so forth and so has to be resisted. The Buddha also spoke of how fixed positions and interpretations generate suffering, showing how attachment gives rise to pain because it involves a denial of the changing nature of our experience.

We seek to predict the responses of others and then set about engaging with the environment to bring us what we want. But what we want is rarely enduring and even when our own desire is stable the environment in which we seek its gratification is undoubtedly changing and so frustration is never far away (Figure 18.2). Prolonged frustration undermines our necessary sense of self-efficacy, and through that our sense of self-esteem,

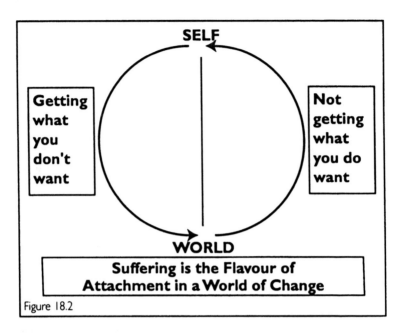

Figure 18.2

leading to a pervasive low-level depression and self-dislike, for, especially under the legacy of a Protestant work ethic, we feel if only we had worked harder things would be better and we could have got what we wanted.

THE NYINGMA VIEW

Luckily the Buddha, in his compassion, has pointed out that this view is just another punitive fantasy of ego omnipotence and that the rots of suffering go much deeper than this. The Buddha taught that attachment arises from ignorance, from not seeing things as they really are. In the Nyingma tradition of Tibetan Buddhism ignorance is described as having three stages (see Figure 18.3).

Before ignorance there is primordial Buddha nature. Buddha nature continues during ignorance and after enlightenment: it is unassailable. To forget it, to not be aware of it, is ignorance. To remember it, to be aware of it, is enlightenment. It is neither destroyed by ignorance nor created by enlightenment. However an interruption does occur in this open awareness free of the constraints of time and space, which is described as being like a shock, like a drunk man falling down a flight of stairs: 'Oh! Ah! What! That! Me!' Consciousness seeks to make sense of the

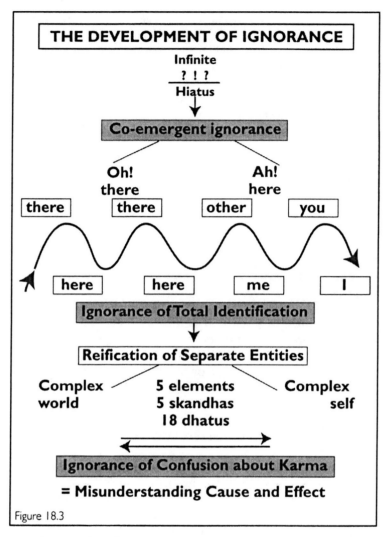

THE DEVELOPMENT OF IGNORANCE

Infinite
? ! ?
Hiatus

Co-emergent ignorance

Oh!
there

Ah!
here

there   there   other   you

here   here   me   I

Ignorance of Total Identification

Reification of Separate Entities

Complex
world

5 elements
5 skandhas
18 dhatus

Complex
self

Ignorance of Confusion about Karma

= Misunderstanding Cause and Effect

Figure 18.3

experience rather than letting it pass as just another moment in the infinity of awareness. Open awareness becomes fixed as a questioning, involved consciousness. This is called 'co-emergent ignorance' since openness and its closure are arising together.

As consciousness tries to strengthen itself by working out what is going on, a process of naming and recognition commences giving rise to a sense of a complete world full of diverse, discrete entities being experienced sensorily by a complex individual. This is the operation of the ignorance of total identification where nothing, including self, escapes definition and the ascription of essential being, true self-existence. This is like a pinball machine, in which the subject shoots about like a ball, setting off lights and bells, ricocheting yet somehow believing it is in control, desperately trying to score lots of points before momentary oblivion and then the start of a new game.

Due to all this busyness we find ourselves born again and again, each time entering a new environment which offers us a new set of values and teleological explanations. A lot is going on and we learn a lot of reasons why it's going on, but these reasons tend to be limited only to the particularities of precise inter-actions, as for example in the notion currently dominant in Western psychoanalytic psychotherapy that the environment surrounding the infant has a powerful influence on the child's development. That is to say the true existence of the child and its environment is taken for granted. This is a mode of the ignorance of confusion regarding karma and it is this misreading of cause and effect that creates the impulses that bring us into further painful situations in the future.

These three stages of ignorance represent the movement from infinite presence to a sense of particular, finite being operating within the constraints of a linear sequence of past, present and future and the dichotomising of me and not me. Of course they could also be used to reflect on psychological development in one life and have some interesting parallels with the work of Daniel Stern[3] especially in terms of an originatory curiosity or intentionality, an urge to order, leading to the arising of structures of differentiation and the evolution of sustainable patterns of self-affirming activity.

The word karma is often used in a very general way to mean the impact of past actions on the present and this weak usage gives it the feel of being not much different from luck. But karma also has a technical usage which is more illuminating.

The *basis* arises from the three stages of ignorance and is the sense of being a subject separate from an environment of objects (Figure 18.4). Although I may be aware of others as having a subjectivity similar to my own, the usual impulse is to interact with the environment in terms of the primacy of my own needs, desires, wants. That is, I experience *intentions* towards another in terms of needs that I have, especially my desire to avoid getting what I don't want and to not get what I do want. This leads to an *enactment* in which subject comes more fully into contact with object, as their connection is manifest in the world. Then follows *satisfaction* or finalisation in which the subject reviews what has

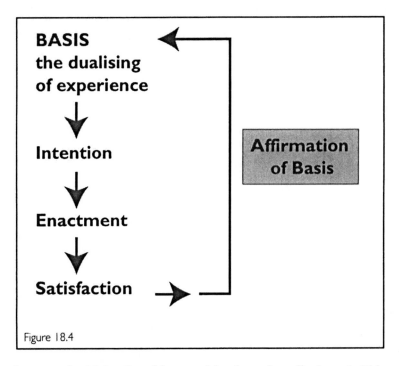

BASIS
the dualising
of experience

↓

Intention

↓

Enactment

↓

Satisfaction

Affirmation
of Basis

Figure 18.4

happened with/to the object, and is pleased or displeased. This leads to an affirmation of the basis, the view of subject and object as inherently real and separate. When all four steps are unimpeded in intensity this creates a powerful 'charge', an impulse to affirm and act on that concretised view of experience. This then leaves the subject open to great distress when things change and the world acts on the subject as if it were an object. As a brief example, I see you put your purse in your bag (basis). I think it would be easy to steal it and I indulge that thought until it becomes an intention. I then wait for the opportunity and then act. Later I open your purse and am pleasantly surprised at how wealthy I now am. Having felt no qualms during or remorse after the incident, I become even more fully committed to exploiting you and getting away with it.

This sequence of cognition, perception, intention, action, review, and affirmation of cognitive structure is self-perpetuating and tends to be so until interrupted by the pain of latterly manifesting consequences. The affective force that powerfully drives these sequences is conceptualised as the five poisons (Figure 18.5).

In giving rise to the sense of a separate self, ignorance establishes a 'self-referencing function' to use Maturana's[4] term, a

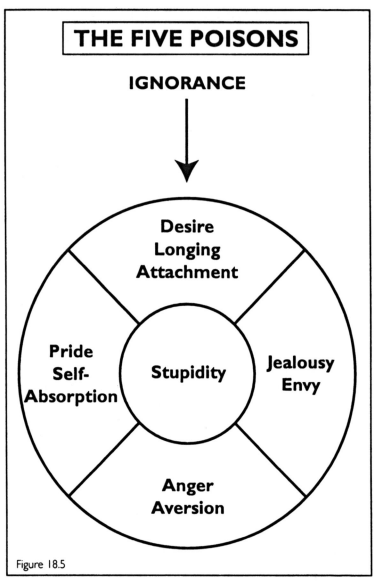

THE FIVE POISONS

IGNORANCE

Desire Longing Attachment

Pride Self-Absorption

Stupidity

Jealousy Envy

Anger Aversion

Figure 18.5

function which can ascribe any content to itself as it moves like a demented cuckoo from nest to evanescent nest with a sense of full proprietorial rights in each and every one. This activity of protecting a territory which is always changing causes a diminution of phenomenological attention since so much has to be ignored in order to maintain the continuity and centrality of self. This is known as stupidity and a great deal of intelligence can be utilised in its continuity, for what stupidity is dull or stupid *about* is precisely the mind's own structurally embedded limitation on awareness. Within that attitude, great intelligence can be displayed in expansion or empowerment, but it does not transcend the 'basic fault', to use Balint's[5] helpful term.

The fragile security of this 'self-existing' self engenders all kinds of boundary issues which are grouped in four segments (see Figure 18.5). *Desire* wants more, reaching out to heal the rupture installed by ignorance. But because it starts from a reified self position to appropriate the other, its satisfaction is grounded in the other's loss of freedom. Any pleasure thus derived is therefore short-lived and perilous and likely to lead to fear and frustration. *Anger* seeks to drive away, crush and punish any threats to the autonomy of this contingent illusory self. However the self is arising in dependent origination[6] with the other and so to drive the other away is to deplete and threaten the self. This in turn promotes a shift to desire in order to bring about replenishment. *Pride* brings both a sense of entitlement over others and a feeling of isolation from their needs. But it also needs a mirror and so is dependent on the other who has to be seduced or bullied into aiding the inflationary task. *Jealousy and envy* are similar in their core fear that what one has is not adequate and is vulnerable. The 'secure base' of self, the self-referencing that adds itself to the apparitional forms as if they were reliable, is revealed as a conceit, as a deceit.

In these ways wave after wave of energetic involvement in the environment is unleashed evoking wave after wave of response from equally reified positions. Like the surface of a pond on the first impact of rain, each individual arises to rock and be rocked by the arising of the others. Within this complex interaction the struggle to remain in control is the prime cause of suffering.

THE COGNITIVE-ANALYTIC VIEW

Many of the elements of this Buddhist model are to be found in modern psychotherapy, particularly in some of the more recent models which seek to integrate historically developed pathological templates from psychoanalysis with the sequential procedural descriptions of the activation and impact of cognitive, and more recently affective, schemas conceptualised in cognitive-behavioural psychotherapy. Aaron Beck's model of depression, though problematic for several reasons, is an interesting early example of cognitive modelling. According to this view, early experience of the environment leads to the development of dysfunctional attitudes, assumptions, or 'schemata' in vulnerable individuals. These remain hidden until activated by resonant environment events. This activation leads to the locking on of negative cognitions which cut the individual off from effective interaction with the environment, resulting in depression. Thus a child whose parents have little time for it may develop the schema 'I am unlovable; the world does not want me.' However through going to school there is enough interaction to keep the child feeling okay. But then later in life a series of abandonments occurs, through redundancy, marital breakdown and so forth, and the underlying schema is powerfully activated in a way that discounts the potentially ameliorating effect of all other life events. This constellates the negative triad shown in Figure 18.6, and so the individual sinks into depression.

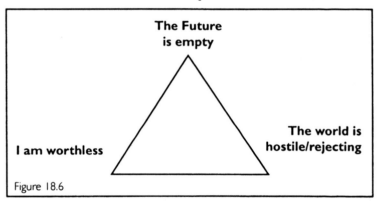

Figure 18.6

The schema is thus in some ways analogous to a karmic potential, for both are activated by precise circumstances. However in Western psychotherapy the originatory cause is generally attributed to the environment rather than to the individual's own attentional, and then latterly ethical, failure, as it is in the Buddhist system.

CAT develops a view of individual identity as arising as the interface between the environment's demands for adaptation and the individual's desire for belonging and meaning (see Figure 18.7).

In this framework, the individual is seen as an interactive sequence, a process of ongoing engagement with the environment, acting and reacting via a ceaseless processing of experience. The great complexity of the multi-dimensional interactive

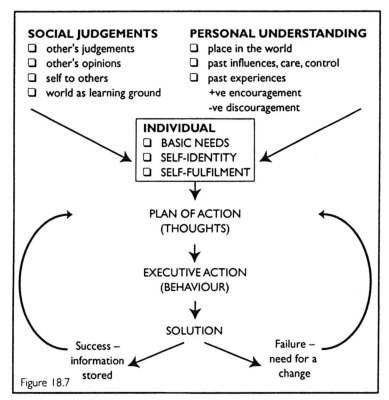

SOCIAL JUDGEMENTS
- ❏ other's judgements
- ❏ other's opinions
- ❏ self to others
- ❏ world as learning ground

PERSONAL UNDERSTANDING
- ❏ place in the world
- ❏ past influences, care, control
- ❏ past experiences
  +ve encouragement
  -ve discouragement

INDIVIDUAL
- ❏ BASIC NEEDS
- ❏ SELF-IDENTITY
- ❏ SELF-FULFILMENT

PLAN OF ACTION
(THOUGHTS)

EXECUTIVE ACTION
(BEHAVIOUR)

SOLUTION

Success –
information
stored

Failure –
need for a
change

Figure 18.7

nature of this process is simplified into a Procedural Sequence
Model (see Figure 18.8): a reaffirming cycle which can operate
with greater or lesser degrees of conscious intentionality.

This dynamic sequencing generates its own energy and seems
to operate like a perpetual motion machine maintaining the
psychosocial life of the individual. There is clearly scope here for
drawing analogies with the twelve links of dependent co-
origination, especially in the circular representation familiar from
the Wheel of Existence.[7]

Each new infant is born ready and willing to engage with the
interactive field it encounters.[8] Key figures in the environment
establish the patterns of response, which have a binary, complementary structure such as criticising – criticised; abandoning –
abandoned; abusing – abused. The more extreme the quality of
the environment, the more intense, narrow and fixed the quality
of these 'reciprocal roles'[9] becomes, leading to the formation of
self states which may have little direct contact with each other.
The infant introjects the pole held originally by a person in the
environment so that these reciprocal roles become basic

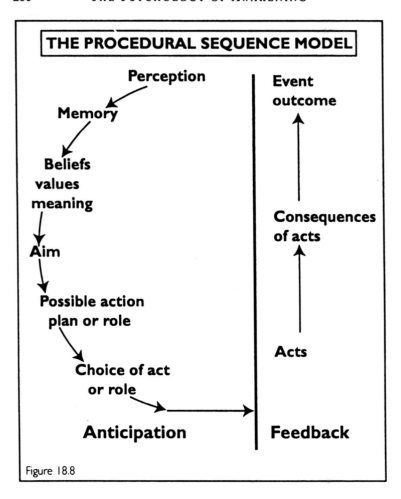

THE PROCEDURAL SEQUENCE MODEL

Perception

Memory

Beliefs
values
meaning

Aim

Possible action
plan or role

Choice of act
or role

Anticipation

Event
outcome

Consequences
of acts

Acts

Feedback

Figure 18.8

organising sites for both self-to-self and self-to-environment experience. Thus self is constructed dialogically[10] as a stream of gestures, a flow of conversation in which self and other cannot be separated as independent monads. Self is a pole of dualistic movement, a pole which is created by that movement and which reveals itself in the interactional responsiveness depicted in the Procedural Sequence Model.

This view would have to regard the autonomous self as a chimera and thus has deep similarities with the Buddhist view described above. Moreover neurotic suffering is generated when the reciprocal role positions resist adaption to the inevitable environmental changes. Thus having grown up in a family where criticising was a primary mode of communication, the adult maintains a criticising–criticised dialogic intention in environments which may be rather more tolerant. This leads to inevitable conflicts which are then processed in terms of criticising–criticised and so the rejected adult can retreat into an angry self-justification alternating with hopeless despair by focusing the criticising pole on either others or self. Suffering for self and other is generated out of entrapment in the rhythm of historical interactive situations which have become condensed as fixed dialogic positions seeking to seduce or coerce the environment into compliance. Thus the open freshness of the potential of the here and now moment is obscured by the imposition of the legacy of past experience.

Clearly in both views reification, fixation, the desire to control others and defend what has been gained become instrumental in the generation of suffering. As the Buddha explained, all sentient beings seek happiness, yet they act continuously in ways which bring about its opposite.

THE CESSATION OF SUFFERING: THE NYINGMA VIEW

Our focus now shifts on to exits, the methods that have been developed to help us extricate ourselves from these pervasive structures of pain. The Buddha Shakyamuni is said to have taught 84,000 Dharmas, both explanations and methods, because sentient beings vary so much. This is an excellent example of the principle that the treatment should be adapted to fit the patient rather than the reverse (though sadly the procrustean bed of ideological foreclosure finds its way into most Dharma centres and psychotherapy institutes).

In the space available we can only touch on some of the Buddhist principles guiding the removal of the causes of suffering. Perhaps three key approaches can be identified: avoidance, regeneration, and disruption. The approach of avoidance seeks to calm the mind by focusing attention on a neutral or reassuring object so that the flow of experience can be experienced as distracting rather than as fascinating. If the object chosen for this focusing is the unborn nature of the mind itself then by recognising it and abiding within it, the very root of *samsara* and all suffering is cut so that all that arises is the ceaseless display of the mind in a state free of reification.[11]

Regeneration occurs when through meditation one goes back

to the ground of all, visualised as a clear blue sky, and with one-pointed attention moves through the three modes of absorption which parallel and deconstruct the three modes of ignorance described above (see Figure 18.9).

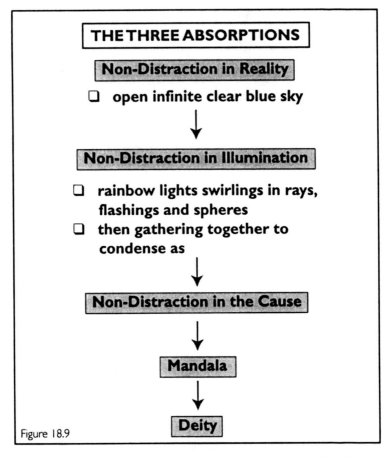

Figure 18.9

Through this process one generates the aesthetically vibrant experience of oneself as a deity in a mandala and the intensity and richness of this experience is used to transform one's daily world at the end of the meditation by enjoying the flavour of the open empty clarity of the mandala in and as all the moments of one's ordinary interactive experience.

This experience of being a deity at the centre of a mandala is the purification and transformation of the five poisons (see Figure 18.5) into the five wisdoms, with the deity manifesting as the integration of the five principles of enlightened and enlightening being-in-the-world. With the awareness of the inalienable openness of being – not being something-as-such, but simply being – the presence of this unborn awareness has no limits and so this infinity is unimpeded no matter what is going on. This is the purification of stupidity, for, rather than experiencing oneself as a self set against the world, self and world arise together as the manifestation of the energy of openness. With this awareness the facticity of impermanence is no longer a threat to identity, an acid inexorably eating away all that we might cling to. Impermanence is the fresh crest of the wave of becoming, on which awareness surfs without ever toppling into the turbulence of the reified splitting of self and other. This is known as the 'wisdom of infinite spaciousness' and it is rich in the confidence of ceaseless generosity, for nothing has been appropriated.

With this at the centre desire and attachment arise as fascination with everything; when nothing is special everything is wonderful, full of the wonder of freshness. As awareness opens to the ceaseless display of becoming, the radiant present frees attention from the determination of linear past-present-future so that surprise is present in each moment. This protects awareness from being shocked out of itself and so ignorance slips by as an unsprung trap. This is called the 'wisdom which is open to everything', an experience rich in discrimination yet free of prejudice and judgement.

Anger and aversion arise only as heightened illumination of the moment, since now the separation from (and retaliation towards) the environment is dissolved in the dislocation of identity. Not being fixed to this body as one's only refuge, awareness becomes a mirror in which self and other carry on their unborn dance of inter-being. With nothing to protect, there is nothing to reject, and so the brilliance of the moment can be enjoyed without threat, even when self is threatened with extinction. This is called the 'mirror-like wisdom', for it reveals appearances to be illusory, essence-less manifestation of nothing at all.

Pride arises only as pride in the infinity of becoming, pride in everything, a pride that deconstructs the isolation of narcissism and self-absorption. 'Where does the world come from? What is the root of me? Of you? Of everything? Why, it is my mind! How wonderful! What is my mind? Where is my mind? Nothing and nowhere – amazing!' The observer self can never observe itself and find something. The motherless mother of all takes pride in all her unborn babies. This is called the 'wisdom of equality', the enjoyment of everything which transcends the petty pleasures of superiority.

Jealousy arises only as a powerful mobilisation free of the paralysis and rage of wondering what others are up to. As awareness welcomes all, nothing can be given or taken away and yet all is connected and so, without shame or anxious excitement, activity moves freely to accomplish whatever is necessary for the benefit of self and others. This is the 'wisdom of accomplishment', of ceaseless unimpeded activity free of the reification of actor, object and connecting activity.

This description of the five wisdoms is necessarily allusive, symbolic and metaphysical since it gestures towards experience on the cusp of language, to a mode of being which cannot be trapped within definitions of this or that. Thus the description invites us into the aesthetic moment of becoming, a moment imbuing language with vibrancy, and yet forever beyond its encapsulation. In this way language itself becomes a means to freedom. This way finds its purest expression in the use of mantra, of 'pure' sound, of sound freshly formed in open awareness, the sound which evokes and sustains the deity and the world of universal liberation through the flow of light, sound and movement.

The third method of liberation, disruption, occurs when one acts on the first level of ignorance by shocking oneself through the use of various techniques, especially the sudden sounding of the syllable Phat![12] One attempts to disrupt the flow of one's thoughts in order to gain a moment's experience of the open state before confusion; and then through that window of opportunity to see the arising of thoughts in quite a different light.

In these various methods the richness of embodied experience, our capacity for thought, feeling, sound, movement, is mobilised in the service of subverting the structure of suffering by settling the dichotomising urge within the simplicity of one-pointed attention.

THE CESSATION OF SUFFERING: THE CAT VIEW

The task of alleviating suffering is construed rather differently in CAT where a three-stage approach is employed (see Figure 18.10).

The 'accurate description' is distilled by the therapist from the first three sessions. Then, in the fourth session of the therapy, the therapist reads out a letter to the patient in which the patient's

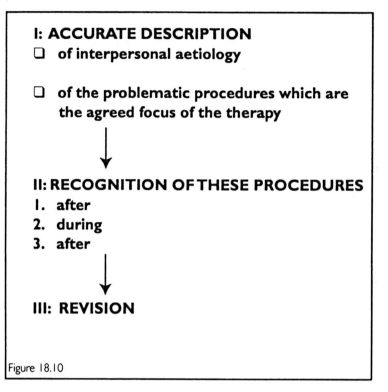

I: ACCURATE DESCRIPTION
❑ of interpersonal aetiology

❑ of the problematic procedures which are
   the agreed focus of the therapy

II: RECOGNITION OF THESE PROCEDURES
1. after
2. during
3. after

III: REVISION

Figure 18.10

presenting problem is refined into a target problem and a historical account is given of the evolution of this target problem via a description of the reciprocal roles and procedures which sustain it. These are then discussed and agreed and become the focus for the therapy i.e. a specific, defined procedural sequence is established as the object of change.

Working with the patient in a collaborative manner the therapist structures the key elements of the description into a diagram, a sequential diagrammatic reformulation.[13] Figure 18.11 illustrates how a reciprocal role structure initiates and is sustained by an interpersonal procedure.

The second stage involves the recognition of these procedures as they operate inside and outside the consulting room. At first they are often only recognised after they have occurred, then one learns to be aware of them as they are going on, and finally one begins to see the conditions in oneself and in the environment which activate the procedures. This of course is very similar to the development of mindfulness in the first style of meditation mentioned above.

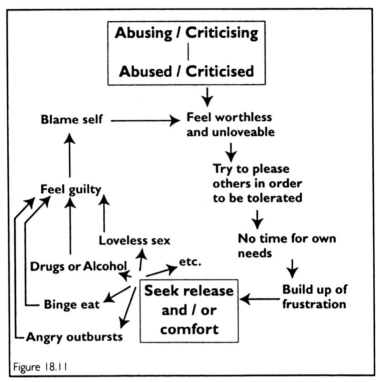

Figure 18.11

Once the process of entrapment in the sequence of habitual limiting responses is clearly established in consciousness, the third stage, revision, can occur. There are many ways to do this but a central focus is always the strengthening of the observing self, especially where the patient's experience of self and other is fragmented.

The Procedural Sequence Model[14] can be used as a basis for discussing specific items of revision (see Figure 18.12).

Clarity and specificity are vital for increasing a sense of self-esteem and self-efficacy and there is an emphasis on homework tasks and evaluation of progress through rating sheets. This again is similar to the Buddhist focus on stages of development and signs of achievement. Precision of evaluation through rating sheets, etc., strengthens the observing self, increasing the space for reflection while also turning the patient's attention away from absorption in habitual thoughts and feelings and towards a more fresh and realistic phenomenological experience.

One question which is very alive in CAT is whether the core reciprocal role positions are an inherent mode of psychological functioning, or whether they can be relaxed until they become

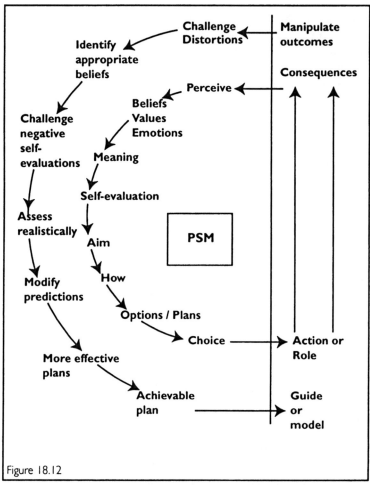

Figure 18.12

'flavours' or 'moods' of interaction rather than determinants of it. Clinically the description of fixed positions in family structure is very helpful in providing a focus for recognition. However the tendency to reify descriptions and to hypothesise the existence of entities is difficult to resist. From the Buddhist viewpoint outlined above, the danger would be that the revision could promote a further concretisation of self and other. In freeing oneself from the encapsulation of a specific reciprocal role determinism, self is established as having a quasi autonomy. This then has to be maintained by attempting to influence the patterns of dualistic interaction through making the best possible choices to achieve the self's goals.

A recent development in CAT has been the use of Bakhtin's

notion of the dialogic structure underpinning all human communication. All speech acts and bodily gestures are taken to be expressions of an intention towards another, a specific other who is the necessary addressee, necessary because without them speech would be a schizoid scream.

Work by Leiman[15] has focused on seeing reciprocal roles as dialogic positions with the suggestion that we develop a necessary core repertoire which then becomes influential if not determinant in our interaction with the environment. In this formulation we again see the reductive move to prediction and stabilisation which, while offering clarification, moves inexorably towards foreclosure. However we can also highlight the potential openness of the field of the dialogic where each position reflects and connects, driving and distorting the energy of interpersonal being. Intentionality is then but a flicker in a hall of mirrors. This is to see the total dialogic field as being like Indra's net, an infinite web of mirror-like crystals which dazzlingly display each other in themselves until self and other are impossible to separate. This motif has of course already been made use of by R.D. Laing[16] in a similar critique of fixed positions in family structures.

The dialogic view allows us to describe dualistic experience in a much more dynamic interactive way, revealing the living inseparability of subject and object, of self and other. This Western view decentres the subject from the splendid isolation of pseudo autonomy and invites the emergence of a responsive awareness moving like a shuttle through the warp and woof of subject-object inter-being. In this way the relative truth[17] experience of entities is reconceptualised allowing a flexibility which gestures towards the openness of absolute truth. Extending the terms of the *Heart Sutra*[18] we can say that the dialogic is emptiness, emptiness is the dialogic.

THE ROLE OF THE TEACHER/THERAPIST

So far we have looked at a range of methods for influencing or even uprooting these structures of suffering without considering how they are imparted. In the Nyingma tradition the teacher or guru is very important for the authenticity of the transmission comes through him – the guru is usually male. The teacher gives instructions on different kinds of meditation, how to do them and how to deal with any difficulties that arise. But he also directly transmits through the quality of his being an experience which gives a living bond with the authenticity of the practice and of oneself. That is to say that the teacher is the gateway to oneself, acting to disrupt the patterns of karma, and their object relations concomitants, which support the false notion of self that then mediates experience. The path to enlightenment is not the journey of a lonely hero or heroine but is a movement between the wisdom that is revealed to us by another and the compassion that we develop in turn for others. The task of meditation cannot be separated from relationship (see Figure 18.13).

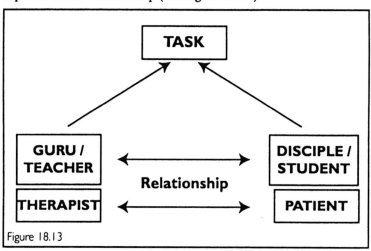

Figure 18.13

In CAT the therapist is both an educator, showing the patient how to attend to the process of her life, and also a potential point of awakening, through non-compliance with the habitual positions that the patient tries to install in the therapeutic relationship. Too much 'task' and the work can be rather cold and formal, lacking the warmth of welcome and conviviality. Too much focus on relationship and the pull of complex connections can ensnare both parties so that the space to think is usurped by a melange of feelings both intoxicating and deadening. If both parties can keep the task in mind, then when the force of the reciprocal roles arises powerfully, causing a rupture in the therapeutic alliance,[19] the experience can be considered via the distilled shared analysis represented in Figures 18.10 and 18.11.

CONCLUSION

Psychotherapy does not seek to facilitate enlightenment in the

Buddhist sense and there have been frequent debates about its goals: for example whether social adaptation is a necessary aim of 'treatment', or whether 'seeking oneself' is often an other-attacking self-indulgence. The Western approaches neither identify nor seek to extirpate the root of suffering as it is set out in the Nyingma view. But perhaps an awareness of the Buddhist vision of infinite freedom of being, and in particular of its commitment to openness and compassion, has a lot to offer psychotherapy. Therapists need an 'inner space' in which to reflect on the process they are involved in, and mindfulness of the open nature of being may be the best inner supervisor[20] for clinical practice. The Buddha suggested that just as a boat is useful for crossing a river but becomes a burden if we carry it with us on our journey, so concepts can be helpful for part of the way but may become heavy and restrictive when the context no longer requires them. Many creative helpful concepts and techniques have been developed in psychotherapy but they can become restrictive, acting as the basis for sectarian identity rather than as useful boats for part of the way. 'Boatism' occurs when we can't move on, when we think we've found a resting-place for this life. Buddhism, with its insistence that whatever is constructed will come apart, provides many methods for deconstruction so that we can stay attuned to the changing rhythm of the world, and through this attain the enlightenment that does not rest anywhere.

But psychotherapy also has much to offer those who practise Buddhism in the West. The Buddhist analysis of experience breaks it down into a wide range of building blocks, *skandhas*, *dhatus*, *samskaras*[21] and so on which can be very alien to current Western thinking. These building blocks are used both for the analysis of experience and, especially in tantra, as points of symbolic transformation. My suggestion would be that the kind of description of the 'components' of interpersonal being developed in CAT provides the basis for a more easily accessible vocabulary to aid analysis and transformation. After all, within the realm of relative truth, our usual mode of experience, what we call truth is always contingent. The important thing is to gain the direct experience of the open nature of awareness and any changes in analytical concepts which aid this process for people at this time is surely to be welcomed. The interplay of Buddhist non-dual openness and Bakhtinian dialogic responsiveness has rich potential to develop a vision that sees through the structures of suffering.

Lucid Dreaming: Exerting the Creativity of the Unconscious

Tarab Tulku

(Compiled and edited by Lene Handberg)

INTRODUCTION

Lucid dreaming is a very old practice indeed. We have written accounts of lucid dream practice in the Indian tradition dating back to the fourth century – but probably the oral tradition dates back much further.

The Buddhist dream-yoga tradition was adopted by Tibetans in the tenth century. It has been practised since then both in Tibet, and since 1959, among Tibetan communities in exile. However, the pre-Buddhist culture of Tibet, named Bön, already had its own well-developed lucid dream tradition. This old shamanistic culture used lucid dreaming for telling the future, for gaining further insight into matters otherwise inaccessible, and for dealing with adverse conditions in terms of negative spirits.

Before the Bön culture Tibet had a so-called folk-religious culture which also used lucid dreaming, in particular for dealing with spirits. In this culture, which is fully alive today in Tibet, and which could very well be many thousands of years old, children learn from an early age how to deal with negativity in their dreams.

On the basis of my experience and understanding of the essential points behind the function of the original Tibetan dream-yoga, as well as that of the ancient shamanistic and folk-religious dream methods, I have developed the psychotherapeutic dream method

'Unity in Duality' as well as methods for personal development. 'Unity in Duality' is a system of Tibetan psychology and psycho-therapy which is based on traditional Tibetan and Indian Buddhist texts as well as my own experience with the Sutras and Tantras. The term 'Unity in Duality' refers to the interdependent relationship between matter and energy, body and mind, as well as subject and object. This understanding is basic to original Tibetan Buddhist philosophy and psychology as well as the dream work presented in this paper.

I. THE TIBETAN VIEW OF THE DREAM STATE

In the Tibetan tradition the dream state is considered as a more subtle state of being, since body and mind are cooperating more closely. The sense perceptions we have in the dream state, and in a state of clear vision, are more subtle than those of ordinary waking consciousness, because our perception in this state is not directly dependent on the physical senses. Even though we do have sense experiences in the dream state, we do not see with the physical eyes, hear with the physical ears, etc. The dream senses are a function of the 'mind'. The five senses we use in the dream state and in the state of clear vision, are of an 'energy' nature, implying that the dream/vision type of sense perception is not necessarily limited in space and time, as is the case with sense perceptions that arise in dependence upon matter.

However, we do not normally experience the dream state as being special, as the impact of normal conceptual mind and the normal roles of physically bound existence carries over into the dream state. As long as we are not lucid, i.e. not aware of dreaming when dreaming, we have a tendency to believe the dream experiences to belong to normal reality – which we assume to be accordingly limited – and the dream state therefore does not strike us as particularly special. Nonetheless, occasionally we have dreams where we fly or are able to go through walls, and thus in various ways are able to break the normal rules of physically bound reality.

Another important view of the dream state, according to the Tibetan tradition, is that the dream state always has both a subject and an object. It is the subject in the dream state which perceives the object and experiences the dream. If there were no subject to perceive and to experience the dream, there would not be any dream.

This point needs to be kept in mind, since the subject/object relationship in the dream state is very important in order to perform the Unity in Duality type of dream psychotherapy.

II. THE TIBETAN VIEW OF THE ORIGIN OF DREAMS

In accordance with the Tibetan view, all impressions during life, from very early childhood, even from the time in the mother's womb, have made imprints in the basic level of mind. There are many types and levels of imprints and many ways in which they influence us. Three types in particular can be distinguished:

a) imprints which determine our concepts, which have a great impact on our apperception;
b) imprints which determine our feeling/emotion, i.e. our self-feeling and self/other reference;
c) imprints which determine the manifestation of appearances.

Imprints emerge all the time in everyday life. Yet they are often unnoticed, since we mistake our experiences for being determined by outer reality alone, and not for what they to a great extent are, subjective creations due to imprints of former experiences. The imprints naturally appear in the dream state, and it is with those imprints that we are most concerned in this paper.

The Tibetan dream tradition categorises three types of causes for dreams to appear, two of which relate to imprints:

Type I: Most dreams appear due to neutral daytime residuals: any kind of daytime experience is to a great extent determined by former imprints, which again create new imprints. Any of these layers and types of imprints subsequently can give rise to dreams. Nonetheless, included in this first category are those neutral imprints which give rise to ordinary or non-spectacular dream experiences.

Type II: The so-called – from a normal Western psychotherapeutic point of view – 'interesting' dreams, are those that rise from imprints caused by experiences in which one is unbalanced, violated, etc. These are impressions we normally have a strong tendency to repress. No matter what difficult times we have been through physically or mentally, the impressions left by them are retained in the basic level of mind. Many people lack the proper support in early or later childhood that they need. This is a very important time in forming basic mental structures and relations to external reality, i.e. an important time for laying the basis of self-reference and reference to others, which is basic to the individual's subsequent creation and experience of reality.

All these types of experience form deep and lasting impressions in the basic mental, physical and 'energy' structure of ourselves, and they then occur in our dreams. According to the Tibetan view of dreams, it is the dream's natural function to be the experiential space where those imprints with which we have been insufficiently concerned or which, for different reasons, we have repressed, occur. These types of imprint generally cause imbalances to our being (both physically, mentally and in terms of subtle body/mind 'energy'). It is the natural function of dreams to balance these often terrible imbalances of our basic mental structures.

Many of these experiences are connected with fear, which generally relates back to a basic fear of either losing one's identity or one's existence. Such experiences are those in which our identity has been violated, frightened and/or degraded, resulting in a weak self-reference and personality structure, which is easily provoked, thus leading to an experience of fear that one's self-identity will be destroyed.

These impressions arise in dreams in the form of special dream-subject/object constellations, most often as the type of scene set by some sort of aggressor and a weak experiencer (subject).

Type III: In addition to these two types of dreams, which are more or less determined by former impressions, the Tibetan dream tradition also includes a third type of dream. This third type includes those dreams in which the individual naturally appears to have special abilities that allow him or her to transgress the spacio-temporal limitations of the physical body. This also includes dreams relating to past and future events, and to subtle levels of reality that we otherwise have no access to in our normal state of being.

III. Types of Dreams Suitable for Practising the Actual Dream-Yoga

When one's dreams basically consist of unproblematic daytime residuals of Type I, one is considered ready to begin training in the original Tibetan dream-yoga. This implies that the original Tibetan dream-yoga is to be practised only by persons of great stability of mind.

If one has the second type of dreams mentioned above, it is advised to deal with them before starting the original Tibetan dream-yoga practice. This is because this type of dream indicates an, at least partly, unbalanced personality structure/weak self-identity, which has to be dealt with and healed before entering into any of the yoga practices. In order to deal with the underlying unbalances we can re-enter these types of recalled dreams, and use some of the methods from the dream-yoga, i.e. we can use the Unity In Duality dream method (see below).

Dreams of the third type obviously cause no obstruction to the original Tibetan dream-yoga practice.

IV. The Four Stages of Traditional Tibetan Dream-Yoga

These four stages are as follows:

1. *rMi-lam bzung-ba*, 'to hold the dream'.
2. *rMi-lam sbyang-ba*, 'to purify or master the dream'.
3. *sGyu-ma ltar slab-pa*, 'to conjure up illusions or miracles'.
4. *De-kho na-nyid sgom-pa*, 'meditation on thatness'.

1. *rMi-lam bzung-ba*, 'To Hold The Dream' – As Seen from the Perspective of Psychotherapy and Self-development

This stage corresponds to what in the West we refer to as the 'lucid dream technique'. 'To hold the dream' implies to go consciously into the dream state and know that you are dreaming.

In the Tibetan tradition there are two basic methods for cultivating lucid dreaming. The first (a) uses will power, while the second (b) uses 'energy' power.

a) *The method of will power*. Traditionally this method is

connected with different rituals and meditations. The practitioner visualises different deities in connection with which he performs rituals. The purpose of these practices is to draw on the deity's power to help strengthen one's own will power. This enables one to keep one's awareness alert and clear throughout the process of falling asleep. In addition, the practitioner commonly visualises and experiences a red energy-light-ball in the throat chakra area, through which he or she enters the dream state.

b) *The method of 'energy' power.* There are many different energy practices the practitioner can use in order to train himself to attain a subtle body/mind level of being. These include: 'vase breathing', *'tumo'* (inner heat), and various 'chakra-energy' practices. With the subtle body/mind level attained through accomplishing these practices, the practitioner is able to consciously enter the dream state, thus attaining lucid dreaming at will. The method of using 'energy' power relates to highly advanced tantric practices, which do not only imply physical and mental 'energy' experiences but also existential changes.

The practices of this first stage of dream-yoga are useful for those gifted people who wish to use the dream state for spiritual development. However, these methods – without the deity rituals – are also useful simply for (a) training oneself to remember one's dreams; (b) for attaining lucid dreaming; (c) for strengthening the sense of subjectivity in the dream state; and (d) being more present in the body/mind sensation of oneself in the waking state. These types of training therefore naturally enhance a more healthy mental state of being. It falls out of the context of this paper, however, to elaborate further on this first stage of dream-yoga.

2. *rMi-lam sbyang-ba*, 'To Purify or Master the Dream' – As Seen from the Perspective of Psychotherapy and Self-development

In the Tibetan expression *rMi-lam sbyang-ba*, *rMi-lam* means 'dream', and *sbyang-ba* can mean 'to purify', 'to practise', and 'to master'. *sByang* can also mean to get rid of mental disturbances in the sense of 'purification'.

This second stage of dream-yoga is mainly a training in mastering the dream body/mind in the dream state, in order to gain the ability to make one's own decisions to act in the dream. This is the basis for being able actively to deal with the dream-object, or, more precisely, to deal with the dream-subject/object constellation. The basic practice is first of all to use the dream senses in order to be able to perceive more fully the details of the object one has decided to focus on.

a) *Dealing with imprints appearing in the dream.* Impressions in the deeper level of mind (whether neutral day residuals, disturbing repressed impressions from early childhood, or even imprints from threats to one's identity in adult life) form a mental structure which, as mentioned above, has a great impact on the conceptual and mental feeling we have of ourselves, our self-reference and self-identity.

In the dream state, these impressions rise and manifest in the 'energy' or non-material form-constellation revealed in the relationship between the dream-subject and the dream-object.

If one is able to actively engage the dream-subject to deal with the dream-object, there are possibilities for changing the underlying mental structure, which otherwise would reinforce a continuous weakening of one's self-feeling or identity. Through this method of strengthening the dream-subject, not just in imagination but in the actual energy-relationship with the dream-object, it is possible to strengthen and heal the damaged self-feeling or weakened identity.

b) *Imaginary-dream or fantasy-dream for psychotherapy and personal development.* In dealing psychotherapeutically with the dream we can, by using these methods, jump the first stage of the original dream-yoga and go directly to the second stage. But we do this on an imaginary-dream level rather than in the dream state itself.

Dealing with one's difficulties and fears represented by the particular subject/object constellation in the dream state does have a much stronger effect than dealing with one's difficulties and fears in the state of dream-imagination or fantasy-dream. Still we have found that dream-yoga methods of the second level do have a strong healing and balancing effect on the client, even when practised in a state of dream-imagination – by working, for instance, with recalled dreams. But should one have lucid dream abilities these can certainly and effectively be used for psychotherapeutic healing. However, first of all one has to learn the methods, which can be developed through working in a state of dream-imagination.

For this kind of dream work the client is guided into a deeper or more subtle state of being – a state in between the dream state and the waking state – in which it is possible to make the body and mind cooperate more closely. In this state the client is still aware, and he therefore knows that the appearances he works with are not of his normal waking-state reality. To lose himself in the imaginary dream does not have the same consequences as it would have had in the normal waking-state reality, a knowledge which allows him more freedom to go through otherwise challenging episodes that normally would provoke too much fear.

In dealing with the challenges met by the client in the recalled dream or imaginary dream, we make use of the special Tibetan knowledge of this state, the special instructions of how to act and deal with the dream-object as described in the second stage of dream-yoga, as well as the dream methods of Tibetan folk tradition and old Tibetan Bön tradition.

c) *To finish the dream*. According to the Tibetan understanding, the natural function of the dream is to be the space in which imprints – especially those we have repressed – can arise. It is thus a healthy function of dreams to balance the imbalances of our basic mental structures.

It is therefore very important to finish one's dreams. If we are aware of it, we will see that many of our dreams have not finished. We often wake up either when something frightening happens or when something really good is about to take place. We very seldom allow ourselves to go through these dreams to the very end. This means that the natural dream function is not fulfilled. Since the problematic mental structures underlying such dreams are part of one's self-reference/other-reference, and since one's normal conceptual experience of self and other has a great impact also in the dream state, the natural healing process of the dream state is most often prevented.

d) *The first three aspects of the psychotherapeutic means of the Tibetan dream-practice.*

i)   First and foremost it is necessary to remember the dreams.
ii) Secondly, we should allow the natural healing process of the dream state to take place, which means to consciously allow the dream to terminate naturally.
iii) Thirdly, the Tibetan psychotherapy Unity in Duality implies working among other things with confronting dream-subject/

object constellations in the recalled dreams, by guiding the client into this particular part of the dream, and dealing with it in one of the ways that are schematically presented below.

e) *How to deal with confrontations in the dream state as well as in the imaginary-dream state.* First of all the dream-subject needs to be mastered. Often in dreams the dream-subject is not experienced very strongly. Sometimes one is more like a shadow figure, or one is just an observer watching the dream-film going on, without a real sense of being the dream-subject. When the dream-subject is hardly present, the dreamer may not have a proper experience of himself in the dream. In this case the dreamer has little possibility of dealing with the dream-object. The dream just runs on of its own accord.

To master the dream-subject entails mastering the dream-senses. The client is therefore encouraged to train in seeing, hearing and feeling the dream-scene more clearly, and in particular to feel his own dream-body. Also, in order to establish himself properly, he should try to look down at himself, noticing his hands and feet. But when doing this, it is advised not to leave one's dream-body, i.e. to look at the dream-body from outside, as this would again leave one with no ability to deal with the dream-object. Thereafter, the dream-body is trained to move around in the dream-scene and use the dream-senses as consciously as possible.

To use the dream-senses and to feel the dream-body establishes the whole dream-subject/dream-object relationship on an experiential level. The dream-reality can be experienced even more vividly than one's normal experience in the waking state.

Next, while maintaining the feeling of the dream-body, the client can try to feel the sensation of whatever dream-object he has chosen to focus on. In this way it is often possible to feel beyond the manifest dream-object, sensing the original mental problem to which it is pointing. One thus comes to sense the original mental problem represented by the particular dream-subject/dream-object constellation.

The client in the form of the dream-subject then chooses which strategy feels right to adopt in the situation. We will now discuss three strategies the adept or client may adopt to work directly with fear when confronted with a negative feature of the dream-scene (or dream-object). The three strategies are: a) flight, b) fight, and c) surrender.

i) *Flight.* First of all, according to the Tibetan psychotherapy method of Unity in Duality, the adept is advised never to flee the negativity, but either to fight it, or better still, to let the negativity destroy himself, i.e. to *unite* with the negativity. However, in order to understand how this method works, we must understand the dynamism between the negativity and the dream-subject confronting it. Generally, we experience pleasant feelings when the object is supportive, and unpleasant feelings when one's identity is threatened. Thus, in dreams, the constellation of a weak dream-subject and an aggressor represents the fear of having one's identity destroyed. In this case, the dream-subject is the weak part and the dream-object is the strong part. The dreamer is thus identified with a weak identity. In fleeing the aggressor, the dreamer then misses the opportunity to work with his weak identity. Instead, he again manifests his weaknesses.

ii) *Fight*. The dreamer feels strengthened by fighting that which attacks his dream-subject identity. There are basically two ways in which the dreamer can become stronger: either by identifying with a more subtle body/mind level of himself or by contacting help from outside. This help can be of many types: it may be of the nature of a subtle universal 'energy', religious symbols or images, heroes or trusted friends – according to the client's beliefs. The help can either deal directly with the dream-aggressor, or be used to strengthen the dream-subject, e.g. to make the subject identify with his more subtle mental/physical forces, giving a more genuine feeling-experience of oneself.

iii) *Surrender*. Thirdly, the dreamer can let the aggressor destroy his dream-subject, i.e. he can unite with the negativity. When the negativity destroys the dream-subject, it destroys that with which one identifies. However, once this weak identity has been destroyed, one naturally goes beyond the weak identity and reaches a more subtle, authentic layer of being. In no longer identifying with the weak identity, there is nothing to sustain the interaction between the fear and the negativity, because neither any longer exist. If one is able to go through with this method completely, underlying psychological problems can be healed.

f) *The process of transformation*. The strategy of surrender can lead to a process of transformation, which resembles the process of death. According to both the Abhidharma literature of the Sutra tradition as well as texts of the Tibetan Tantric tradition, when dying we go through different experiences of dissolution that take us from a solid form level into an 'energy' level of being. This process of dying is used in shamanic as well as Tantric practices. It describes how one changes from one state into another. This is often expressed as the 'elements' or the 'energy-origins' dissolving into one another. First the 'earth element' dissolves into the 'water element' and gives rise to certain experiences. Then water dissolves into fire, fire into air, and air into space, each phase being characterised by a different experience. Finally, the air element dissolves into the space element, leading to four different stages of experiences before reaching the 'clear light' of unity of body/mind and subject/object.

Throughout this transformative process of the dying of one's former weak identity, one experiences a change from a solid level of the problematic subject/object interrelation to an 'energy' level beyond the conceptual and emotional construction of the object. In this 'energy' state the subject (one's self-feeling) and the object (one's experience of the object) are no longer separate. This gives an experience of full inner strength, wholeness of oneself, and the regaining of a genuine self-feeling. From this 'energy' level a new 'form' appears, purified of the former artificially constructed identity and all the projections connected to it.

Another way of describing this process would be as follows. Through dream appearances (*sNang-ba*) in the form of a particular subject/object relationship (which has emerged because of former imprints) the underlying and related feeling/emotion (*Myong-ba*), which was previously repressed, is allowed to arise. By letting oneself completely identify with this process of transformation beyond conceptualisation (*rTog-pa*), one is taken through the natural process of exhausting the original problematic self/other structure and its related feeling/emotion (which created the weak subject and the aggressor and other experiences of negativity) to a genuine feeling of wholeness of oneself.

If one is able to go completely beyond conceptualisation, it is possible to be part of this transformation process, which is the dying of the problematic identity structure. But even though one can only partly go beyond the naming and description of experiences in connection with this process, it will nonetheless bring one into touch with a more genuine self-feeling. The less conceptualisation, the more we can allow ourselves to be part and parcel of the actual changing process, and the better and deeper is the result.

g) *Using the abilities of the second stage of the dream-yoga in the dream state or in the imaginary-dream state for gaining knowledge*. Having developed the ability to 'master the dream', it is possible to engage in many different and even extraordinary activities in both the dream state and imaginary-dream state. If, for instance, one wishes to understand certain topics in the arts or the sciences, there are methods whereby one can contact or tune into the 'energy-lines' of that particular field. The dream state and the subtle imaginary-dream state make this possible because of their special nature of stronger unity between body/mind and subject/object.

3. *sGyu-ma ltar slab-pa*, 'to Conjure up Illusions or Miracles'

To complete this paper we will just briefly mention the last two stages of the original dream-yoga. However, these stages are not used for dealing psychotherapeutically with the dream or for normal personal development. Such practices are undertaken in the dream state itself and require a high level of attainment. They are only relevant for those engaged in advanced 'spiritual practice'.

The third stage is 'to conjure up illusions or miracles'. The core of actual dream-yoga practice is to break the roles of dualistic existence in order to go beyond them. At this third stage the adept learns to break some of our strongest beliefs: the belief in the solidity and absoluteness of the object; the belief in separateness between subject and object; and the belief in the linearity of time and fixity in space.

In order to change the dream-object, the adept has to develop the subtle inner will power of the dream body/mind to contact his basic structuring energy, thus also enabling him to contact the structuring level of the dream-object. Through directly contacting this energy, the adept is able to change the object and/or create new objects at will. When, in the dream state, the adept can tune into this subtle structuring energy of subject and the object and use it for changing the object, thus breaking the ordinary natural laws of separateness, solidity of matter, etc. On attaining this ability, it is possible through using will power to transgress the ordinary limitations of space and time.

4. *De-kho na-nyid sgom-pa*, 'Meditation on Thatness'

The fourth and last stage of dream-yoga is 'to merge with the unity of the subtle body/mind'. Here the adept is no longer working with the dream-object or dream appearances. He now works directly with the unified subtle feminine and masculine energies of the dream-subject, enabling him to go beyond dream-appearances. He can now manifest himself in another form within the ordinary waking-state reality, thus attaining a state of being closely connected to that called 'the illusory body' (*sGyu-lus*). Nonetheless, at the fourth level of dream-yoga, he still trains to break the natural laws of dualistic existence, especially in regard to temporal and spacial limitations.

SUMMARY

From the point of view of traditional Tibetan dream-yoga, for the adept to use the potentialities of the dream state, he has to train and build up his abilities step by step. First he has to train to go consciously into the dream state, thus invoking the state of lucid dreaming. Thereafter, he must develop his own power in the dream state, thus establishing himself firmly in the dream. The mastery of this last step is strongly emphasised in dream-yoga, because the quality of the adept's skill in dealing with the dream-subject, and through that with the dream-object, depends on the development of his own power as the dream-subject. This step is followed by training the adept's abilities in using the dream body/mind, first in connection with the dream-object, then in dealing directly with the subtle energy levels of the subject, and finally in a transference to the waking-state reality of the abilities and knowledge he has obtained in the dream-state.

In general, however, any practice that leads towards awakening and developing subtle energies of body/mind – whether in the dream or waking state – will have an impact on one's ability to create clear dreams, develop the dream-power necessary for creating lucid dreams at will, and work directly with dream appearances in the dream.

In doing dream work on a psychological level, as briefly outlined above, the development of skills in the imaginary dream as well as in the dream itself is as important as in traditional dream-yoga practice. For when these skills are developed, psychological transformation takes place on a more subtle energy level of being. In other words, the psychological changes are existentially of a deeper nature.

Mindfulness of Breathing and Contemporary Breathwork Techniques

Joy Manné

This paper takes a meditation case history and proposes that the problem could have been treated more efficiently through the use of conscious breathing techniques.[1] My position is that knowledge of meditation practice and technique enhances therapeutic breathwork, and knowledge of therapeutic breathwork techniques makes meditation more effective.

1. A MEDITATION CASE HISTORY

Mark Epstein, in his book, *Thoughts without a Thinker: Psychotherapy from a Buddhist Perspective*, contains a meditation case history that demonstrates some very basic features of breathwork meditation.[2] The first is that the breath is not a neutral object. Joe, a participant during a meditation retreat, '(finds) himself quite fearful of watching his breath . . . (as) it felt dangerous and made him anxious'. It takes three full days before Joe is able to concentrate on his breath again. We see from this that observing the breath has profound psychological consequences. This is hardly surprising as observing the breath is observing the process of consciousness itself.

The second feature is the close connection between breathwork meditation and bodywork. The next stage in Joe's breathwork meditation was a peak experience 'immediately followed by the feeling of an iron band constraining his abdomen, hurting him and restricting his breath'. These feelings were so intense and unpleasant that meditation could not help Joe through them in any way: 'No amount of attention, no change in position, no associated thoughts or feelings, no advice from his teachers seemed to affect the intensity of the sensations.'

The third feature is the close connection between breathwork meditation and both primal therapy and regression therapy. Joe finally stopped fighting his process. He stopped trying to induce the suggested meditative altered states of consciousness and he stopped trying to please his meditation teachers. Instead he surrendered to what was happening. Lying in one position and overcome by sadness, he 'sobbed and shook for several hours'. Eventually, he remembered a traumatic childhood incident during which he had hidden from his raging father in the closet with his mouth filled with rags. This was when he had learned to hold his breath and to 'bind all of his fear and rage and despair in the muscles of his abdomen'.

In spite of the evidence which he cites, and despite his own observation (quoted above) that Joe's unpleasant sensations could not be alleviated through any advice whatever from his meditation teachers, Epstein nevertheless asserts the efficacy of meditation, claiming that Joe's realisation came through the meditative state rather than through therapy. He does, however, add this proviso: '(Joe's) years of therapy obviously helped him see the experience through in a way that many other such traumatised people could not.'

There is a gentle way of working with the breath therapeutically that would have brought Joe through his problem probably in one or two hours.

2. *ANAPANASATI* AND PSYCHOTHERAPY

Joe's experience was evoked in the context of the Buddhist meditation on the breath, *anapanasati*.[3] This practice concerns much more than the awareness of breathing. It shows the Buddhists using the breath in order to attain non-ordinary states of consciousness. If we analyse the sequence in the text, we see that the basic requirement is to have sufficient concentration to be able, for an extended period, *to breathe with awareness*.

The exercises begin with directing one's attention towards *the duration of one's breath*. I think that everyone who has tried meditation will agree that it is impossible to be aware of the duration of one's breath without also becoming aware of its rhythm, the quantity of air one is inhaling and exhaling, the way the air is flowing into and out of the body and the movement of and feelings in the body as the air flows in and out of it. There is also awareness of whether the breath is easy or blocked and where it may be blocked. We are thus immediately in the realm of today's breath and body therapies and indeed Joe's case history shows that comparable experiences will be evoked. Watching the breath can indeed feel fearful and dangerous and induce anxiety. Many traumatic situations result in the habit of holding or blocking the free flow of one's breathing.[4]

The next part of the exercise too has similarities with today's breath and body therapies. It uses the breath to *experience the whole body*. Experiencing the whole body may bring up various physical tensions such as the feelings of restricted or obstructed breathing or tension in the abdomen that came up in Joe's case. As Epstein says: 'Joe's story illustrates the power of meditation to focus us in on the places in our bodies where fear has taken hold.' The exercise then goes on to using the breath to *calm bodily activity*. It is difficult to calm bodily activity without becoming aware of where the bodily activity is agitated, and working through *psychotherapeutically* the causes of the agitation. Epstein describes these as 'the internalised remnants of chronic defensive reactions, fossilised within the body out of reach of our usual awareness'. In the case history, Joe's breath was constrained by the feeling of an iron band around his abdomen and this problem had to be worked through to the point of catharsis. As Epstein says, 'when there has been a specific trauma, there is often a specific focal point in the body that needs to be experienced'. This is classically the language and the process of body therapy.

The text then passes to using the breath to cultivate the particular emotional states of *joy*, and *happiness*. We read in the texts that the mind of someone who is happy is concentrated.[5] The purposeful cultivation of joy and happiness is likely to evoke the awareness of their absence, and also the experience of their opposites, sorrow and suffering, as well as emotions such as passion, hatred and delusion[6] which are considered particularly dangerous and harmful in the Buddhist texts.[7] Joy and happiness become possible when we have resolved enough of our life's suffering and when we have attained some degree of freedom from our intense emotions, hatreds and wrong ideas.

In this exercise, being able to produce states of joy and happiness at will, supported by the breath, is a prerequisite for confronting the mind. Only then does the meditator have enough concentration to use the breath to focus awareness upon *experiencing mental activity*, i.e. to become conscious of what is happening in her/his mind. Experiencing mental activity is what happens in every psychotherapy, unfortunately without the preparation of being able to enter stages of joy and happiness at will. The meditation continues with using the breath to *calm mental activity*. This includes purifying the mind by getting rid of certain hindrances which can be regarded as negative thought patterns, among them covetousness for the world, ill-will, apathy, agitation, regret and doubt.[8] Working through these mental states is also part of today's psychotherapies.

The breath is then used to *experience mind*: this is a state of being able to watch the mind without becoming involved with its multiple processes. This peaceful state cannot come about unless practitioners have worked through and integrated many of their life's problems. Otherwise, as is well known in psychotherapy, these keep coming up.

The next stage is to *please the mind*, keeping it contented and peaceful, so that it is possible to *concentrate the mind*, and *release the mind*. One can then use the breath to *observe impermanence, freedom from passion, cessation* and *renunciation*.

All of these exercises and the states of consciousness that they induce are supported and energised by the breath. For most parts of this exercise, and certainly for practitioners on all but the highest levels, this is, in today's terms, psychotherapy using the breath as the means to gain access to the unconscious.

3. REBIRTHING AND MEDITATION

The use of connected breathing techniques in personal and spiritual development was developed by Leonard Orr and Sondra Ray in 1977 as *Rebirthing*.[9] If you spend a moment observing your breathing you will notice that there is a pause between the inhale and the exhale, and again between the exhale and the inhale. Traditionally rebirthing is taught as strong and rapid connected breathing in the top of the chest, the pause between inhale and exhale being avoided. This is what I will mean when I refer to rebirthing in what follows. Hyperventilation is often connected with Rebirthing, not always justifiably.[10]

Rebirthing got its name because its method of breathing frequently caused clients to relive their birth trauma. In fact, Rebirthing is a powerful psychotherapy and brings up the same material as psychoanalysis.[11] The breath is the 'royal expressway' to the unconscious. Rebirthing goes further than psychoanalysis, however: breathwork induces transpersonal experiences as the Buddhist text on awareness of the breathing shows.

There are certain common problems between practitioners of meditation and clients in Rebirthing, usually called rebirthees. In Rebirthing, as in meditation, there are people who can just do it. Rebirthing and meditation work for these clients. They have good concentration and awareness. They cope with the experiences that come up, remain stable, integrate what happens and make good progress. There are people who can neither meditate nor do Rebirthing. In meditation, they have insufficient concentration: their minds wander, they daydream or they fall asleep.[12] In this way they escape the experiences that meditation may induce. Another outcome for meditators who have insufficient awareness is that they become very rigid in their minds and bodies through fighting out of their consciousness with sheer will power the experiences they cannot integrate. These meditators hold on to the meditation object with grim determination which they mistake for concentration. In Rebirthing there is a second person present, so mind-wandering and daydreaming are more difficult, although clients do sometimes fall asleep.[13] Further, there is a witness there to draw the client's attention to rigid body holding. Rebirthing clients may also suffer from tetany, a temporary painful paralysis of the hands and sometimes of the mouth, too, during sessions. Tetany is said to be caused by hyperventilation.[14] Hyperventilation forces into consciousness painful experiences, or evokes non-ordinary states of consciousness, that the client may not be ready to integrate. This accounts for the hysteria frequently present in groups where hyperventilation is practised. Tetany is the psyche's way of preventing this abuse from taking place.

Both meditation and Rebirthing can bring up extreme experiences. These may be traumatic memories, ecstatic states, and other altered states of consciousness.[15] The incident in the case history cited above is an example of a traumatic event evoked through meditation. When the foundation of personal development is insufficient for the integration of these experiences, various more or less serious problems may ensue. The strong ecstatic experiences can cause people without a solid foundation to lose contact with reality and to become flippy. There are many examples in the Buddhist texts of people who wanted to out-Buddha the Buddha, imagining they knew more than he did. One Sarabha claimed that he gave up being a follower of the Buddha for the reason that he understood the Buddha's teaching. The Buddha challenged Sarabha to repeat this claim in his presence. Sarabha could not, and so his claim was exposed as false.[16] Contemporary meditators, too, may come to believe that they are enlightened, boast about it and start playing the 'Teacher'.[17] In Rebirthing, practitioners may take up various types of rather odd religious beliefs (belief in the possibility of physical immortality is frequent[18]) or fall into other types of unrealistic beliefs or superstitious thought.[19]

These are the main kinds of outcome that I have noticed with both meditation and Rebirthing. These outcomes are not mutually exclusive. Many clients will go beyond tetany after a number of sessions and be able to open up and integrate the material that comes up. Many meditators and rebirthees who have spent some time being unrealistic will become realistic. With confidence and knowledge, people who have sought safety in rigid defences become more flexible.

4. MEDITATION INFLUENCES REBIRTHING

My experience with *vipassana* meditation, the Buddhist breathing exercises,[20] and my study of Buddhist texts influenced my practice of Rebirthing, and eventually I came to an adaptation which I now call 'Conscious Breathing Techniques'. This is a six-part structure for using the breath in therapy and for personal and spiritual development. The structure is:

Part 1. Awareness work with the breath and analytical breathwork
Part 2. Introduction to independent breathwork
Part 3. Inducing conscious connected breathing
Part 4. Working the breath
Part 5. Advanced energy work with the breath
Part 6. Advanced awareness work with the breath.[21]

This influence was not systematic except for one point: as in the exercises the breath is used as a support for awareness and the cultivation of specific states of consciousness.

5. CONSCIOUS BREATHING TECHNIQUES
INFLUENCE MEDITATION

I will briefly describe the various stages of the structure and relate them to the experiences Joe went through in his meditation practice to show hypothetically how Conscious Breathing Techniques could contribute to a more effective practice of meditation.

Many people do not naturally have basic awareness and have to learn it. The Buddha says, 'the practice of mindfulness of breathing in and out is not for one who is careless in mindfulness or inattentive'.[22] So the first step in working with the breath is to teach awareness and *analysis*. The one leads to the other.

In Joe's case history, his fearfulness of watching his breath could have been treated through awareness in the following way: When Joe feels an iron band around his stomach, he can be encouraged to breath into that area and to use his breath to explore the iron band. In other words, to increase his awareness of the situation he describes and to explore it with his awareness. The realisation and consequent release usually come very quickly. In this case, it was some days before the meditator realised that, 'all of his fear and rage and despair in the muscles of his abdomen, (and) the iron band around his diaphragm was the feeling that resulted from his sobbing and holding his breath (stifling his reactions so as not to set off his father), with his diaphragm rising and falling until it cramped'.

Joe's fear could also have been treated analytically through the use of precisely relevant questions or instructions while he was attending to his breathing, e.g. 'Tell me about this fear of watching your breath', or 'What is your relationship with your breath?' or 'Do you often have feelings of tension in your abdomen?' or 'Tell me about feelings of tension in your abdomen.' Again, one would expect the client to come rather quickly to realise that he had a habit of holding his breath, and to connect that to his father's treatment of him and possibly to other traumatic events. Joe's fidgeting could be similarly treated with awareness and analysis. Here the technique would either be to avoid it or to enhance it. In order to avoid it the instruction would be: 'Be aware of your urge to fidget, but do not do it. Just keep connected to your breath and be aware of this urge.' In order to enhance it the instruction would be 'Fidget consciously. Make the movements your body wants to make. Really go into this, and all the time remain connected to your breathing.' Here I would expect that after only a few minutes Joe's body would have ended up repeating the position in the cupboard. Whatever the instructions, the breathing is at all times the anchor, the source of grounding, the support for mindfulness. In both awareness work with the breath and analytical breathwork, clients remain grounded in their breathing, speaking only on their out-breath, so that their conscious breathing continues to energise their process. Both methods: awareness work and analysis, would be likely to result in catharsis, understanding and integration.

The second step of the structure is the introduction to independent breathwork. This happens when clients are aware of what is happening in their minds and bodies and can concentrate on it. With regard to our hypothetical treatment of Joe's case history: if he had been capable of this level of conscious breathwork, he would spontaneously have had his attention on his bodily feelings and have been able to keep it there. He would have known how to observe these feelings, analyse them and integrate what he discovered as he worked. It is easy for the trained breathworker to support a client in such a situation if the client can work at this level. Good accompaniment would have helped Joe to move through his fear of his breath and to integration of the traumatic event that caused it. Many conscious-breathing techniques that facilitate discharge of tension are available. In this situation one possibility is to invite the client to breathe into the area of tension and to release the tension on the out-breath.

Effective meditation depends on competence in these first two stages of conscious breathwork.

Inducing conscious connected breathing is the third part of this structured way of doing breathwork. This means inviting the client to breathe in such a way that pauses between in- and out-, and out- and in-breaths are eliminated. This is done once clients have a good foundation: i.e. they are grounded, their self-awareness is good, their awareness of their body is good, and their self-esteem is good. Then they are ready to integrate stronger experiences. Connected breathing is more likely to lead to trance states although it will not necessarily do so. It will certainly lead to strong experiences and that is why it should only be induced with clients who have already developed a sufficiently solid foundation to be able to integrate these. Connected breathing may be proposed, but it should never be imposed. Connected breathing is not hyperventilation.

From the case history, it seems possible that Joe was in a breathing trance: it seems that his breath was breathing him into an experience and holding him there. He could not get out of the process or shake it off, but had to work it through. Augmented breathing (see fourth stage below) and connected breathing give energy to such a process. Although what has to be gone through may be unpleasant, the support of the breathworker makes it easier and gives ongoing guidance. In this process, what might have happened to Joe if he had been working at this level is an intensification of the feeling of choking over a short period (usually only minutes) followed by the realisation of its cause and a discharge of the tension held through childhood.

The fourth stage is working the breath. Rebirthing is also called 'conscious connected breathing' as the in-breath and the out-breath are connected and form a continuous cycle. It is unfortunately often associated with rapid breathing in the upper chest area, which is an unnecessarily limiting way of using connected breathing. Conscious connected breathing can take any form and rhythm and can be focused on any body zone. Working the breath means any rhythm of consciously connected breathing intentionally undertaken and worked purposefully and with discipline like a physical exercise. This *consciously augmented* breathing is not to be confused with hyperventilation,[23] which I categorically exclude from my practice: there is nothing meditative or conscious in hyperventilation.

When working the breath, the goals for the session are discussed and an appropriate rhythm of breathing and part of the body where the breath should happen is proposed. There is an agreement between client and therapist that if what has been proposed does not happen, whatever is happening will be honoured, as the true practice of awareness in meditation demands (and which, incidentally, does not seem to have been proposed by Joe's meditation teachers). The breath is an honest guide on the path of development.

This way of breathing induces intense emotional experiences, regressions and higher states of consciousness. When we have learned to contain ourselves and can integrate strong experiences, we are ready to work with the consciously connected breath without fear. We are ready to play with our breath and have adventures with it. Breathwork consciously undertaken, in strength and not through an overwhelming upsurgence of the unconscious, can lead to shamanic experiences at this stage. Stanislav Grof's Holotropic Breathwork™ belongs in this part of this structure.

Epstein's account of Joe's case history does not say what kind of breathing took place at which stage, and so I cannot comment on it in this part of the structure.

Parts 5 and 6 are not relevant to Joe's case history. In advanced energy work with the breath advanced practitioners use their breath to purposefully clear out from their energy-field – their aura and chakras – unproductive thoughts, habits and attitudes, unnecessary influences, old relationship problems and tendencies towards relationship problems, and the energy left over from past life problems and experiences. These clients are able to practise all the parts of the *anapanasati* exercise. Advanced awareness work with the breath is meditation. A client who has reached this stage no longer needs to be accompanied by a therapist.

6. ACCOMPANIED MEDITATION

Conscious breathing techniques are a form of meditation for two, which is how David Brazier describes his Zen therapy.[24] The therapist holds the space, helps the client to keep her or his attention on what is happening, and supports the client through difficult experiences. This form of 'supported meditation' is an effective therapeutic method which surely has its uses in the teaching and practice of meditation. It would certainly prevent meditators from getting lost in their process for long periods of time, as happened to Joe.

Hospitality Beyond Ego: Working with Exchange

Karen Kissel Wegela

In Contemplative Psychotherapy, 'exchange' refers to our direct experience of another person's state of being. As we work with others in psychotherapy, we may feel as though we have 'caught' or taken on their feelings or their mood. While some traditions might regard this as a problem, in contemplative psychotherapy it is treated as an opportunity to deepen our understanding of our clients, to recognise our connection with others, and to go beyond our own obstacles to entering into genuine relationship. The technique of 'body/speech/mind' presentation has been developed to help therapists and other helpers work with exchange. In this chapter this technique will be explored, together with the phenomenon of exchange and how to work with it.

EXCHANGE

Since 1975, The Naropa Institute in Boulder, Colorado, has been offering a Master of Arts degree in what has come to be called 'Contemplative Psychotherapy'. This approach to training clinicians has its roots both in the wisdom traditions of Buddhism and Shambhala and also the method of psychotherapy as it has been developed in the West. An important part of this training is learning to work with exchange. Let us begin by looking at an example taken from a recent training interview engaged in by two contemplative psychotherapy students.

Karl is conducting an interview with Kristina. She begins by saying that she is looking for something safe to talk about, but that she is having a hard time doing so because she is going through 'something really extreme'. As she continues, a theme of intense ambivalence becomes increasingly clear. Tearfully she describes how she wants to remain in her current relationship rather than falling into her old pattern of leaving at the first sign of trouble. On the other hand, she feels tremendous fear and feels that staying in the relationship is so personally threatening that it could lead to her death.

As Karl listens and reflects back what he is hearing from Kristina, he becomes increasingly hesitant. He starts to shift the conversation away from the intense emotionality Kristina is expressing, and starts to ask questions which require factual answers. He feels like he is losing track of the interaction and begins to feel quite awkward. Then he begins to worry that he is doing a bad job altogether. He doesn't know what to do or how to proceed. He feels stuck and anxious.

At this point Karl is feeling much the same way as Kristina. He doesn't know what to do; he feels frightened and confused; he doesn't want to make a mistake yet he wants to do something to get away from his feelings of terror and helplessness. Karl is experiencing exchange with the client. As Karl described his feelings following the interview, Kristina said, 'Yes! That's it. That's what it's like for me right now.'

Exchange is a common phenomenon. It seems to go on all the time, yet often we are not aware of it. When we are with a friend who is sad, we may start to feel sad ourselves – not just in response to what our friend tells us, but also through a direct experience of our friend in the moment. Lately I have been visiting a close friend who is dying of cancer. Louise is often drowsy and forgetful, perhaps because of painkillers she is taking. I find that when I am visiting, I easily lose track of my own thoughts. I have been late twice following these visits – losing track of the passage of time myself. Often when I enter the room in which she is lying on the couch, her family is sitting around, nodding sleepily. This is not just their own fatigue; this is also exchange with Louise's current state of mind.

Exchange goes in both directions at once. Not only do Louise's family and friends pick up on what she is experiencing, she also responds to what they bring to her. A team of friends who are trained in mindful attendance are providing basic care around the clock. The atmosphere in the home is often peaceful and wakeful, and many times Louise (and everyone else) picks up on this as well.

As therapists it is important that we are familiar with this phenomenon of exchange. If we are unaware of it, we can readily fall into many errors. We might get sidetracked into trying to figure out why we are feeling a particular way. Or, we might distract our clients to interrupt what are uncomfortable feelings for us. We might judge clients as good, bad or difficult, depending upon our own abilities to work with the exchange that they evoke.

Instead, if we know about exchange, it can provide us with a deeper understanding of what is going on for the client in the moment. Deep understanding often leads to compassion. It can help us join our clients and show them that they are being heard and understood.

Exchange reflects our lack of solidity. Most of us regard ourselves as solid and separate. We tend to believe that there is something inside us which is unchanging, permanent. The Buddhist teachings suggest that this is not the case. Instead of having a self or ego of this kind, we are constantly changing. Buddhist teachings ask us to look into our experience and find this unchanging self. Close examination fails to locate any such thing.

Instead of being separate, we are touched by all we come into contact with. We are permeable. In the contemplative psychotherapy training, students practise 'maitri space awareness'. Undertaken in the context of community and in conjunction with basic mindfulness/awareness sitting meditation, this practice done in five specially constructed rooms is designed to evoke the energies of the five 'Buddha families' identified in Tibetan Vajrayana Buddhism. The Ratna room, for example, is a golden colour with large round windows. The windows are translucent yellow with light shining behind them. The practitioner holds the posture specific to this room: lying on the back with arms and legs spread wide, hands open and fingers extended. Ratna energy is associated with richness and equanimity. It is also associated with the 'neurotic' manifestation of the same energy: arrogance, pride, and hunger.

In practising in this room and in the other four rooms, practitioners come to see how these energies occur in themselves. The practice tends to evoke or even exaggerate these five basic styles of relating to phenomena. People doing the Ratna room might find that they want to possess things that they never cared about before. They might feel arrogant and proud; or they might feel the opposite: worthless and poverty-struck. Recently I did the Ratna room for a week. I went shopping for a new refrigerator that I didn't need.

The room practice has many implications, but the point I'd like to make here is that it highlights our lack of solidity. The maitri practice shows us that even as small an act as lying in a coloured room for forty minutes has profound effects on our state of mind. This discovery can be frightening if we want to hang on to a sense of ourselves as solid and separate. We have the same obstacles to recognising exchange. We would rather feel that we have control of our own experience, but working with exchange undermines this view again and again.

WORKING WITH EXCHANGE

The most important thing in working with others is to be present. If we are not present, we cannot help our clients, and we cannot recognise or work with the exchange. The foundation of the contemplative psychotherapy training is the sitting practice of mindfulness/awareness meditation. As taught at Naropa, this meditation practice is designed to give us the opportunity to make friends with all aspects of our experience. Sitting practice leads to the development of mindfulness, which is precise attentiveness to the details of moment-to-moment experience. It also cultivates awareness, which is a broader sense of the context and environment in which mindfulness takes place. Mindfulness can be likened to a ballroom dancer knowing exactly how to do the tango, paying attention to the steps of the dance and to his posture as he guides his partner. Awareness would be his consciousness of where all the other dancers are and where the empty spaces are on the ballroom floor so that he can tango along without crashing into anyone.

In this meditation technique the eyes are left open with a soft downward gaze. The breath is used as a reference point in the present moment and the practitioner identifies with and 'goes out' along with it. The emphasis is thus on recognising the texture and experience of the present moment and also letting it go. We use the term 'touch and go' to describe this aspect of the practice. Sometimes we try to misuse our practice as a way to escape from unpleasant experiences. Instead of touching our experience, we just 'go'. Alternatively, sometimes we touch and then hang on. We grasp our experience, think it over, wallow around in it. This is touching without going. We need to find a balance in which we momentarily but completely touch and then also go. Sitting meditation allows us to develop this natural way of relating to the flow of our experience.

Finally, we need to relate to the process of thinking as it arises while we are practising. Part of being human is thinking. When we sit, this is what we experience as well. Sitting, thinking, breathing, more thinking and so it goes. In this technique when we get lost in our thoughts we acknowledge that we have been thinking by saying the label, 'thinking', silently to ourselves. We are not trying to change who we are or trying to get ourselves to stop thinking. We are simply looking into and seeing whatever we find.

As we practise in this way, we not only learn to be more present with all the changing aspects of our experience, we also start to develop 'maitri'. Maitri is unconditional friendliness toward whatever arises in our minds. This fearless and gentle attitude develops slowly through our practice. Together with the cultivation of mindfulness/awareness, maitri leads to unconditional confidence. If we can remain present and open – even friendly! – to all aspects of our own experience, then we can be present with whatever is brought to us by exchange. Ongoing meditation practice is thus a crucial aspect of working with exchange.

If we are able to join mindfulness and maitri with our experience, then this is what we bring to the exchange ourselves. Often, having this kind of hospitality toward our own experience is the most important gift we have to offer to a client. As I'm sitting with an angry client, I may begin to feel the physical, emotional, and cognitive experiences which I might label as anger. I might notice that I am holding my jaw tightly and tensing my shoulders. I am starting to feel heat on the back of my neck. A feeling of speed and urgency is arising in my mind. I'd like to hit the person my client is describing. If I can bring mindfulness and maitri to these experiences, these qualities might be what the client can then experience in the exchange. If I'm scared of this angry experience in myself, then I will be adding fear to our relationship's flavour in the moment. This cannot be faked. If I'm afraid, then I'm afraid. Perhaps I can be curious or mindful of the fear, bringing curiosity and mindfulness to the exchange. Or perhaps, I will try to ignore my experience and so add a cloudiness to the environment. The point is that the exchange will go both ways, and if I practise diligently with my own mind both on my meditation cushion and in the session with my client, I am more likely to bring an atmosphere of maitri and mindfulness into the therapeutic encounter. Sometimes this may be the first experience a client has of these qualities.

When I am in session, I work with the technique of 'touch and go', as I have learned to do in my sitting practice. In the above example, I touch the anger: feel its indications in my body and then let it go. In meditation the letting go happens along with the out-breath. In session I might or might not make use of the breath in this way. Often, being willing to touch naturally leads to letting go of this momentary experience and opens the way for touching the next moment. Fully touching and letting go are simultaneous.

So, the technique of touch and go is the first and most important way to work with the exchange that arises from moment to moment.

Another important point here is that it is not generally helpful to try to figure out whether our experiences come from exchange or from ourselves while we are in session. Because of our ongoing meditation practice we become intimately familiar with our own patterns of emotion and thought. It is likely that we can tell what is our own habitual style of reacting and what is not. It is good to think about this and sort things out, but it is generally best to do this after a session not in the middle of it. Getting caught up in this kind of figuring out tends to take us away from the client. However our experience arises, once we are having it, it is 'ours', and we need to work with our minds on the spot.

Exchange happens in a moment. It is direct and immediate. Generally, we then react as we do to any experience: we tend to judge it or think about it. We might try to push it away, draw it to ourselves or ignore it. It differs from empathy or countertransference. For most people (but not all), empathy refers to our ability to imagine what someone else is feeling. Exchange is more direct. Countertransference involves our reaction to the exchange and so is an extra step compared to the simplicity and directness of the exchange. It is based not in the immediacy of the present moment, but in our habitual responses which themselves are based in the past. Of course, we might easily have countertransference reactions as well as the experience of exchange.

Whatever the source of our experience is, we work with it in the same way: we touch it, recognise it, and then we let it go along, let it go.

Sometimes therapists become worried that they will get caught in the exchange. We are afraid that if we are truly open to a depressed client, for example, then we will feel as hopeless and despairing as he does. After a session we feel that we are still carrying a heavy emotional load. Often this is exchange which we have touched but which we have not let go again. Or, we have felt the same kind of despairing sadness as the client and we have 'bought' the story the client is telling himself. 'It's hopeless, I might as well kill myself.' We start to believe this is the only option for this client too, or we feel we are helpless as his therapist. It is important to tease apart the experience of exchange from the story about it.

The first thing to do is to return again to our meditation cushion. We practise touch and go with whatever it is we are feeling. We recognise thinking as thinking. Often this is very important. Exchange is a momentary experience free from commentary. By recognising the thoughts we have added, and which tend to perpetuate a story about our experience, we can often let go.

In addition, we can talk with colleagues, especially if we can do this mindfully. Complaining tends to dig us in deeper. Also, we can engage in body/speech/mind presentation groups.

BODY/SPEECH/MIND PRESENTATIONS

Body/speech/mind presentations provide an opportunity to deepen our understanding of our relationships with our clients. Unlike other forms of peer supervision, body/speech/mind groups do not focus on problem-solving or diagnosis. Their purpose is to illuminate the relationship that is occurring between the therapist and the client. We generally say we are presenting a client, but we are really presenting the relationship. It is a good idea to present a client when we feel stuck or when we feel confused. It can help us to reconnect with our hearts and our inspiration to be of help.

Body/speech/mind is a group mindfulness/awareness practice. The job of the presenter is to bring the client into the room as fully as possible by providing an exhaustive description of the client's body, speech and mind. The task of the other group members is to track their own experiences mindfully and to describe them for the presenter.

As the presenter describes the client, the various members of the group tend to experience aspects of the exchange going on between the therapist and the client. They can then describe their own experience, providing a mirror for the therapist. Sometimes different members reflect back different aspects of the client. One member might pick up on and manifest the sharpness of the client's mind. Another might begin to feel frightened and young.

The assumption we make is that whatever happens during a presentation is relevant to the relationship being presented. So, if one member of the group is feeling sleepy and bored, this is regarded as valuable information. We ask everyone to be descriptive and not evaluative. We also ask that everyone describes his experience rather than acting it out. So, I might say 'I feel like hitting you right now', instead of taking some aggressive action of body or speech.

Body/speech/mind groups can be used by any helpers. Their usefulness is not limited to therapists. Small groups of four or five people can meet, presenting on a rotating basis. Generally we take an hour and a half or so to present a client. If group members are also meditation practitioners, they have a better foundation for being able to track their experience and work with it through touch and go.

The form itself requires that the presenter begin with describing the client's body. This includes not only physical details but also the environment in which the client lives. Nothing is too trivial to include. The process often thrives on abundance, so we try to include as much as we can. We describe hair, eyes, skin-tone, ears, eyebrows, mouth, posture, torso, gait, and anything else we can think of. We include any physical ailments, addictions, medications. We describe how clients dress, how they spend their time, what they eat, what's in their refrigerators.

In the speech section we describe all the ways in which the client expresses himself. This includes how he speaks, gestures, and interacts with others. Relationships are described here including the therapy relationship. Again, we only describe, we do not use evaluative words. We say, for example, this client is often in disagreement with his wife and they often yell at each other. We would not say, this is an argumentative man who tries to impose his views on his wife.

In the speech section the presenter also describes how he feels when he is with the client. How does he feel in anticipation of a session with this client?

Other questions arise: How does this client deal with emotions? Which ones does he experience? Which ones are absent? Is he expressive? How? With whom does this client have significant relationships? Co-workers? Family? Pets?

In the mind section we focus on the nature of the client's awareness and the content of his thoughts. Is his awareness narrow? Is he confused? Clear? When? What activities does he engage in which are mindfulness practices – formal or informal? How does he cultivate mindlessness? Sometimes in this section we describe the client's mind as a landscape. Unlike body and speech we can sometimes observe, mind relies on inference and client report. What assumptions does this client seem to make about the world? About his own nature?

We often find that we cannot remember or don't know things. That's fine. We include whatever we know. Group members can help by asking questions. Some groups like to let the presenter cover one section before asking questions; other ask all through the presentation. Groups find their own rhythms with this.

We also regard the process of the group as a relevant piece of information. One presenter couldn't think of much to say, and the group found itself asking him many questions to which he gave one word answers. As group members described their frustration with this, the presenter recognised his own frustration with the client who often provided brief answers to his own questions. He also discovered sympathy for this client when he realised how painful it was to be on the receiving end of such a barrage of inquiries.

Often a presentation will reach a point in which many people feel stuck or confused. This may be what the therapist is feeling in this relationship. If the group can bring mindfulness and friendliness to these experiences, sometimes they begin to shift. When we don't try to push away what we are feeling, we can then touch. Often this is followed by an opening up of a larger view or a softening of a solid stance. Toward the end of a presentation, members sometimes offer suggestions about how to proceed, but just as often no suggestions are given.

An important function of body/speech/mind groups is to identify how we are resisting the experience of exchange. We might recognise obstacles in ourselves to being fully open and hospitable to a particular client. We can experience this as the presenter and sometimes as a group member. If we are uncomfortable, for example, in allowing the experience of exchange with a very angry client, we might see how we are avoiding the same experience when we present this client. Or a group member might describe feeling rage which we have overlooked in this client.

When we notice these obstacles we can often go beyond them. 'Oh, I can be with that anger. It's scary but I can accommodate it.' Other times we realise that we have more work to do of our own before we can be truly helpful to a specific client. 'I'm not ready to deal with this kind of anger. It is too much like my own issues which I haven't worked through yet. I can see that I'm going to keep deflecting this client's experience.' Then we have to decide how to proceed. The group can be helpful with this decision too.

Many times presenting in a body/speech/mind group can help us reconnect with our commonality with our clients. We recognise that our pain and joy are no different from theirs. When we can see deeply into our clients' and our own experiences, we often find tenderness and compassion.

I taught this technique to a workshop group in Australia a few years ago. A psychiatrist made a presentation of a client with whom he was having a hard time working. As he proceeded through the various sections, the group listening became increasingly restless and bored. 'This technique is a waste of time.' 'I'm not getting anything out of this.' The presenter carried on. Group members started to become irritated and impatient. Some expressed the desire to leave. Soon people were beginning to make suggestions about how the presenter could change his approach to this client. In turn, he began to feel more and more hopeless about what he was doing. The presenter realised that the group was treating him the way he usually treated his client. He hated the feeling of helplessness and boredom that arose when he worked with this client. This was what the group was reflecting to him. It made him feel useless and ineffectual. He realised that this, in itself, was the obstacle to his being able to be with this client and really hear him. As this became clear, the group began to relax. Some described a feeling of peaceful resting. There was a quality of space free from demand. This group had exchanged with the relationship, had then become stuck and restless, and finally, seeing the presenter give in to the experience of what was arising, was able to let go of its expectations. This was very helpful to the presenter who was able to let go of his own at the same time. He described a feeling of anticipation and curiosity as he now thought of seeing this client.

Recognising and working with exchange through meditation

practice and body/speech/mind presentations gives us the
opportunity again and again to extend hospitality to ourselves
and to others and to go beyond the narrow confines of the
illusion of ego.

Four Noble Truths for Counselling: A Personal Reflection

Eric Hall

My first memory of hearing about the Four Noble Truths of Buddhism was on a television documentary some thirty years ago. The programme was filmed in a high mountain village and a senior monk was inducting a novice into the order. They appeared to be shouting at each other and the subtitles explained what they were saying.

> 'What is the first Noble Truth?' demanded the monk. The novice shouted back, 'The first Noble Truth is suffering.' 'What is the second Noble Truth?' 'The second Noble Truth is the origin of suffering.' 'What is the third Noble Truth?' 'The third Noble Truth is the cessation of suffering.' 'What is the fourth Noble Truth?' 'The fourth Noble Truth is the path which leads to the cessation of suffering.'

Strangely, this short sequence stuck in my mind, but at the time it just seemed like an anthropological curiosity. As the years passed, I came across the 'Truths' in books on Buddhism from time to time and thought that they were interesting ideas, but could not grasp how they could possibly apply to my life and work. Even so, my continuing fascination with Buddhism led me to attend several extended meditation retreats and the importance of the Truths suddenly seemed to dawn – as if dropping into an empty space. I did not gain this insight through learning by rote or at a shout or by reading books. Only by creating an inner reflective space did I give myself permission to form a clearer perception of what had been going on all the time.

In this chapter, I propose to share the insights gained and explore the implications of the Four Noble Truths of Buddhism for the process of counselling. The development and application of these ideas is based on my experience of *vipassana* meditation within a Theravadin tradition, rather than on Buddhist scholarship or theory. I would like to think that this is in line with a tradition which has carried on honourably down the centuries. However, I do not intend to dwell at length on the theory of Buddhism and its links with psychotherapy and counselling, which is described eloquently in other chapters. My intention is simply to explore practical examples of the way the 'Truths' are relevant to the practice of counselling and to everyday living.

In recent decades, a number of writers and practitioners have emphasised the spiritual dimensions of counselling and therapy (Claxton, 1981; 1996; Epstein, 1995; Rowan, 1993; Watts, 1971). It is possible to argue that spiritual development may be at the core of what constitutes personal growth, healing and the resolution of illness whether it be somatic or psychosomatic. If the counselling relationship is fundamentally concerned to enable the individual to struggle with existential questions about the meaning of life then counselling, by definition, has strong links with spirituality. Five years ago, when I first started to formulate the ideas outlined in this chapter, the Four Noble Truths did not seem to attract the widespread attention of writers on counselling and were presented only as a part of a wider discussion of Buddhist philosophy. Recently there has been a surge of interest in the Four Noble Truths and perhaps the time is right to examine their relevance to our lived daily experience. There are minor variations in the texts from the various systems of Buddhism and the source I am familiar with is the *Visuddhimagga* (Buddhaghosa, 1976) and the interpretation used in this text is taken from this source.

Suffering or *dukkha*, the First Noble Truth, seems to have dogged me most of my life. As a young person I seemed to be cut off from my feelings but couldn't understand why I felt so unhappy at times. It was only later when problems with relationships, financial and work difficulties emerged that the clear realisation came that I was not a happy person. Now, in my sixties with the inevitable experiences of a higher incidence of the sadness of bereavement and the loss of those close to me, frustration about unfulfilled career aspirations and an increasing experience of the effects of aging, the awareness of suffering becomes more vivid. However, it required a combination of expressive bodywork and sitting meditation to realise the great store of suffering that had built up over the years. In the bodywork, this suffering appeared to literally ooze out of every muscle in my body, was expressed through movement and shouting, and was exhaled with the released breath. This therapeutic experience appeared to make it easier to 'sit still' and added to the effectiveness of the meditation.

My sense of personal suffering was compounded by the illusion that there were other people around who were happy, because their lives appeared to be going smoothly and I would compare myself unfavourably with them. Comparing relative suffering is probably a fruitless activity, although I have to admit that I am repeatedly humbled by the way some individuals cope with extreme physical and mental adversity. In spite of the comments on my own sense of suffering, I have undoubtedly led a privileged life compared to most of the clients I work with in an inner-city urban counselling agency. It seems to me that engaging in the process of counselling and psychotherapy does provide a profound insight into the extent of the 'sea of suffering' and many counsellors and psychotherapists have taken on the work because of their own struggle with suffering. On the other hand, it may be a mistake for the counsellor or psychotherapist to regard themselves to be suffering any less than their clients. Our own suffering is not mitigated by meeting others whose life situations and past experience is worse than ours. What I didn't understand was that it was the thoughts, fears and anxieties that went endlessly round in my head which constituted the source of suffering and not the events in themselves. This is central to the understanding of the Second Noble Truth.

I want to pay more attention to the Second Noble Truth – the cause of suffering, which is craving or desire. It does not take much insight to recognise that we often engage in craving and desire. We only have to spend an evening watching advertisements on television to see how cravings are created and sustained for material possessions. What seems to be missing is an awareness of how much time and psychological energy is spent in this endless craving. This may be revealed in the persistent thoughts that pass through our heads during meditation, but craving also occurs in the same way in our ongoing thoughts and daydreams throughout the day and probably during sleep as well. The difference is that we are not being encouraged to pay attention to this activity. I often ask clients to tell me about their daydreams, which are probably a clearer indication of dissatisfaction than sleeping dreams, which present issues in a more complex and symbolic mode. It is not uncommon for clients to be asked to keep a dream diary by their therapists. It may be equally productive to keep a daydream diary. Mine would be filled with running and winning marathons, climbing Everest, coping Dorian Gray-like with my desire not to age. In my imagination I lead organisations and political parties to cope with my lack of temporal power. Sexual imagery reflects grief for my waning sexual potency. These are just a few of the themes which run through my daydreaming life and talking to other people in workshop settings where members are encouraged to be more open, suggests that this is a universal experience. I had hoped that with the practice of concentration this internal dialogue would slowly diminish. This does not appear to be true for me and with an ageing brain there appears to be even more random firing of cells to produce idiosyncratic memories and thoughts in a way which is sometimes described as 'dullness of mind'.

The current British national obsession with the Lottery and the thoughts and feelings that go with it, provide a powerful social manifestation of this form of suffering and this is only one of many possible examples from my own wide repertoire of craving. Association with the unloved, a phrase taken from the *Visuddhimaga*, is represented for me in all the uncharitable thoughts I have for colleagues and associates I see in a less than positive light. I have a similar set of thoughts and feelings for the people that are close to me when they fail to provide me with what I want or desire.

A useful summary of suffering is that it consists of 'not wanting what you have' and 'wanting what you haven't got'. All of the examples given so far are forms of craving which fit into these two categories. People who come for counselling or therapy often express a desire to change and are clearly unhappy with who they are or where they are going. They want to feel better, be more satisfied with life and to have better, more fulfilling relationships. In short, they want what they do not have at the present time. They crave rest from the experience of their suffering and believe that the counselling relationship can provide a temporary shelter from it.

A disciplined examination of what goes through our minds indicates that most of our thoughts are a variation of one of these two processes of not wanting what you have and wanting what you haven't got. This form of thinking, which is the basis of what we might describe generally as worry, is probably the major source of stress for people whose lives do not currently involve any major form of external stress, bereavement, injury or illness (Fisher, 1986). This discussion of suffering could be interpreted as devaluing the experience of those who are experiencing intense physical or psychological pain. I believe I have not had the experience of extreme physical pain or emotional suffering. I have also fortunately avoided the extremes of social and economic deprivation which Smail (1993) offers as the cause of much contemporary suffering and stress. This notwithstanding, I am convinced that an understanding of the causes of suffering as outlined here is helpful in the experience of extremes of suffering.

All of the clients who present themselves for counselling describe themselves or believe themselves to be suffering in some way, much in the same way as their counsellors and their counsellors' supervisors. Invariably the client's goal is to be 'cured' of their suffering or to become 'happy'. Buddhism reminds us that this creates a double-bind, as the craving to be cured or the craving for happiness are just other manifestations of suffering, which may explain why many personal problems seem to be very intractable and as soon as one set of problems is apparently solved, another set appear to take their place. Feelings and behaviour may change, but this does not bring an end to the experience of suffering.

From a Buddhist perspective, an understanding of these processes could be achieved simply by 'seeing things clearly'. This is a possible translation of the Pali word *vipassana*, which describes the form of meditation which I found useful to gain a better understanding of the Four Noble Truths and their application to everyday life. It could also be a description of 'enlightenment' which would provide an understanding of suffering, although it does not set out to prevent it. However, there has been a suggestion recently that depressed people may actually be able to see their situations more accurately than others and with just cause become depressed. Perhaps they are closer to enlightenment than the so-called 'normal' person. Part of the counsellor's or therapist's role is to help their clients to see things more clearly.

Another important aspect of craving is the desire for permanence. The universe exists in a state of change or impermanence. It does not require a belief in the cycle of birth and rebirth to come to a realisation that everything is continually in the process of change. Every aspect of our lives illustrates this truth. Our bodies are in a continuous state of development and decay and after our early twenties, it all seems to be in a process of steady deterioration. Cars, houses, technology, information, knowledge provide further clear examples of ongoing change and as with our bodies many of us are struggling to keep them the same, or worse, trying to pretend that the changes are not taking place. It is relatively easy to accept Prigogine's assertion (Prigogine and Stengers, 1985) that all living forms maintain their appearance by a constant dissipation of energy and yet most of us lead our lives as if this was not the case.

Indeed, many clients describe themselves as being in fixed states, such as depressed, anxious, having a poor opinion of themselves and so on. Listening to them talk suggests that they are changing all the time and there are times when they are happy, calm and confident. Reflecting this back to the client enables them to realise that they are capable of change and that change is in fact a part of their ongoing experience. On occasions, when clients have reported feeling better, I have suggested that they are likely to experience a cyclical process of ups and downs. This is invariably the case, but the client then knows that there is a good chance that they will feel better at some later time after feeling bad. In effect they are coming into contact with the truth and the knowledge that psychological states are not intractable.

In spite of the overwhelming evidence that experience can be defined as a condition of ongoing change, notions of permanence permeate many aspects of counselling both in terms of the reported experience of the clients and the models, techniques and behaviour of counsellors. This denial of ongoing change is understandable as it would otherwise be difficult to handle the mass of continually changing information generated by a complex human being. Some degree of permanence is necessary to think about people, their behaviour and to make sense of the continuity of our lives. However, if I plan what to raise in the next meeting with a client, invariably their situation has changed so much that this planning is at best redundant and may even be harmful. It is the areas where this sense of permanence ceases to be helpful that I intend to explore.

We provide ourselves with a strong sense of permanence by ascribing labels to the other person. This is particularly true when clients are given psychiatric diagnoses or personality types. These forms of labelling usually relate to patterns of behaviour which occur in some contexts and not in others; at some times and not at others. I behave in an extroverted way in front of a large group, but in an introverted way in a small group of two or three. However, I don't think that it is helpful for me to be labelled an introvert or an extrovert, which could encourage me to perceive my patterns of behaviour as fixed and reduce the possibility of widening my choices. I have personally been given three radically different psychiatric classifications by expert international group leaders, all of which could be seen to describe aspects of my behaviour, but I am sure that the labels contributed nothing to my development of self-understanding or created possibilities for change.

People who present themselves for counselling or psycho-therapy may seize on the labels ascribed to them by experts, in spite of their negative connotations, and clutch them to their hearts because they provide a feeling of permanence and a false resolution of the suffering caused by impermanence. Not all counselling models encourage labelling, but the process certainly seems to make life easier for some counsellors or therapists as they provide apparent predictability and control. A client can be controlled by the label and treatment can be organised to fit the diagnosis which fits the client. This may be appropriate for making decisions about the medication of a small number of clients displaying extreme forms of disturbance, but hardly necessary for most people who come for counselling. The whole labelling process is neatly satirised by Levy (1992) in what I would see as an elegant lampooning of *The Diagnostic and Statistical Manual of Mental Disorders* (American Psychiatric Association, 1994) by suggesting the addition of a new category, 'Pervasive Labelling Disorder'.

Bandler and Grinder (1975) describe this use of nouns to label processes as 'nominalisation' and suggest that the criteria for whether a noun is appropriate is if it can be put into a wheelbarrow. If 'introversion' can't be put into a wheelbarrow then it should be considered as a process and defined using a verb, which describes behaviour used in a particular time and place. Try putting ego-states, empathy, defence mechanisms, sub-personalities, transference, schizophrenia, depression . . . and many other key notions from the counselling and psychotherapy vocabulary into the wheelbarrow. The paradox for this article is that it would not be possible to put 'truth' into a wheelbarrow.

The Third Noble Truth is of the cessation of suffering and

involves the notion of 'no-self'. I find this is the most difficult of the notions involved in the Four Noble Truths for me to incorporate into my ongoing life experience. Not that it is difficult to understand cognitively, but the problem for me is to be able to live as if it were true, given that all my conditioning has given me a sense of a continuing self. The self is not a thing which can be grasped and examined objectively, or indeed put into a wheelbarrow. It is more a morass of changing thoughts and associated feelings which change dramatically from moment to moment. The need to have a sense of a permanent self is a powerful example of the denial of impermanence. Nevertheless, I still cling to a sense of a permanent self, which is largely based on memory and probably a false sense of my own importance in the world.

A point of view is that if you look into yourself and peel away all the layers of the onion, you will eventually discover your 'real self', or 'transcendent self'. A similar view is that by turning inwards with activities such as guided imagery, focusing or meditation you will discover a spiritual dimension of yourself. The deep sense of relaxation and of being in a parasympathetic state is sometimes interpreted as spiritual bliss or a higher transpersonal level (Rowan, 1993). Even though these physiological states may be healthy to attain in terms of stress reduction and can create the conditions for positive change, the search for them may be just another manifestation of suffering.

There are many activities which produce a stilling of the mind providing a sense of 'no-self'. Most of them involve paying attention to sense data, which may be simple concentration in some forms of meditation. Other more active forms would include deep breathing, chanting, rhythmic movement, hatha yoga, guided imagery, hypnosis, deep relaxation and a whole range of body therapies. These techniques all involve a focus on immediate experience in the 'here and now', which precludes engaging in the cognitive process which generates suffering. They all tend to produce what Tart (1969) describes as altered states of consciousness. In these states, it appears possible to have experiences which are very different from ordinary experience such as memories of past lives, clairvoyance, out of body experiences, to see auras and so on, which are described as transpersonal experiences. However, a Theravadin teacher might suggest that these phenomena are quite common, but are in fact distractions from right practice. To be simply aware of present experience in the 'here and now' could also be described as transpersonal in the sense that it is not common to ordinary experience and that this is more important than the more unusual phenomena which are sometimes linked to spirituality.

My own experience of meditation is that extensive practice can produce a deep sense of relaxation and stillness, but that distractions from the mind and body still themselves intrude and are forms of impermanence and suffering. I am in fact arguing here that there is nothing else to the self than these thoughts. The process of meditation may provide a state of bliss, but more importantly provides a technique for seeing things more clearly. This hopefully translates into everyday life with other people, which offers a far more complex and difficult arena for working on spiritual issues than sitting on a cushion in an ashram. A difficult domestic situation, a row at work, or a counselling session which is not going too well may be much sterner tests of a sense of 'no-self'.

It is difficult for a counsellor to be in a state of 'no-self' working with a client because cognitive processes have to be engaged in order to respond and to make appropriate decisions on how to relate to the client. This becomes even more difficult when the client's story triggers emotional reactions in the counsellor related to the counsellor's own life. It is at these moments that I feel least competent, even though I have shared experience with the client and the countertransference process provides the illusion that our experiences were the same.

There are occasions when as a counsellor, I appear to put aside my own thoughts and feelings and take in the client as a sensory experience and become deeply relaxed, like a form of self-hypnosis. From this position it seems to be possible to respond to the client without any interference from the parallel processes that are going on in me. My own thoughts, feelings and memories that intrude can be noted without attachment. This state seems to be a form of deep empathy or intuition in which my own interventions always seem appropriate and in particular risky interventions appear to work extremely well. I would guess that my experiences during meditation have enabled me to be more effective in this mode. To be fully with another person would be an advanced form of empathy and by staying with their issues and their own interpretations of experience, it becomes possible to lose your own sense of self.

My own view of the 'real self' or 'spiritual self' is that it is best observed in our interactions with other people. It is easy to say that our behaviour may be cruel, obnoxious or inappropriate but underneath all of that there is a 'real self' which will emerge when I have had enough counselling, therapy, personal development and meditation. This is another good example of wanting what you haven't got, which is a source of suffering. At that moment in time, the 'real self' is cruel, obnoxious and inappropriate. Endlessly looking inwards can be an avoidance of dealing with interpersonal issues. This is not to devalue the inner search or spiritual journey as an important element in the counselling process or in personal development, but my own view is that its value lies in providing an experience which offers a deeper understanding of impermanence and suffering which will provide a more meaningful way of engaging with the world and other people.

So what can be done to lose the sense of self which is necessary for the cessation of suffering? Certainly it would not be helpful to strive for this as it, would in turn, only become another form of suffering. The solution is to allow the causes of suffering to fade away, a state which has been described as *nibbana*. This condition may be the experience of being fully present in the 'here and now' and there is a good chance that we have all had glimpses of this state. I doubt if there are enlightened masters who are permanently in the 'here and now' and would agree with Wren-Lewis (1994) that gurus and enlightened teachers are as human as the rest of us, with typical addictions such as for power, sex, alcohol or self-mortification.

My own view is that being present in the 'here and now' provides an indication of what it is like to suspend your sense of self. This can involve awareness of what is going on both internally and externally. This is not, of course, a new concept for psychotherapy and counselling. Being in the 'here and now' is central to person-centred counselling. Gestalt therapy (Perls, Hefferline and Goodman, 1973) has always placed a strong emphasis on immediate experience. It was useful for me to attend a workshop by Douglas Harding (Harding, 1986; Lang, 1994) in which we were invited to explore what we could actually see. This certainly did not involve much of one's 'self' apart from a blurred outline at the periphery of vision, parts of the lower part of the body and the arms. In a group, most of what can be seen is the other people and not yourself. In spite of this, group members are often obsessed with themselves. This model is limited to vision and does not work so well when all the senses are involved. A form of therapy which takes a similar approach to all aspects of bodily and mental experience is Core Process psychotherapy (Donington, 1994) and it is interesting that it has a

Theravadin Buddhist influence. Seeing things as they really are, or as close as is possible to an approximation of this, is basically what the phenomenological process is about and is central to existential psychotherapy (Deurzen-Smith, 1988). I would regard Psychosynthesis as an extremely useful system, with powerful techniques for contacting immediate experience. However the notion of a 'transcendent self' (Assagioli, 1965) suggests permanence and the desire to contact it implies craving. It also implies a form of dualism which is rejected by Buddhism.

It may be the search for the 'self', let alone the 'real self' should be outwards and not inwards and that we are only 'real' when we are in relationships. This notion can be accepted in the relationship between mother and infant, but having spent our lives struggling to develop an independent existence it is difficult to acknowledge that the internal activity related to this idea of an independent self is the cause of our suffering. We change in every relationship we engage in so it becomes more real to consider the patterns of relationships rather than the individuals involved. I become a different person with every client I see and neither of us are fully in control of this process. This fits neatly into the processes of general systems theory (Capra, 1983; Watzlawick, Beavin and Jackson, 1967). This is one of the few theoretical positions which accepts that dis-ease is part of a pattern of relationships rather than the nature of the individuals in the pattern. This model has been accepted in family therapy but is rarely applied to the one-to-one counselling setting.

The Fourth Noble Truth is of the paths leading to the cessation of suffering. These are right view, right thinking, right speech, right action, right livelihood, right effort, right mindfulness and right concentration. Reframing, cognitive restructuring, externalising inner speech, finding the right job and relationships, regaining energy, staying in the present and concentration are all aspects of positive outcomes of counselling. The continual use of the word 'right' has a strong moralistic flavour. However, if the word 'appropriate' is substituted for 'right', this shifts the onus for deciding what is 'right' on to the person concerned. 'Skilful' is the term which is often used in Buddhist discussions of ethical behaviour (Wray, 1996) and skilful behaviour is that which produces the effects listed at the beginning of this paragraph.

I am not suggesting that counsellors and therapists should take up meditation and then train their clients to do the same and my certainty that it would be productive is another example of my own craving. I am putting forward a point of view which is divergent from the systems that offer cure and happiness. The notion that we are all suffering, apart from when we are in the 'here and now', appears to be a bleak picture and not likely to sell, so the other counselling and psychotherapeutic systems need not be dismayed. Paradoxically, 'happiness' may simply be understanding that all of life is suffering.

I will conclude by considering an event that took place at the conference that provided the basis for this book. One of the speakers suggested that some people spent many years in sitting meditation, but still carried a great deal of unexpressed or repressed anger. This did not seem surprising to me, but it seemed to strike a raw nerve in the audience and the anger in the room seemed palpable. This condition was then labelled schizoid by a member of the audience as if this in some way solved the problem. At the beginning of this chapter I referred to a combination of expressive bodywork and sitting meditation. It has long been my view that people gravitate to the activities which provide the most comfort, but are perhaps the least helpful. I was attracted to sitting meditation because it helped me to avoid the difficult engagement with interpersonal relationships and fitted neatly into my strongly conditioned Protestant ethic of hard work and struggling to achieve. Some clients in counselling and therapy go because they enjoy the involvement in feelings, which they are already familiar with, and have indulged for most of their lives. A middle path would be to engage in both, but I also know mature well-balanced people who can put their own needs to one side who have engaged in neither therapy nor sitting meditation.

References
and Bibliographies

Chapter 2

1. The aggregates of body, feeling, perception, volitional and formatory factors, and consciousness. These are known as *skandha* (literally meaning 'heaps' or 'aggregates') in Buddhist discourse and are perceived as together constituting an individual's personal existence.

2. Ratnavali, v.35, P no.5658. All references to classical Sanskrit texts cited here are to the Peking (P) edition of the Tibetan Buddhist canon (Tokyo-Kyoto: Tibetan Tripitaka Research Foundation, 1956). For an English translation of *Ratnavali*, see Jeffrey Hopkins, *et al.* (1975) *The Precious Garland and the Song of Four Mindfulnesses*, New York: Harper & Row.

3. *The Dhammapada*, verses 153-4. The above translation is based on Juan Mascaro's translation (1973) of *The Dhammapada*, Harmondsworth: Penguin, with some alterations. All translations cited in this chapter are mine unless otherwise stated.

4. *Drang nges legs bshad snying po* (1991) Mundgod: Soku Publications, p.142. Robert F. Thurman translates them as 'habitual modes of intellectual and unconscious reifications'. See *Tsongkhapa's Speech of Gold. Reason and Enlightenment in Tibetan Buddhism* (1984), Princeton, NJ Princeton University Press, p.291.

5. For an enriching account of the interface between Buddhism and psychotherapy, see Mark Epstein (1995) *Thoughts Without a Thinker: Psychotherapy from a Buddhist Perspective*, New York: Basic Books, HarperCollins.

6. A hymn from the *sadhana* (practice manual) of Varayogini meditation.

7. Vajrayana Buddhism can be roughly characterised as the esoteric school of Mahayana Buddhism. Amongst others the principal features of this school include a thoroughly non-dualistic perspective on self and the world, an application of emotional states into the path of awakening, and a novel approach towards sexual energy as a means of liberation. All the four main schools of Tibetan Buddhism claim to belong to Vajrayana Buddhism. For a brief description of this dimension of Tibetan Buddhism, see my 'The Buddhist Context: An Overview' in The Dalai Lama, *et al.* (1996) *The Good Heart*, London: Routledge.

8. *Catushataka*, VI:10, P no. 5246. An English translation of this work exists in Karen Lang (1986), *Aryadeva's Catuskoti: On the Boddhisattva's Cultivation of Merit and Knowledge*, Indiske Studier VII, Copenhagen: Akademisk Forlag.

9. *Mahayanottaratantrashastra*, P no. 5525. For an English translation of this work, see J. Takasaki (1966) *A Study of Ratnagotravibhaga*, Rome: IS. M.E.O.

10. See, for example, Vasubhandu's *Abhidharmakosha*, Chapter 3.

11. This is used as one of the grounds in the *Uttaratantra* to argue for the existence of Buddha nature in all sentient beings.

12. *Dharanishvarajaparipracchasutra*. Cited by Tsongkapa in *Essence of True Eloquence*, p.197. See Thurman (1984) note 4 above, pp.353-4.

13. Buddhagosa. Visuddhimagga. XIV, 114, trs. Bhikkhu Nyanamoli. *The Path of Purification* (1991), Kandy: Buddhist Publication Society, Fifth edition, p.460.

14. *Abhidharmakoshabhasya*, Chapter 9.

15. *Sautanantarasiddhi*, P no. 5716.

16. *Madhyamakavatara*, VI:61. For an English translation of this verse, see C.W. Huntington, Jr. (1989) *Emptiness of Emptiness*, Honolulu: University of Hawaii, p.164.

17. Quoted by Tsongkhapa in *Elucidation of the Intent* (1974) Sarnath: Pleasure of Elegant Sayings, p.285. Source unknown.

Chapter 4

1. In a most interesting recent collection of essays on this topic, P. Young-Eisendrath and J.A. Hall (eds.) (1987) *The Book of the Self: Person, Pretext & Process*, one contribution alone is dedicated to the terminology of Ego and Self, and that merely amongst Freudians and Jungians.
2. Locke (1975) *Essay Concerning Human Understanding*, II 27.9.
3. James (1981) p.279.
4. Varela, Thompson and Rosch (1991) p.9.
5. *Ibid.*, p. 80.
6. Udana 10.8. Unless otherwise stated, quotations from the canon are from PTS editions.
7. For a detailed exposition, see Hamilton (1996) Chapter VI.
8. *Samyutta Nikaya III. 1-5.*
9. *Madhupinkika Sutta* of *Majjima Nikaya. Middle Length Discourses of the Buddha*, p.208.
10. Notably, Hamilton (1996) and Sprung (1979).
11. Willis (1979).
12. Crook (1980); Claxton (1994). Also see Dennett (1993) and Baars (1997).
13. Engler (1984) p.28.
14. James Hillman and Michael Ventura (1992).
15. D. Loy (1992) p.174.
16. 'the deep problem . . . with the merely theoretical discovery of mind without self in as powerful and technical a context as late twentieth century science is that it is almost impossible to avoid embracing some form of nihilism.' Varela, Thompson and Rosch (1991) p.127.
17. Bateson (1973) p.440.
18. Heidegger describes this in 'The Age of the World Picture', whereby in this age of great subjectivism and individualism, there is at the same time great objectivism, as the world has become impoverished as 'representation'. See Heidegger (1977) p.128.
18. Dogen (1972) p.133.

Baars, B. (1997) *In the Theatre of Consciousness*, Oxford: Oxford University Press.
Bateson, G. (1973) *Steps to an Ecology of Mind*, London: Granada. 1973.
Bennington, G. and Derrida, J. (1993) *Jacques Derrida*, Chicago: University of Chicago Press.

Bruner, J. (1986) *Actual Minds, Possible Worlds*, Cambridge, Mass.: Harvard University Press.

Bruner, J. (1990) *Acts of Meaning*, Cambridge, Mass.: Harvard University Press.

Claxton, G. (1994) *Noises From the Darkroom*, London: Aquarian.

Crook, J. (1980) *The Evolution of Human Consciousness*, Oxford: Oxford University Press.

Dennett, D.C. (1993) *Consciousness Explained*, London: Penguin.

Dogen, 'Genjokoan' (1972) in *Eastern Buddhist*, 5(2), trs. M. Abe and N. Waddell.

Donaldson, M. (1992) *Human Minds*, London: Allen Lane.

Edelman, G. (1992) *Bright Air, Brilliant Fire*, London: Allen Lane.

Engler, J. (1984) 'Therapeutic aims in psychotherapy and meditation: developmental stages in the representation of the self', *Journal of Transpersonal Psychology*, 16(1).

Hamilton, S. (1996) *Identity and Experience*, London: Luzac. Hamilton, S. 'Passionlessness in Buddhism', typescript.

Heidegger, M. (1977) 'The age of the world picture', in *The Question Concerning Technology and other Essays*, trs. W. Lovitt. New York: Harper & Row.

Hillman, J. and Ventura, M. (1992) *We've Had a Hundred Years of Psychotherapy – And the World's Getting Worse*, New York: HarperCollins.

Holquist, M. (1990) *Dialogism: Bakhrtin and his World*, London: Routledge.

James, W. (1981) *Principles of Psychology*, Cambridge, Mass.: Harvard University Press.

Locke, J. (1975) *Essay Concerning Human Understanding*, ed. P.H. Nidditch, Oxford: Oxford University Press.

Loy, D. (1988) *Nonduality*, New Haven: Yale University Press.

Loy, D. (1992) 'Avoiding the Void: the lack of self in psychotherapy and Buddhism', *Journal of Transpersonal Psychology*, 24(2).

Middle Length Discourses of the Buddha (Majjima Nikaya), trs. Nånamoli and Bodhi (1995), Boston: Wisdom Publications.

Mitchell, S. (1989) *The Enlightened Heart*, New York: Harper & Row.

Nånanda, Bhikku (1971) *Concept and Reality in Early Buddhist Thought*, Kandy: Buddhist Publication Society.

Reat, N.R. (1987) 'Some fundamental concepts of Buddhist psychology', *Religion* **17**.

Rorty, R. (1989) *Contingency, Irony and Solidarity*, Cambridge: Cambridge University Press.

Sprung, M. (1979) *Lucid Exposition of the Middle Way*, London: Routledge & Kegan Paul.

Taylor, C. (1989) *Sources of the Self*, Cambridge, Mass.: Harvard University Press.

Varela, F., Thompson, E. and Rosch, E. (1991) *The Embodied Mind*, Cambridge, Mass.: M.I.T. Press.

Willis, J. (1979) *Knowing Reality. The Tattvårtha Chapters of Asåga'sBodhisattvabhËmi*, New York: Columbia University Press.

Young-Eisendrath, P. and Hall, J.A. (eds.) (1987) *The Book of the Self: Person, Pretext and Process*, New York: New York University Press.

Chapter 5

1. For this term and a useful description of its application to and spread within modern American culture, see the editors' introduction in Richard Wightman Fox and T.J. Jackson Lears (eds.) (1983) *The Culture of Consumption: Critical Essays in American History 1880-1980*, New York: Pantheon Books.

2. 'The politics of a simple monk: His Holiness the Dalai Lama in conversations with Jerry Brown and Orville Schell', *Inquiring Mind* 14(2), Spring: 6.

3. Nancy Schnog (1997) 'On inventing the psychological', in Joel Pfister and Nancy Schnog (eds.), *Inventing the Psychological: Toward a Cultural History of Emotional Life in America*, New Haven, CT: Yale University Press, p.4.

4. Robert Bellah *et al.*, ([1985] 1996) *Habits of the Heart: Individualism and Commitment in American Life*, second edition, Berkeley, Cal.: University of California Press, pp.98, 101, 133.

5. Putnam is quoted in Bellah *et al.*, *ibid.*, p.xvii.

6. Maurice Merleau-Ponty ([1962] 1989) *Phenomenology of Perception*, trs. Colin Smith, London: Routledge, p.xvii.

7. Stephen Batchelor, 'The freedom to be no one: Buddhism, mind and experience', unpublished manuscript, p.14.

8. This reference amounts to no more or less than a tossing up of my hands. I came across this quote from Freire's work twenty years ago somewhere in Adrienne Rich's writing,

wrote it out and committed it to memory, and subsequently lost all track of exactly where I had found it. My apologies for this all-too-characteristic bibliographic amnesia . . .

9.   Donald Lowe (1982) *The History of Bourgeois Perception*, Chicago, Ill.: University of Chicago Press; Morris Berman (1981) *The Reenchantment of the World*, Ithaca, NY: Cornell University Press; Charles Taylor (1985) *Sources of the Self: The Making of the Modern Identity*, Cambridge, Mass.: Harvard University Press; Carl Schorske (?) in *Fin-de-Siècle Vienna?*; Ellen Herman (1995) *The Romance of American Psychology: Political Culture in the Age of Experts*, Berkeley, Cal.: University of California Press; Joel Pfister (1997) 'Glamorizing the psychological: the politics of the performances of modern psychological identities', in Pfister and Schnog, (eds.) *Inventing the Psychological: Towards a Cultural History of Emotional Life in America*, New Haven: Yale University Press, pp.167-213.

10.   Kaja Silverman (1983) *The Subject of Semiotics*, New York and London: Oxford University Press, pp.126, 130.

11.   I have drawn the Foucault quote from p.83 of the work by Judith Butler I will be discussing shortly; see reference 14, below.

12.   Quoted from the useful and accurate preface written by Neal Bruss and I.R. Titunk to V.N. Volosinov (1976) *Freudianism: A Marxist Critique*, trs. I.R. Titunk, New York: Academic Press, pp.vii, viii.

13.   Stephen Batchelor, 'The freedom to be no one: Buddhism, mind and experience', unpublished manuscript, p.7.

14.   Judith Butler (1997) *The Psychic Life of Power; Theories in Subjection*, Stanford, Cal.: Stanford University Press, pp.3–4, 20, 28, 29 and 30.

Chapter 6

1.   Noam Chomsky (1981) *Radical Priorities*, Montreal: Black Rose Books, pp.19-20.

2.   Miguel Covarrubias (1937) *Island of Bali*, London: Cassell, p.50.

3.   Kirkpatrick Sale (1990) *The Conquest of Paradise*, London: Papermac, p.112.

4.   Steven Batchelor (1997) *Buddhism without Beliefs*, London: Bloomsbury, p.112.

Chapter 7

1. F. Varela, E. Thompson and E. Rosch (1991) *The Embodied Mind: Cognitive Science and Human Experience*, Cambridge: MIT Press.

2. J. Martinerie, C. Adam, M. Le van Quyen, M. Baulac, B. Renault and F.J. Varela (1998) 'Epileptic crisis can be anticipated by non-linear analysis', *Nature Medicine* 4:1173-6.

3. Le Van Quyen, M.J. Martinerie, C. Adam, J-Ph. Lachaux, M. Baulac, B. Renault and F. Varela (1997) 'Temporal patterns in human epileptic activity are modulated by perceptual discriminations', *Neuroreport* 8:1703-10.

4. Provinelli, D.J. and T.M. Preuss (1995) 'Theory of mind: evolutionary history of a cognitive specialization', *Trends in Neuroscience* 18:418-24.

5. Stern, D. (1992) *Diary of a Baby*, New York: Basic Books.

6. Meany, M.J. *et al.* (1996) 'Early environmental regulation of forebrain glucocorticoid receptor gene expression: Implications for adrenocortical responses to stress', *Developmental Neuroscience*, 18:49-72.

7. These themes (empathy and intersubjectivity) can be given a rigorous philosophical foundation; they are the hidden iceberg of Husserl's later works, slowly emerging thanks to the publication of his massive studies on constitution (passive synthesis) and on intersubjectivity (cf. *Husserliana* XI, XIV-XVI).

8. Varela, F. (1996) 'Neurophenomenology: A methodological remedy for the hard problem', *Journal of Consciousness Studies* 3:330-50.

9. F. Varela and J. Shear (eds.) (1999) 'The view from within: first person methods in the study of consciousness', *Journal of Consciousness Studies* 6(2-3).

10. P. Vermersch (1999) 'Introspection as Practice', in F. Varela and J. Shear, 'The view from within: first-person methods in the exploration of consciousness', *Journal of Consciousness Studies* 6(2-3).

11. F. Varela 'The specious present; the neurophenomenology of time consciousness', in J. Petitot, F. Varela, B. Pachoud and J.M. Roy (eds.), *Naturalized Phenomenology*, Stanford: Stanford University Press (in press).

12. S. Gallagher and A. Meltzoff (1996) 'The earliest sense of self- and others: Merleau-Ponty and recent developmental studies', *Philosophical Psychology* 9:211-32.

13. F. Varela (1997) 'The naturalization of phenomenology as the transcendence of nature: searching for generative mutual constraints', *Alter: Revue de Phénoménologie* 5: 355-85 (Paris).

Chapter 8

Capra, F. and Steindl-Rast, D. (1991) *Belonging to the Universe*, San Francisco: HarperSanFranciso.

Churchland, P.S. (1986) *Neurophilosophy: Towards a Unified Science of the Mind/Brain*, Cambridge Mass.: MIT Press.

Claxton, G.L. (1994) *Noises From the Darkroom: The Science and the Mystery of the Mind*, London: Aquarian.

Claxton, G.L. (1997) *Hare Brain, Tortoise Mind: Why Intelligence Increases When You Think Less*, London: Fourth Estate; Hopewell, NJ: Ecco Press.

Dawkins, R. (1976) *The Selfish Gene*, Oxford: Oxford University Press.

De Bono, E. (1969) *The Mechanism of Mind*, London: Jonathan Cape.

Ferguson, J. (1976) *An Illustrated Encyclopedia of Mysticism*, London: Thames & Hudson.

Goleman, D. (1985) *Vital Lies, Simple Truths*, New York: Touchstone.

Greenwald, A.G. (1980) 'The totalitarian ego', *American Psychologist*, 35:7, 603-18.

Grush, R. and Churchland, P.S. (1995), 'Gaps in Penrose's toiling', *Journal of Consciousness Studies*, 2:10-29.

Hebb, D.O. (1949) *The Organisation of Behavior*, New York: Wiley.

James, H. (1990) *The American*, New York: Buccaneer Books.

James, W. (1958) *Varieties of Religious Experience*, New York: New American Library.

Jantsch, E. (1980) *The Self-Organising Universe*, Oxford: Pergamon.

Jung, C.G. (1958) *The Undiscovered Self*, London: Routledge & Kegan Paul.

Kahneman, D. (1973) *Attention and Effort*, Englewood Cliffs, NJ: Prentice Hall.

Kinsbourne, M. (1988) 'Integrated field theory of consciousness', in A.J. Marcel and E. Bisiach (eds.), *Consciousness in Contemporary Science*, Oxford: Clarendon Press.

Lewontin, R. (1983) 'The organism as the subject and object of evolution', *Scientia*, 118:63-82.

Minsky, M. (1988) *The Society of Mind*, London: Picador.

Nanavira Thera (1987) *Clearing the Path*, Colombo, Sri Lanka: Path Press.

Penrose, R. (1994) *Shadows of the Mind*, Oxford: Oxford University Press.

Rumelhart, D.E., McClelland, J.L. and the PDP Research Group (1986) *Parallel Distributed Processing: Explorations in the Microstructure of Cognition*, Cambridge, Mass.: MIT Press.

Suzuki, D.T. (1969) *The Zen Doctrine of No Mind*, London: Rider.

Varela, F., Thompson, E. and Rosch, E. (1991) *The Embodied Mind: Cognitive Science and Human Experience*, Cambridge Mass.: MIT Press.

Watts, A.W. (1961) *Psychotherapy East and West*, New York: Pantheon.

Whyte, L.L. (1978) *The Unconscious Before Freud*, London: Julian Friedmann.

Wilber, K. (1977) *The Spectrum of Consciousness*, Wheaton, Ill.: Theosophical Publishing House.

Wilber, K. (1979) *No Boundary*, Boulder, Col.: Shambhala.

Wilber, K. (1982) *The Holographic Paradigm*, Boulder, Col.: Shambhala.

Yeats, W.B. (1958) *Collected Poems*, London: Macmillan.

Zohar, D. (1990) *The Quantum Self*, London: Bloomsbury.

Chapter 9

Cavalli-Sforza, L.L. and Feldman, M.W. (1981) *Cultural Transmission and Evolution: A Quantitative Approach*, Princeton NJ: Princeton University Press.

Churchland, P.S. and Sejnowski, T.J. (1992) *The Computational Brain*, Cambridge, Mass.: MIT Press.

Crook, J.H. (1980) *The Evolution of Human Consciousness*, Oxford: Clarendon Press.

Crook, J.H. (1995) 'Psychological processes in cultural and genetic coevolution', in E. Jones and V. Reynolds (eds.), *Survival and Religion: Biological Evolution and Cultural Change*, Chichester: Wiley, pp.45-110.

Darwin, C. (1859) *On the Origin of Species by Means of Natural Selection*, London: John Murray.

Dawkins, R. (1976) *The Selfish Gene*, Oxford: Oxford University Press.

Dawkins, R. (1993) 'Viruses of the mind', in B. Dahlbom (ed.), *Dennett and His Critics*, Oxford: Blackwell, pp.13-27.

Dawkins, R. (1996) *Climbing Mount Improbable*, London: Viking.

Dean, G., Mather, A. and Kelly, I.W. (1996) 'Astrology', in G. Stein (ed.), *The Encyclopedia of the Paranormal*, New York: Prometheus, pp.47-99.

Dennett, D.C. (1991) *Consciousness Explained*, London: Little, Brown & Co.

Dennett, D. (1995) *Darwin's Dangerous Idea*, Harmondsworth: Penguin.

Durham, W.H. (1991) *Coevolution: Genes, Culture and Human Diversity*, Palo Alto, Cal.: Stanford University Press.

Humphrey, N. (1986) *The Inner Eye*, London: Faber & Faber.

Kapleau, P. (1965) *The Three Pillars of Zen*, San Francisco: John Weatherhill (and Doubleday, 1989).

Lumsden, C.T. and Wilson, E.O. (1981) *Genes, Mind and Culture: The Co-evolutionary Process*, Cambridge, Mass.: Harvard University Press.

Chapter 10
Bowlby, J. (1971) *Attachment and Loss, Volume 1: Attachment*, Harmondsworth: Pelican.

Damasio, A.R. (1994) *Descartes' Error: Emotion, Reason and the Human Brain*, New York: Putnam. (Published in the UK in 1995 by Picador.)

Koestler, A. (1967) *The Ghost in the Machine*, Harmondsworth: Penguin.

Kraemer, G.W. (1992) 'A psychobiological theory of attachment', *Behavioural and Brain Sciences*, 15:493-541.

Lama Anagarika Govinda, (1961) *The Psychological Attitude of Early Buddhist Philosophy*, London: Rider.

Lewis, M. and Haviland, J.M. (eds.) (1993) *Handbook of Emotion*, New York: Guilford.

Lewis, M. and Rosenblum, L.A. (1974) *The Effect of the Infant on its Caregiver*, New York: Wiley.

Meadows, S. (1993) *The Child as Thinker*, London & New York: Routledge.

Oatley, K. and Jenkins, J. (1996) *Understanding Emotion*, Oxford: Blackwell.

Schaffer, H.R. (1977) *Studies in Mother-Infant Interaction*, London: Academic Press.

Schore, A.N. (1994) *Affect Regulation and the Origin of Self: The Neurobiology of Emotional Development*, New Jersey: Lawrence Erlbaum.

Schore, A.N. (1996) 'The experience-dependant maturation of a regulatory system in the orbital prefrontal cortex and the origin of developmental psychopathology', *Developmental Psychopathology*, 8:59-87.

Sroufe, L.A. (1989) 'Relationships, self, and individual adaptation', in A.J. Sameroff and R.N. Emde (eds.) *Relationship Disturbances in Early Childhood*, New York: Basic Books, pp.70-94.

Stern, D.N. (1995) *The Motherhood Constellation*, New York: Basic Books.

Stone, J.L., Smith, H.J. and Murphy, L.B. (1974) *The Competent Infant*, London: Tavistock.

Trevarthen, C. (1993) 'The self born in intersubjectivity: The psychology of an infant communicating', in U. Neisser (ed.), *The Perceived Self: Ecological and Interpersonal Sources of Self-knowledge*, New York: Cambridge University Press, pp.121-73.

Trevarthen, C. and Aitken, K.J. (1994) 'Brain development, infant communication, and empathy disorders: intrinsic factors in child mental health', *Developmental Psychopathology*, 6: 597-633.

Wei Wu Wei, (1966) *The Tenth Man*, Hong Kong: Hong Kong University Press.

Chapter 11

1. Although living an otherworldly life was more common in traditional Asia, I am not suggesting that all or even most Asian adepts display this otherworldly strain. Many have lived in the world and displayed a high degree of personal integration of their spiritual realisation. Under the right circumstances spiritual practice by itself does appear to have the power to transform the personality in noticeable ways – for instance, under the close personal guidance of a great teacher, or in a person with strong innate aptitudes, or in spiritual retreat of many years' duration. (In Tibet, certain kinds of transformation were said to require a twelve-year retreat.) Nonetheless, the major emphasis in many Eastern traditions is on realising absolute true nature, rather than on developing an individuated, personal expression of that nature.

2. This is of course a generalisation. I am speaking here of most Tibetans who have grown up in a traditional family/ community context. I do know some modern Tibetans, even

teachers, who seem to be suffering from psychological wounding on the personal level, for whom psychological work might be of some benefit.

3. Of course, there are many distinctions that one could make between different Asian cultures and traditions, and even between different lineages within a single tradition, such as Buddhism. In this discussion, and throughout this paper, I am choosing not to address these find distinctions, which would require a much longer, more scholarly treatment. Instead, I have chosen to focus on certain broad outlines in order to develop a particular line of reasoning.

4. One telling sign of the difference between childrearing influences East and West: Tibetan teachers, who traditionally begin compassion practices by instructing students to regard all sentient beings as their mothers, have been surprised and dismayed by the difficulty many American students have in making their mothers a useful starting-point for developing compassion.

5. Roland reports an interesting case of two Indian women married to American men whom he worked with, for whom 'it took many years of psychoanalysis with a warm, supportive analyst gradually to be able to have a more individualized self' and thus function normally in American society (1988: 198).

6. This is not to say that most Westerners are truly individuated or even interested in this. For most people, individualism – which is a lower-level approximation – is the closest they come. Nevertheless, genuine individuation is a real possibility here, and those who feel most alienated are often those who feel most called in this direction.

7. As Karlfried Graf Dürckheim points out, for most Eastern teachers, 'the individual form acquired in the process [of spiritual awakening] is not taken seriously as such . . . This, however, is the very thing that counts for Western masters . . . [freedom] *to become* the person that one individually is. For us in the West, it is more important that a new worldly form should emerge *from* true nature and witness to Being . . . than that the ego should dissolve *in* true nature and *in* Being' (1992: 100).

Speaking of the Japanese Zen masters he studied with, Dürckheim notes: 'As masters, they appear in a supreme form in which every personal element has been converted into something suprapersonal, almost remote from the world, or at least not involved in it. One rarely, if ever, meets the happy or suffering individual, through whose joy-filled, sorrow-filled eye the otherworldly glimmers in a unique personal sense . . . Is such a master a person in our sense of the term?' (1992: 101).

8. Teachers from the far East – often from China, Japan, or Korea – who emphasise the earthy aspect of life in their teaching are an exception to this. For example, teachers of Tai Chi, Chi Kung, and Aikido always stress the belly centre in their work. And many Zen teachers rarely speak of spiritual realisation, but instead have their students attend to the earthy details of chopping wood and carrying water.

9. Of course, personal psychological work is not in itself sufficient for spiritual transformation or for the integration of being into personal functioning. In addition to finding a spiritual teacher or practice that strips away egocentricity, particular individuals may also need to work on their body, their livelihood, their intimate relationships, or their relation to community. But psychological work can help people recognise the areas where they need work and clear away some obstacles in these areas.

Aurobindo (n.d.), *Letters on Yoga*, vol. 1, Pondicherry: Sri Aurobindo Ashram Birth Centenary Library.

Dürckheim, K.G. (1977) *Hara: The Vital Center of Man*, London: Unwin.

Dürchkheim, K.G. (1992) *Absolute Living: The Otherworldly in the World and the Path to Maturity*, New York: Arkana.

Greenberg, S. and Mitchell, S. (1983) *Object Relations in Psychoanalytic Theory*, Cambridge: Harvard University Press.

Klein, A. (1995) *Meeting the Great Bliss Queen: Buddhists, Feminists, and the Art of the Self*, Boston: Beacon.

Roland, A. (1988) *In Search of Self in India and Japan: Toward a Cross-cultural Psychology*, Princeton: Princeton University Press.

Schlipp, P. and Friedman, M. (eds.) (1967) *The Philosophy of Martin Buber*, LaSalle, Ill.: Open Court.

Welwood, J. (1984) 'Principles of inner work: psychological and spiritual', *Journal of Transpersonal Psychology*, **16**(1).

Welwood, J. (1996) *Love and Awakening: Discovering the Sacred Path of Intimate Relationship*, New York: HarperCollins.

Chapter 12

1. See E.A. Burtt (ed.) (1955) *The Teachings of the Compassionate Buddha*, New York: Mentor Books, pp.98-100.
2. Wallace Stevens (1990) *The Collected Poems of Wallace Stevens*, New York: Vintage Books, p.93.
3. Winnicott, D.W. (1965) 'Communicating and not communicating leading to a study of certain opposites', in *The Maturational Processes and the Facilitating Environment*, New York: International Universities Press, pp.185-6.
4. *Ibid.*, p.61.
5. *Ibid.*, p.59-60.

Chapter 13

Besserman, P. and Steger, M. (1991) *Crazy Clouds: Zen Radicals, Rebels and Reformers*, Boston, Mass.: Shambhala.

Dehing, J. (1993) 'The transcendent function: a critical re-evaluation', *Journal of Analytical Psychology*, 38(3): 225-35.

Dreyfus, H. (1972) *What Computers Can't Do: A Critique of Artificial Reason*, New York: Harper & Row.

Dreyfus, H.L. and Dreyfus, S.E. (1986) *Mind Over Machine*, New York: Free Press.

Gendlin, E. (1962) *Experiencing and the Creation of Meaning*, New York: Free Press of Glencoe.

Merleau-Ponty, M. (1962) *Phenomenology of Perception*, trs. Colin Smith, New York: Humanities Press.

Polanyi, M. (1966) *The Tacit Dimension*, Garden City, NY: Doubleday.

Todres, L. (1990) 'An existential phenomenological study of the kind of therapeutic self-insight that carries a greater sense of freedom', unpublished Ph.D. dissertation, Rhodes University.

Todres, L. (1993) 'Psychological and spiritual freedoms: reflections inspired by Heiddegger', *Human Studies*, 16: 255-66.

Wilber, K. (1995) *Sex, Ecology, Spirituality*, Boston, Mass.: Shambhala.

Chapter 14

1. Stephen Batchelor (1997) *Buddhism Without Beliefs: A Contemporary Guide to Awakening*, London: Bloomsbury.

Chapter 15

1. Lachs, S. (1994) 'A slice of Zen in America', *New Ch'an Forum*, 10. The New Ch'an Forum is the house journal of the newly formed Western Ch'an Fellowship. It contains Dharma translations, talks by contemporary Zen teachers, social criticism, poetry and retreat reports. Copies available from P. Howard, 22 Butts Rd., Chiseldon, Wilts. SN4 0NW, UK. 01793 740659 (phoward@raychem.com).
   Crook, J.H. (1996) 'Authenticity and the practice of Zen', *New Ch'an Forum*, 13. Also in Pickering, J. (ed.) (1997) *The Authority of Experience*, London: Curzon Press.

2. Schaef, A.W. (1985) *Co-dependence – Misunderstood, Mistreated. Understanding and Healing the Addictive Process*, San Francisco, Cal.: Harper & Row. Also: Whitfield, C. (1984) 'Co-dependency – an emerging issue among professionals', in *Co-dependency – An Emerging Issue*, Pompano Beach, Florida: Health Communications.

3. As quoted by Epstein, M. (1996) *Thoughts Without a Thinker: Psychotherapy from a Buddhist Perspective*, London: Duckworth, p.77.

4. *Ibid.*

5. Berner created this approach through comparing the practice of Zen interview with co-counselling and I was taught to run his 'Enlightenment Intensives' by Jeff Love in the 1970s. Berner has provided a manual for those directing such events. For the Western Zen retreat see Chapters 8 and 13 in Crook, J.H. and D. Fontana, (eds.) (1990) *Space in Mind: East-West Psychology and Contemporary Buddhism*, Shaftesbury, Dorset: Element.

6. The 'True man of the Way'. See Schloegl, I. (1975) *The Zen Teaching of Rinzai*, Berkeley, Cal.: Shambala.

7. Hellinger, Bert (1991) 'For love to flourish: the systemic preconditions for love', trs. Hunter Beaumont, typescript.

8. These are the technical definitions from the literature, given me by Stephen Batchelor.

9. 'Flow' is a term not idly used here. The notion has become of considerable importance in self psychology and the study of consciousness: see Csikszentmihaly, M. and Csikszentmihalyi, I.S. (1988) *Optimal Experience: Psychological Studies of Flow in Consciousness*, Cambridge: Cambridge University Press.

Chapter 16

1. I must acknowledge here a contribution by my good friend Brian Thorne: paper presented to the 3rd International Conference on Client-Centred and Experiential Psychotherapy, Gmunden, Austria (Thorne 1996).

2. For Freud see Bakan (1990). Jung was the son of a Protestant pastor, a fact which was of particular significance for him, and the spiritual dimension of his work is well known (see Franz, 1993; Van der Post, 1976; Moacanin, 1986 and many other works). Rogers was training to become a Protestant minister when he decided to become a psychologist instead and a mystical dimension is visible in his later works (Rogers, 1980). Moreno, inventor of psychodrama and arguably the originator of group psychotherapy as a whole, had a strong mystical sense which comes through powerfully in many of his works (e.g. Moreno, 1971).

3. The term dukkha is a key element of Buddhist terminology. There has been controversy about how it should be best translated, so I will leave it in its Pali/Sanskrit form. Dukkha, according to the Buddha, means birth, ageing, sickness, death, separation from what is loved, association with what is hated, not getting what one wants, and the whole process by which attachment works upon our mentality (*Samyutta Nikaya 56. 11*).

4. E.g. see Hanh (1988, 1990, 1993).

Akong (1987) *Taming the Tiger*, Eskdalemuir: Dzalendara.

Bakan, D. (1990) *Sigmund Freud and the Jewish Mystical Tradition*, London: Free Association Books.

Brazier, D.J. (1994) 'Is Buddhism a therapy?', in Raft: *The Journal of the Buddhist Hospice Trust*, **10**:3-9.

Brazier, D.J. (1995) *Zen Therapy*, London: Constable.

Franz M-L. von (1993) *Psychotherapy*, London: Shambhala.

Hanh, N. (1988) *Breathe! You are Alive: Sutra on the Full Awareness of Breathing*, Berkeley, Cal.: Parallax.

Hanh, N. (1990) *Transformation and Healing: Sutra on the Four Establishments of Mindfulness*, Berkeley, Cal.: Parallax.

Hanh, N. (1993) *Thundering Silence: Sutra on Knowing the Better Way to Catch a Snake*, Berkeley, Cal.: Parallax.

Moacanin, R. (1986) *Jung's Psychology and Tibetan Buddhism*, London: Wisdom.

Moreno, J.L. (1971) *The Words of the Father*, New York: Beacon House.

Reynolds, D.K. (1976) *Morita Psychotherapy*, Berkeley, Cal.: University of California Press.

Reynolds, D.K. (1984) *Playing Ball on Running Water*, New York: William Morrow.

Reynolds, D.K. (1989) *Flowing Bridges Quiet Waters*, Albany, NY: State University of New York Press.

Rogers, C.R. (1980) *A Way of Being*, New York: Houghton Mifflin.

Sogyal Rinpoche (1992) *The Tibetan Book of Living and Dying*, London: Rider.

Thorne, B. (1996) 'Person-centred therapy: the path to holiness', in R. Hutterer, G. Pawlowsky, P. Schmid and R. Stipsits (eds.) *Client-Centered and Experiential Psychotherapy: A Paradigm in Motion*, Vienna: Peter Lang, pp.107-16.

Van der Post, L. (1976) *Jung and the Story of Our Time*, Harmondsworth: Penguin.

Chapter 17

Bernhard, J., Kristeller, J. and Kabat-Zinn, J. (1988) 'Effectiveness of relaxation and visualization techniques as a adjunct to phototherapy and photochemotherapy of psoriasis', *Journal of the American Academy of Dermatology*, **19**:572-3.

Kabat-Zinn, J. (1982) 'An out-patient programme in behavioral medicine for chronic pain patients based on the practice of mindfulness meditation: theoretical considerations and preliminary results', *General Hospital of Psychiatry*, **4**:33-47.

Kabat-Zinn, J. (1994) *Mindfulness Meditation for Everyday Life*, London: Piatkus.

Kabat-Zinn, J. (1996) *Full Catastrophe Living: How to Cope with Stress, Pain and Illness using Mindfulness Meditation*, London: Piatkus.

Kabat-Zinn, J., Lipworth, L. and Burney, R. (1985) 'The clinical use of mindfulness meditation for the self-regulation of chronic pain', **8**:163-90.

Kabat-Zinn, J., Lipworth, L., Burney, R. and Sellers, W. (1986) 'Four year follow-up of a meditation-based programme for the self-regulation of chronic pain: treatment outcomes and compliance', *Clinical Journal of Pain*, **2**:159-73.

Kabat-Zinn, J. and Chapman-Waldrop, A. (1988) 'Compliance with an outpatient stress reduction programme: rates and predictors of completion', *Journal of Behavioral Medicine*, **11**:333-52.

Kabat-Zinn, J., Massion, A.O., Kristeller, J., Peterson, L.G., Fletcher, K., Pbert, L., Linderking, W. and Santorelli, S.F. (1992) 'Effectiveness of a meditation-based stress reduction programme in the treatment of anxiety disorders'. *American Journal of Psychiatry*, **149**:936-43.

Kabat-Zinn, J., Chapman, A. and Salmon, P. (1997) 'The relationship of cognitive and somatic components of anxiety to patient preference for alternative relaxation techniques', *Mind/Body Medicine*, **2**:101-9.

Kabat-Zinn, J., Wheeler, E., Light, T., Skillings, A., Scharf, M.S., Cropley, T.G., Hosmer, D. and Bernhard, J. (1998a) 'Influence of a mindfulness-based stress reduction intervention on rates of skin clearing in patients with moderate to severe psoriasis undergoing phototherapy (UVB) and photochemotherapy (PUVA)', *Psychosomatic Medicine*, **60**:625-632.

Kabat-Zinn, J., Massion, A.O., Herbert, J.R. and Rosenbaum, E. (1998b) 'Meditation', (ed.) Jimmie Holland, *Textbook of Psycho-oncology*, Oxford: Oxford University Press, pp.767-79.

Kabat-Zinn, M. and Kabat-Zinn, J. (1997) *Everyday Blessings: The Inner Work of Mindful Parenting*, New York: Hyperion, pp.302-7.

Miller, J., Fletcher, K. and Kabat-Zinn, J. (1995) 'Three-year follow-up and clinical implications of a mindfulness-based stress reduction intervention in the treatment of anxiety disorders', *General Hospital of Psychiatry*, **17**:192-200.

Pascal, Blaise (1909) *Pensées*, fifth edition (ed.) L. Brunschveig, ii. 139.

Salmon, P., Santorelli, S., and Kabat-Zinn, J. (1998) 'Intervention elements promoting high adherence to mindfulness-based stress reduction programmes in the clinical behavioral medicine setting', in *Handbook for Health Behavior Change*, (2nd Edition) Sally A. Shumaker, Eleanor B. Schron, Judith K. Ockene, Wendy L. McBee (eds.), Springer, pp.239-66.

Santorelli, S. (1999) *Healthy Self: Lessons on Mindfulness in Medicine*, New York: Random House

Suzuki, D.T. (1934) *Introduction to Zen Buddhism*, Kyoto, rcpr. 1949, New York: Philosophical Library.

Chapter 18

1. A good overview of the Nyingma approach can be found in Dudjom Rinpoche (1992) *The Nyingma School of Tibetan Buddhism*, London: Wisdom Books. For a translation of a related text by Nuden Dorje, founder of the Khordong Lineage, see Chapter 8 of James Low (1998) *Simply Being*, London: Vajra Press.

2. Dr Anthony Ryle, the creator of CAT, has written an introduction to both theory and practice (1991) *Cognitive Analytic Therapy: Active Participation in Change*, Chichester: Wiley.

3. See, for example, Daniel Stern (1985) *The Interpersonal World of the Infant*, New York: Basic Books.

4. Humberto Maturana (1979) 'Neurophysiology of cognition', in P. Garvin (ed.) *Cognition: a Multiple View*, New York: Spartan.

5. Michael Balint (1968) *The Basic Fault*, London: Tavistock Publications.

6. James Low (1990) 'Buddhist developmental psychology', in J. Crook and D. Fontana (eds.) *Space in Mind*, Shaftesbury, Dorset: Element Books.

7. *Ibid.*

8. Stern (1985).

9. Ryle (1991).

10. For example, M.M. Bakhtin (1981) *The Dialogic Imagination: Four Essays*, Austin, Tex.: University of Texas Press.

11. J. Low (1998), Chapters 8 and 9.

12. J. Low (1998), Ch. 11.

13. Ryle (1991).

14. See Figure 18.8.

15. Mikael Leiman (1994) 'Integrating the Vygotskian theory of sign-mediated activity and the British objects relations theory', *University of Joensuu Publications in Social Sciences*, **20**, Joensuu, Finland.

16. See Laing, R.D., Phillipson, H. and Lee, R. (1966) *Interpersonal Perception: A Theory of Method and Research*, London: Tavistock Publications.

17. See for example Patrul Rinpoche in Chapter 7 of Low, J. (1998) *Simply Being*, Boston: Wisdom.

18. See for example Lopez, D.S. (1998) *The Heart Sutra Explained*, Ithaca, NY: State University of New York.

19. See for example Safran, J.A. and Segal, Z.V. (1990) *Inter-*

personal Process in Cognitive Therapy, New York: Basic Books.

20. Casement, P. (1985) *Learning from the Patient*, London: Tavistock Publications.

21. For a westernised view see Trungpa, C. (1985) *Glimpses of Abhidharma*, Boulder, Col.: Prajna Press. For a more conventional presentation see Govinda, A. (1969) *The Psychological Attitude of Early Buddhist Philosophy*, New York: Samuel Weiser.

Chapter 19

Ajitamitragupta (1981) *The Tibetan Tripitaka*, D.G. edition no. 2832: *Rmi-lam dri-ma med-pa bsgom-pa*, Berkeley, Cal.: Dharma Press. (Note: Provides information on *rMi-lam bsgom-pa*, 'dream-yoga'.)

Dharmakirti (1981) *The Tibetan Tripitaka*, D.G. edition, no. 4210: *Tshad-ma rnam-hgrel gyi tshig-lehur byas-pa* (the Tibetan translation of *Pramanavarttikakarika*), Berkeley, Cal.: Dharma Press. (Note: Provides information on *'Du-shes* ('perception') in Chapter 1, and *mNgon-sum* ('direct awareness') in Chapter 3.)

rGyal-tshab dar-ma rin-chen (1974-5) *Tsong-kha-pa's Collected Works*, vol. ca: *Rnam-hgrel gyi bsdus-don, Thar-lam gyi de-nid gsal-byed*, printed in Varanasi, India. (Note: Provides further information on *'Du-shes* and *mNgon-sum*.)

Guenther, Herbert V. (1963) *The Life and Teachings of Naropa*, Oxford: Oxford University Press.

Kong-sprul Blo-gros mtha'-yas (1971) *Zab-lam su-kha chos-drug gi brgyud-pa'i gsol-'debs bde-chen char-'bebs*, compiled by 'Jam-mgon Kon-sprul Blo-gros-mtha'-yas, *gDams-ngag mdzod*, vol. VIII, printed in Delhi. (Note: Provides information on *rMi-lam bsgom-pa*, 'dream-yoga' and *sGyu-lus*, 'Illusory Body'.)

Thang-stong rGyal-po (1971) *Ye-shes mkha'-'gro ni-gu ma'i chos-drug gi khrid-kyi gnad-yig snying-po kun-'dus & Ni-gu'i yan-lag phyag-chen ga'u-ma'i khrid*, compiled by 'Jam-mgon Kon-sprul Blo-gros-mtha'-yas, *gDams-ngag mdzod*, vol. VIII, printed in Delhi. (Note: Provides information on *rMi-lam bsgom-pa*, 'dream-yoga' and *sGyu-lus*, 'Illusory Body'.)

Tsong-kha-pa (1979) *Tsong-kha-pa's Collected Works*, vol. ta: *Zab-lam na-rohi chos-drug gi sgo-nas hkhrid-pahi rim-pa, yid-ches gsum ldan & Na-rohi chos-drug gi dmigs-skor lag-tu len tshul bsdus-pa*, New Delhi, India. (Note: Provides information on *rMi-lam bsgom-pa*, 'dream-yoga' and *sGyu-lus*, 'Illusory Body'.)

Chapter 20

1. Manné (1994), (1995a), (1997a).
2. See Epstein (1995), pp.168-70 and my review, Manné (1997b).
3. *Majjhima-Nikāya III*. pp.82f.
4. Boadella (1994); Conway (1994); Proskauer (1994).
5. Joy Manné (1995b).
6. *rāga, dosa, moha*.
7. Joy Manné (1995c); Brazier (1995).
8. *abhijjhā loke, vyāpāda, thīna, middha, uddhacca, kukkucca, vicikicchā. Manné (1995b).*
9. Orr and Ray (1983).
10. Manné (1995).
11. Manné (1994, 1995).
12. Engler (1984) pp.33.
13. Taylor (1994), pp.81-3.
14. See Albery (1985) pp.84-120; Karl Raab (1992) pp.155-67.
15. Engler (1984) p.26; Manné (1997a).
16. Anguttara Nikāya, I 187, see Manné (1996a).
17. Engler (1984) pp.33, 37.
18. Manné (1995a), (1996b), (1997a).
19. See Albery, p.68f and elsewhere: Manné (1995a).
20. Manné (1995a).
21. Manné (1995a), (1997a).
22. *Majjhima Nikāya* III, 84.
23. Manné, forthcoming.
24. Brazier, 1995, p.61.

Albery, Nicholas (1985) *How to Feel Reborn: Varieties of Rebirthing Experience* – an exploration of rebirthing and associated primal therapies, the benefits and dangers, the facts and fictions. London: Regeneration Press.

Anguttara Nikāya, vol. I (1989), Oxford: Pali Text Society.

Boadella, David (1994) 'Styles of breathing in Reichian therapy', in Timmons, B.H. and Ley, R. (eds.) (1994) *Behavioral and Psychological Approaches to Breathing Disorders*, New York: Plenum, pp.233-42.

Brazier, David (1995) *Zen Therapy*, London: Constable.

Conway, Ashley (1994) 'Breathing and feeling', in Timmons, B.H. and Ley, R. (eds.) (1994), *Behavioral and Psychological*

Approaches to Breathing Disorders, New York: Plenum, pp.243-52.

Engler, Jack (1984) 'Therapeutic aims in psychotherapy and meditation: developmental stages in the representation of the self', *Journal of Transpersonal Psychology*, 16(1).

Epstein, Mark (1995) *Thoughts Without a Thinker: Psychotherapy from a Buddhist Perspective*, New York: Basic Books.

Majjhima-Nikāyā, vol. III (1977) London: Pali Text Society. Translated as *Middle Length Sayings*, I.B. Horner. London: Pali Text Society.

Manné, Joy (1994) 'Rebirthing, an orphan or a member of the family of psychotherapies?' *International Journal of Prenatal and Perinatal Psychology and Medicine*, 6(4):503-17.

Manné, Joy (1995a) 'Rebirthing – is it marvellous or terrible?' *The Therapist: Journal of the European Therapy Studies Institute*, Spring.

Manné, Joy (1995b) 'Case histories from the Pāli Canon I: The Sāmaññaphala Sutta hypothetical case history – or how to be sure to win a debate', *Journal of the Pāli Text Society*.

Manné, Joy (1995c) 'Case histories from the Pāli Canon, II: *sotāpanna, sakadāgāmin, anāgāmin, arahat* – the Four Stages case history *or* spiritual materialism and the need for tangible results', *Journal of the Pāli Text Society*.

Manné, Joy (1996) 'Sīhanāda – the lion's roar or what the Buddha was supposed to be willing to defend in debate', *Buddhist Studies Review*.

Manné, Joy (1996b) 'On teaching physical immortality', *Breathe International*.

Manné, Joy (1997a), *Soul Therapy*, Berkeley, Cal.: North Atlantic Books.

Manné, Joy (1997b) 'Creating a contemporary Buddhist psychotherapy', a review-article of David Brazier's *Zen Therapy*, London: Constable, 1995 and Mark Epstein's *Thoughts without a Thinker: Psychotherapy from the Buddhist Perspective*, New York: Basic Books, 1995, in *The Authority of Experience: Readings in Buddhism and Psychology*, ed. John Pickering, London: Curzon Press, 1997.

Manné, Joy (forthcoming) 'Hyperventilation vs conscious breathing techniques.' *The Inner Door*.

Minett, Gunnell (1994), *Breath and Spirit: Rebirthing as a Healing Technique*, London: Aquarian/Thorsons.

Orr, Leonard and Sondra Ray (1983) *Rebirthing for the New*

Age (revised edition), California: Trinity Publications.

Proskauer, Magda (1994) 'Breathing therapy', in Timmons, B.H. and Ley, R. (eds.) (1994) *Behavioral and Psychological Approaches to Breathing Disorders*, New York, Plenum, pp.253-60.

Raab, Karl (1992) 'Die Bedeuting des Hyperventilations-Syndroms im Rebirthing-Atemprozess', in *Rebirthing – Integrative Atemarbeit in Theorie und Praxis : Vorträge und Seminare des 2.* Deutscher Rebirthing-Kongress, Dusseldorf, Oktober 1992.

Taylor, Kylea (1994) *The Breathwork Experience: Exploration and Healing in Nonordinary States of Consciousness*, Santa Cruz, Cal.: Hanford Mead.

Timmons, B.H. and Ley, R. (eds.) (1994) *Behavioral and Psychological Approaches to Breathing Disorders*, New York: Plenum.

For further information about breathwork of all kinds, contact the *International Breathwork Foundation*, General Secretary: Gunnel Minett, 6 Middlewatch, Swavesy, GB – Cambridge CH4 5RN, Fax. 0044 1954 232 019.

Chapter 22

American Psychiatric Association: Task Force of DSM-1V (1994) *Diagnostic and Statistical Manual of Mental Disorders* (Fourth edition) Washington D.C.: American Psychiatric Association.

Assagioli, R. (1965) *Psychosynthesis: A Manual of Principles and Techniques*, New York: Hobbs Dorman.

Bandler, R. and Grinder, J. (1975) *The Structure of Magic 1*, Paulo Alto, Cal.: Science and Behaviour Books.

Buddhaghosa, B. (1976) *The Path of Purification: Visuddhimagga*, trs. Bhikkhu Nyanamoli, Berkeley, Cal.: Shambala.

Capra, F. (1983) *The Turning Point*, London: Fontana.

Claxton, G. (1981) *Wholly Human: Western and Eastern Visions of the Self and its Perfection*, London: Routledge & Kegan Paul.

Claxton, G. (1996) *Beyond Therapy: the Impact of Eastern Religions on Psychological Theory and Practice*, Dorset: Prism Press.

Deurzen-Smith, van E. (1988) *Existential Counselling in Practice*, London: Sage.

Donington, L. (1994) 'Core Process psychotherapy', in D. Jones, (ed.) *Innovative Therapy*, Buckingham: Open University Press.

Epstein, M. (1995) *Thoughts without a Thinker*, New York: Basic Books.

Fisher, S. (1986) *Stress and Strategy*, London: Lawrence Earlbaum.

Harding, D. (1986) *On Having No Head: Zen and the Rediscovery of the Obvious*, London: Arkana.

Lang, R. (1994) 'The Headless Way', in D. Jones, (ed.) *Innovative Therapy*, Buckingham: Open University Press.

Levy, D.A. (1992) 'A proposed category for the Diagnostic and Statistical Manual of Mental Disorders (DSM): pervasive labelling disorder', *Journal of Humanistic Psychology*, 32(1), Winter.

Perls, F.F., Hefferline, R. and Goodman, P. (1973) *Gestalt Therapy*, Harmondsworth: Penguin.

Prigogine, I. and Stengers, I. (1985) *Order out of Chaos: Man's New Dialogue With Nature*, London: Fontana.

Rowan, J. (1993) *The Transpersonal in Psychotherapy and Counselling*, London: Routledge.

Smail, D. (1993) *The Origin of Unhappiness: A New Understanding of Personal Distress*, London: Harper & Row.

Tart, C.T. (1969) *Altered States of Consciousness*, New York: Wiley.

Watts, A. (1971) *Psychotherapy East and West*, London: Jonathan Cape.

Watzlawick, P., Beavin, J.H. and Jackson, D.D. (1967) *The Pragmatics of Human Communication*, New York: Norton.

Wray, I. (1996) 'Buddhism and psychotherapy: a Buddhist perspective', in G. Claxton (ed.) *Beyond Therapy: the Impact of Eastern Religions on Psychological Theory and Practice*, Dorset: Prism Press.

Wren-Lewis, J. (1994) 'Death knell of the guru system? Perfectionism versus enlightenment', *Journal of Humanistic Psychology*, 34(2) Spring.

Contributors

Christopher Titmuss
Christopher Titmuss, co-founder of Gaia House retreat centre, South Devon, teaches awakening and insight meditation worldwide. A poet and a writer, his books include *Light on Enlightenment*, *An Awakened Life*, The *Profound and the Profane* and *The Power of Meditation*. A former Buddhist monk in the East, he is a member of the international founding board of the Buddhist Peace Fellowship. He lives in Totnes, Devon.

David Brazier
Dr David Brazier is Buddhist teacher to the Amida Trust, an international, non-profit, inter-denominational, Buddhist, humanitarian network. He has created projects and trainings in Buddhist psychology, engaged Buddhist practice, social work, aid work and community building. He is author of *Zen Therapy*, three other books, and numerous writings. He is a registered psychotherapist. He and his wife live in a UK based Buddhist community. He travels, lectures and leads retreat events extensively.

Eric Hall
Eric Hall combines an interest in Buddhist psychology with his work on experiential courses in Human Relations and Counselling in the School of Education at the University of

Nottingham (UK). His work on awareness integrates talking, thinking, imagery, breathing and bodywork in a systemic approach to the personal and professional development of educators. His recent research has examined the long-term outcomes of small-group training with professionals and promoting the emotional development of students in inner-city schools.

Francisco J. Varela

Francisco J. Varela holds a doctoral degree in biological sciences from Harvard University (1970). He is the author and editor of thirteen books including *The Embodied Mind* (MIT Press, 1992) and, more recently, *Naturalizing Phenomenology* (Stanford University Press, 1999) and *The View from Within* (Imprint Academic, London, 1999). Currently he lives and works in France, where he is Director of Research at the Centre Nationale de la Recherche Scientifique (CNRS), a senior member of CREA, Ecole Polytechnique, and Head of the Neurodynamics Unit at LENA (Laboratory of Cognitive Neurosciences and Brain Imaging) at Salpetrié Hospital, Paris. He is a Buddhist practitioner, interested in dialogue between Dharma and science and has published articles and books on this subject including *Sleeping, Dreaming and Dying* (Wisdom, 1997), the fourth of the *Mind and Life* dialogues he started ten years ago.

Fred Pfeil

Fred Pfeil has been practising Buddhist meditation for nine years, and writing for thirty. He lives in Hartford, Connecticut, professes English and American Studies at Trinity College, and is the author of a novel, two collections of short fiction, and two collections of essays in cultural criticism and contemporary cultural theory. His most recent books are *White Guys: Studies in Postmodern Domination and Difference* (Verso, 1995) and *What They Tell You to Forget* (Pushcart, 1996).

Gay Watson

Gay Watson trained as a psychotherapist with the Karuna Institute and received her PhD from the School of Oriental and African Studies at the University of London for a thesis on Buddhism and psychotherapy. She is the author of *The Resonance of Emptiness*, published in 1998 by Curzon Press, a member of Sharpham College, and a Trustee of the Dartington Hall Trust.

Guy Claxton
Guy Claxton is Visiting Professor at the University of Bristol Graduate School of Education. Previously he was a founding faculty member of Schumacher College in South Devon. His book *Hare Brain, Tortoise Mind: Why Intelligence Increases When you Think Less* (Fourth Estate, 1997) was Anthony Storr's 'Book of the Week', and formed the basis of John Cleese's keynote address to the Chicago '99 International Business Convention. Guy's latest book, *Wise Up: The Challenge of Lifelong Learning*, is published by Bloomsbury in the UK and the USA.

Helena Norberg-Hodge
Helena Norberg-Hodge is the director of the International Society for Ecology and Culture, which promotes ecological regeneration and community renewal while raising awareness of the impact of economic globalisation. She is also author of *Ancient Futures: Learning from Ladakh*, which has been translated into 30 languages.

James Low
James Low studied Tibetan language and Buddhism in India for ten years and subsequently trained in psychotherapy in London. Currently he is Consultant Psychotherapist at Guy's Hospital, London and teaches several approaches to psychotherapy in different training institutes. He also teaches Buddhist meditation in Europe.

John Crook
John Crook PhD, Dsc, formerly Reader in Ethology (Animal Behaviour) in Bristol University's Psychology Department, now teaches Ch'an (Chinese Zen) from his centre in Wales. A long-term practitioner of Zen, John was given transmission to teach Dharma from Master Sheng Yen of Taiwan and New York and is very much concerned with the role of Buddhism in our time and the relations between Asian and European cultures. He is the author of *The Evolution of Human Consciousness* (Oxford, 1980), *Catching a Feather on a Fan* (Element, 1991), *Hilltops of the Hong Kong Moon* (Minerva, 1998) and, with James Low, *The Yogins of Ladakh* (Motilal Banardsidass, 1977). He continues to research the Social Anthropology of Ladakh. He edits *New Ch'an Forum*, the journal of the Western Ch'an Fellowship.

John Welwood

John Welwood, PhD, is a psychotherapist in San Francisco, teacher, and Associate Editor of the *Journal of Transpersonal Psychology*. He received his PhD in clinical psychology from the University of Chicago, where he studied existential psychology with Eugene Gendlin, and has been a student of Tibetan Buddhism and other Eastern spiritual traditions for more than thirty years. His innovative work, which focuses on psychological work in a spiritual context, integrates Eastern contemplative teachings with Western psychotherapeutic insight. He has published more than fifty articles on relationship, psychotherapy, consciousness and personal change, as well as seven books including *Journey of the Heart: The Path of Conscious Love*; *Love and Awakening: Discovering the Sacred Path of Intimate Relationship*; *Awakening the Heart: East/West Approaches to Psychotherapy and the Healing Relationship* and *Ordinary Magic: Everyday Life as Spiritual Path*.

Jon Kabat-Zinn

Jon Kabat-Zinn, PhD, is Executive Director of the Center for Mindfulness in Medicine, Health Care, and Society at the University of Massachusetts Medical School and the UMass-Memorial Medical Center (UMMMC). He is the founder and former director of the UMMMC Stress Reduction Clinic. He is also Associate Professor of Medicine. He is the author of two bestselling books: *Full Catastrophe Living: Using the Wisdom of Your Body and Mind to Face Stress, Pain and Illness* (Delta, 1991), and *Wherever You Go, There You Are: Mindfulness Meditation in Everyday Life* (Hyperion, 1994). He is also co-author, with his wife Myla, of *Everyday Blessings: The Inner Work of Mindful Parenting* (Hyperion, 1997).

Joy Manné

Joy Manné began Vipassana meditation in 1965, became interested in Buddhist psychology, learned Sanskrit and Pali, and wrote her PhD on 'The Debates and Case Histories in the Pali Canon'. She teaches and writes about Breathwork and works as a Breathwork psychotherapist. She is the author of *Soul Therapy* (North Atlantic, Berkeley, CA, 1997), editor of the internet, peer review journal *The Healing Breath: a journal of Breathwork Practice, Psychology and Spirituality* (www.i-breathe.com), and editor of the International Breathwork Foundation's newsletter.

Karen Kissel Wegela

Dr Wegela is a core faculty member of the Naropa University in Boulder, Colorado, in the MA Psychology: Contemplative Psychotherapy programme. She served as the director of the programme for about fifteen years and currently is a member of the department's faculty leadership team. She is a psychologist in private practice, and she is also the author of many articles and a book, *How to Be a Help Instead of a Nuisance*.

Leslie Todres

Dr Les Todres, PhD, is a clinical psychologist and Reader in Interprofessional Care at the Institute of Health and Community Studies, Bournemouth University. His previous occupational roles have included head of a student counselling service and director of a clinical psychology training programme. He has also worked within NHS clinics and GP practices. He has published in the areas of phenomenological psychology and integrative psychotherapy. He has a long-standing interest in Buddhist psychology.

Mark Epstein

Mark Epstein MD is a psychiatrist in private practice in New York City, contributing editor to *Tricycle: The Buddhist Review* and the author of *Thoughts Without a Thinker: Psychotherapy from a Buddhist Perspective* (Basic Books) and *Going to Pieces Without Falling Apart* (Broadway Books and Thorsons UK). He has been a student of Buddhist meditation for the past twenty-five years.

Maura Sills

Maura Sills is the Programme Director of the Karuna Institute, Devon, England which offers a recognised four and a half year training in Core Process Psychotherapy which is inspired and informed by Buddhist practice and psychotherapy. Maura has had experience as a therapist and teacher in the UK and USA. She is a Trustee and founding member of the Association of Accredited Psychospiritual Psychotherapists. She was a Buddhist nun under the most Venerable Taungpulu Sayadaw of Burma and trained with Dr Rina Sicar in Buddhist studies.

Stephen Batchelor

Stephen Batchelor was born in Scotland and educated at Watford Grammar School, England, and in Buddhist monasteries in India, Switzerland and Korea. He has translated and written several books on Buddhism, including *Alone with Others, The Faith to Doubt, The Awakening of the West* and *Buddhism Without Beliefs*. He lectures and conducts meditation retreats worldwide, is a contributing editor to *Tricycle: the Buddhist Review* and Director of Studies of the Sharpham College for Buddhist Studies and Contemporary Enquiry, Devon, England.

Susan Blackmore
Susan Blackmore is Reader in Psychology at the University of the West of England, Bristol, and Perrott-Warrick Researcher studying psychic phenomena in borderline states of consciousness. She has a degree in psychology and physiology from Oxford and an MSc and PhD from Surrey University. She is author of more than fifty scientific articles. Her books include *Dying to Live: Near-death experiences* (1993), an autobiography *In Search of the Light* (1996) and *The Meme Machine* (1999). She writes for several magazines and newspapers, and is a frequent contributor and presenter on radio and television. She has been training in Zen for many years.

Tarab Tulku
Tarab Tulku is a Tibetan lama, the 11th incarnation of Tarab Tulku. He holds the Geshe Llaram degree from Drepung Monastery, and is the head of the Tibetan section of the Royal Library and the University of Copenhagen. He has established Tarab Institutes in Denmark, France, Belgium, Germany and Austria, and has started a psychotherapy training programme in Brussels.

Terence Gaussen
Terence Gaussen read psychology and biology at Keele and has worked as a teacher and psychologist in education and the NHS. He is now a Consultant Clinical Psychologist in Developmental Paediatric Psychology in community services in Leeds and meets with the effects of atypical developmental processes on a daily basis. He has a long term interest in Buddhist practice and its interface with modern psychological understanding of being human.

Thupten Jinpa
Geshe Thupten Jinpa has been the principal interpreter to HH the Dalai Lama since 1986, and has translated and edited several

of his books. He holds the Geshe Llaram degree from Ganden Monastery, and a BA and PhD from Cambridge University where he was a research fellow at Girton College. His latest work is an anthology of Tibetan religious poetry to be published by HarperCollins.